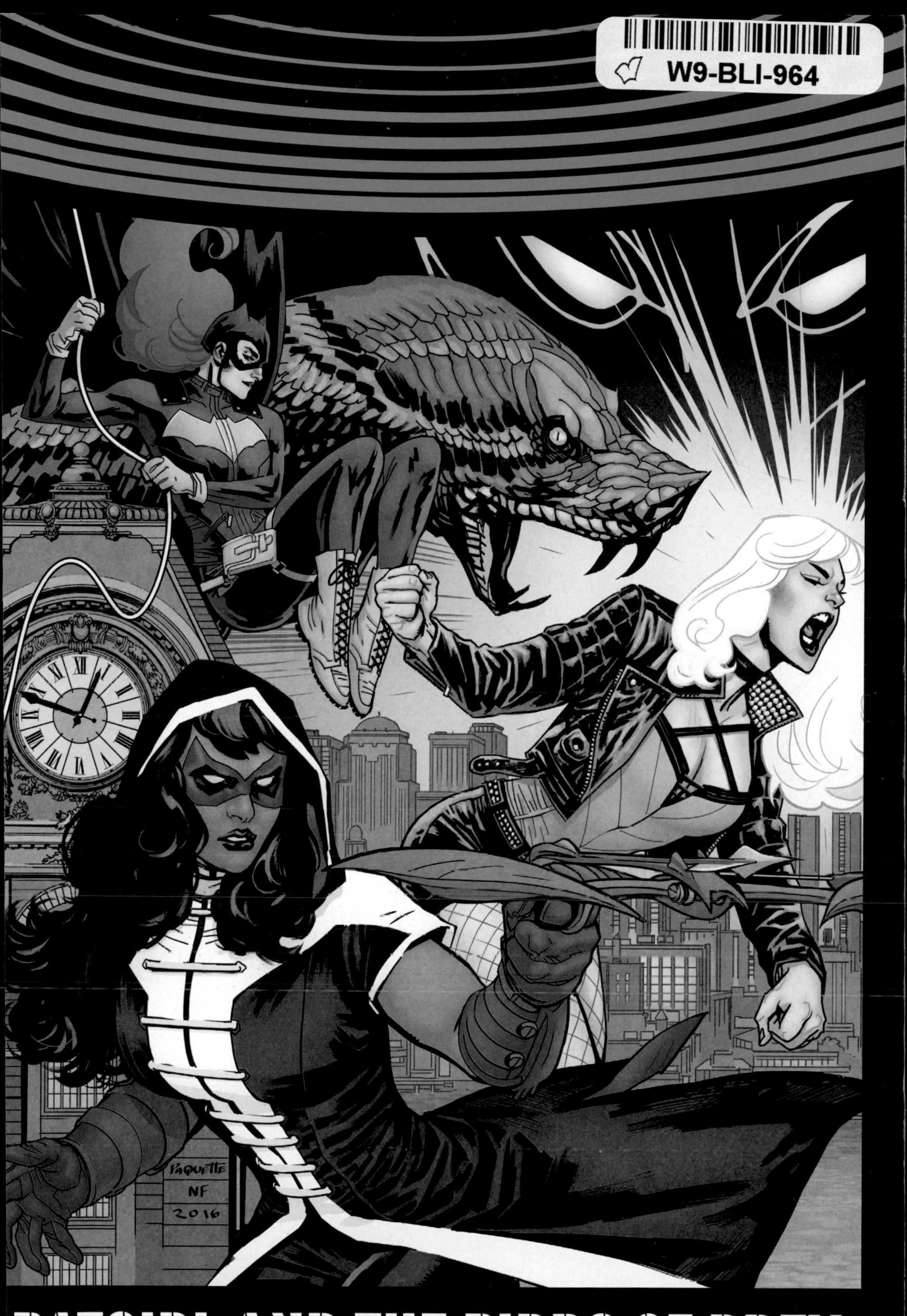
PAQUETTE
NF
2016

BATGIRL AND THE BIRDS OF PREY

VOL.1 WHO IS ORACLE?

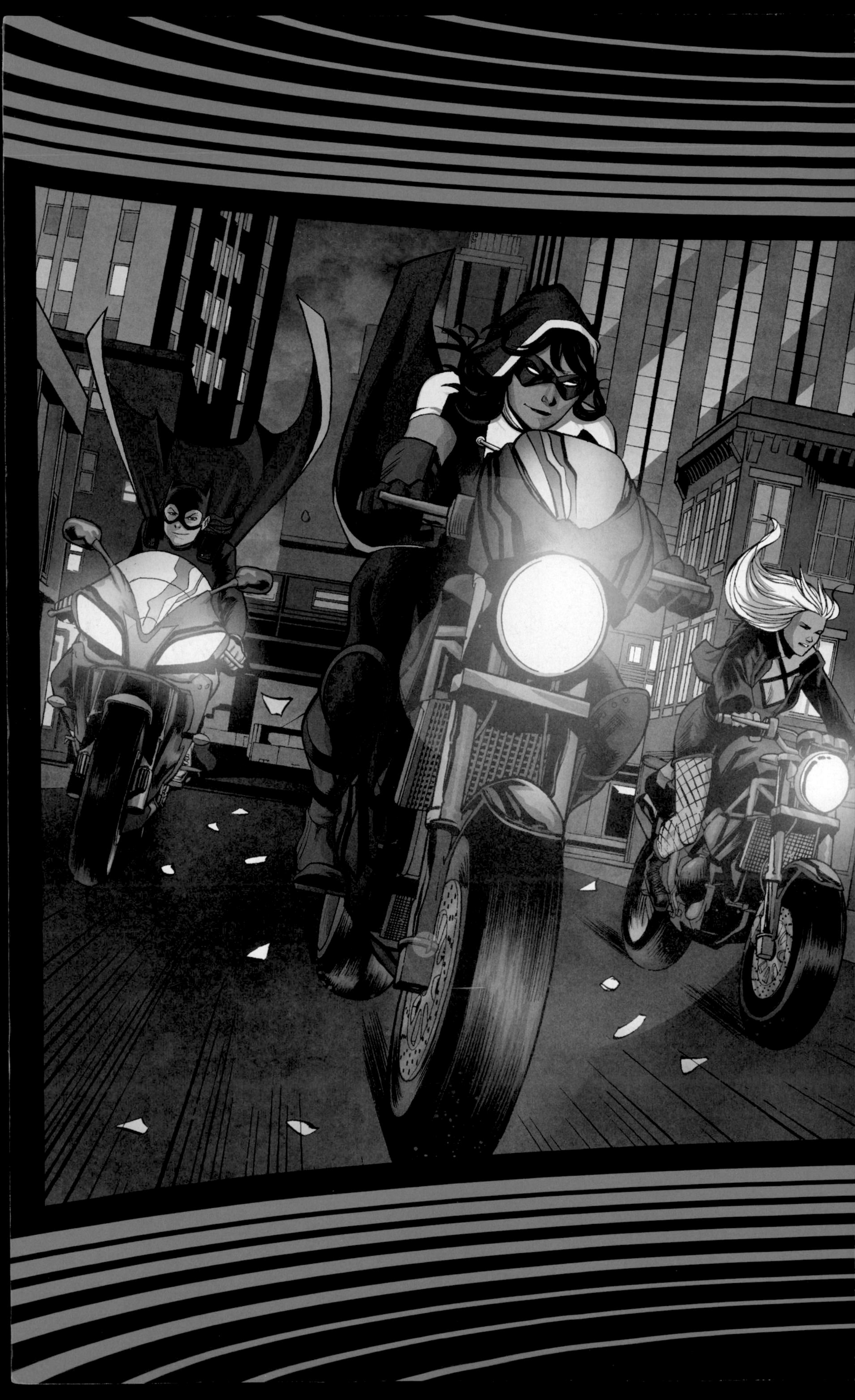

BATGIRL AND THE BIRDS OF PREY
VOL.1 WHO IS ORACLE?

JULIE BENSON
SHAWNA BENSON
writers

CLAIRE ROE
ROGE ANTONIO
artists

ALLEN PASSALAQUA
HI-FI
colorists

STEVE WANDS
DERON BENNETT
letterers

YANICK PAQUETTE and **NATHAN FAIRBAIRN**
series and collection cover artists

BATMAN created by **BOB KANE** with **BILL FINGER**

CHRIS CONROY Editor – Original Series • **DAVE WIELGOSZ** Assistant Editor – Original Series
JEB WOODARD Group Editor - Collected Editions • **LIZ ERICKSON** Editor - Collected Edition
STEVE COOK Design Director - Books • **MONIQUE GRUSPE** Publication Design

BOB HARRAS Senior VP - Editor-in-Chief, DC Comics

DIANE NELSON President • **DAN DiDIO** Publisher • **JIM LEE** Publisher • **GEOFF JOHNS** President & Chief Creative Officer
AMIT DESAI Executive VP - Business & Marketing Strategy, Direct to Consumer & Global Franchise Management • **SAM ADES** Senior VP - Direct to Consumer
BOBBIE CHASE VP - Talent Development • **MARK CHIARELLO** Senior VP - Art, Design & Collected Editions
JOHN CUNNINGHAM Senior VP - Sales & Trade Marketing • **ANNE DePIES** Senior VP - Business Strategy, Finance & Administration
DON FALLETTI VP - Manufacturing Operations • **LAWRENCE GANEM** VP - Editorial Administration & Talent Relations
ALISON GILL Senior VP - Manufacturing & Operations • **HANK KANALZ** Senior VP - Editorial Strategy & Administration
JAY KOGAN VP - Legal Affairs • **THOMAS LOFTUS** VP - Business Affairs
JACK MAHAN VP - Business Affairs • **NICK J. NAPOLITANO** VP - Manufacturing Administration
EDDIE SCANNELL VP - Consumer Marketing • **COURTNEY SIMMONS** Senior VP - Publicity & Communications
JIM (SKI) SOKOLOWSKI VP - Comic Book Specialty Sales & Trade Marketing • **NANCY SPEARS** VP - Mass, Book, Digital Sales & Trade Marketing

BATGIRL AND THE BIRDS OF PREY VOL. 1: WHO IS ORACLE?

Published by DC Comics. Compilation and all new material Copyright © 2017 DC Comics. All Rights Reserved.
Originally published in single magazine form in BATGIRL AND THE BIRDS OF PREY 1-6 and BATGIRL AND THE BIRDS OF PREY: REBIRTH 1 © 2016, 2017 DC Comics.
All Rights Reserved. All characters, their distinctive likenesses and related elements featured in this publication are trademarks of DC Comics.
The stories, characters and incidents featured in this publication are entirely fictional.
DC Comics does not read or accept unsolicited submissions of ideas, stories or artwork.

DC Comics, 2900 West Alameda Ave., Burbank, CA 91505. Printed by LSC Communications, Salem, VA, USA. 3/3/17.
First Printing. ISBN: 978-1-4012-6867-1

Library of Congress Cataloging-in-Publication Data is available.

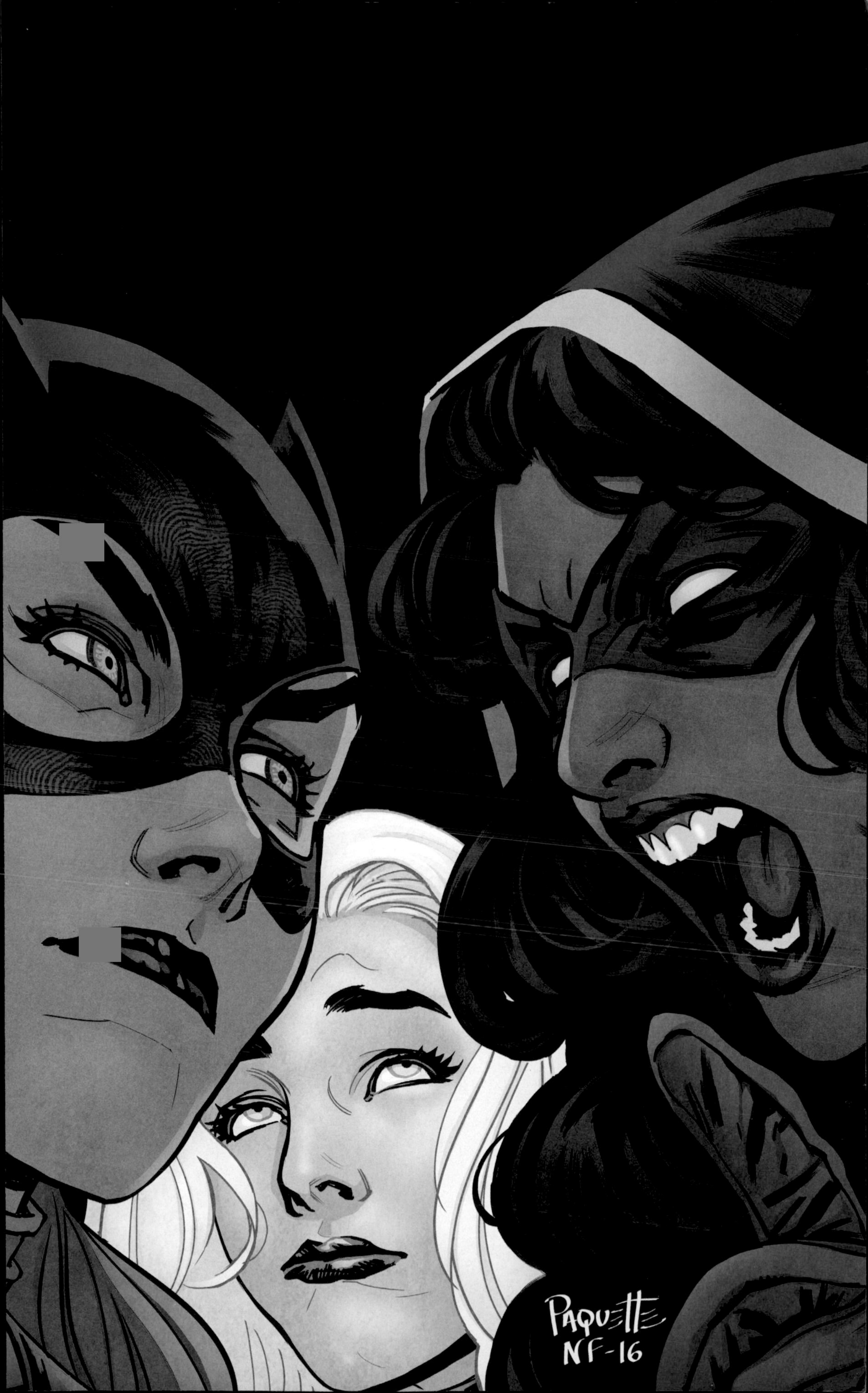
PAQUETTE
NF-16

REBIRTH

JULIE and SHAWNA BENSON writers * CLAIRE ROE artist

ALLEN PASSALAQUA colorist * STEVE WANDS letterer

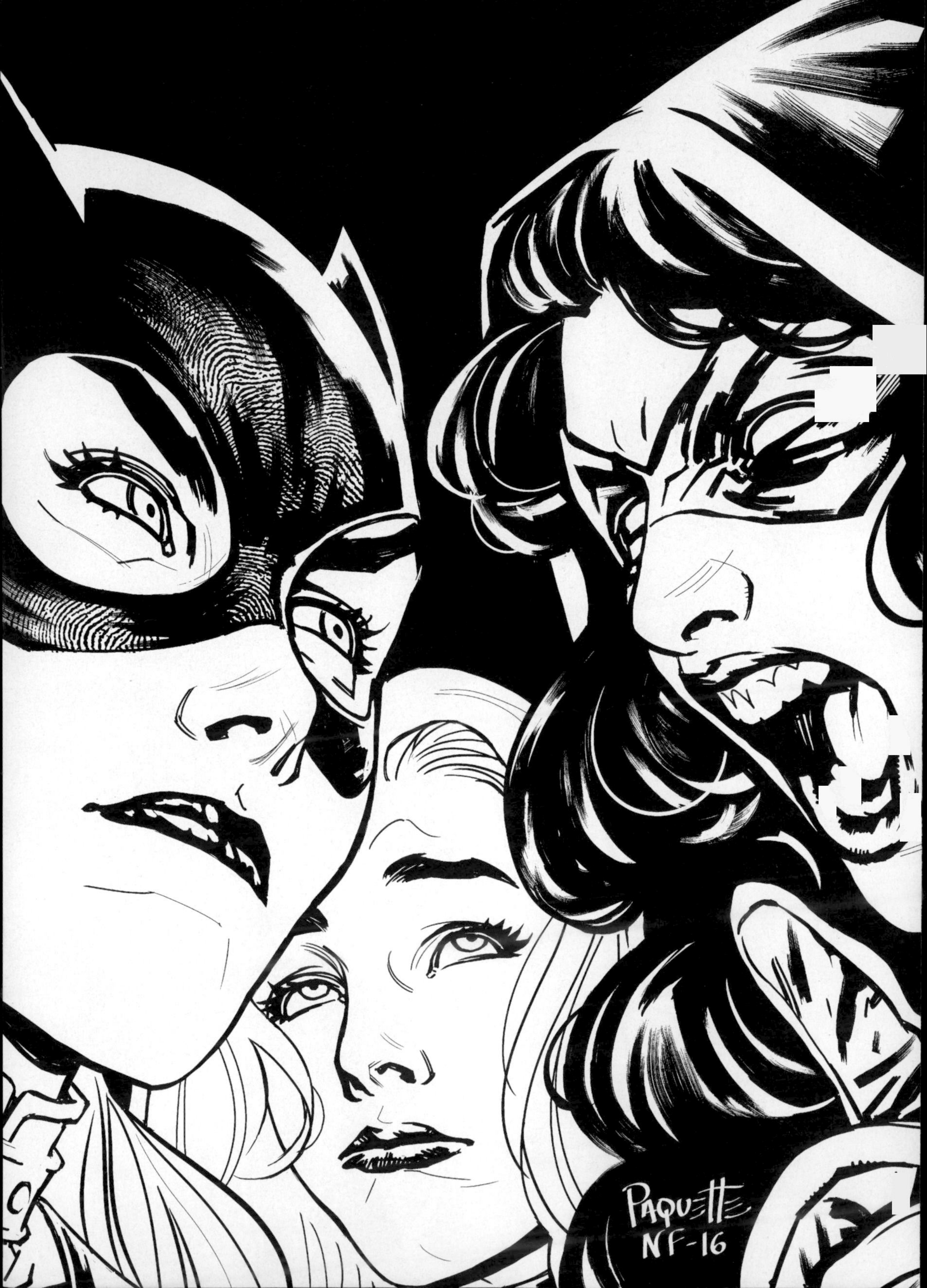
PAQUETTE
NF-16

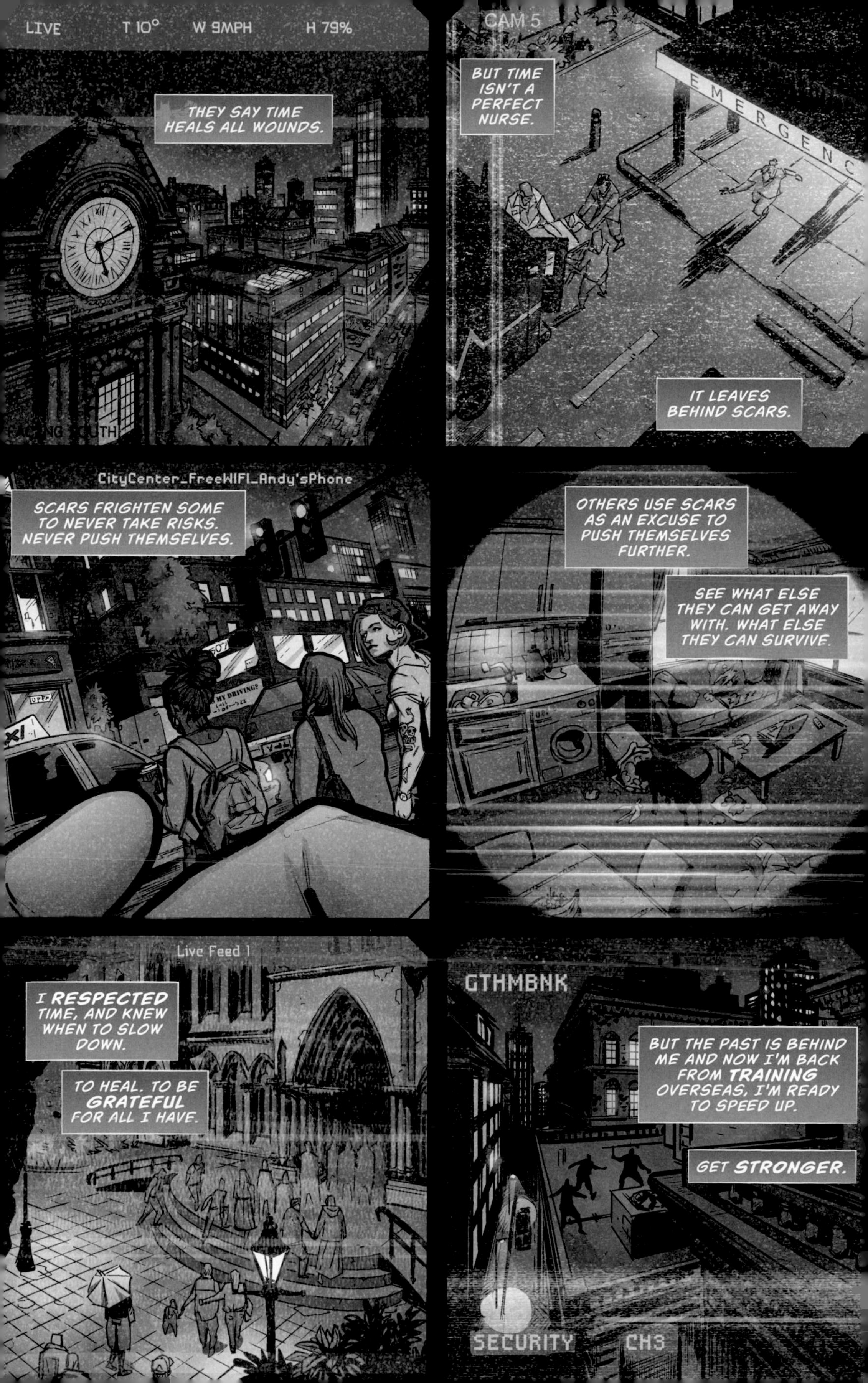
LIVE T 10° W 9MPH H 79%
THEY SAY TIME HEALS ALL WOUNDS.
CAM 5
BUT TIME ISN'T A PERFECT NURSE.
EMERGENC
IT LEAVES BEHIND SCARS.
CityCenter_FreeWIFI_Andy'sPhone
SCARS FRIGHTEN SOME TO NEVER TAKE RISKS. NEVER PUSH THEMSELVES.
OTHERS USE SCARS AS AN EXCUSE TO PUSH THEMSELVES FURTHER.
SEE WHAT ELSE THEY CAN GET AWAY WITH. WHAT ELSE THEY CAN SURVIVE.
Live Feed 1
I RESPECTED TIME, AND KNEW WHEN TO SLOW DOWN.
TO HEAL. TO BE GRATEFUL FOR ALL I HAVE.
GTHMBNK
BUT THE PAST IS BEHIND ME AND NOW I'M BACK FROM TRAINING OVERSEAS, I'M READY TO SPEED UP.
GET STRONGER.
SECURITY CH3

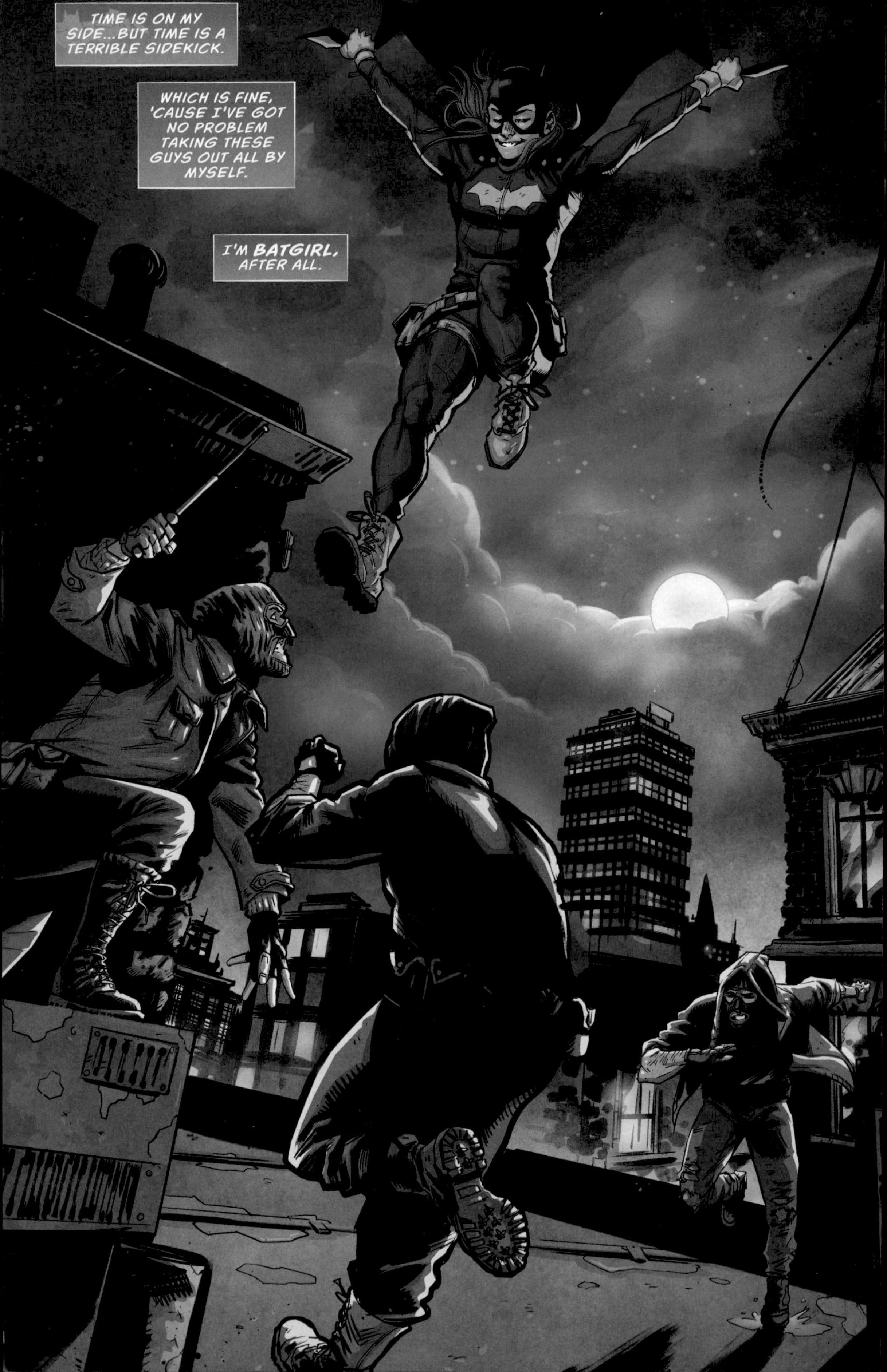
TIME IS ON MY SIDE...BUT TIME IS A TERRIBLE SIDEKICK.
WHICH IS FINE, 'CAUSE I'VE GOT NO PROBLEM TAKING THESE GUYS OUT ALL BY MYSELF.
I'M BATGIRL, AFTER ALL.

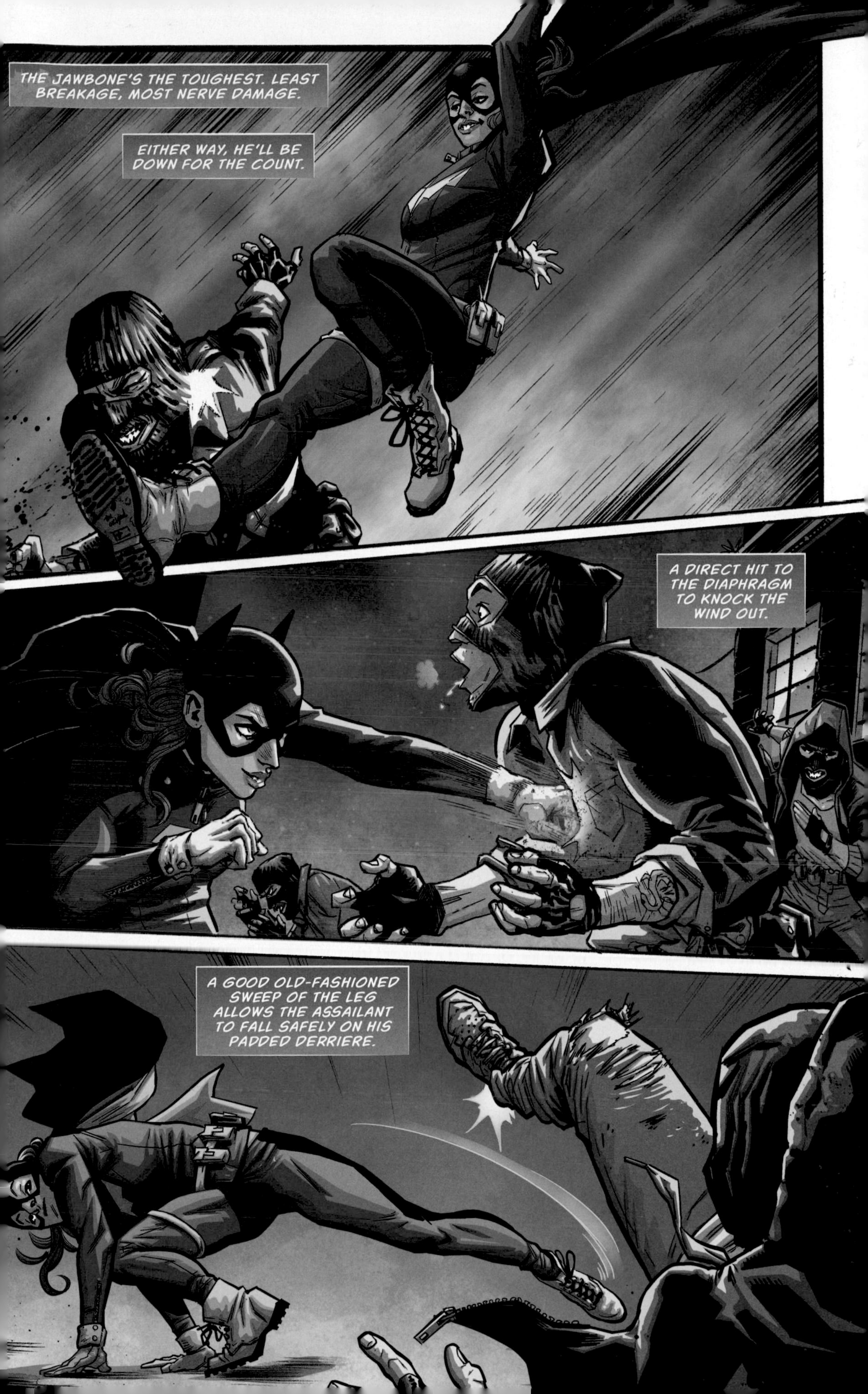
THE JAWBONE'S THE TOUGHEST. LEAST BREAKAGE, MOST NERVE DAMAGE.
EITHER WAY, HE'LL BE DOWN FOR THE COUNT.
A DIRECT HIT TO THE DIAPHRAGM TO KNOCK THE WIND OUT.
A GOOD OLD-FASHIONED SWEEP OF THE LEG ALLOWS THE ASSAILANT TO FALL SAFELY ON HIS PADDED DERRIERE.

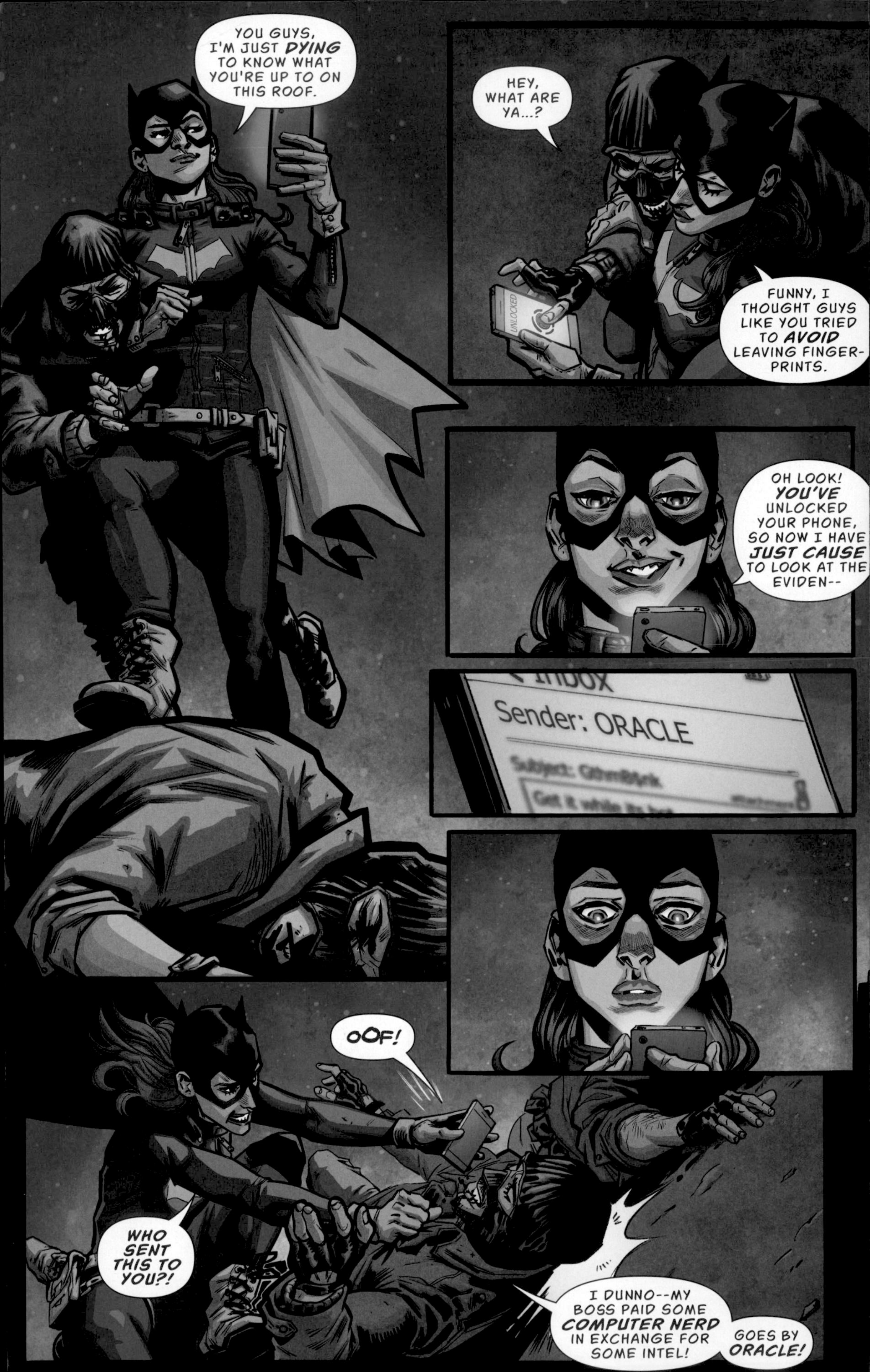
YOU GUYS, I'M JUST DYING TO KNOW WHAT YOU'RE UP TO ON THIS ROOF.
HEY, WHAT ARE YA...?
UNLOCKED
FUNNY, I THOUGHT GUYS LIKE YOU TRIED TO AVOID LEAVING FINGER-PRINTS.
OH LOOK! YOU'VE UNLOCKED YOUR PHONE, SO NOW I HAVE JUST CAUSE TO LOOK AT THE EVIDEN--
Inbox
Sender: ORACLE
OOF!
WHO SENT THIS TO YOU?!
I DUNNO--MY BOSS PAID SOME COMPUTER NERD IN EXCHANGE FOR SOME INTEL!
GOES BY ORACLE!

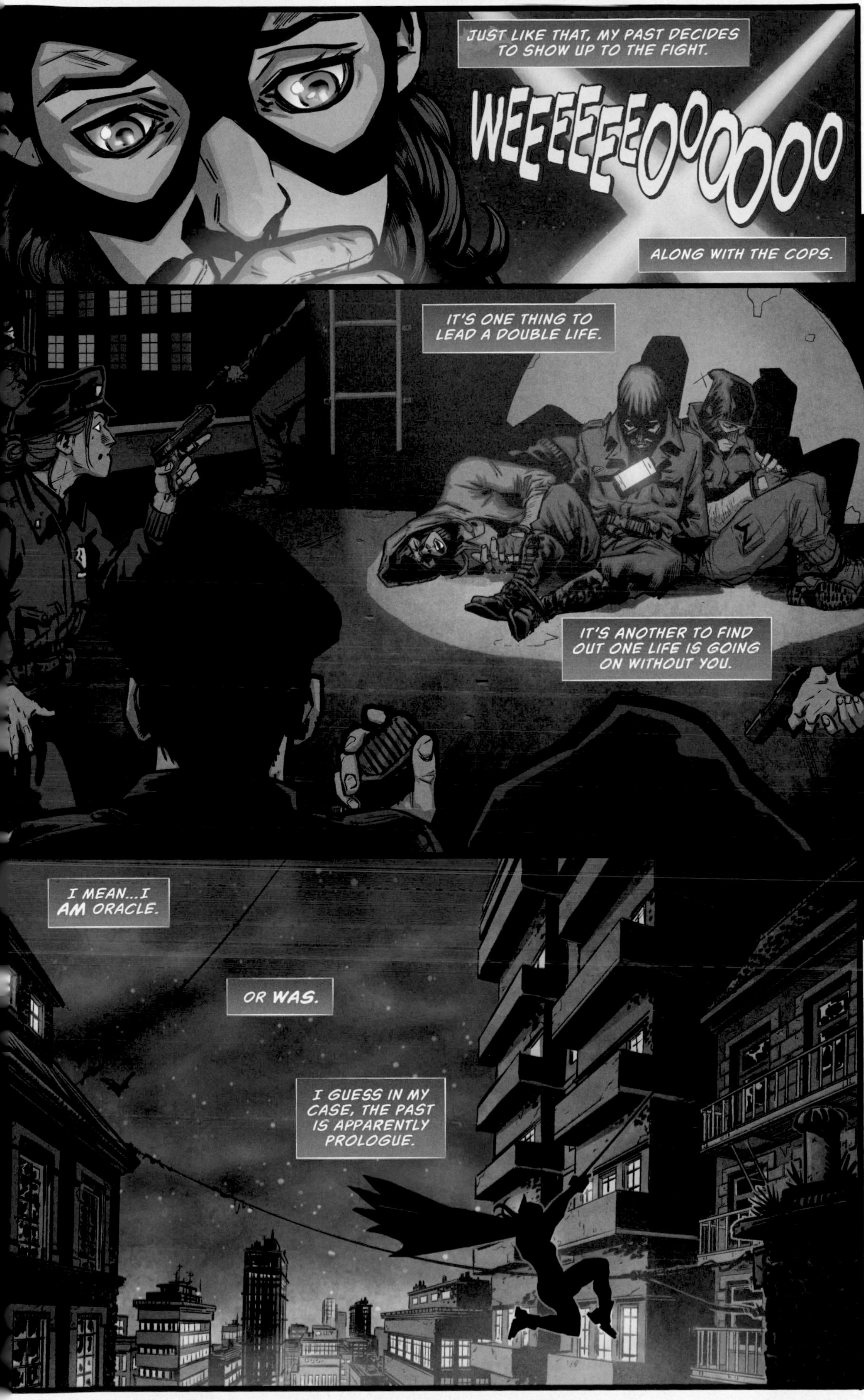
JUST LIKE THAT, MY PAST DECIDES TO SHOW UP TO THE FIGHT.
WEEEEEEOOOOOO
ALONG WITH THE COPS.
IT'S ONE THING TO LEAD A DOUBLE LIFE.
IT'S ANOTHER TO FIND OUT ONE LIFE IS GOING ON WITHOUT YOU.
I MEAN...I AM ORACLE.
OR WAS.
I GUESS IN MY CASE, THE PAST IS APPARENTLY PROLOGUE.

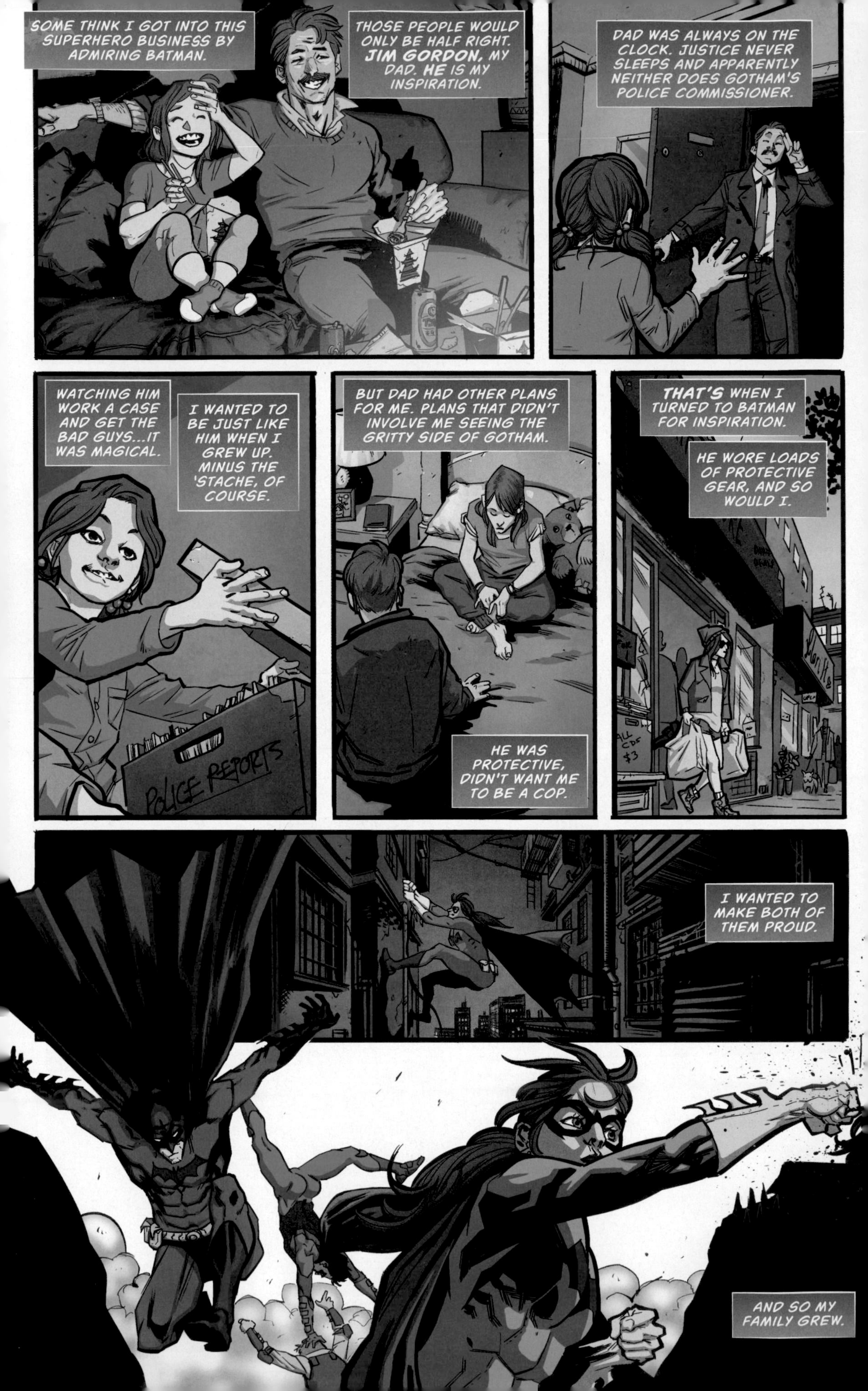
SOME THINK I GOT INTO THIS SUPERHERO BUSINESS BY ADMIRING BATMAN.
THOSE PEOPLE WOULD ONLY BE HALF RIGHT. JIM GORDON, MY DAD. HE IS MY INSPIRATION.
DAD WAS ALWAYS ON THE CLOCK. JUSTICE NEVER SLEEPS AND APPARENTLY NEITHER DOES GOTHAM'S POLICE COMMISSIONER.
WATCHING HIM WORK A CASE AND GET THE BAD GUYS...IT WAS MAGICAL.
I WANTED TO BE JUST LIKE HIM WHEN I GREW UP. MINUS THE 'STACHE, OF COURSE.
POLICE REPORTS
BUT DAD HAD OTHER PLANS FOR ME. PLANS THAT DIDN'T INVOLVE ME SEEING THE GRITTY SIDE OF GOTHAM.
HE WAS PROTECTIVE, DIDN'T WANT ME TO BE A COP.
THAT'S WHEN I TURNED TO BATMAN FOR INSPIRATION.
HE WORE LOADS OF PROTECTIVE GEAR, AND SO WOULD I.
I WANTED TO MAKE BOTH OF THEM PROUD.
AND SO MY FAMILY GREW.

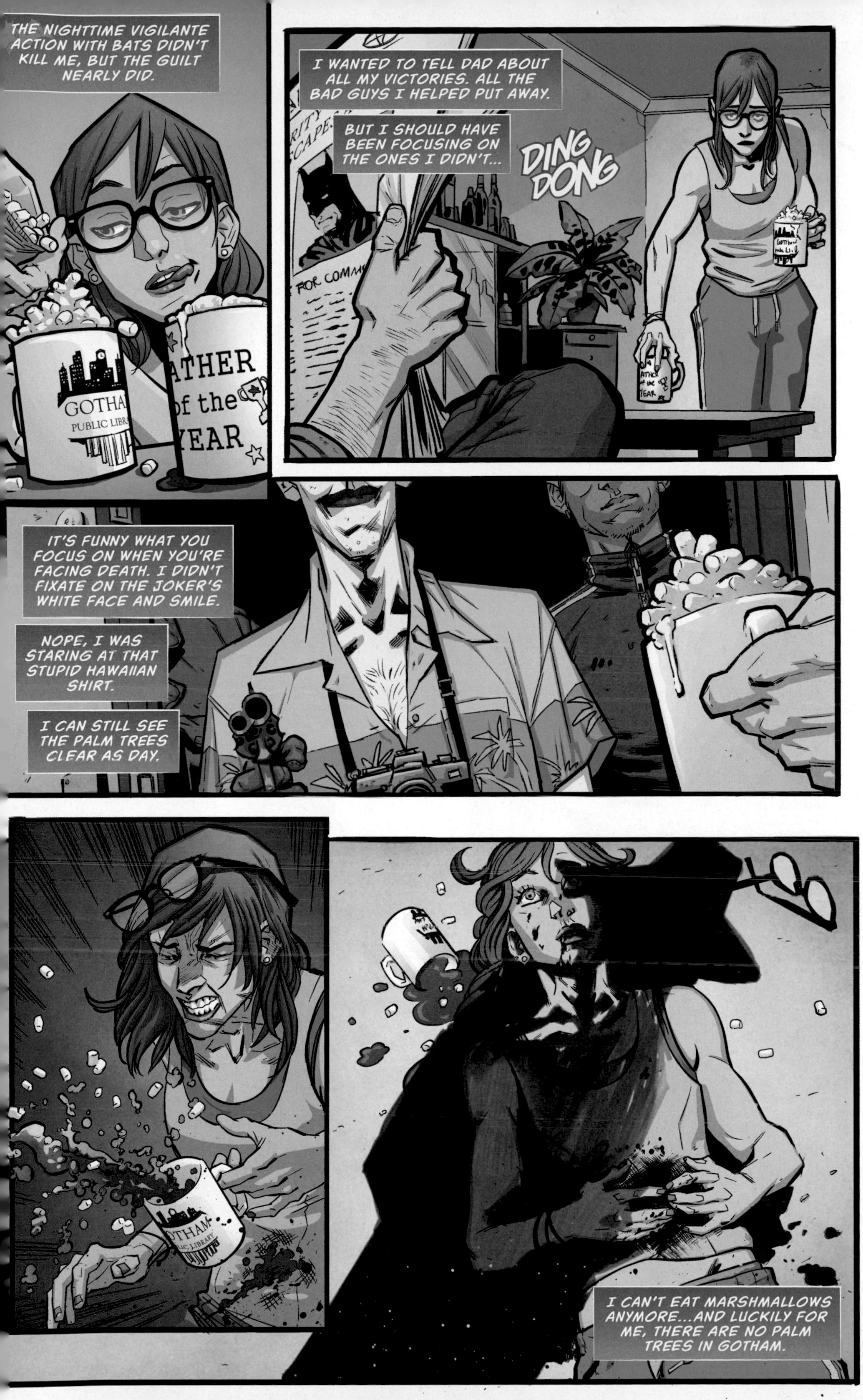
THE NIGHTTIME VIGILANTE ACTION WITH BATS DIDN'T KILL ME, BUT THE GUILT NEARLY DID.
GOTHAM PUBLIC LIBRARY
FATHER of the YEAR
I WANTED TO TELL DAD ABOUT ALL MY VICTORIES. ALL THE BAD GUYS I HELPED PUT AWAY.
BUT I SHOULD HAVE BEEN FOCUSING ON THE ONES I DIDN'T...
DING DONG
IT'S FUNNY WHAT YOU FOCUS ON WHEN YOU'RE FACING DEATH. I DIDN'T FIXATE ON THE JOKER'S WHITE FACE AND SMILE.
NOPE, I WAS STARING AT THAT STUPID HAWAIIAN SHIRT.
I CAN STILL SEE THE PALM TREES CLEAR AS DAY.
I CAN'T EAT MARSHMALLOWS ANYMORE...AND LUCKILY FOR ME, THERE ARE NO PALM TREES IN GOTHAM.

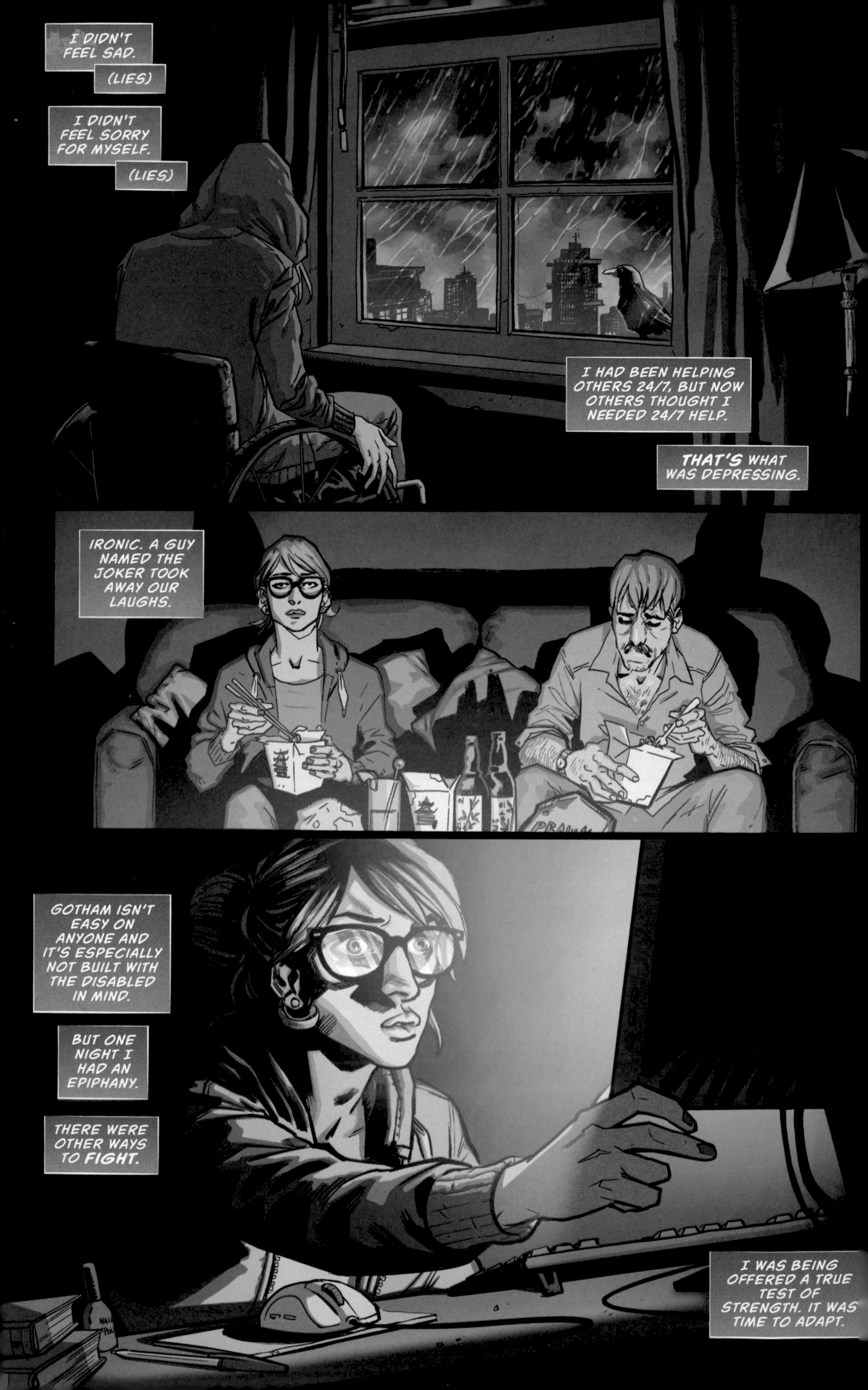
I DIDN'T FEEL SAD.
(LIES)
I DIDN'T FEEL SORRY FOR MYSELF.
(LIES)
I HAD BEEN HELPING OTHERS 24/7, BUT NOW OTHERS THOUGHT I NEEDED 24/7 HELP.
THAT'S WHAT WAS DEPRESSING.
IRONIC. A GUY NAMED THE JOKER TOOK AWAY OUR LAUGHS.
GOTHAM ISN'T EASY ON ANYONE AND IT'S ESPECIALLY NOT BUILT WITH THE DISABLED IN MIND.
BUT ONE NIGHT I HAD AN EPIPHANY.
THERE WERE OTHER WAYS TO FIGHT.
I WAS BEING OFFERED A TRUE TEST OF STRENGTH. IT WAS TIME TO ADAPT.

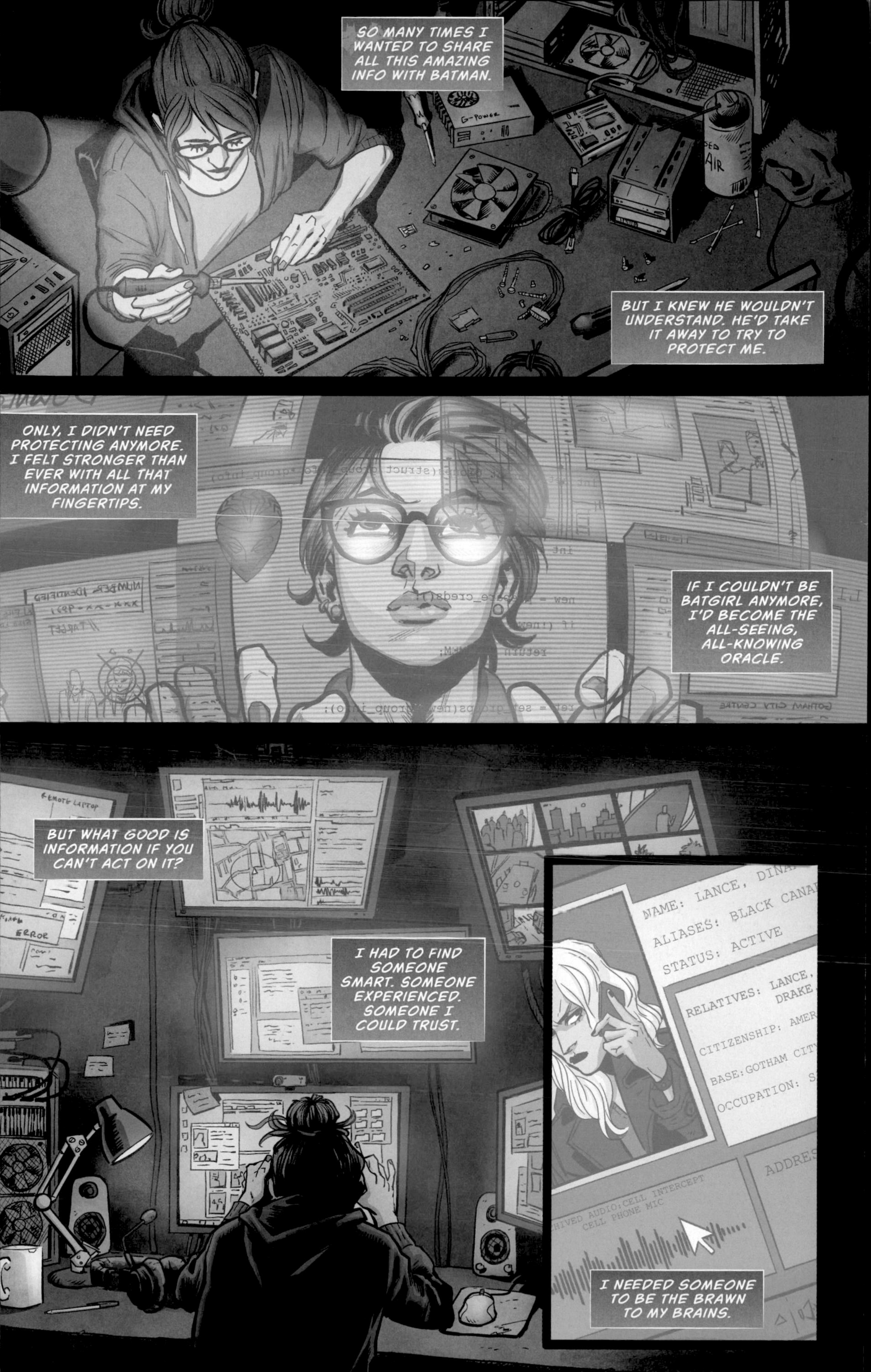

SO MANY TIMES I WANTED TO SHARE ALL THIS AMAZING INFO WITH BATMAN.
G-POWER
AIR
BUT I KNEW HE WOULDN'T UNDERSTAND. HE'D TAKE IT AWAY TO TRY TO PROTECT ME.
ONLY, I DIDN'T NEED PROTECTING ANYMORE. I FELT STRONGER THAN EVER WITH ALL THAT INFORMATION AT MY FINGERTIPS.
IF I COULDN'T BE BATGIRL ANYMORE, I'D BECOME THE ALL-SEEING, ALL-KNOWING ORACLE.
BUT WHAT GOOD IS INFORMATION IF YOU CAN'T ACT ON IT?
REMOTE LAPTOP
ERROR
I HAD TO FIND SOMEONE SMART. SOMEONE EXPERIENCED. SOMEONE I COULD TRUST.
STATUS: ACTIVE
RELATIVES:
CITIZENSHIP:
OCCUPATION:
CELL PHONE MIC
I NEEDED SOMEONE TO BE THE BRAWN TO MY BRAINS.

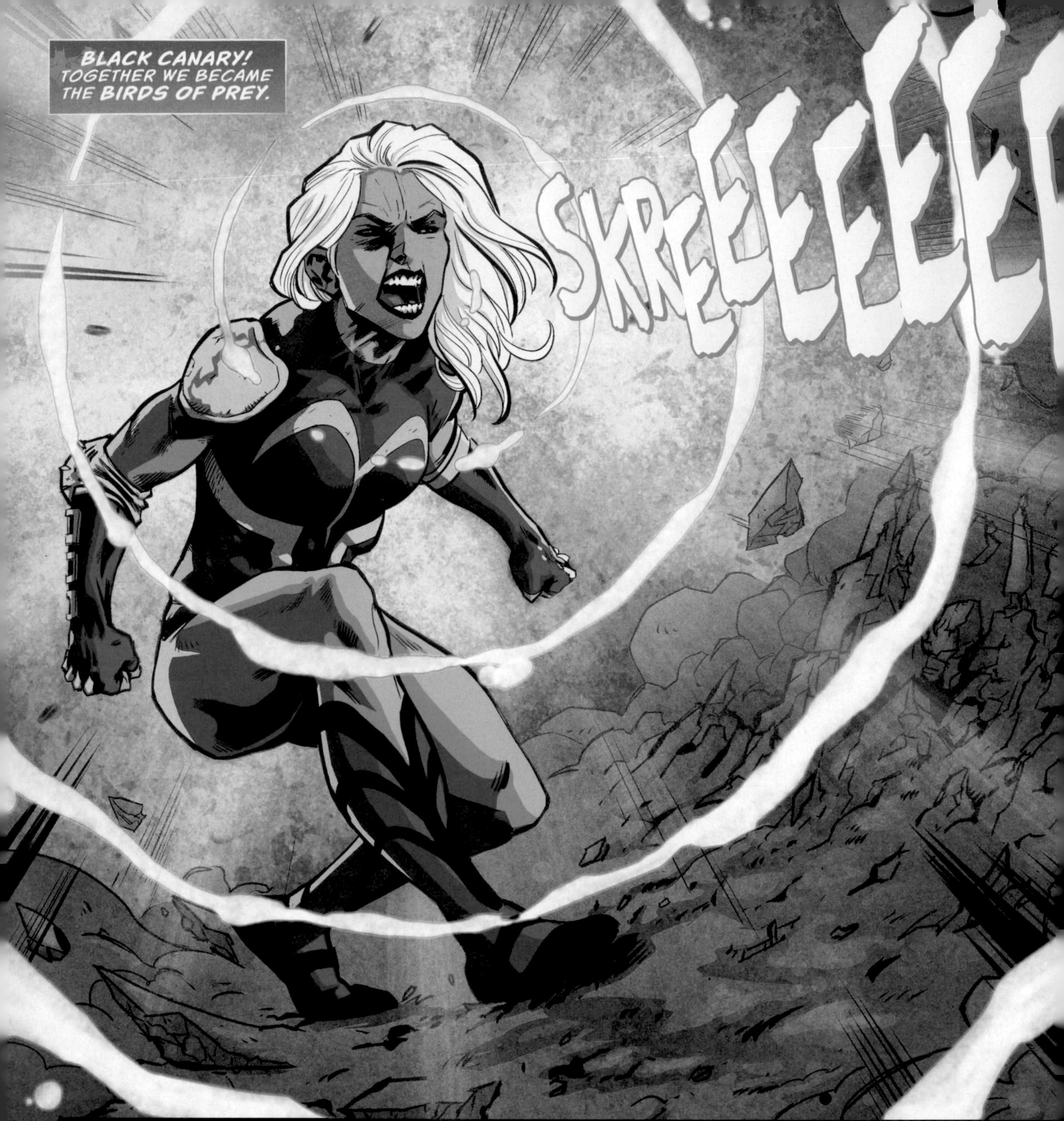
BLACK CANARY! TOGETHER WE BECAME THE BIRDS OF PREY.
SKREEEEEEE

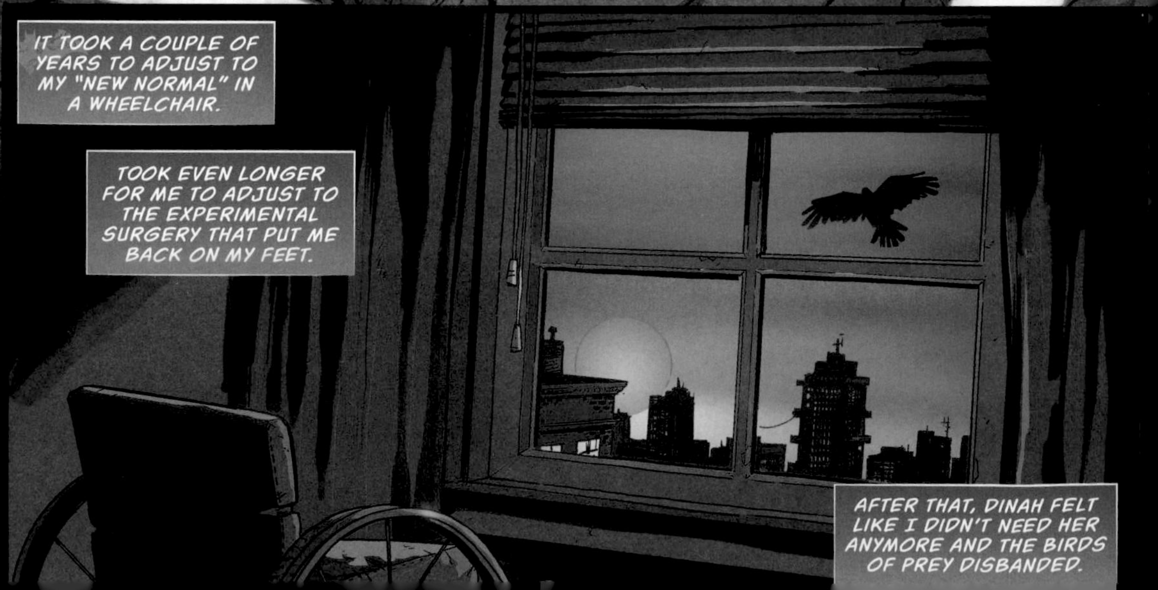
IT TOOK A COUPLE OF YEARS TO ADJUST TO MY "NEW NORMAL" IN A WHEELCHAIR.
TOOK EVEN LONGER FOR ME TO ADJUST TO THE EXPERIMENTAL SURGERY THAT PUT ME BACK ON MY FEET.
AFTER THAT, DINAH FELT LIKE I DIDN'T NEED HER ANYMORE AND THE BIRDS OF PREY DISBANDED.

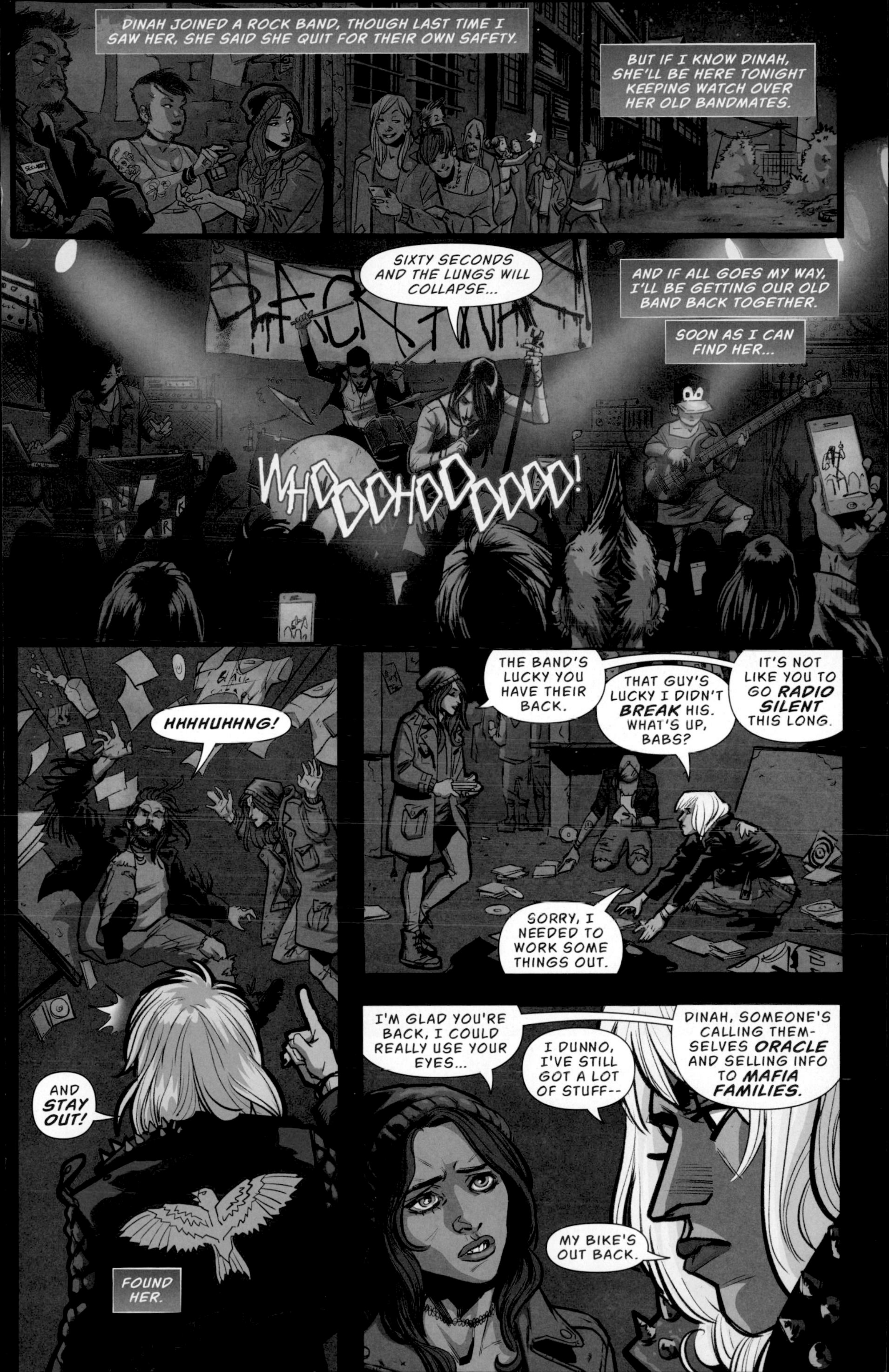
DINAH JOINED A ROCK BAND, THOUGH LAST TIME I SAW HER, SHE SAID SHE QUIT FOR THEIR OWN SAFETY.
BUT IF I KNOW DINAH, SHE'LL BE HERE TONIGHT KEEPING WATCH OVER HER OLD BANDMATES.
SIXTY SECONDS AND THE LUNGS WILL COLLAPSE...
AND IF ALL GOES MY WAY, I'LL BE GETTING OUR OLD BAND BACK TOGETHER.
SOON AS I CAN FIND HER...
WHOOOOHOOOOOOO!
HHHHUHHNG!
AND STAY OUT!
FOUND HER.
THE BAND'S LUCKY YOU HAVE THEIR BACK.
THAT GUY'S LUCKY I DIDN'T BREAK HIS. WHAT'S UP, BABS?
IT'S NOT LIKE YOU TO GO RADIO SILENT THIS LONG.
SORRY, I NEEDED TO WORK SOME THINGS OUT.
I'M GLAD YOU'RE BACK, I COULD REALLY USE YOUR EYES...
I DUNNO, I'VE STILL GOT A LOT OF STUFF--
DINAH, SOMEONE'S CALLING THEMSELVES ORACLE AND SELLING INFO TO MAFIA FAMILIES.
MY BIKE'S OUT BACK.

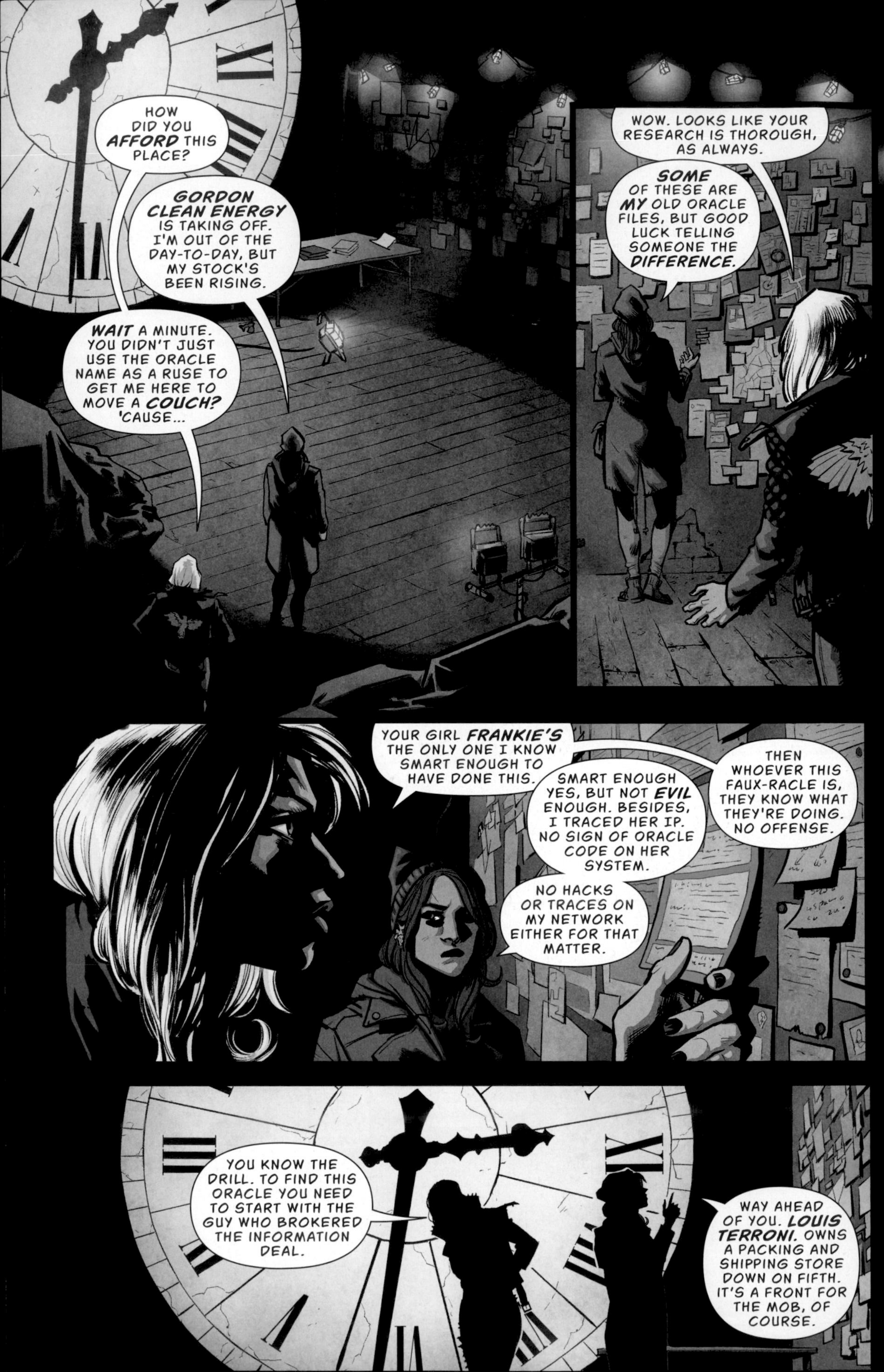
HOW DID YOU AFFORD THIS PLACE?
GORDON CLEAN ENERGY IS TAKING OFF. I'M OUT OF THE DAY-TO-DAY, BUT MY STOCK'S BEEN RISING.
WAIT A MINUTE. YOU DIDN'T JUST USE THE ORACLE NAME AS A RUSE TO GET ME HERE TO MOVE A COUCH? 'CAUSE...
WOW. LOOKS LIKE YOUR RESEARCH IS THOROUGH, AS ALWAYS.
SOME OF THESE ARE MY OLD ORACLE FILES, BUT GOOD LUCK TELLING SOMEONE THE DIFFERENCE.
YOUR GIRL FRANKIE'S THE ONLY ONE I KNOW SMART ENOUGH TO HAVE DONE THIS.
SMART ENOUGH YES, BUT NOT EVIL ENOUGH. BESIDES, I TRACED HER IP. NO SIGN OF ORACLE CODE ON HER SYSTEM.
NO HACKS OR TRACES ON MY NETWORK EITHER FOR THAT MATTER.
THEN WHOEVER THIS FAUX-RACLE IS, THEY KNOW WHAT THEY'RE DOING. NO OFFENSE.
YOU KNOW THE DRILL. TO FIND THIS ORACLE YOU NEED TO START WITH THE GUY WHO BROKERED THE INFORMATION DEAL.
WAY AHEAD OF YOU. LOUIS TERRONI. OWNS A PACKING AND SHIPPING STORE DOWN ON FIFTH. IT'S A FRONT FOR THE MOB, OF COURSE.

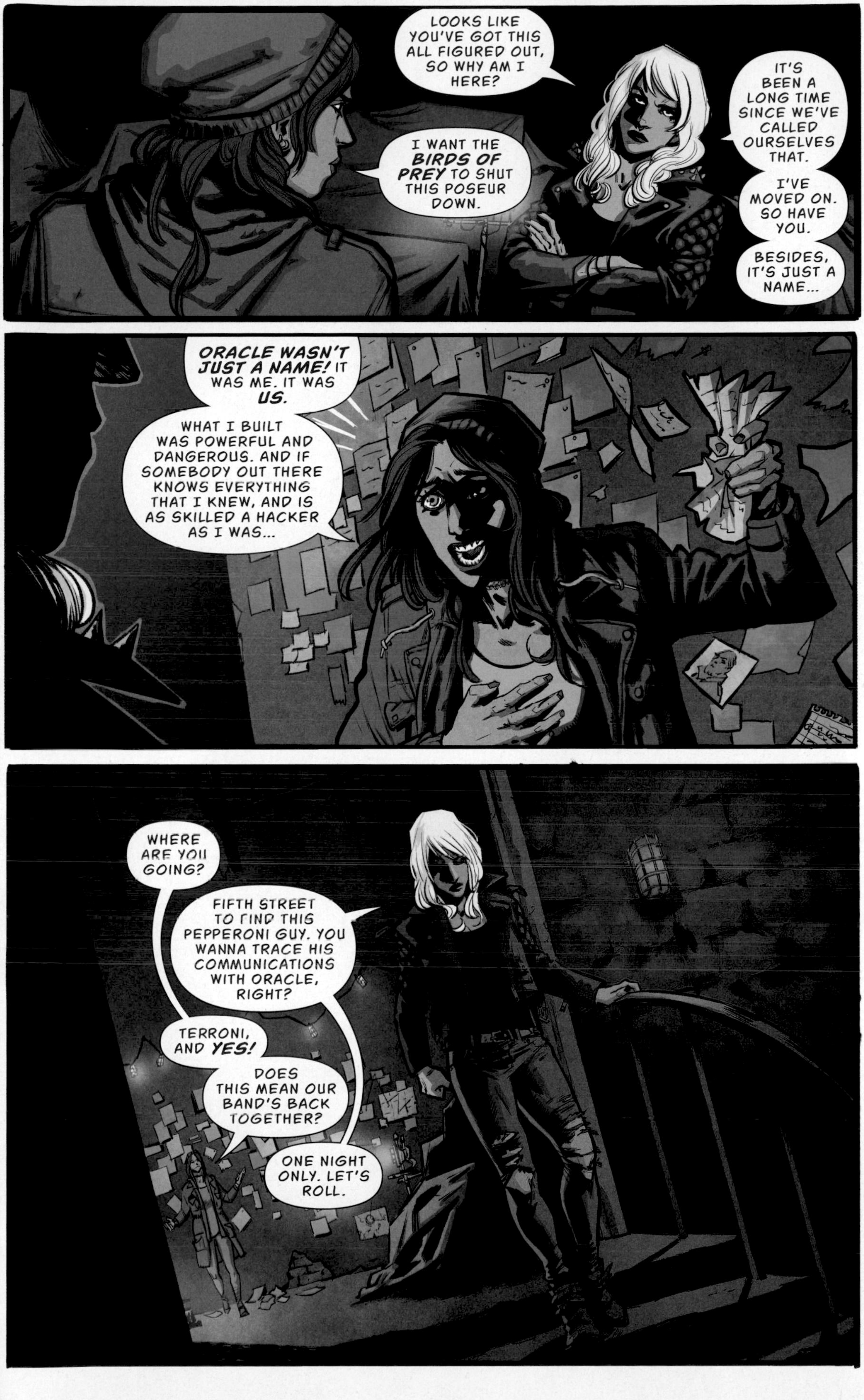
LOOKS LIKE YOU'VE GOT THIS ALL FIGURED OUT, SO WHY AM I HERE?
I WANT THE BIRDS OF PREY TO SHUT THIS POSEUR DOWN.
IT'S BEEN A LONG TIME SINCE WE'VE CALLED OURSELVES THAT.
I'VE MOVED ON. SO HAVE YOU.
BESIDES, IT'S JUST A NAME...
ORACLE WASN'T JUST A NAME! IT WAS ME. IT WAS US.
WHAT I BUILT WAS POWERFUL AND DANGEROUS. AND IF SOMEBODY OUT THERE KNOWS EVERYTHING THAT I KNEW, AND IS AS SKILLED A HACKER AS I WAS...
WHERE ARE YOU GOING?
FIFTH STREET TO FIND THIS PEPPERONI GUY. YOU WANNA TRACE HIS COMMUNICATIONS WITH ORACLE, RIGHT?
TERRONI, AND YES!
DOES THIS MEAN OUR BAND'S BACK TOGETHER?
ONE NIGHT ONLY. LET'S ROLL.

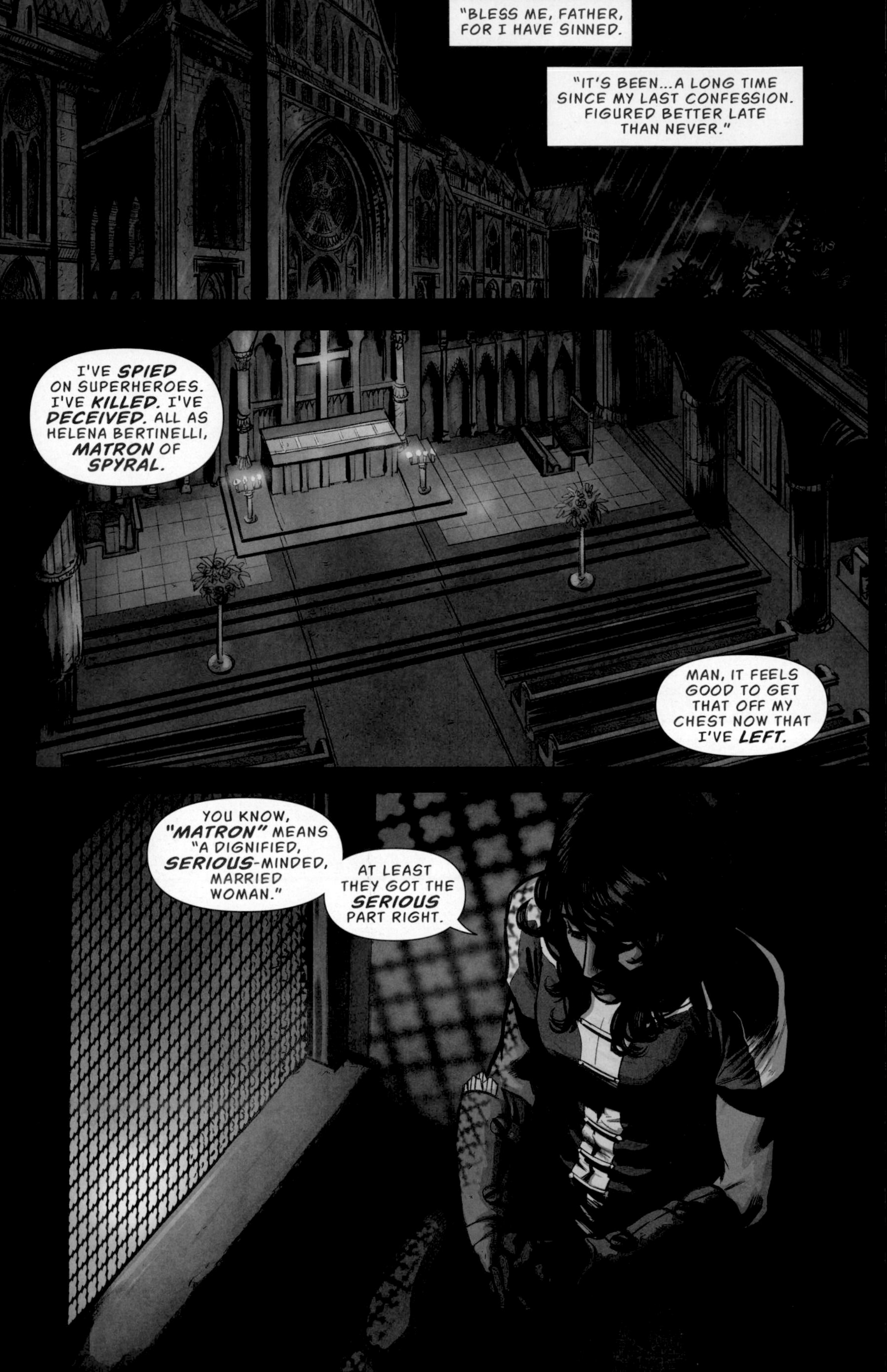
"BLESS ME, FATHER, FOR I HAVE SINNED.
"IT'S BEEN... A LONG TIME SINCE MY LAST CONFESSION. FIGURED BETTER LATE THAN NEVER."
I'VE SPIED ON SUPERHEROES. I'VE KILLED. I'VE DECEIVED. ALL AS HELENA BERTINELLI, MATRON OF SPYRAL.
MAN, IT FEELS GOOD TO GET THAT OFF MY CHEST NOW THAT I'VE LEFT.
YOU KNOW, "MATRON" MEANS "A DIGNIFIED, SERIOUS-MINDED, MARRIED WOMAN."
AT LEAST THEY GOT THE SERIOUS PART RIGHT.

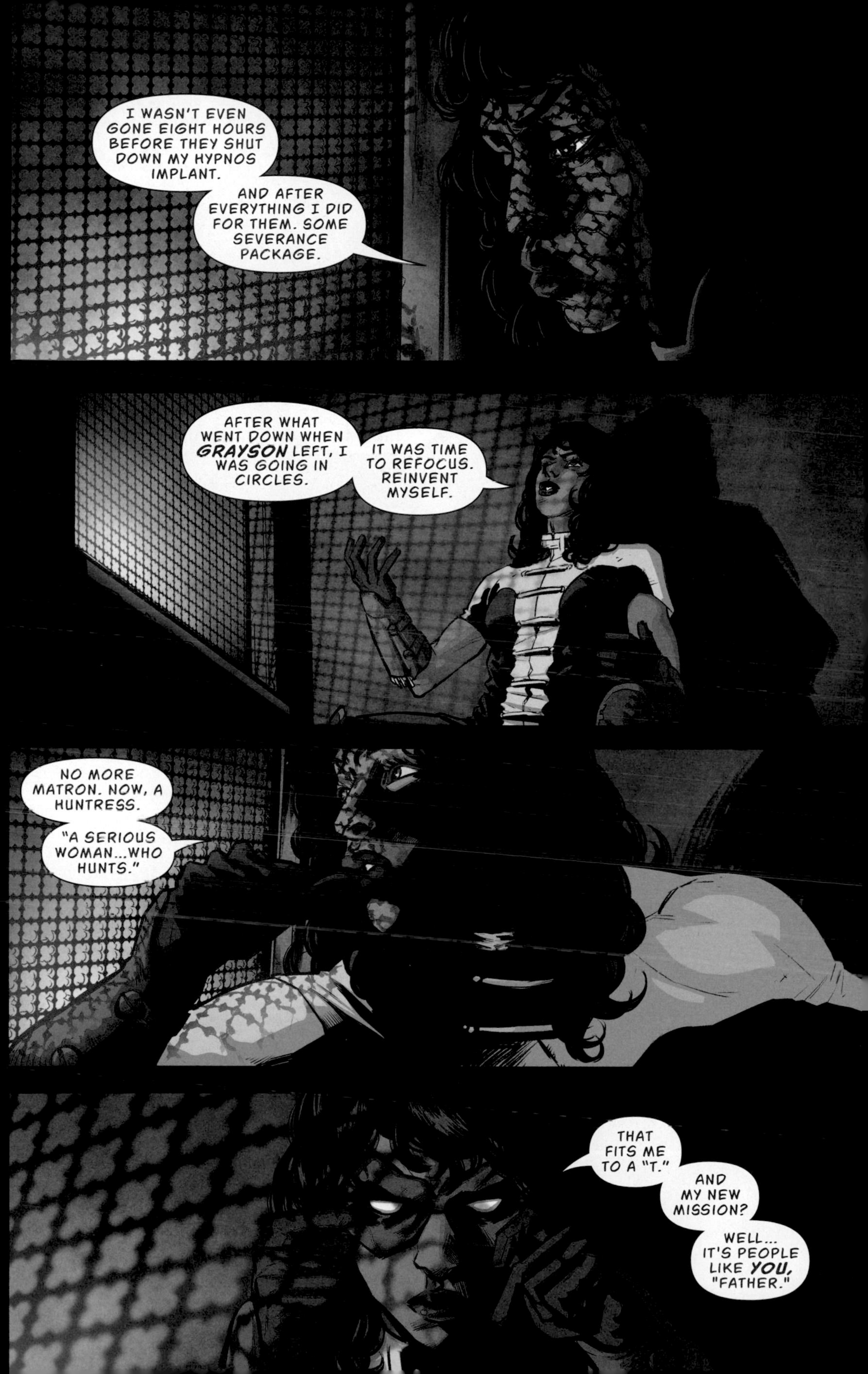
I WASN'T EVEN GONE EIGHT HOURS BEFORE THEY SHUT DOWN MY HYPNOS IMPLANT.
AND AFTER EVERYTHING I DID FOR THEM. SOME SEVERANCE PACKAGE.
AFTER WHAT WENT DOWN WHEN GRAYSON LEFT, I WAS GOING IN CIRCLES.
IT WAS TIME TO REFOCUS. REINVENT MYSELF.
NO MORE MATRON. NOW, A HUNTRESS.
"A SERIOUS WOMAN...WHO HUNTS."
THAT FITS ME TO A "T."
AND MY NEW MISSION?
WELL... IT'S PEOPLE LIKE YOU, "FATHER."

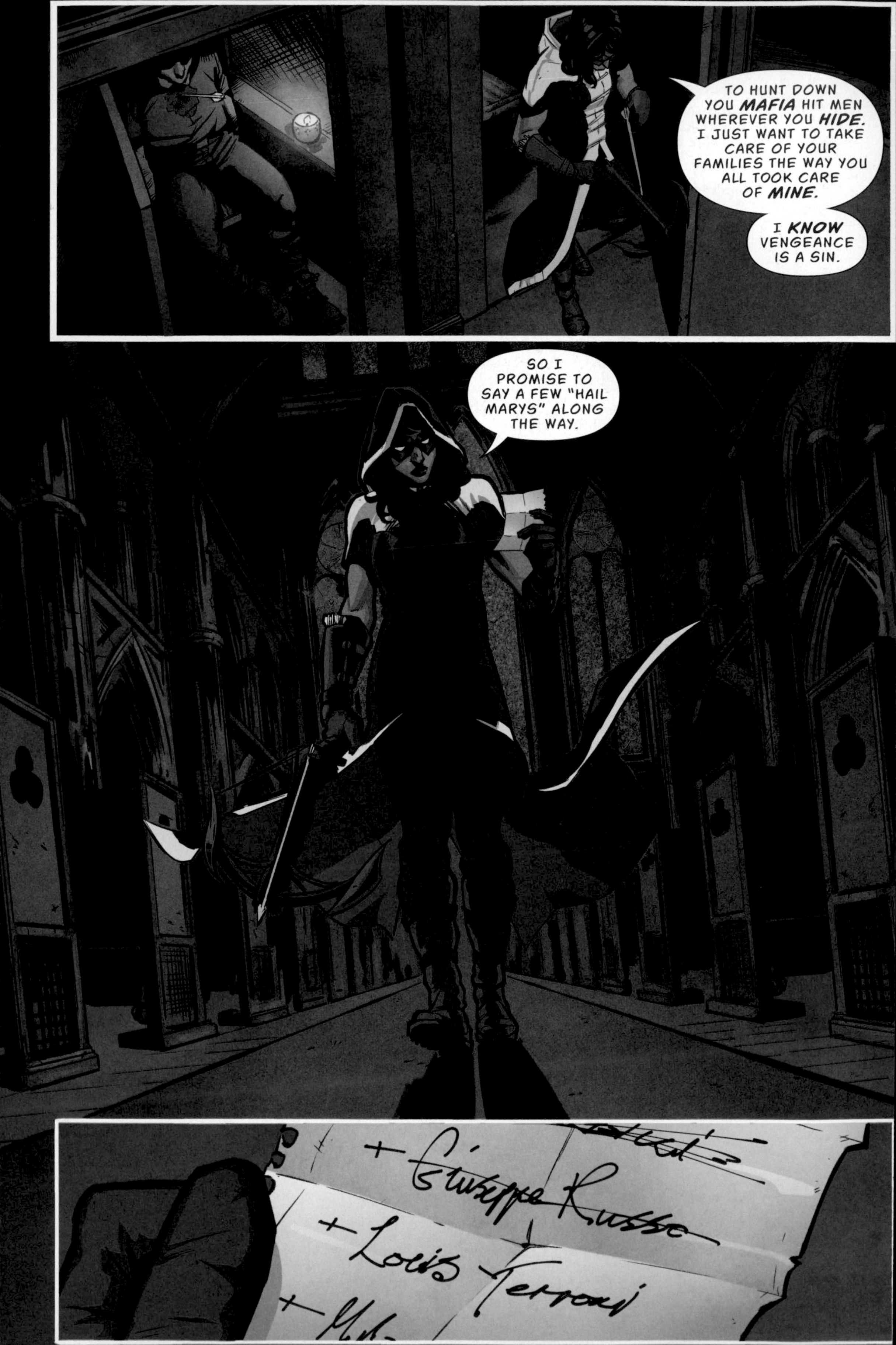
TO HUNT DOWN YOU MAFIA HIT MEN WHEREVER YOU HIDE. I JUST WANT TO TAKE CARE OF YOUR FAMILIES THE WAY YOU ALL TOOK CARE OF MINE.
I KNOW VENGEANCE IS A SIN.
SO I PROMISE TO SAY A FEW "HAIL MARYS" ALONG THE WAY.

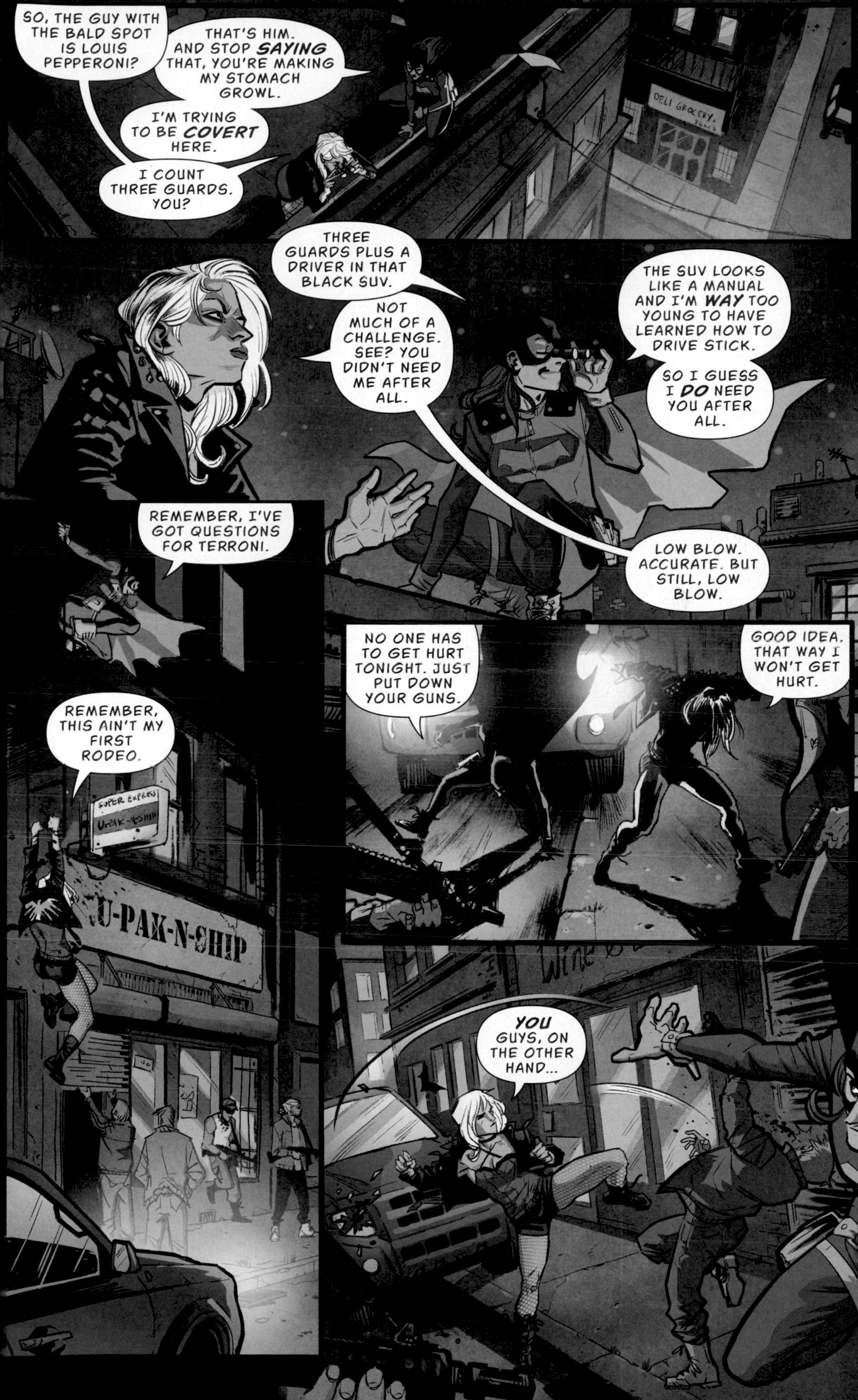
SO, THE GUY WITH THE BALD SPOT IS LOUIS PEPPERONI?
THAT'S HIM. AND STOP SAYING THAT, YOU'RE MAKING MY STOMACH GROWL.
I'M TRYING TO BE COVERT HERE.
I COUNT THREE GUARDS. YOU?
DELI GROCERY.
THREE GUARDS PLUS A DRIVER IN THAT BLACK SUV.
NOT MUCH OF A CHALLENGE. SEE? YOU DIDN'T NEED ME AFTER ALL.
THE SUV LOOKS LIKE A MANUAL AND I'M WAY TOO YOUNG TO HAVE LEARNED HOW TO DRIVE STICK.
SO I GUESS I DO NEED YOU AFTER ALL.
LOW BLOW. ACCURATE. BUT STILL, LOW BLOW.
REMEMBER, I'VE GOT QUESTIONS FOR TERRONI.
REMEMBER, THIS AIN'T MY FIRST RODEO.
SUPER EXPRESS
U-PAK-N-SHIP
NO ONE HAS TO GET HURT TONIGHT. JUST PUT DOWN YOUR GUNS.
GOOD IDEA. THAT WAY I WON'T GET HURT.
YOU GUYS, ON THE OTHER HAND...

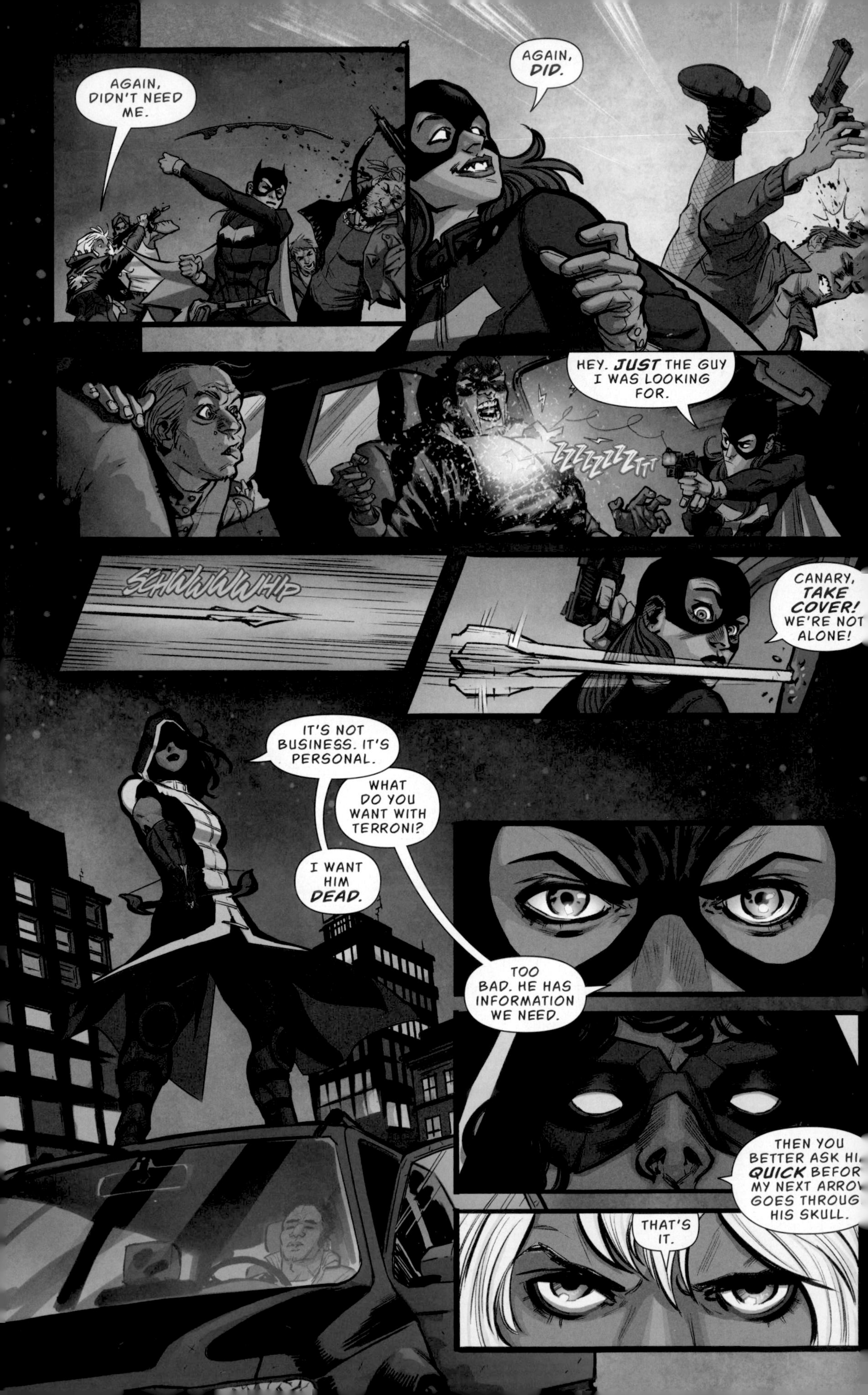
AGAIN, DIDN'T NEED ME.
AGAIN, DID.
HEY. JUST THE GUY I WAS LOOKING FOR.
ZZZZZZZZTTT
SCHWWWWHIP
CANARY, TAKE COVER! WE'RE NOT ALONE!
IT'S NOT BUSINESS. IT'S PERSONAL.
WHAT DO YOU WANT WITH TERRONI?
I WANT HIM DEAD.
TOO BAD. HE HAS INFORMATION WE NEED.
THEN YOU BETTER ASK HI QUICK BEFOR MY NEXT ARROV GOES THROUG HIS SKULL.
THAT'S IT.

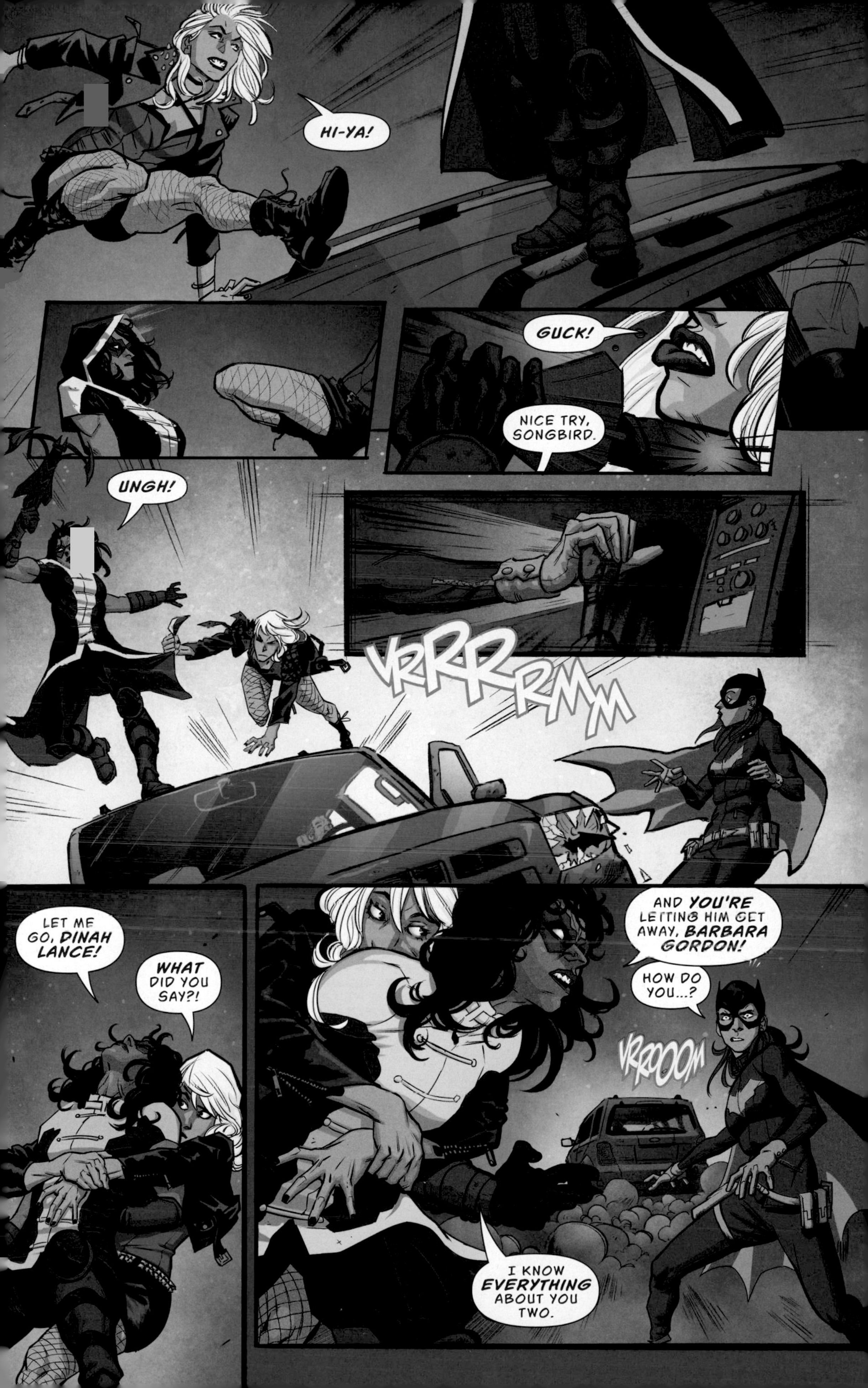
HI-YA!
GUCK!
NICE TRY, SONGBIRD.
UNGH!
VRRRRMM
LET ME GO, DINAH LANCE!
WHAT DID YOU SAY?!
AND YOU'RE LETTING HIM GET AWAY, BARBARA GORDON!
HOW DO YOU...?
VRROOOM
I KNOW EVERYTHING ABOUT YOU TWO.

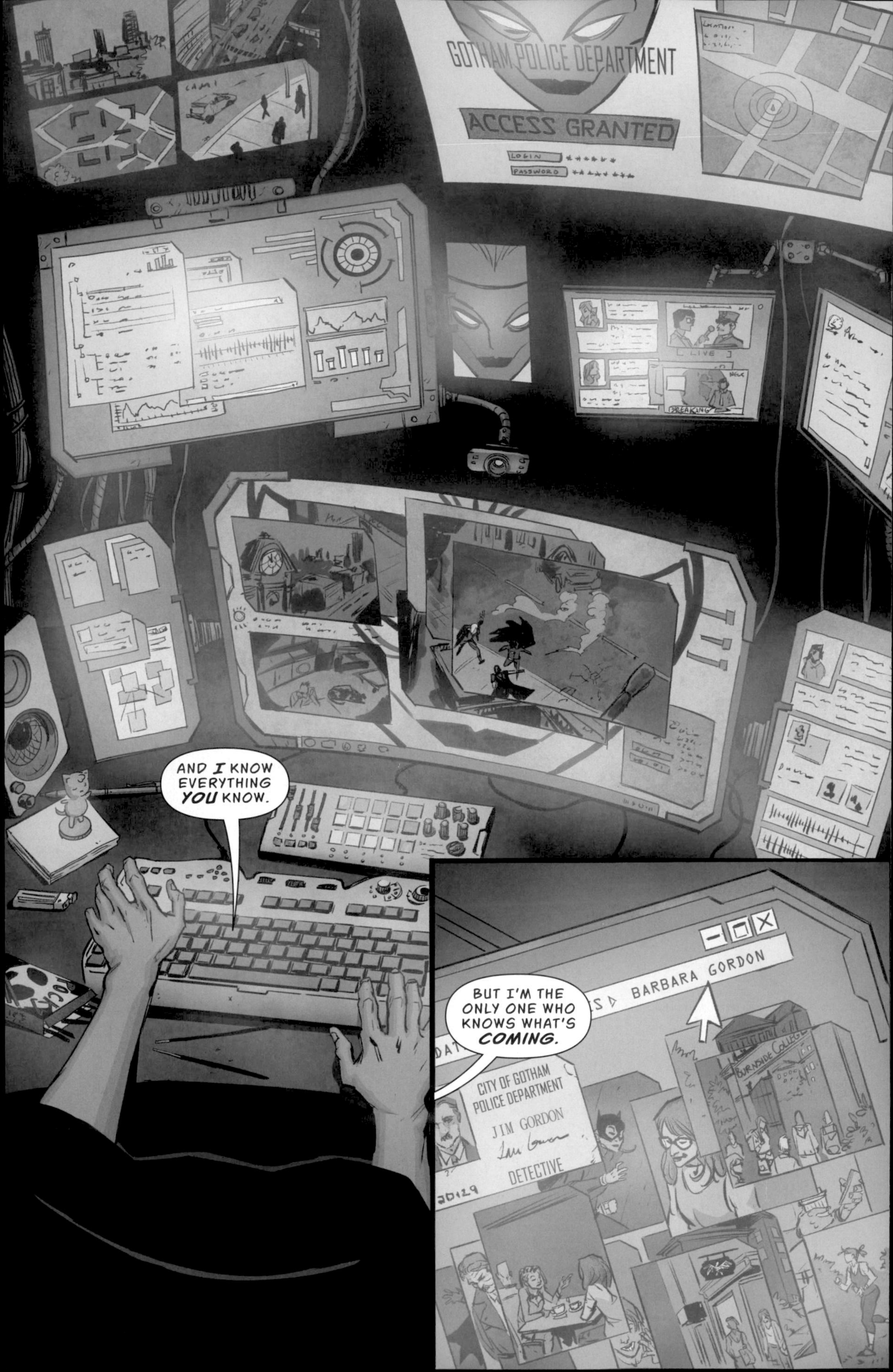
GOTHAM POLICE DEPARTMENT
ACCESS GRANTED
LOGIN
PASSWORD
LIVE
BREAKING
AND I KNOW EVERYTHING YOU KNOW.
BARBARA GORDON
BUT I'M THE ONLY ONE WHO KNOWS WHAT'S COMING.
CITY OF GOTHAM POLICE DEPARTMENT
JIM GORDON
DETECTIVE
BURNSIDE COLLEGE

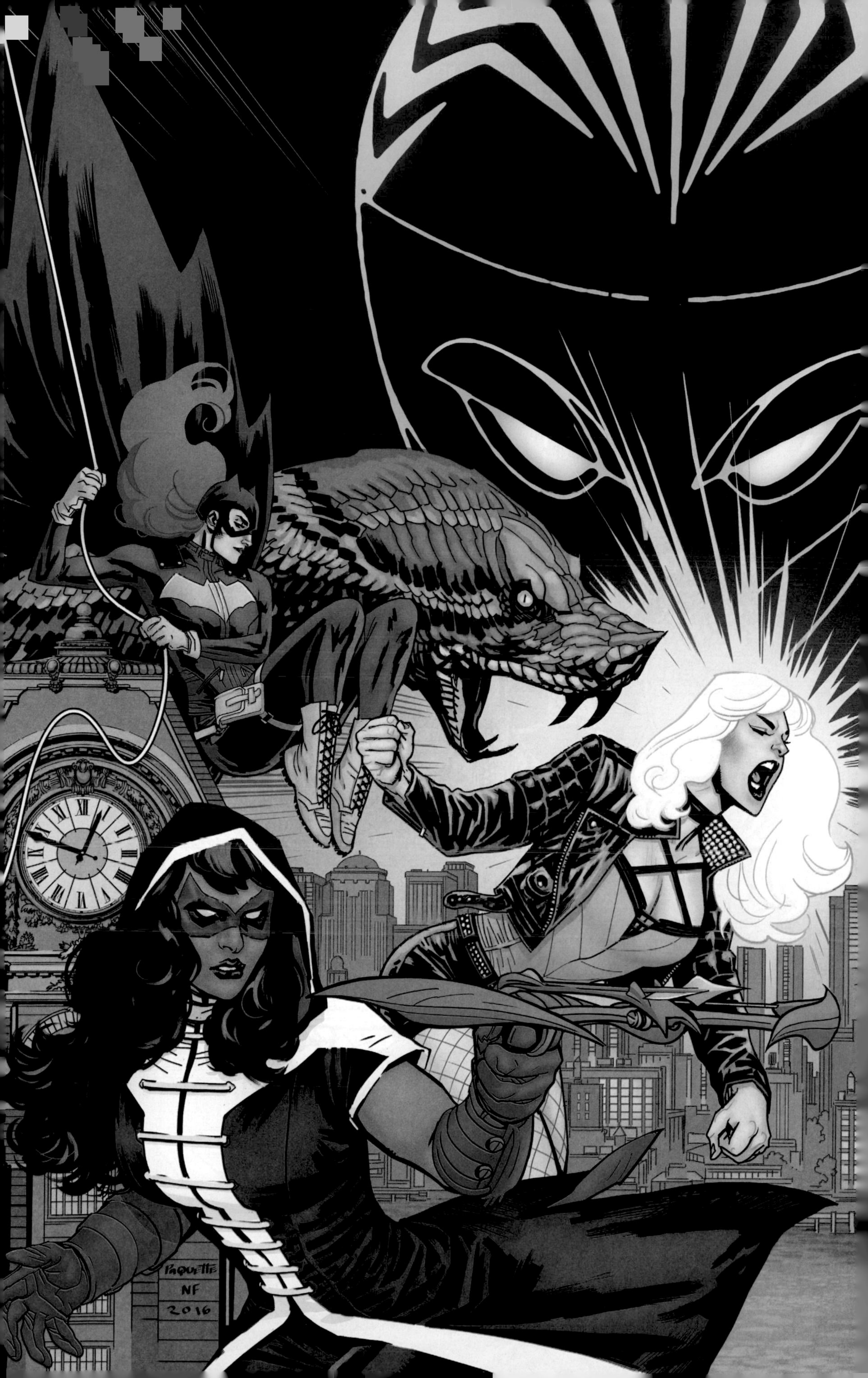
PAQUETTE
NF
2016

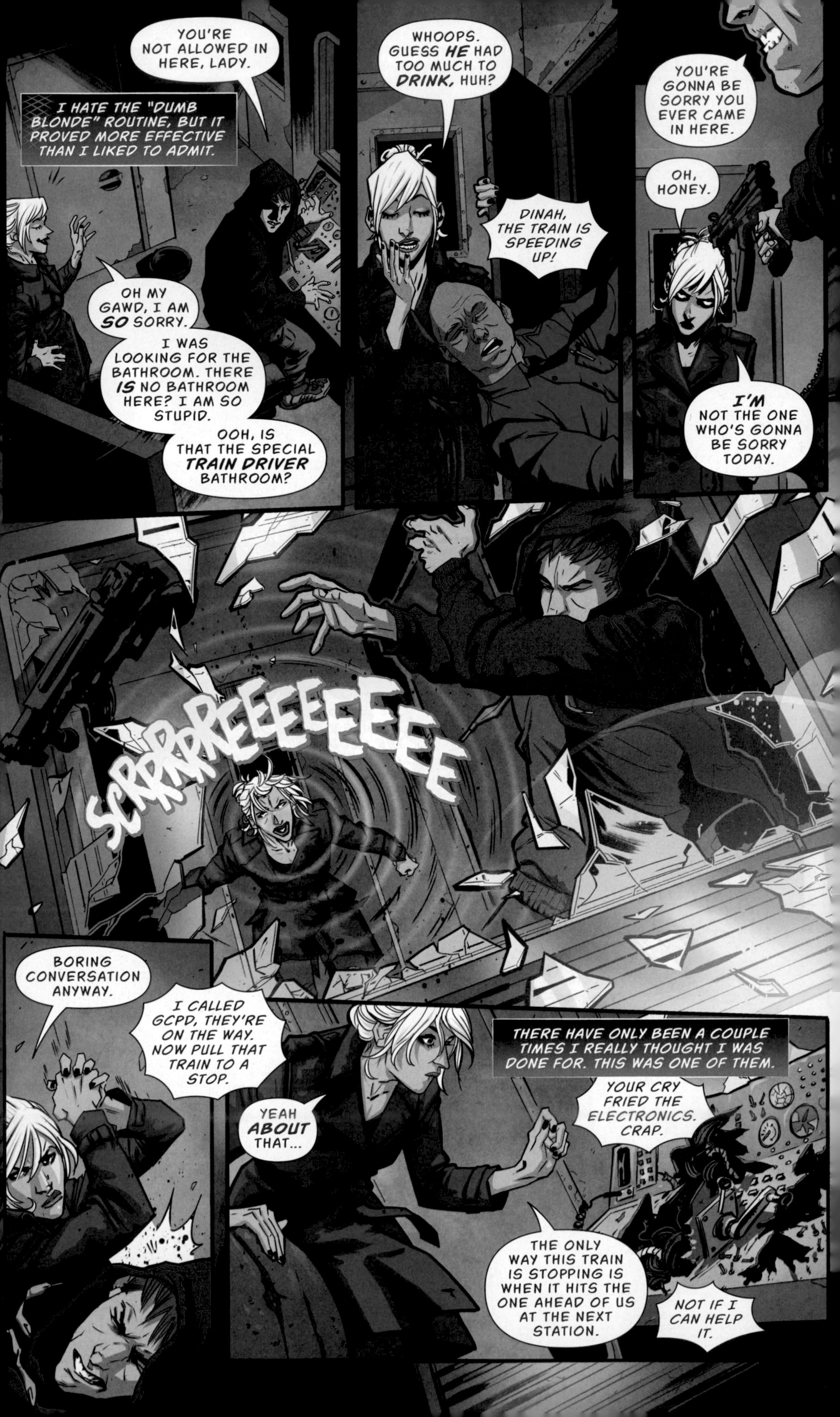
YOU'RE NOT ALLOWED IN HERE, LADY.
I HATE THE "DUMB BLONDE" ROUTINE, BUT IT PROVED MORE EFFECTIVE THAN I LIKED TO ADMIT.
OH MY GAWD, I AM **SO** SORRY.
I WAS LOOKING FOR THE BATHROOM. THERE **IS** NO BATHROOM HERE? I AM SO STUPID.
OOH, IS THAT THE SPECIAL **TRAIN DRIVER** BATHROOM?
WHOOPS. GUESS **HE** HAD TOO MUCH TO **DRINK,** HUH?
DINAH, THE TRAIN IS SPEEDING UP!
YOU'RE GONNA BE SORRY YOU EVER CAME IN HERE.
OH, HONEY.
I'M NOT THE ONE WHO'S GONNA BE SORRY TODAY.
SCRRRREEEEEEEEE
BORING CONVERSATION ANYWAY.
I CALLED GCPD, THEY'RE ON THE WAY. NOW PULL THAT TRAIN TO A STOP.
YEAH **ABOUT** THAT...
THERE HAVE ONLY BEEN A COUPLE TIMES I REALLY THOUGHT I WAS DONE FOR. THIS WAS ONE OF THEM.
YOUR CRY FRIED THE ELECTRONICS. CRAP.
THE ONLY WAY THIS TRAIN IS STOPPING IS WHEN IT HITS THE ONE AHEAD OF US AT THE NEXT STATION.
NOT IF I CAN HELP IT.

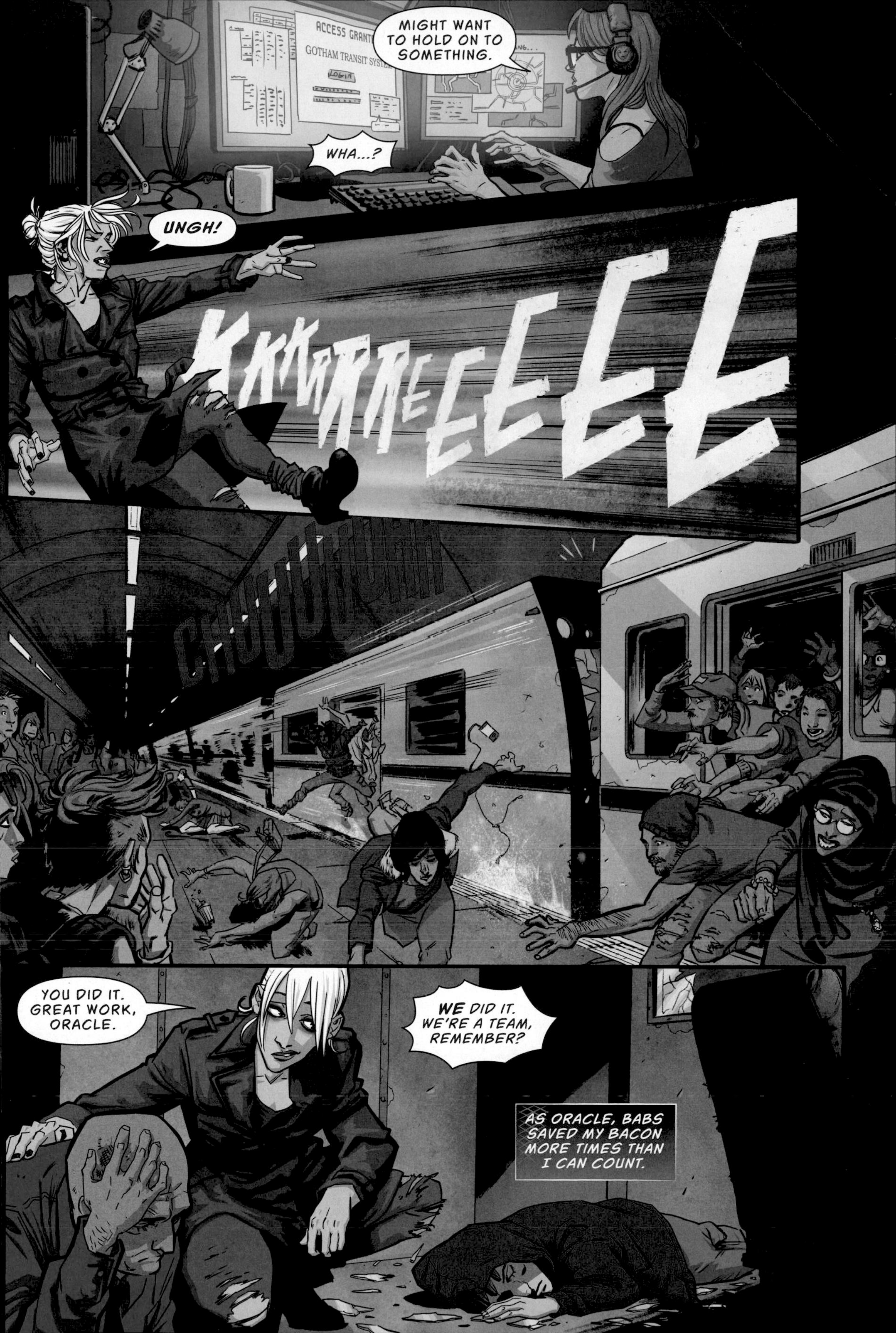
ACCESS GRANTED
GOTHAM TRANSIT SYSTEM
LOGIN
MIGHT WANT TO HOLD ON TO SOMETHING.
WHA...?
UNGH!
KKKRRREEEEE
CHUUUUUUNN
YOU DID IT. GREAT WORK, ORACLE.
WE DID IT. WE'RE A TEAM, REMEMBER?
AS ORACLE, BABS SAVED MY BACON MORE TIMES THAN I CAN COUNT.

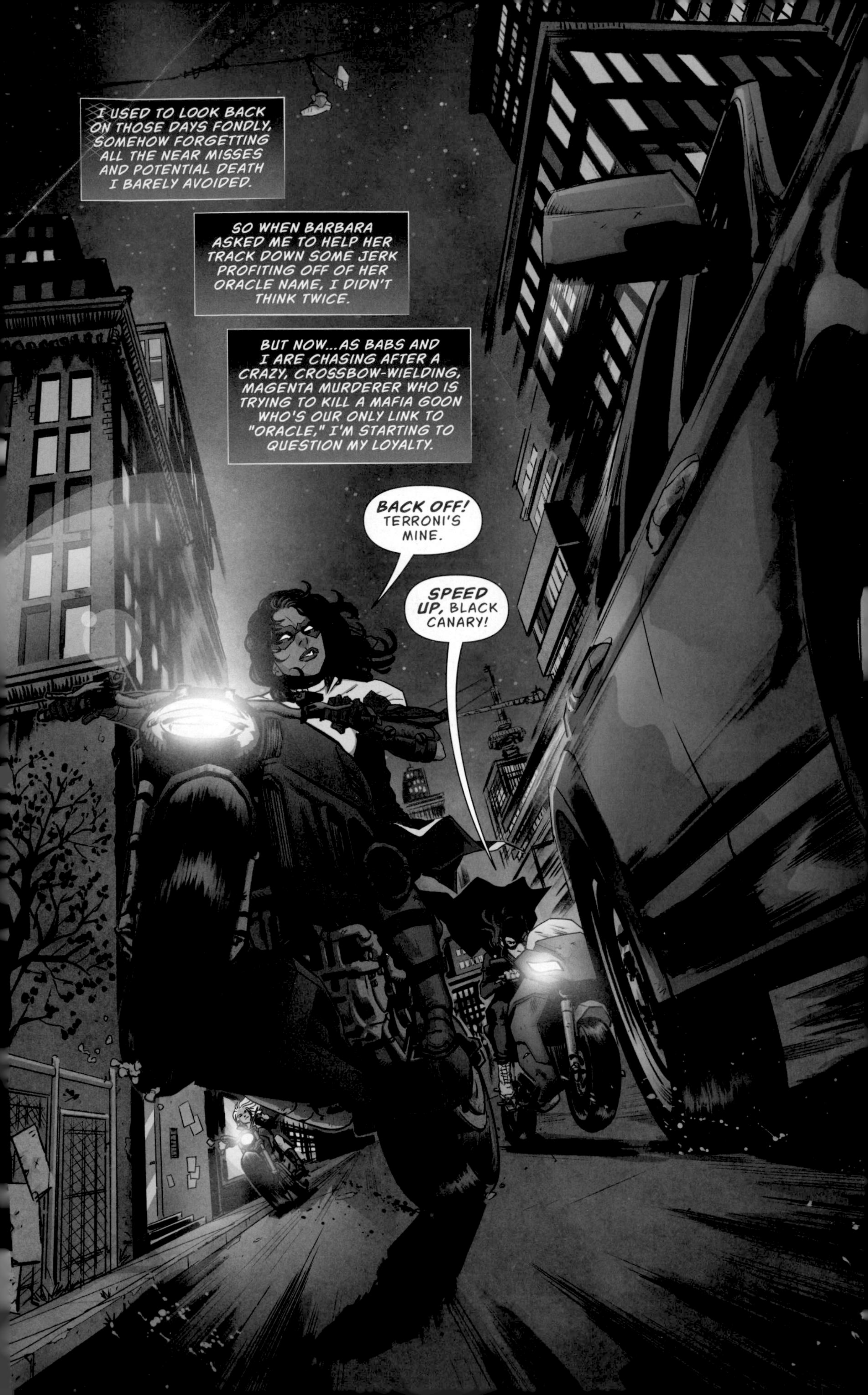
I USED TO LOOK BACK ON THOSE DAYS FONDLY, SOMEHOW FORGETTING ALL THE NEAR MISSES AND POTENTIAL DEATH I BARELY AVOIDED.
SO WHEN BARBARA ASKED ME TO HELP HER TRACK DOWN SOME JERK PROFITING OFF OF HER ORACLE NAME, I DIDN'T THINK TWICE.
BUT NOW...AS BABS AND I ARE CHASING AFTER A CRAZY, CROSSBOW-WIELDING, MAGENTA MURDERER WHO IS TRYING TO KILL A MAFIA GOON WHO'S OUR ONLY LINK TO "ORACLE," I'M STARTING TO QUESTION MY LOYALTY.
BACK OFF! TERRONI'S MINE.
SPEED UP, BLACK CANARY!

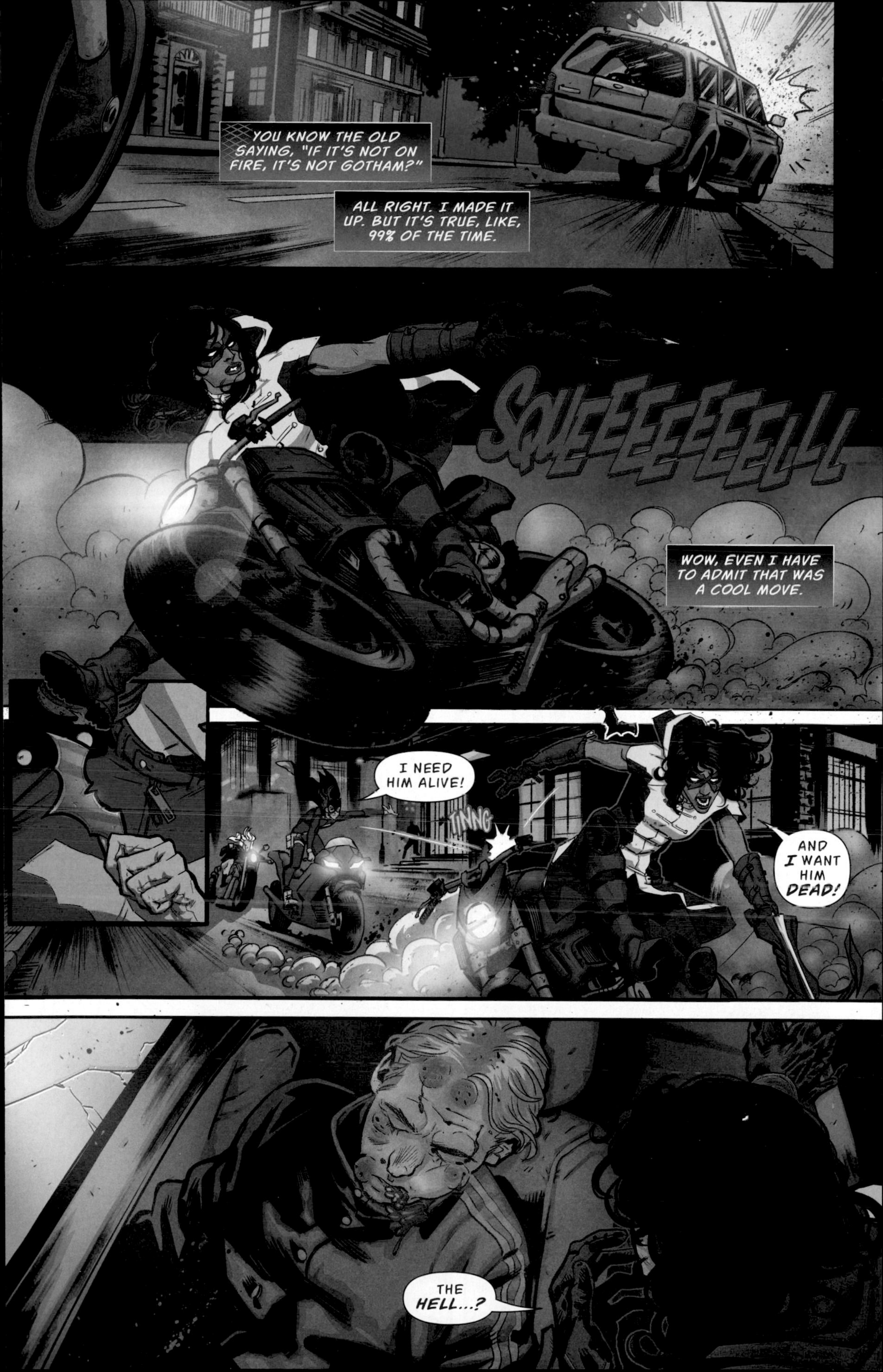
YOU KNOW THE OLD SAYING, "IF IT'S NOT ON FIRE, IT'S NOT GOTHAM?"
ALL RIGHT. I MADE IT UP. BUT IT'S TRUE, LIKE, 99% OF THE TIME.
SQUEEEEEEELLL
WOW, EVEN I HAVE TO ADMIT THAT WAS A COOL MOVE.
I NEED HIM ALIVE!
TINNG
AND I WANT HIM DEAD!
THE HELL...?

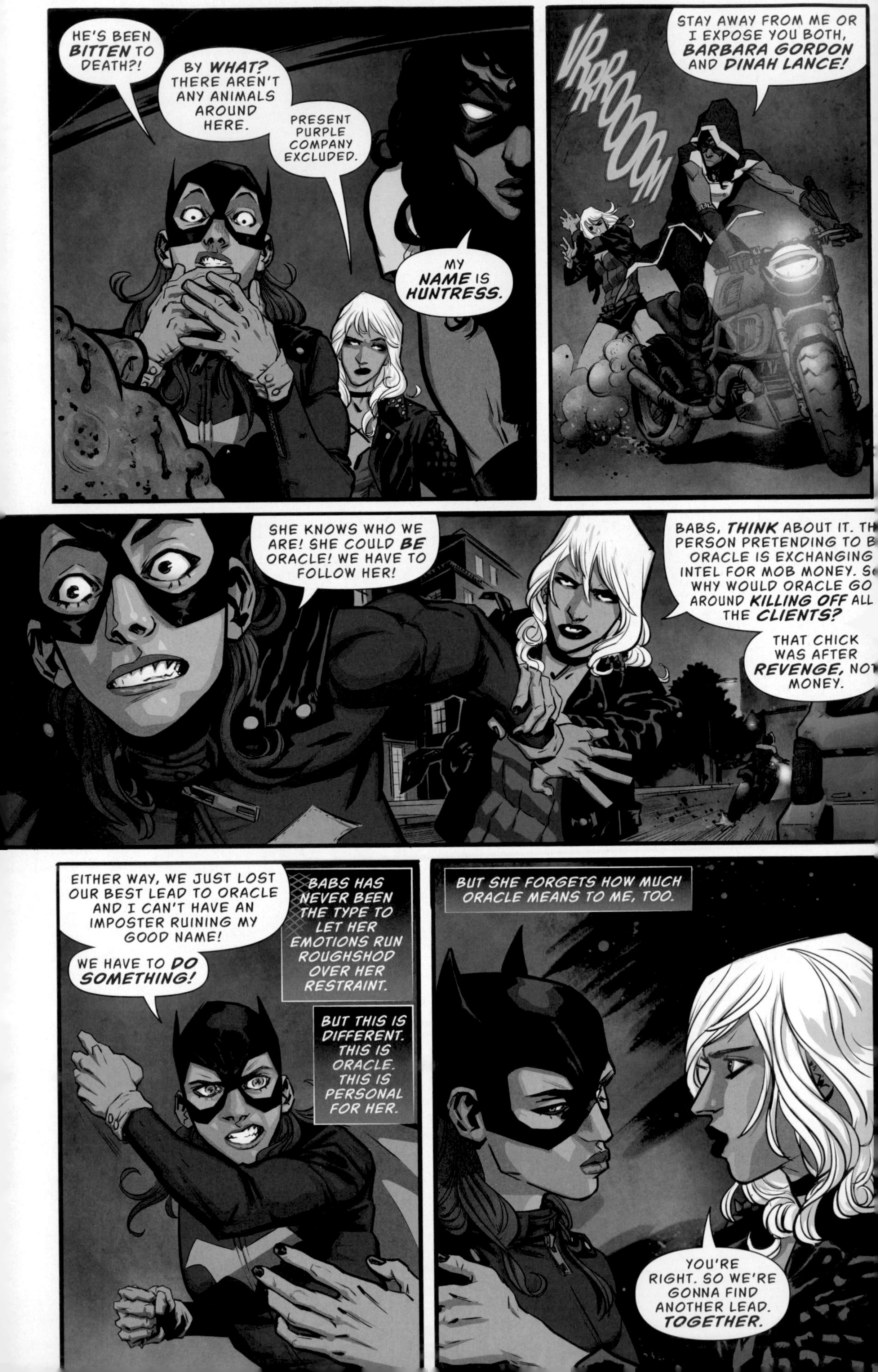
HE'S BEEN BITTEN TO DEATH?!
BY WHAT? THERE AREN'T ANY ANIMALS AROUND HERE.
PRESENT PURPLE COMPANY EXCLUDED.
MY NAME IS HUNTRESS.
VRRROOOOM
STAY AWAY FROM ME OR I EXPOSE YOU BOTH, BARBARA GORDON AND DINAH LANCE!
SHE KNOWS WHO WE ARE! SHE COULD BE ORACLE! WE HAVE TO FOLLOW HER!
BABS, THINK ABOUT IT. TH PERSON PRETENDING TO B ORACLE IS EXCHANGING INTEL FOR MOB MONEY. S WHY WOULD ORACLE GO AROUND KILLING OFF ALL THE CLIENTS?
THAT CHICK WAS AFTER REVENGE, NOT MONEY.
EITHER WAY, WE JUST LOST OUR BEST LEAD TO ORACLE AND I CAN'T HAVE AN IMPOSTER RUINING MY GOOD NAME!
WE HAVE TO DO SOMETHING!
BABS HAS NEVER BEEN THE TYPE TO LET HER EMOTIONS RUN ROUGHSHOD OVER HER RESTRAINT.
BUT THIS IS DIFFERENT. THIS IS ORACLE. THIS IS PERSONAL FOR HER.
BUT SHE FORGETS HOW MUCH ORACLE MEANS TO ME, TOO.
YOU'RE RIGHT. SO WE'RE GONNA FIND ANOTHER LEAD. TOGETHER.

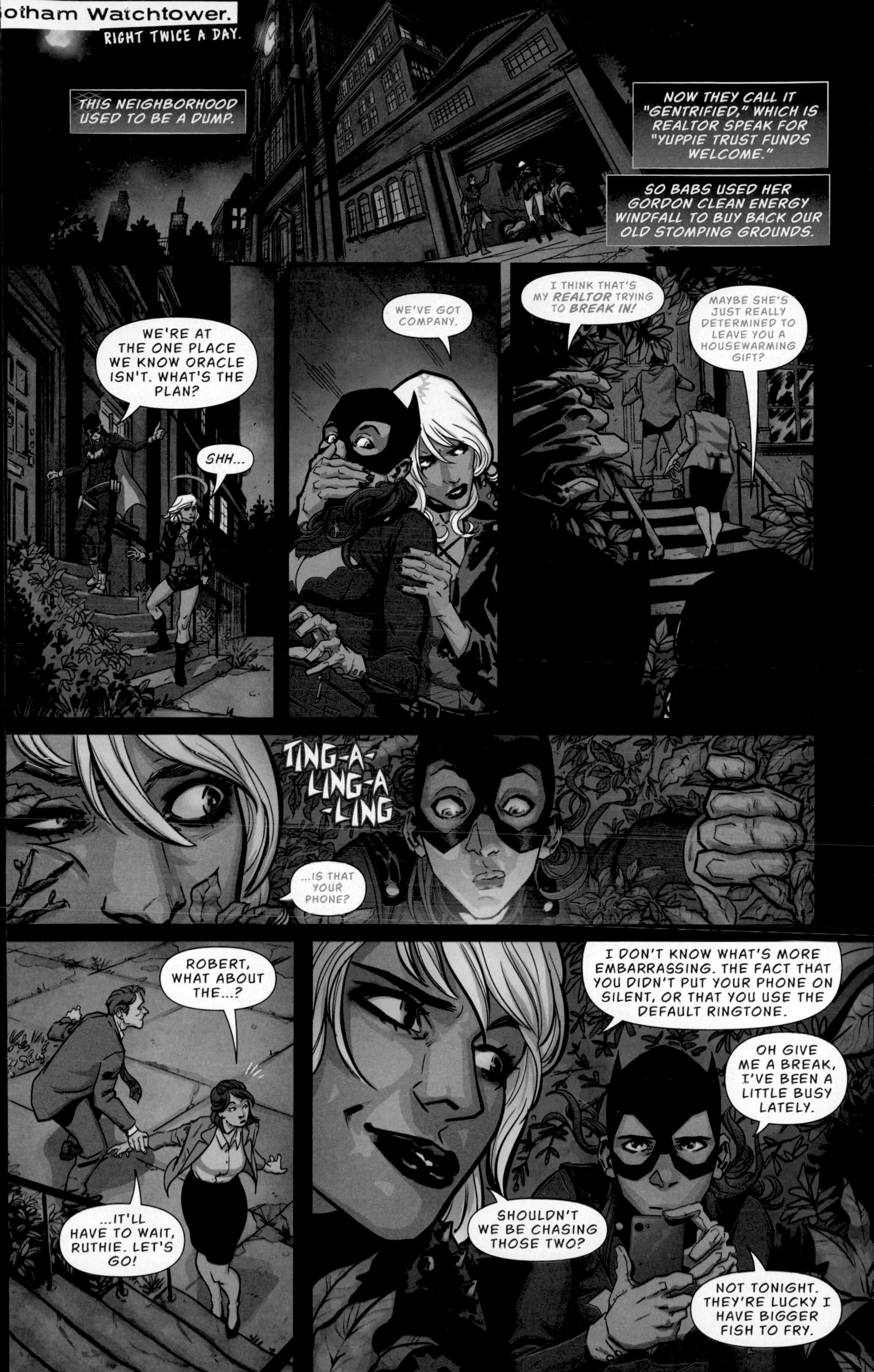

otham Watchtower.
RIGHT TWICE A DAY.
THIS NEIGHBORHOOD USED TO BE A DUMP.
NOW THEY CALL IT "GENTRIFIED," WHICH IS REALTOR SPEAK FOR "YUPPIE TRUST FUNDS WELCOME."
SO BABS USED HER GORDON CLEAN ENERGY WINDFALL TO BUY BACK OUR OLD STOMPING GROUNDS.
WE'RE AT THE ONE PLACE WE KNOW ORACLE ISN'T. WHAT'S THE PLAN?
SHH...
WE'VE GOT COMPANY.
I THINK THAT'S MY REALTOR TRYING TO BREAK IN!
MAYBE SHE'S JUST REALLY DETERMINED TO LEAVE YOU A HOUSEWARMING GIFT?
TING-A-LING-A-LING
...IS THAT YOUR PHONE?
ROBERT, WHAT ABOUT THE...?
...IT'LL HAVE TO WAIT, RUTHIE. LET'S GO!
I DON'T KNOW WHAT'S MORE EMBARRASSING. THE FACT THAT YOU DIDN'T PUT YOUR PHONE ON SILENT, OR THAT YOU USE THE DEFAULT RINGTONE.
OH GIVE ME A BREAK, I'VE BEEN A LITTLE BUSY LATELY.
SHOULDN'T WE BE CHASING THOSE TWO?
NOT TONIGHT. THEY'RE LUCKY I HAVE BIGGER FISH TO FRY.

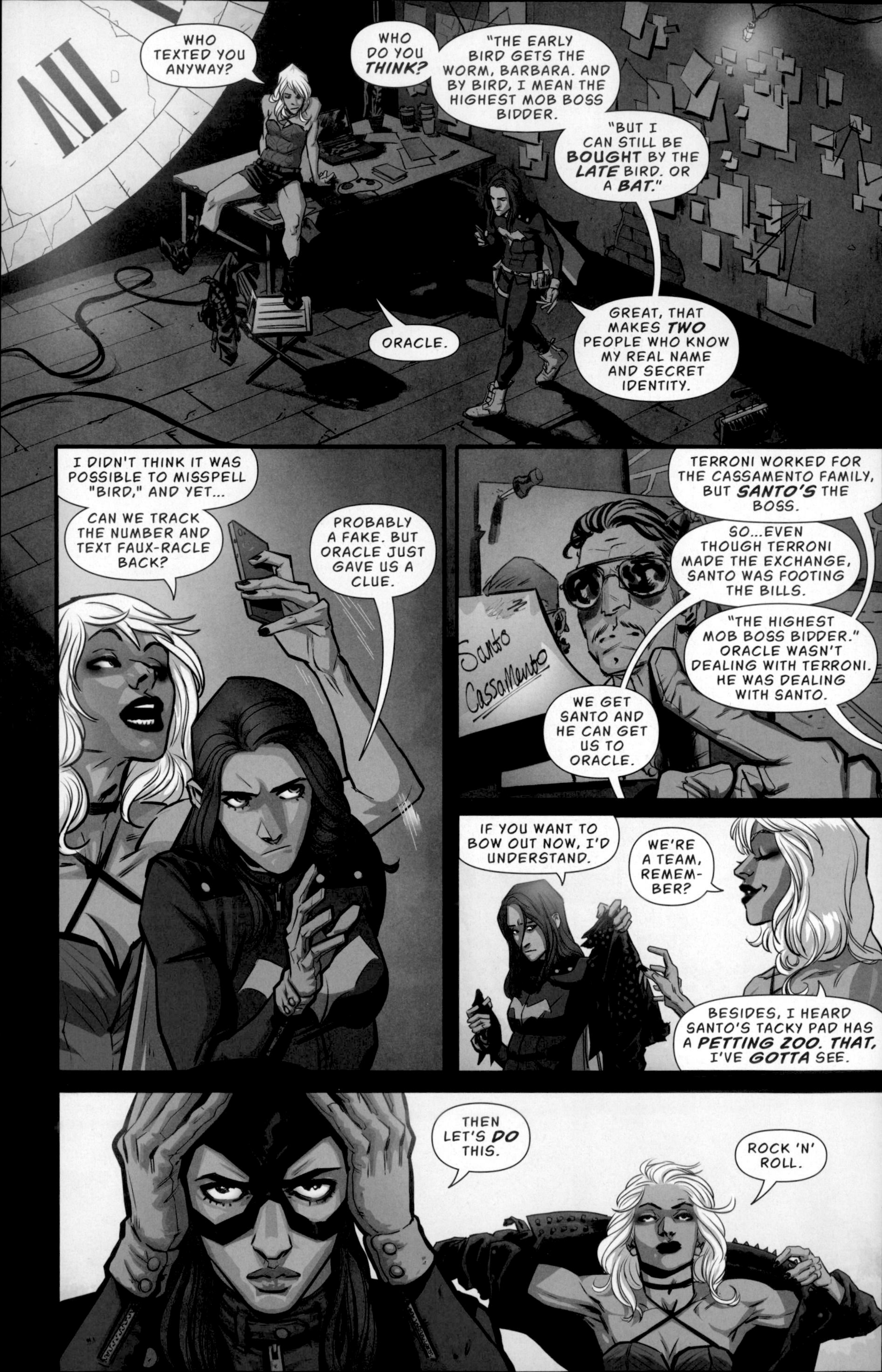

WHO TEXTED YOU ANYWAY?
WHO DO YOU *THINK?*
"THE EARLY BIRD GETS THE WORM, BARBARA. AND BY BIRD, I MEAN THE HIGHEST MOB BOSS BIDDER.
"BUT I CAN STILL BE **BOUGHT** BY THE *LATE* BIRD. OR A *BAT*."
ORACLE.
GREAT, THAT MAKES *TWO* PEOPLE WHO KNOW MY REAL NAME AND SECRET IDENTITY.
I DIDN'T THINK IT WAS POSSIBLE TO MISSPELL "BIRD," AND YET...
CAN WE TRACK THE NUMBER AND TEXT FAUX-RACLE BACK?
PROBABLY A FAKE. BUT ORACLE JUST GAVE US A CLUE.
TERRONI WORKED FOR THE CASSAMENTO FAMILY, BUT *SANTO'S* THE BOSS.
SO...EVEN THOUGH TERRONI MADE THE EXCHANGE, SANTO WAS FOOTING THE BILLS.
"THE HIGHEST MOB BOSS BIDDER." ORACLE WASN'T DEALING WITH TERRONI. HE WAS DEALING WITH SANTO.
Santo Cassamento
WE GET SANTO AND HE CAN GET US TO ORACLE.
IF YOU WANT TO BOW OUT NOW, I'D UNDERSTAND.
WE'RE A TEAM, REMEMBER?
BESIDES, I HEARD SANTO'S TACKY PAD HAS A *PETTING ZOO. THAT,* I'VE *GOTTA* SEE.
THEN LET'S *DO* THIS.
ROCK 'N' ROLL.

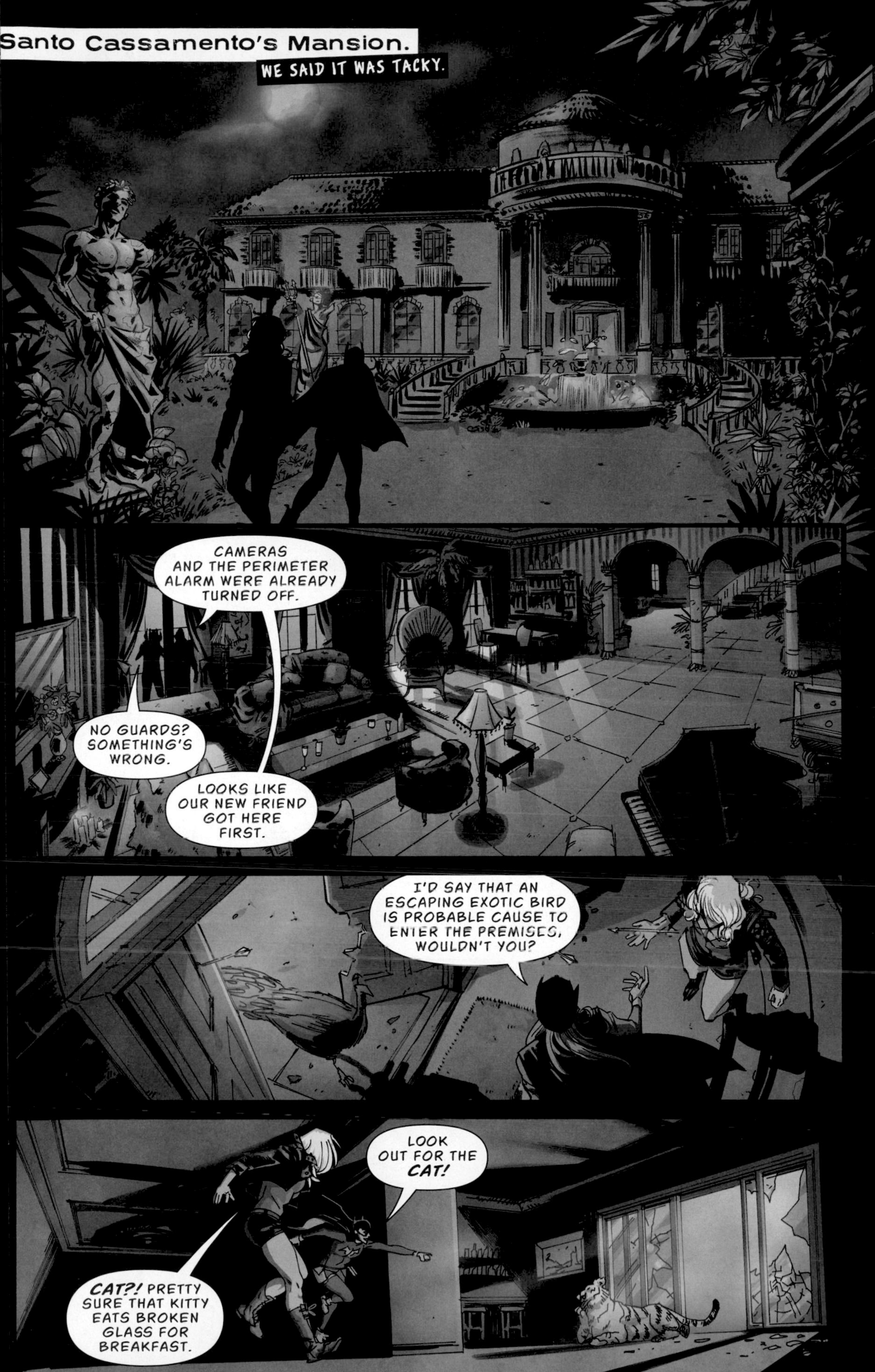
Santo Cassamento's Mansion.
WE SAID IT WAS TACKY.
CAMERAS AND THE PERIMETER ALARM WERE ALREADY TURNED OFF.
NO GUARDS? SOMETHING'S WRONG.
LOOKS LIKE OUR NEW FRIEND GOT HERE FIRST.
I'D SAY THAT AN ESCAPING EXOTIC BIRD IS PROBABLE CAUSE TO ENTER THE PREMISES, WOULDN'T YOU?
LOOK OUT FOR THE CAT!
CAT?! PRETTY SURE THAT KITTY EATS BROKEN GLASS FOR BREAKFAST.

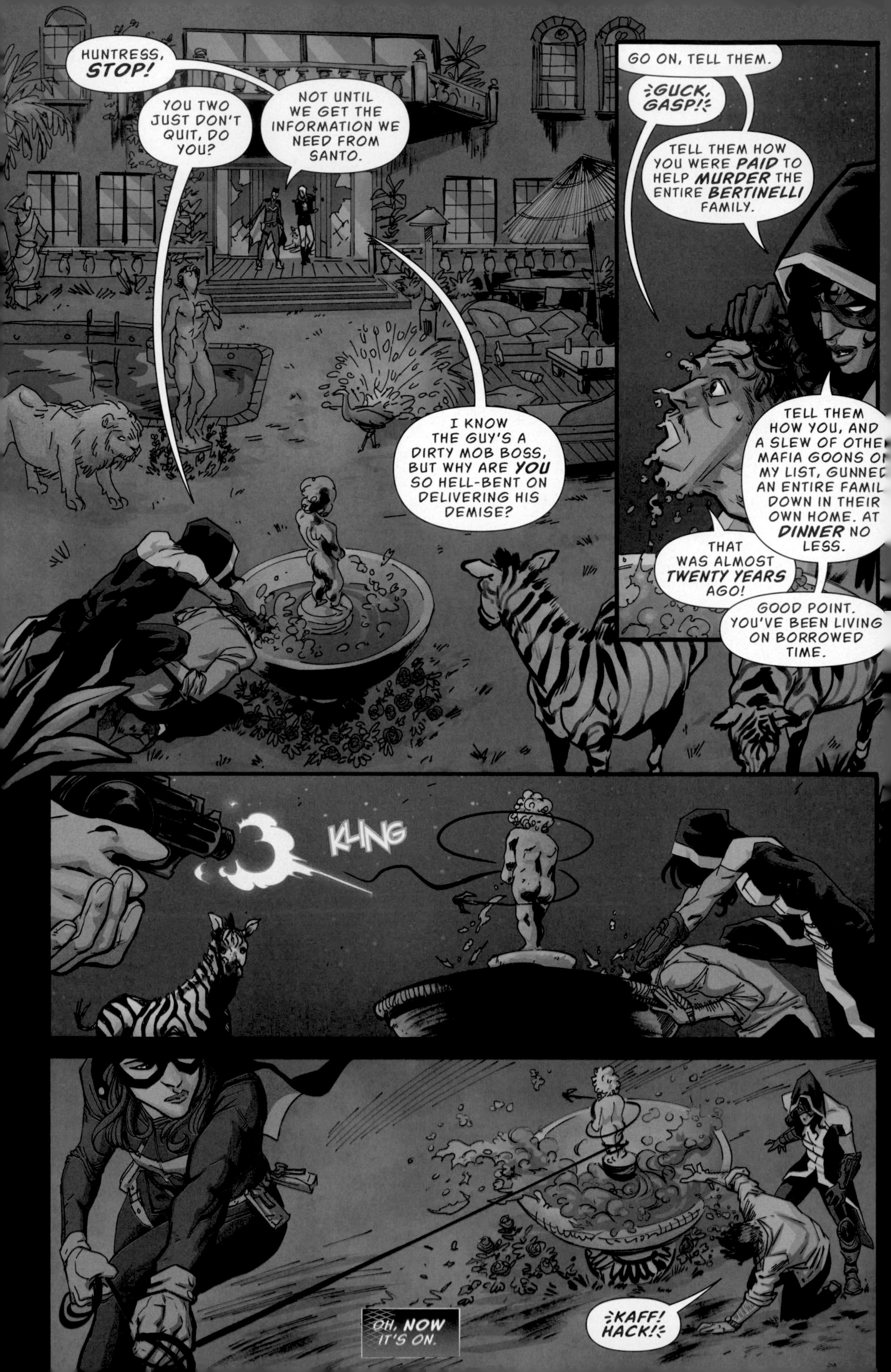
HUNTRESS, STOP!
YOU TWO JUST DON'T QUIT, DO YOU?
NOT UNTIL WE GET THE INFORMATION WE NEED FROM SANTO.
I KNOW THE GUY'S A DIRTY MOB BOSS, BUT WHY ARE YOU SO HELL-BENT ON DELIVERING HIS DEMISE?
GO ON, TELL THEM.
GUCK, GASP!
TELL THEM HOW YOU WERE PAID TO HELP MURDER THE ENTIRE BERTINELLI FAMILY.
TELL THEM HOW YOU, AND A SLEW OF OTHE MAFIA GOONS O MY LIST, GUNNE AN ENTIRE FAMIL DOWN IN THEIR OWN HOME. AT DINNER NO LESS.
THAT WAS ALMOST TWENTY YEARS AGO!
GOOD POINT. YOU'VE BEEN LIVING ON BORROWED TIME.
KLING
OH, NOW IT'S ON.
KAFF! HACK!

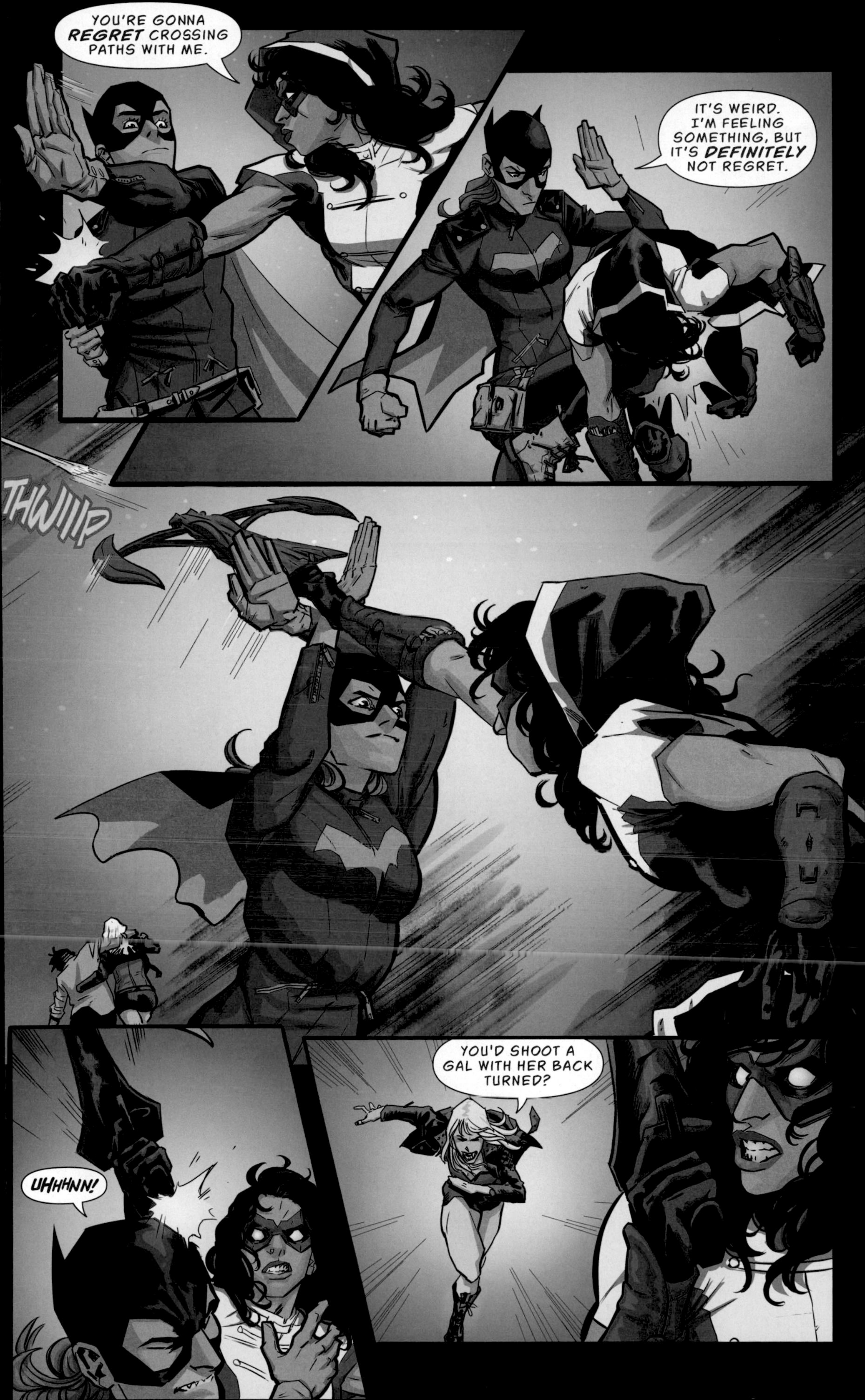
YOU'RE GONNA **REGRET** CROSSING PATHS WITH ME.
IT'S WEIRD. I'M FEELING SOMETHING, BUT IT'S ***DEFINITELY*** NOT REGRET.
THWIIIP
UHHHNN!
YOU'D SHOOT A GAL WITH HER BACK TURNED?

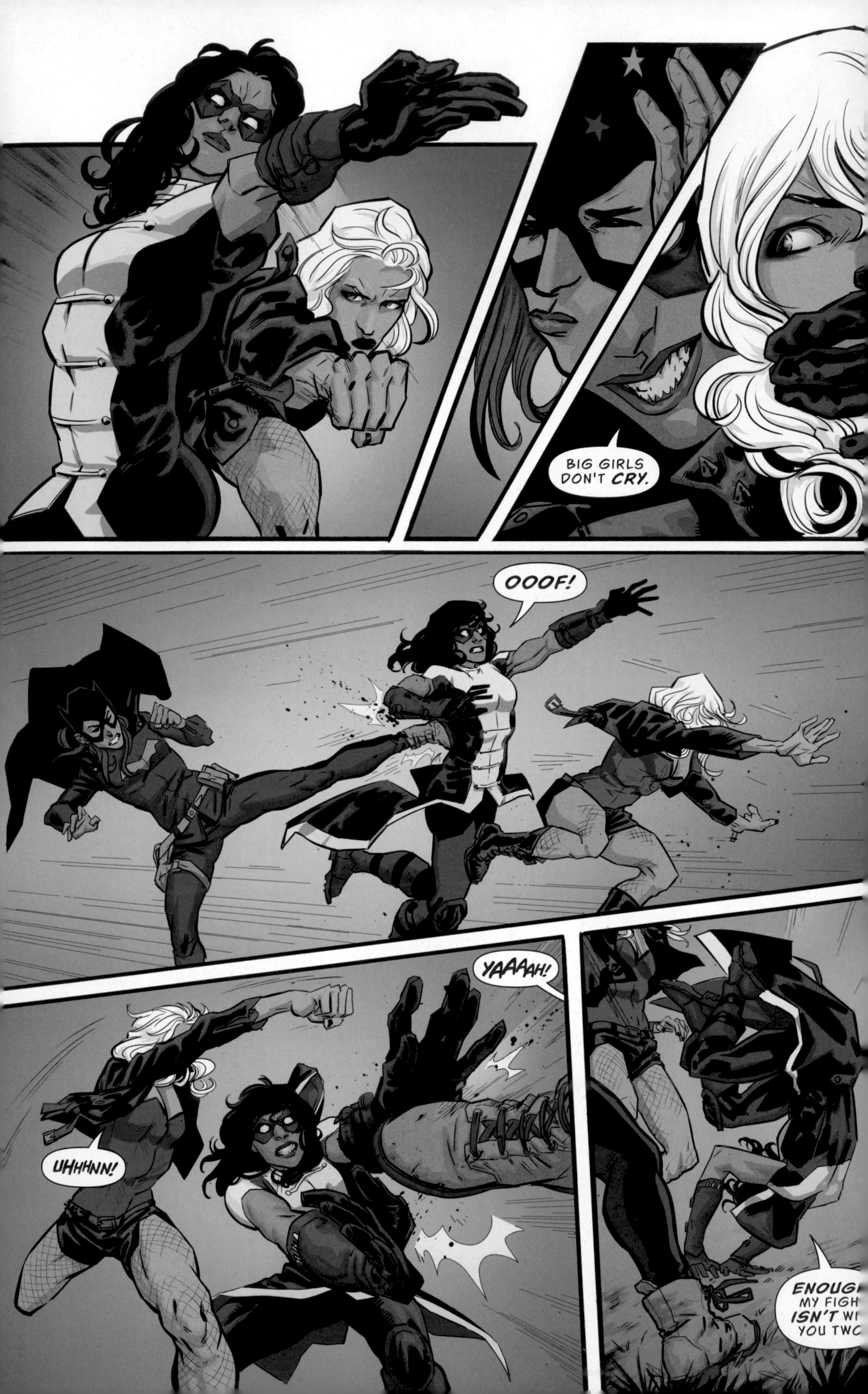
BIG GIRLS DON'T CRY.
OOOF!
YAAAAH!
UHHHNN!
ENOUG
MY FIGH
ISN'T WI
YOU TWO

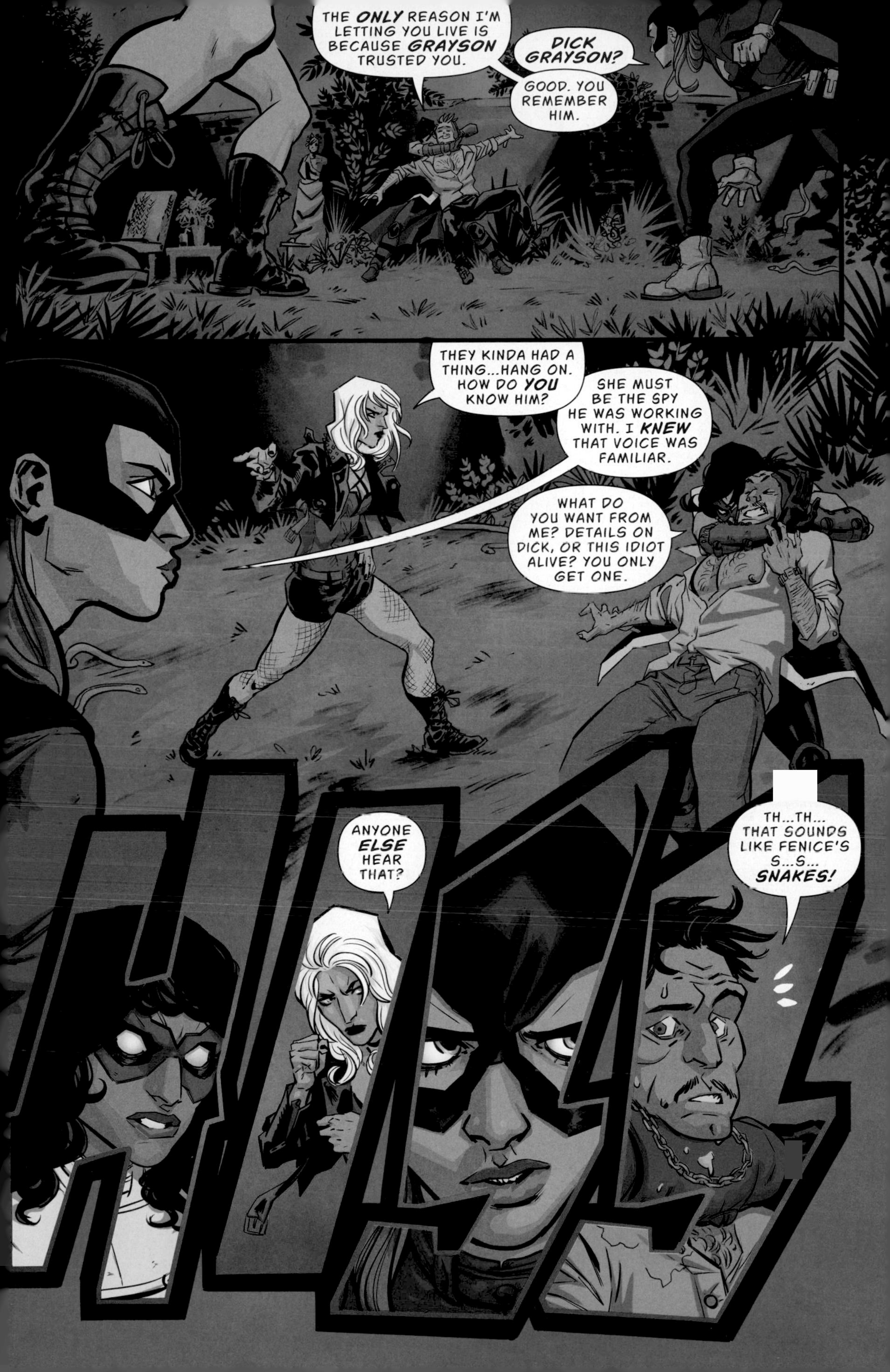
THE ONLY REASON I'M LETTING YOU LIVE IS BECAUSE GRAYSON TRUSTED YOU.
DICK GRAYSON?
GOOD. YOU REMEMBER HIM.
THEY KINDA HAD A THING...HANG ON. HOW DO YOU KNOW HIM?
SHE MUST BE THE SPY HE WAS WORKING WITH. I KNEW THAT VOICE WAS FAMILIAR.
WHAT DO YOU WANT FROM ME? DETAILS ON DICK, OR THIS IDIOT ALIVE? YOU ONLY GET ONE.
ANYONE ELSE HEAR THAT?
TH...TH... THAT SOUNDS LIKE FENICE'S S...S... SNAKES!

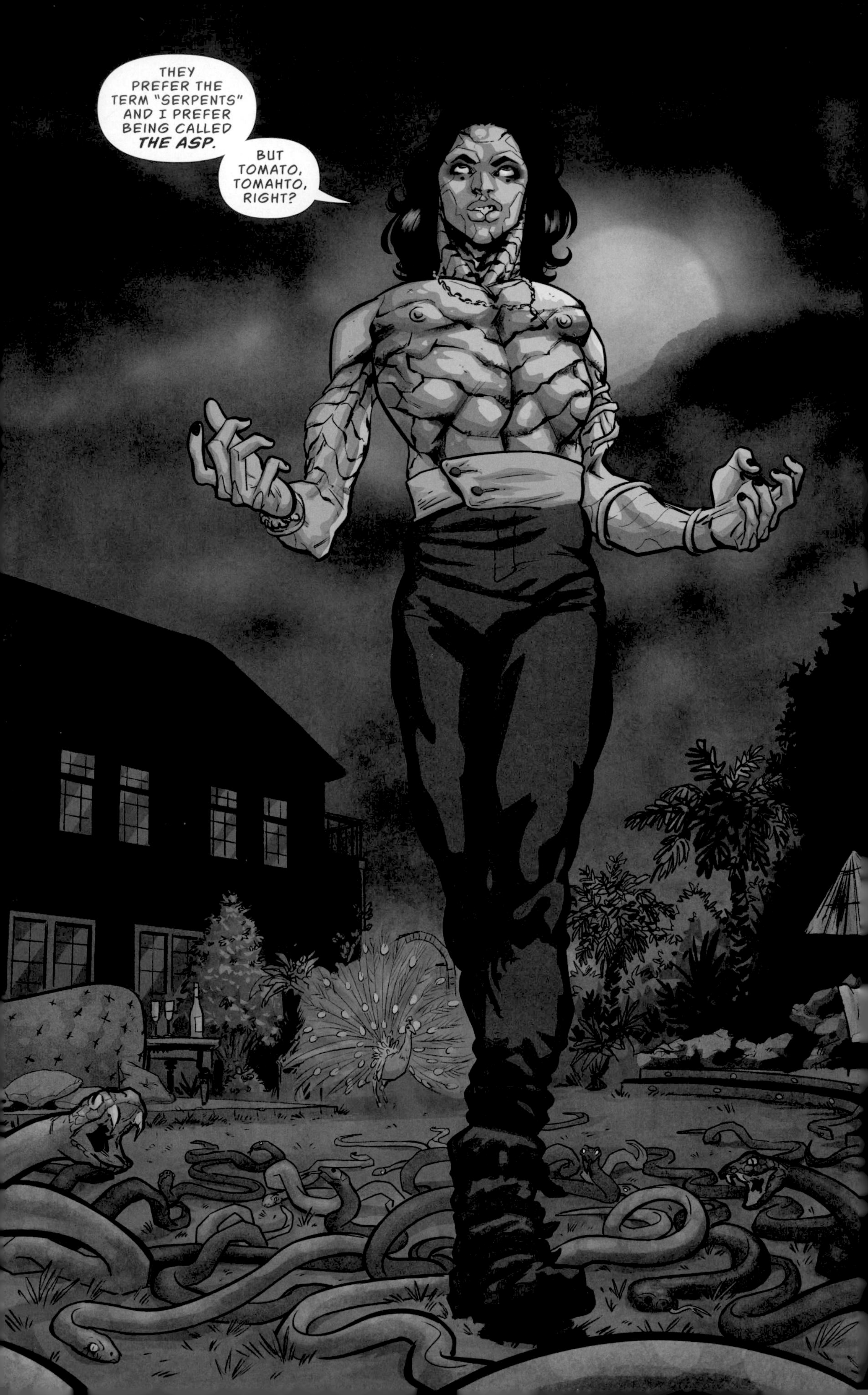
THEY PREFER THE TERM "SERPENTS" AND I PREFER BEING CALLED THE ASP.
BUT TOMATO, TOMAHTO, RIGHT?

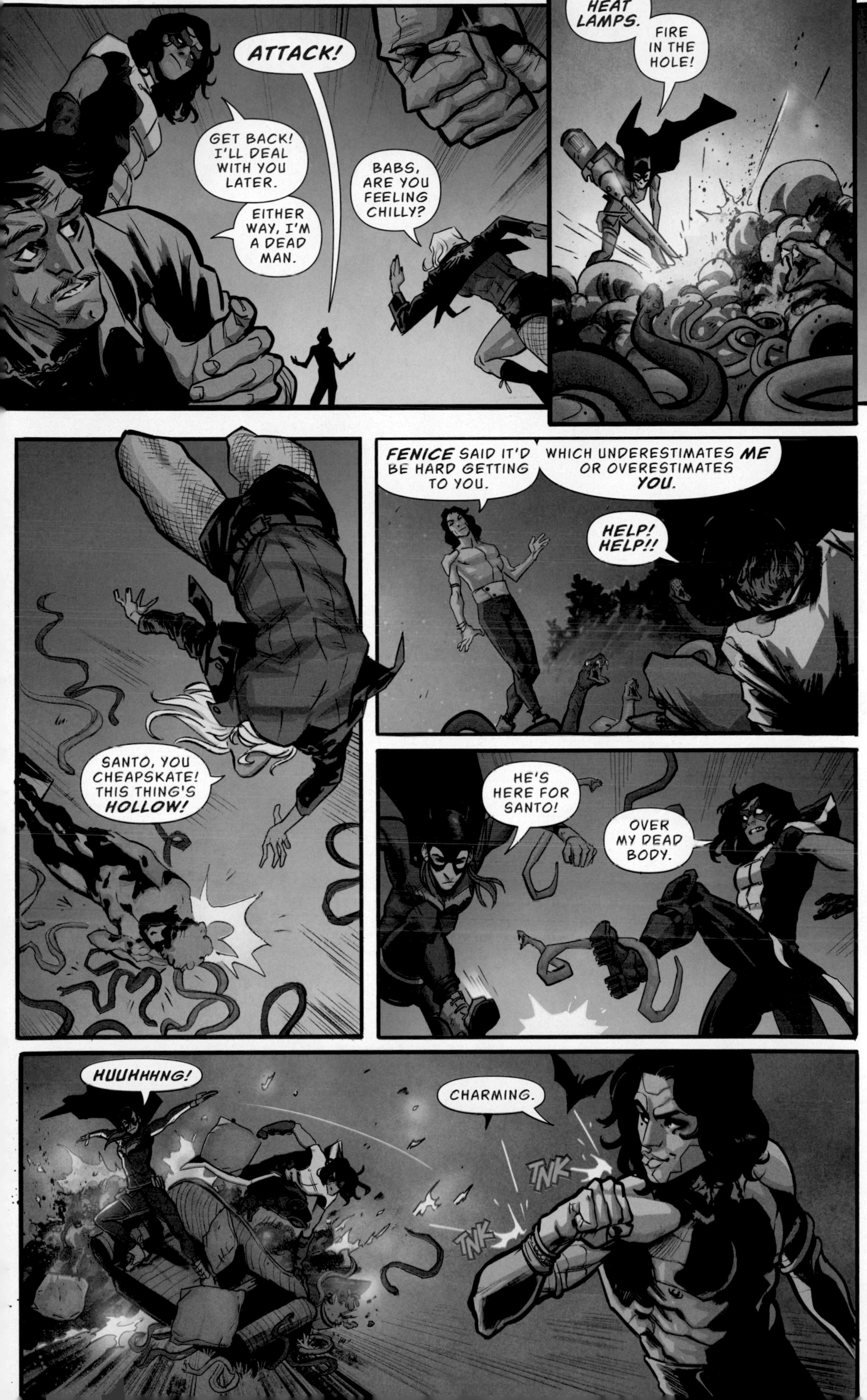
ATTACK!
GET BACK! I'LL DEAL WITH YOU LATER.
EITHER WAY, I'M A DEAD MAN.
BABS, ARE YOU FEELING CHILLY?
THE HEAT LAMPS.
FIRE IN THE HOLE!
SANTO, YOU CHEAPSKATE! THIS THING'S HOLLOW!
FENICE SAID IT'D BE HARD GETTING TO YOU.
WHICH UNDERESTIMATES ME OR OVERESTIMATES YOU.
HELP! HELP!!
HE'S HERE FOR SANTO!
OVER MY DEAD BODY.
HUUHHHNG!
CHARMING.
TNK
TNK

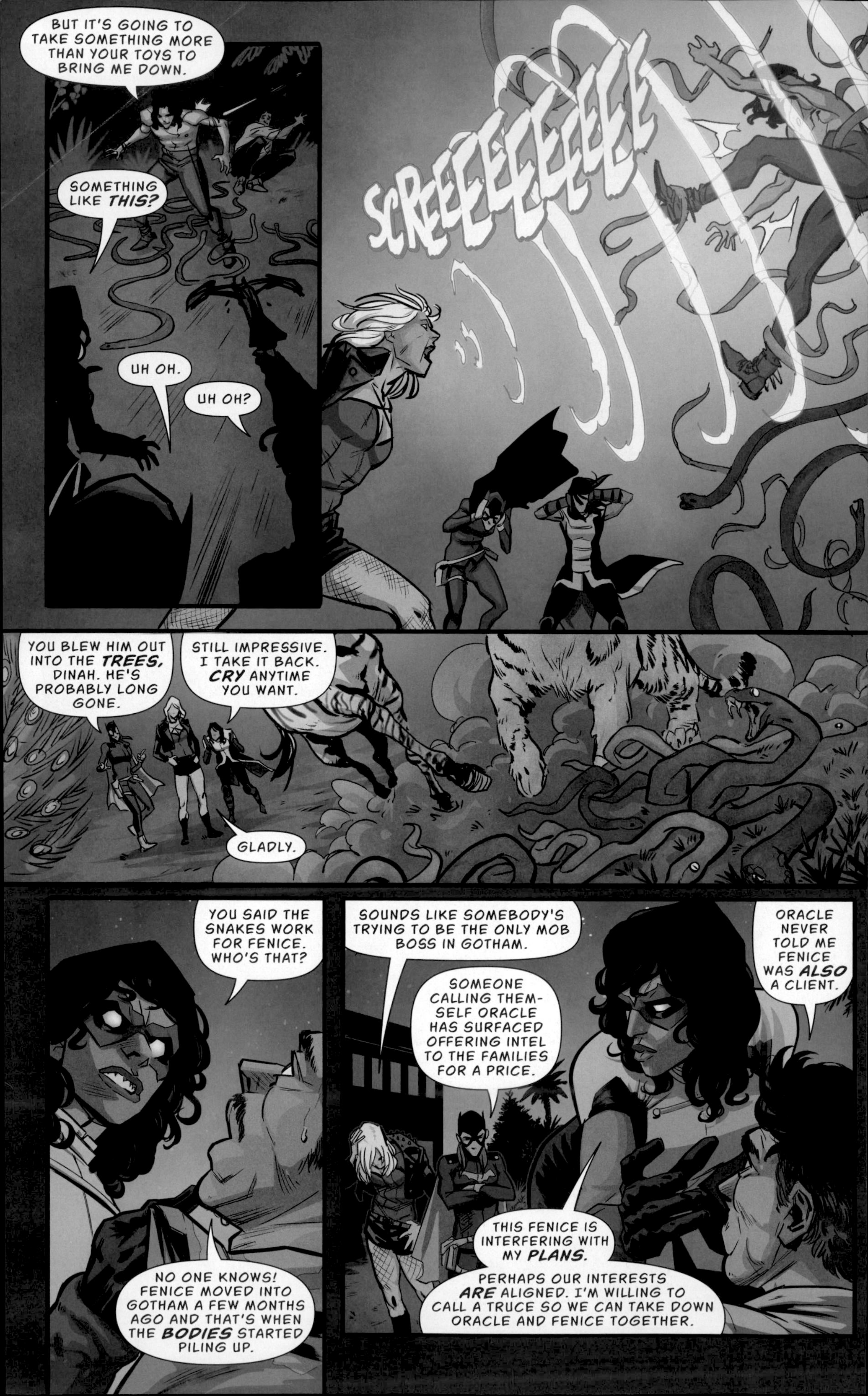
BUT IT'S GOING TO TAKE SOMETHING MORE THAN YOUR TOYS TO BRING ME DOWN.
SOMETHING LIKE THIS?
UH OH.
UH OH?
SCREEEEEEEEEEE
YOU BLEW HIM OUT INTO THE TREES, DINAH. HE'S PROBABLY LONG GONE.
STILL IMPRESSIVE. I TAKE IT BACK. CRY ANYTIME YOU WANT.
GLADLY.
YOU SAID THE SNAKES WORK FOR FENICE. WHO'S THAT?
NO ONE KNOWS! FENICE MOVED INTO GOTHAM A FEW MONTHS AGO AND THAT'S WHEN THE BODIES STARTED PILING UP.
SOUNDS LIKE SOMEBODY'S TRYING TO BE THE ONLY MOB BOSS IN GOTHAM.
SOMEONE CALLING THEMSELF ORACLE HAS SURFACED OFFERING INTEL TO THE FAMILIES FOR A PRICE.
ORACLE NEVER TOLD ME FENICE WAS ALSO A CLIENT.
THIS FENICE IS INTERFERING WITH MY PLANS.
PERHAPS OUR INTERESTS ARE ALIGNED. I'M WILLING TO CALL A TRUCE SO WE CAN TAKE DOWN ORACLE AND FENICE TOGETHER.

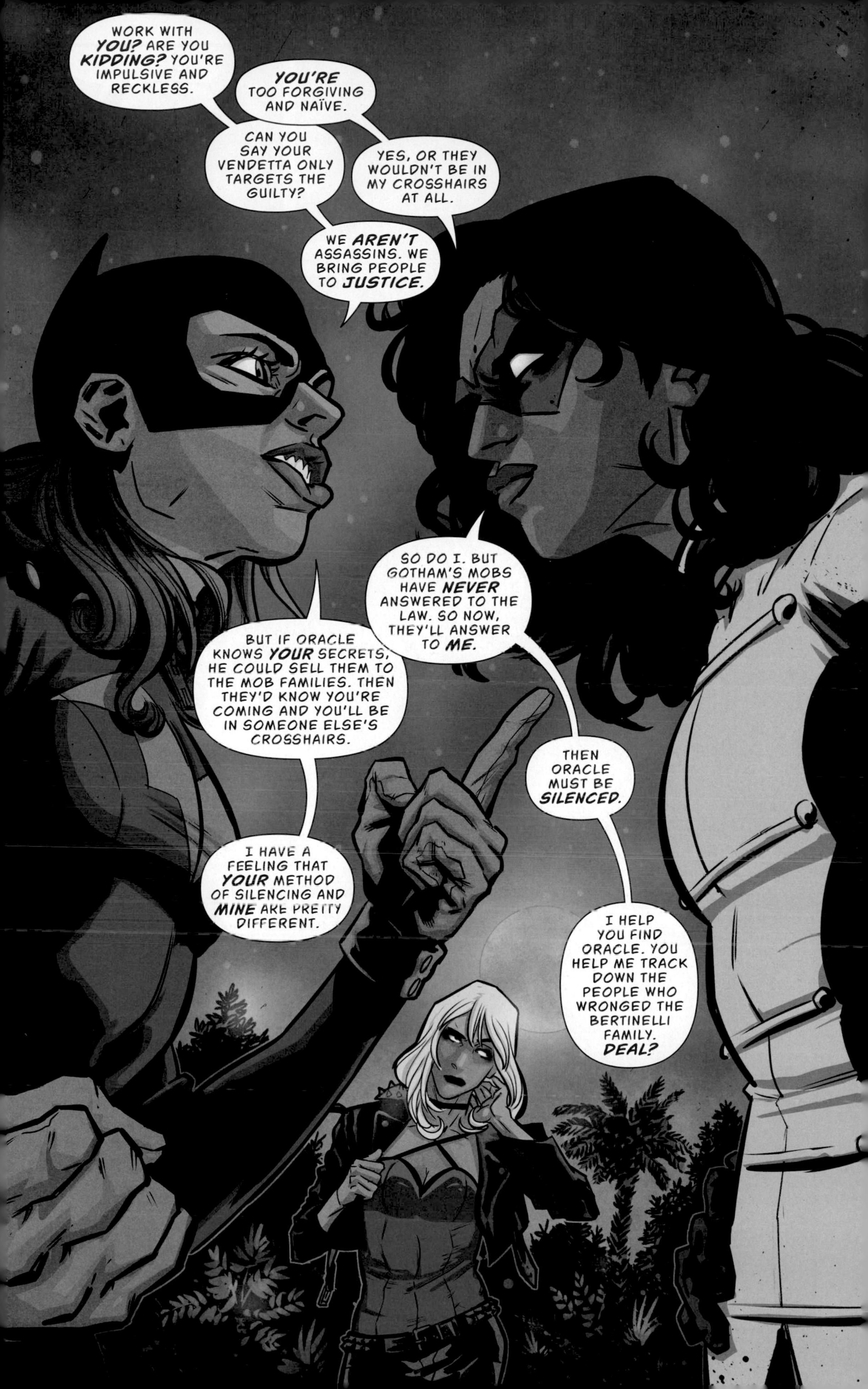
WORK WITH YOU? ARE YOU KIDDING? YOU'RE IMPULSIVE AND RECKLESS.
YOU'RE TOO FORGIVING AND NAÏVE.
CAN YOU SAY YOUR VENDETTA ONLY TARGETS THE GUILTY?
YES, OR THEY WOULDN'T BE IN MY CROSSHAIRS AT ALL.
WE AREN'T ASSASSINS. WE BRING PEOPLE TO JUSTICE.
SO DO I. BUT GOTHAM'S MOBS HAVE NEVER ANSWERED TO THE LAW. SO NOW, THEY'LL ANSWER TO ME.
BUT IF ORACLE KNOWS YOUR SECRETS, HE COULD SELL THEM TO THE MOB FAMILIES. THEN THEY'D KNOW YOU'RE COMING AND YOU'LL BE IN SOMEONE ELSE'S CROSSHAIRS.
THEN ORACLE MUST BE SILENCED.
I HAVE A FEELING THAT YOUR METHOD OF SILENCING AND MINE ARE PRETTY DIFFERENT.
I HELP YOU FIND ORACLE. YOU HELP ME TRACK DOWN THE PEOPLE WHO WRONGED THE BERTINELLI FAMILY. DEAL?

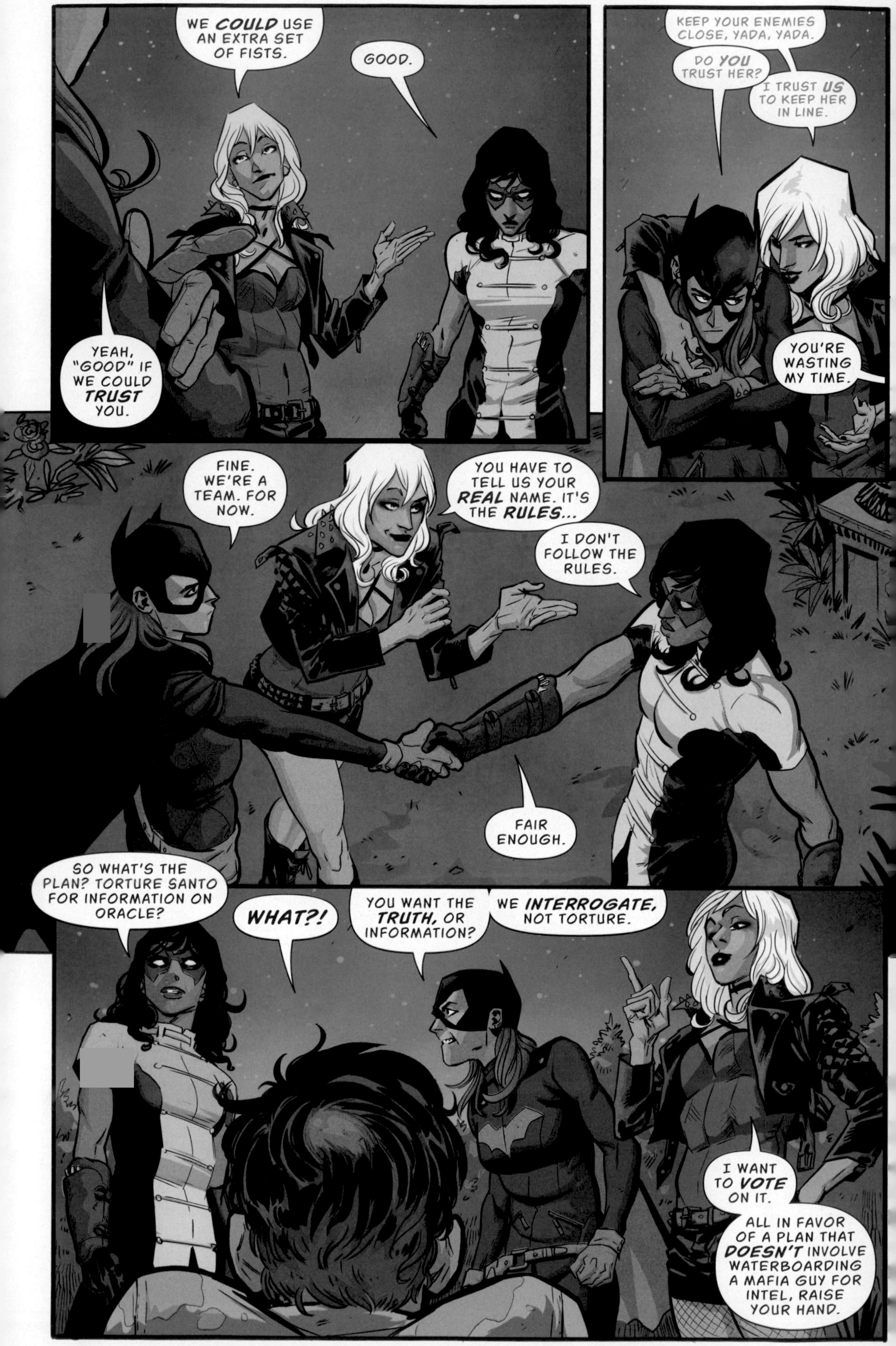
WE COULD USE AN EXTRA SET OF FISTS.
GOOD.
YEAH, "GOOD" IF WE COULD TRUST YOU.
KEEP YOUR ENEMIES CLOSE, YADA, YADA.
DO YOU TRUST HER?
I TRUST US TO KEEP HER IN LINE.
YOU'RE WASTING MY TIME.
FINE. WE'RE A TEAM. FOR NOW.
YOU HAVE TO TELL US YOUR REAL NAME. IT'S THE RULES...
I DON'T FOLLOW THE RULES.
FAIR ENOUGH.
SO WHAT'S THE PLAN? TORTURE SANTO FOR INFORMATION ON ORACLE?
WHAT?!
YOU WANT THE TRUTH, OR INFORMATION?
WE INTERROGATE, NOT TORTURE.
I WANT TO VOTE ON IT.
ALL IN FAVOR OF A PLAN THAT DOESN'T INVOLVE WATERBOARDING A MAFIA GUY FOR INTEL, RAISE YOUR HAND.

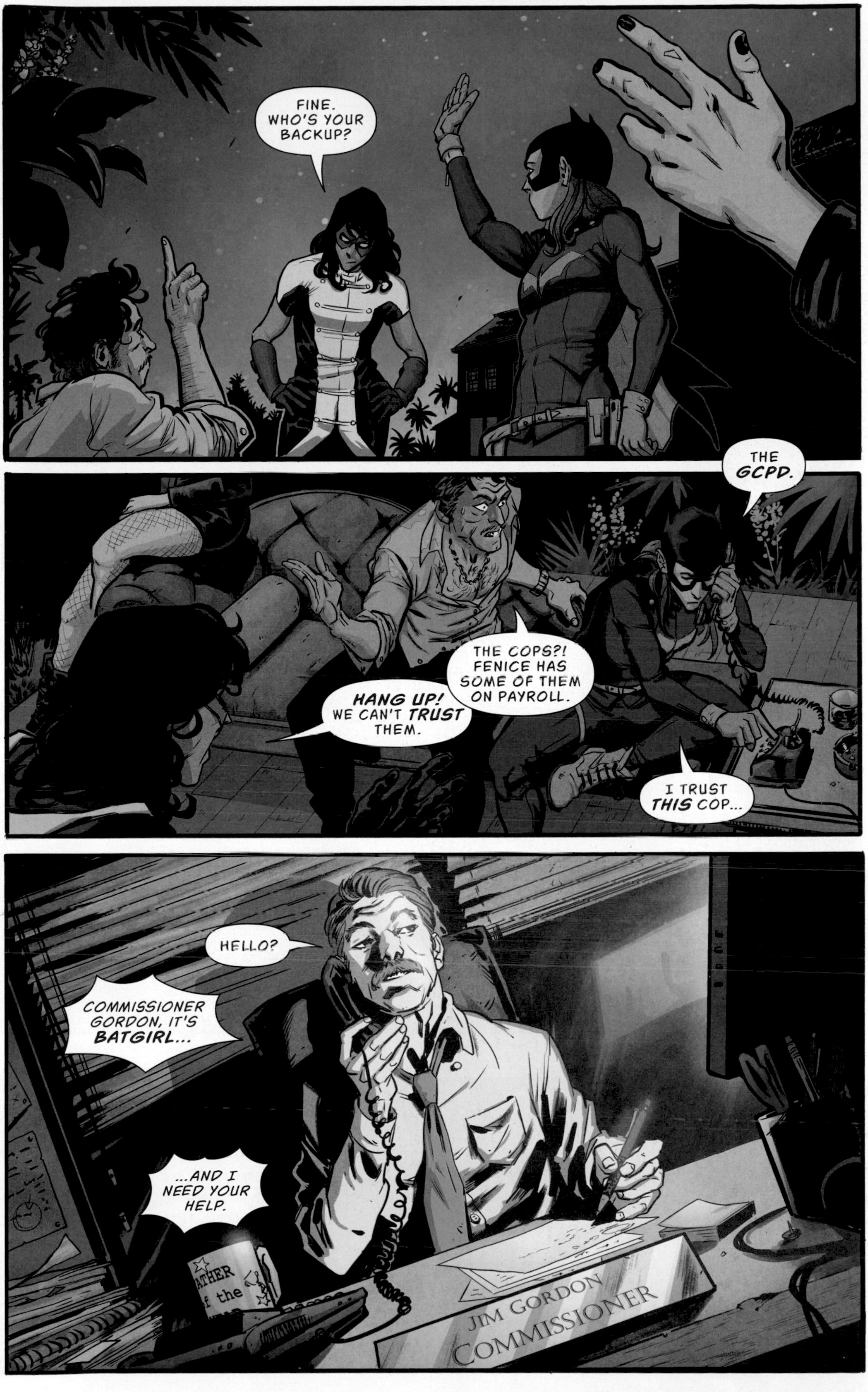
FINE. WHO'S YOUR BACKUP?
THE GCPD.
THE COPS?! FENICE HAS SOME OF THEM ON PAYROLL.
HANG UP! WE CAN'T TRUST THEM.
I TRUST THIS COP...
HELLO?
COMMISSIONER GORDON, IT'S BATGIRL...
...AND I NEED YOUR HELP.
JIM GORDON
COMMISSIONER

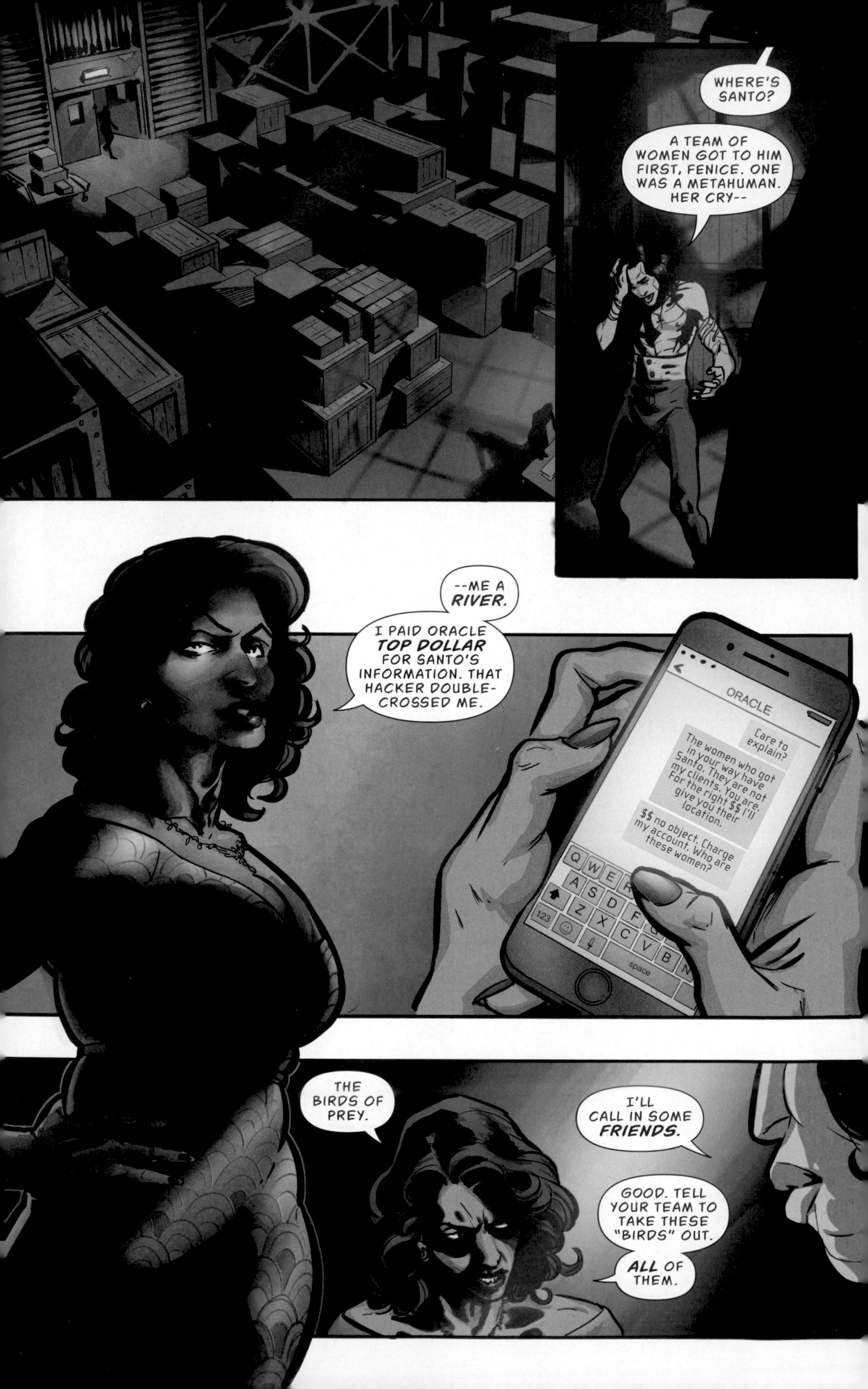
WHERE'S SANTO?
A TEAM OF WOMEN GOT TO HIM FIRST, FENICE. ONE WAS A METAHUMAN. HER CRY--
--ME A RIVER.
I PAID ORACLE TOP DOLLAR FOR SANTO'S INFORMATION. THAT HACKER DOUBLE-CROSSED ME.
ORACLE
Care to explain?
The women who got in your way have Santo. They are not my clients. You are. For the right $$ I'll give you their location.
$$ no object. Charge my account. Who are these women?
THE BIRDS OF PREY.
I'LL CALL IN SOME FRIENDS.
GOOD. TELL YOUR TEAM TO TAKE THESE "BIRDS" OUT.
ALL OF THEM.

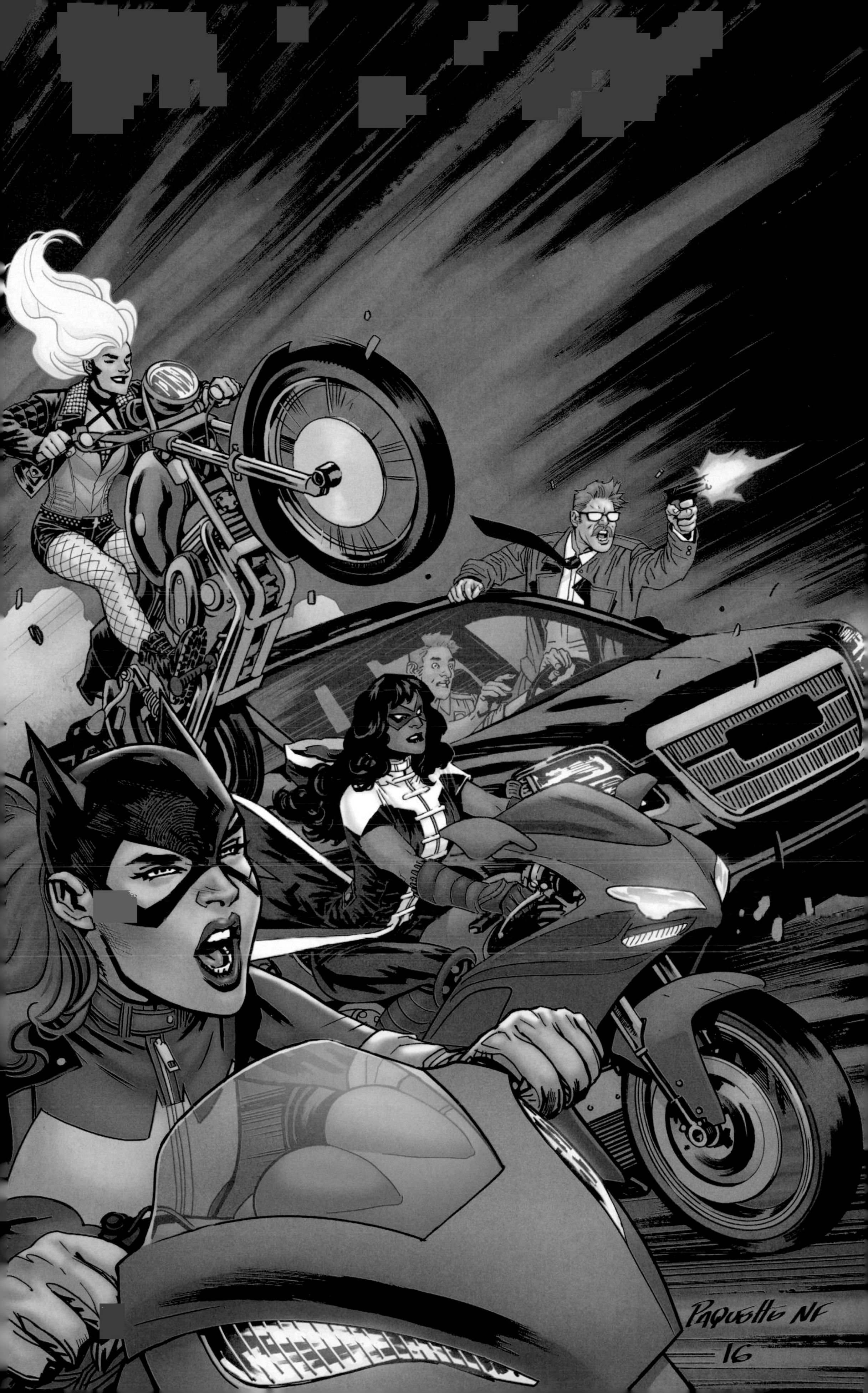
PAQUETTE NF
16

PART TWO: LEARN TO FLY

JULIE and SHAWNA BENSON writers * CLAIRE ROE and ROGE ANTONIO artists
ALLEN PASSALAQUA and HI-FI colorists * STEVE WANDS letterer

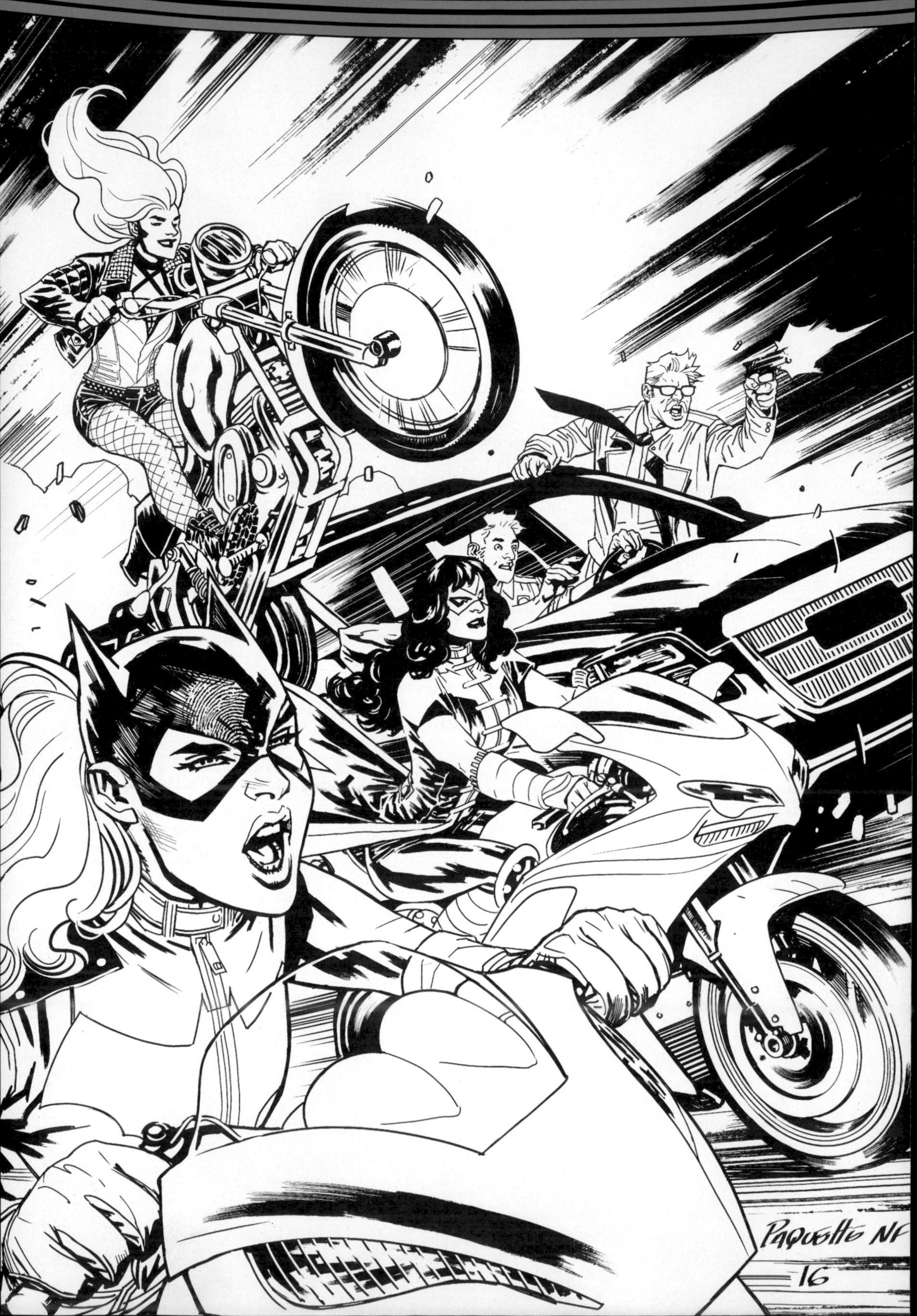

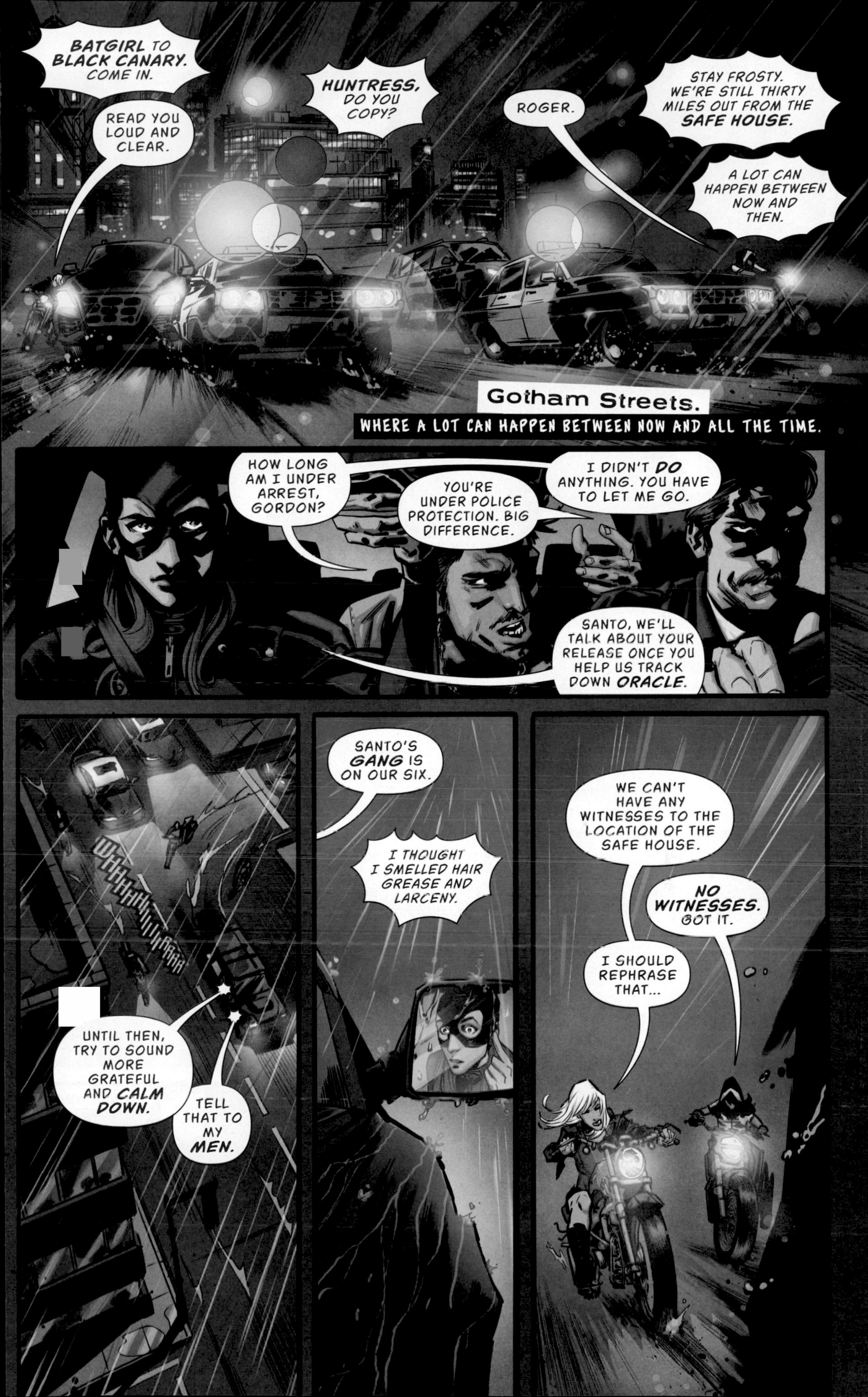
BATGIRL TO BLACK CANARY. COME IN.
READ YOU LOUD AND CLEAR.
HUNTRESS, DO YOU COPY?
ROGER.
STAY FROSTY. WE'RE STILL THIRTY MILES OUT FROM THE SAFE HOUSE.
A LOT CAN HAPPEN BETWEEN NOW AND THEN.
Gotham Streets.
WHERE A LOT CAN HAPPEN BETWEEN NOW AND ALL THE TIME.
HOW LONG AM I UNDER ARREST, GORDON?
YOU'RE UNDER POLICE PROTECTION. BIG DIFFERENCE.
I DIDN'T DO ANYTHING. YOU HAVE TO LET ME GO.
SANTO, WE'LL TALK ABOUT YOUR RELEASE ONCE YOU HELP US TRACK DOWN ORACLE.
UNTIL THEN, TRY TO SOUND MORE GRATEFUL AND CALM DOWN.
TELL THAT TO MY MEN.
SANTO'S GANG IS ON OUR SIX.
I THOUGHT I SMELLED HAIR GREASE AND LARCENY.
WE CAN'T HAVE ANY WITNESSES TO THE LOCATION OF THE SAFE HOUSE.
NO WITNESSES. GOT IT.
I SHOULD REPHRASE THAT...

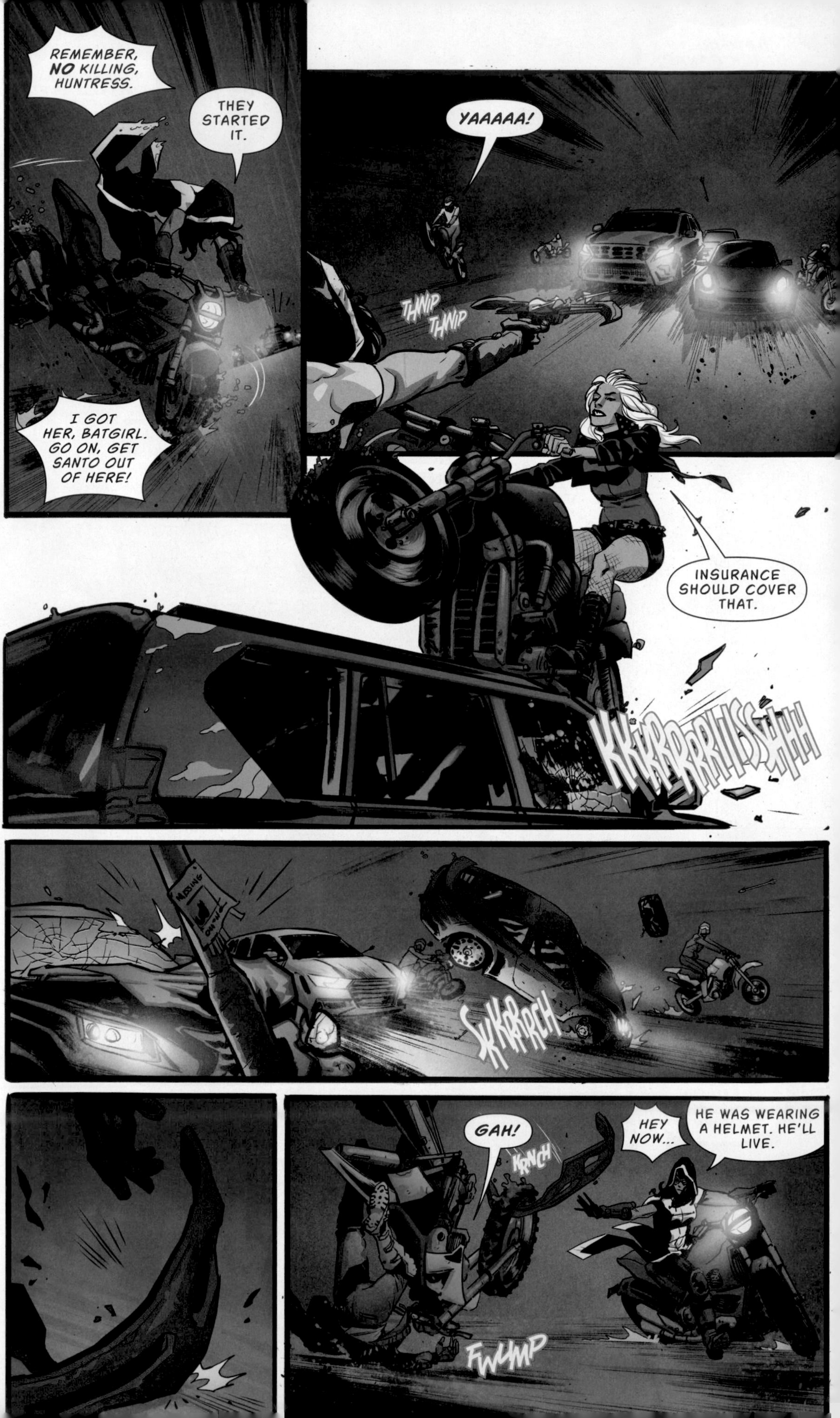

REMEMBER, NO KILLING, HUNTRESS.
THEY STARTED IT.
I GOT HER, BATGIRL. GO ON, GET SANTO OUT OF HERE!
YAAAAA!
THWIP THWIP
INSURANCE SHOULD COVER THAT.
KKKRRRRLLSSHHH
SKKRRRCH
GAH!
KRNCH
HEY NOW...
HE WAS WEARING A HELMET. HE'LL LIVE.
FWUMP

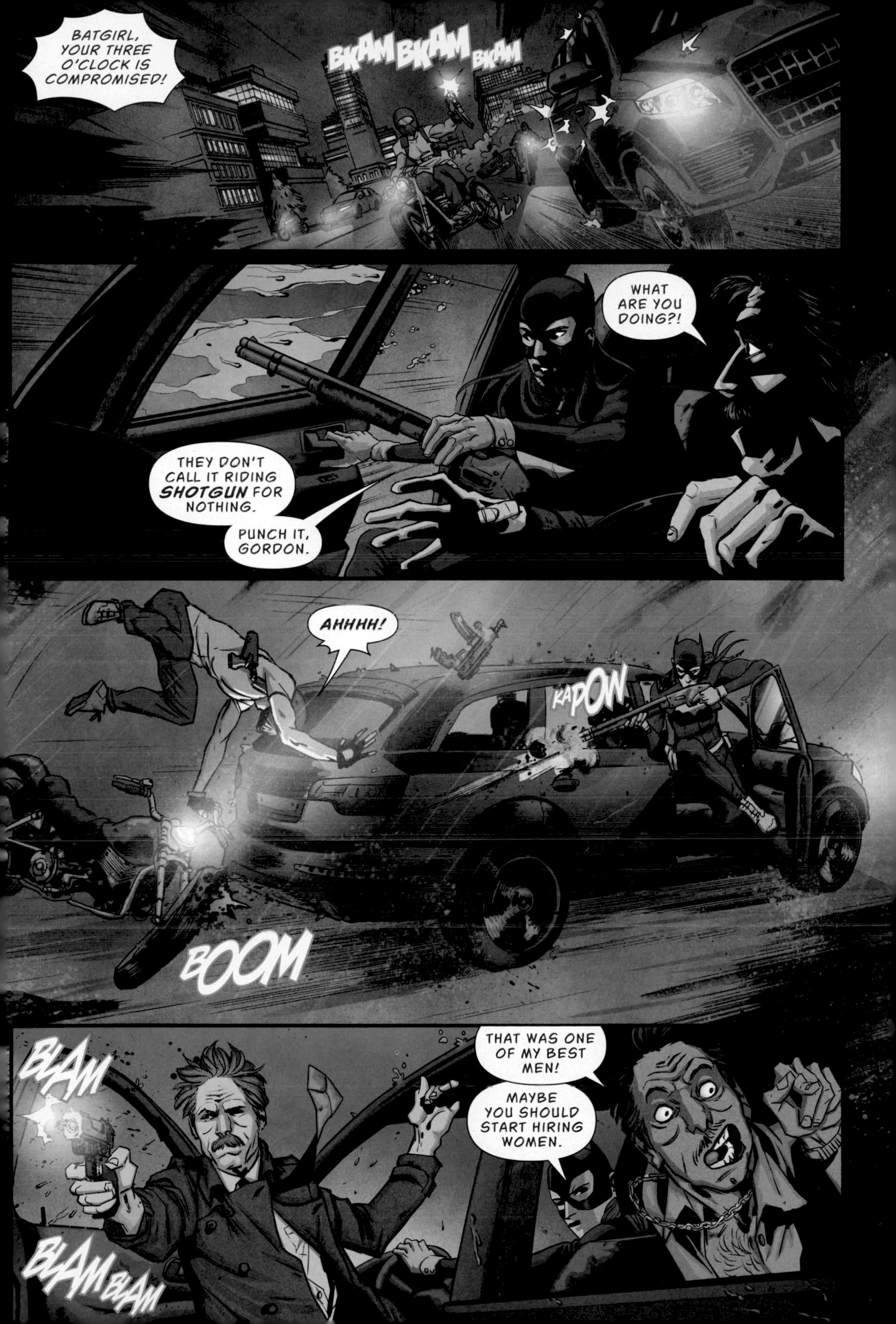
BATGIRL, YOUR THREE O'CLOCK IS COMPROMISED!
BKAM BKAM BKAM
WHAT ARE YOU DOING?!
THEY DON'T CALL IT RIDING SHOTGUN FOR NOTHING.
PUNCH IT, GORDON.
AHHHH!
KAPOW
BOOM
BLAM
THAT WAS ONE OF MY BEST MEN!
MAYBE YOU SHOULD START HIRING WOMEN.
BLAM BLAM

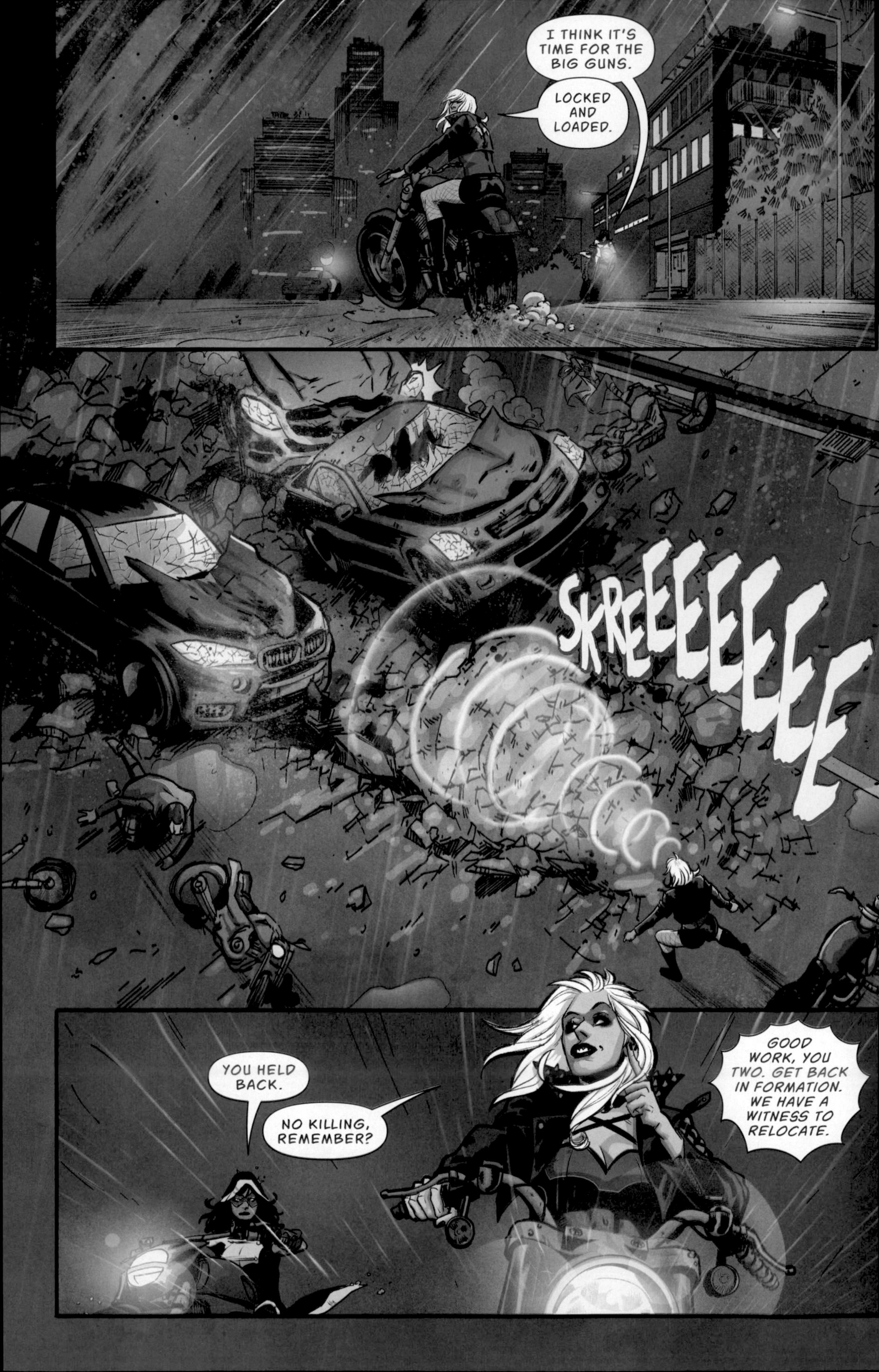
I THINK IT'S TIME FOR THE BIG GUNS.
LOCKED AND LOADED.
SKREEEEEEEE
YOU HELD BACK.
NO KILLING, REMEMBER?
GOOD WORK, YOU TWO. GET BACK IN FORMATION. WE HAVE A WITNESS TO RELOCATE.

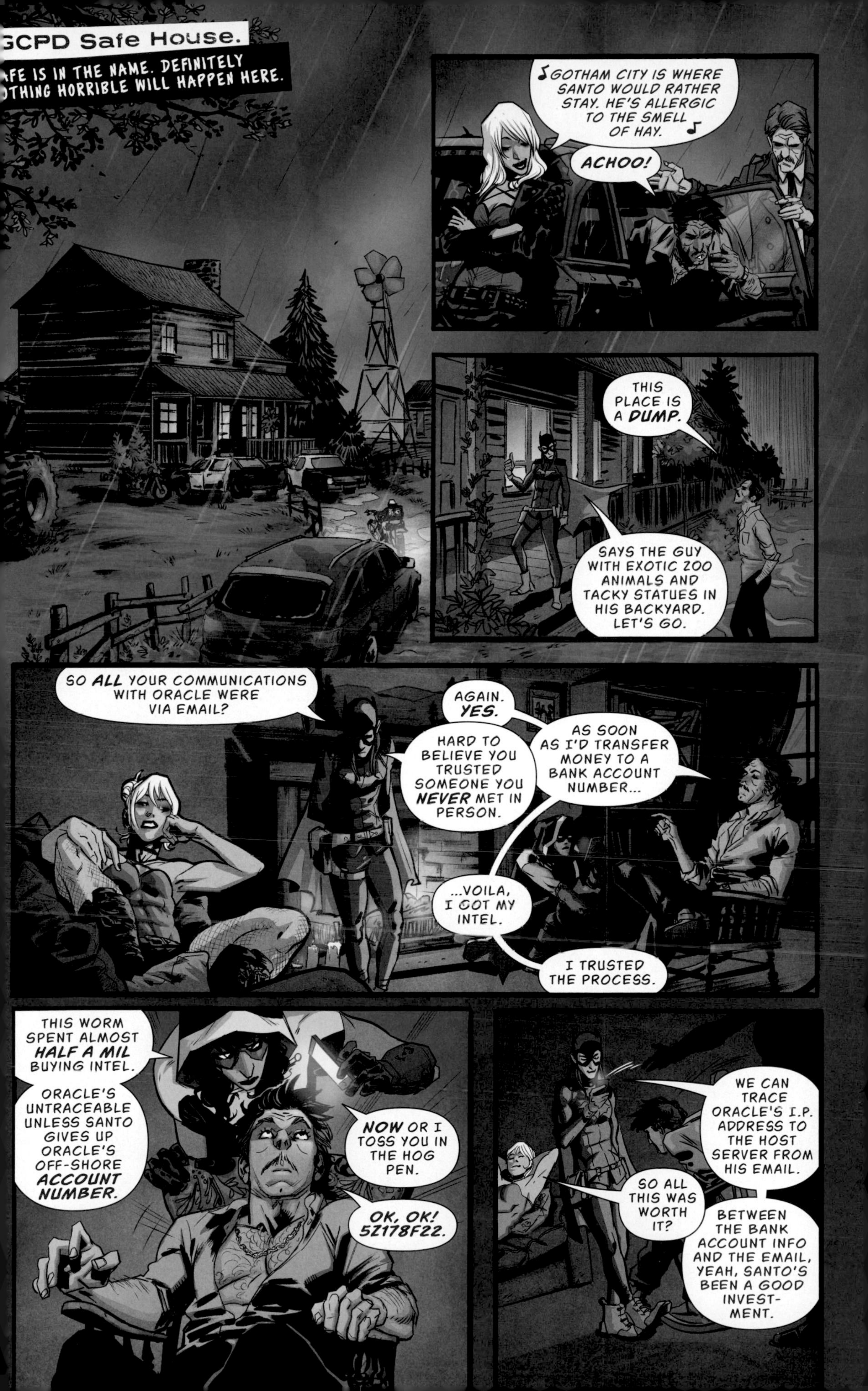
GCPD Safe House.
AFE IS IN THE NAME. DEFINITELY OTHING HORRIBLE WILL HAPPEN HERE.
GOTHAM CITY IS WHERE SANTO WOULD RATHER STAY. HE'S ALLERGIC TO THE SMELL OF HAY.
ACHOO!
THIS PLACE IS A DUMP.
SAYS THE GUY WITH EXOTIC ZOO ANIMALS AND TACKY STATUES IN HIS BACKYARD. LET'S GO.
SO ALL YOUR COMMUNICATIONS WITH ORACLE WERE VIA EMAIL?
AGAIN. YES.
HARD TO BELIEVE YOU TRUSTED SOMEONE YOU NEVER MET IN PERSON.
AS SOON AS I'D TRANSFER MONEY TO A BANK ACCOUNT NUMBER...
...VOILA, I GOT MY INTEL.
I TRUSTED THE PROCESS.
THIS WORM SPENT ALMOST HALF A MIL BUYING INTEL.
ORACLE'S UNTRACEABLE UNLESS SANTO GIVES UP ORACLE'S OFF-SHORE ACCOUNT NUMBER.
NOW OR I TOSS YOU IN THE HOG PEN.
OK, OK! 5Z178F22.
WE CAN TRACE ORACLE'S I.P. ADDRESS TO THE HOST SERVER FROM HIS EMAIL.
SO ALL THIS WAS WORTH IT?
BETWEEN THE BANK ACCOUNT INFO AND THE EMAIL, YEAH, SANTO'S BEEN A GOOD INVEST-MENT.

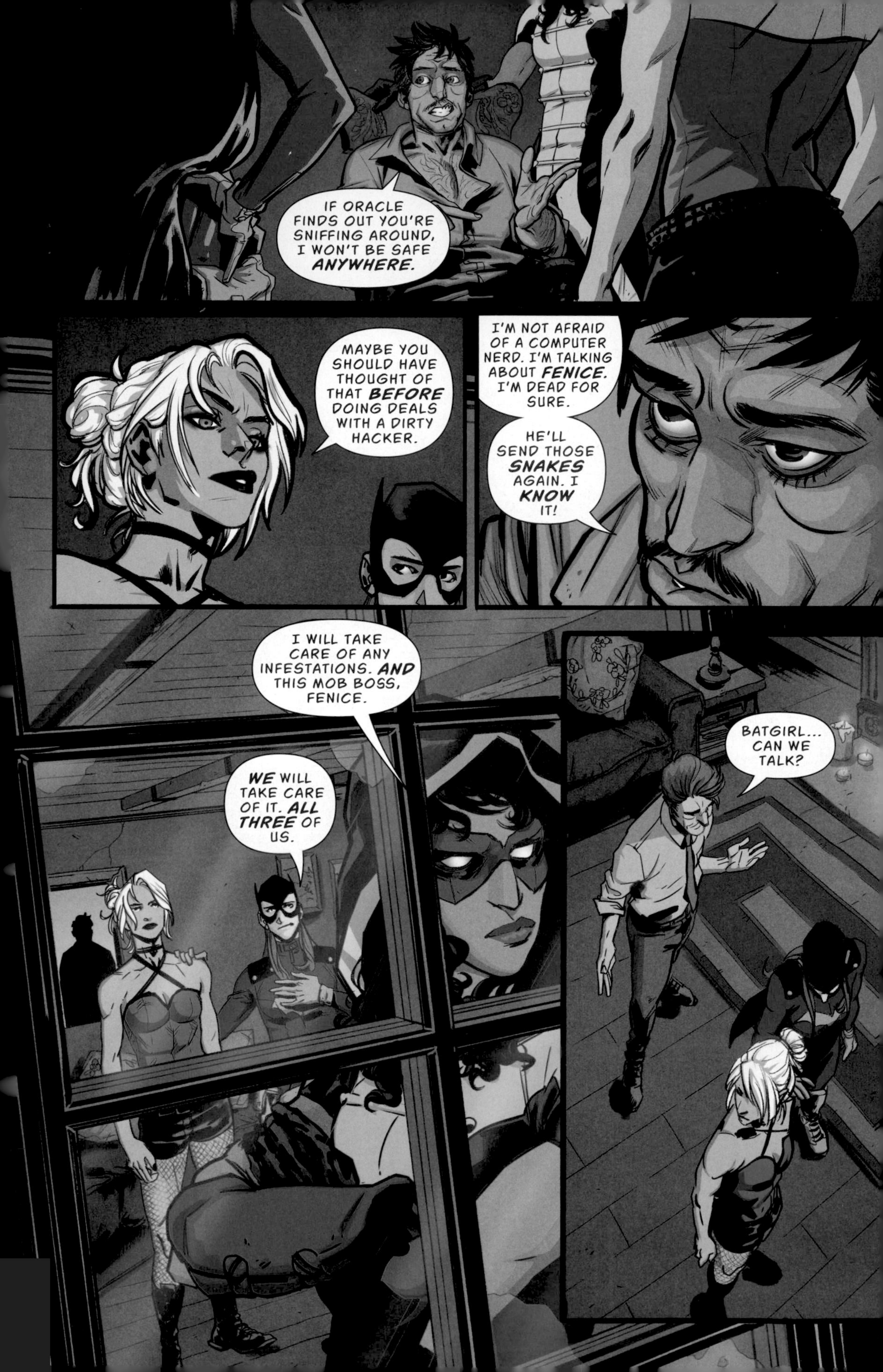
IF ORACLE FINDS OUT YOU'RE SNIFFING AROUND, I WON'T BE SAFE ANYWHERE.
MAYBE YOU SHOULD HAVE THOUGHT OF THAT BEFORE DOING DEALS WITH A DIRTY HACKER.
I'M NOT AFRAID OF A COMPUTER NERD. I'M TALKING ABOUT FENICE. I'M DEAD FOR SURE.
HE'LL SEND THOSE SNAKES AGAIN. I KNOW IT!
I WILL TAKE CARE OF ANY INFESTATIONS. AND THIS MOB BOSS, FENICE.
WE WILL TAKE CARE OF IT. ALL THREE OF US.
BATGIRL... CAN WE TALK?

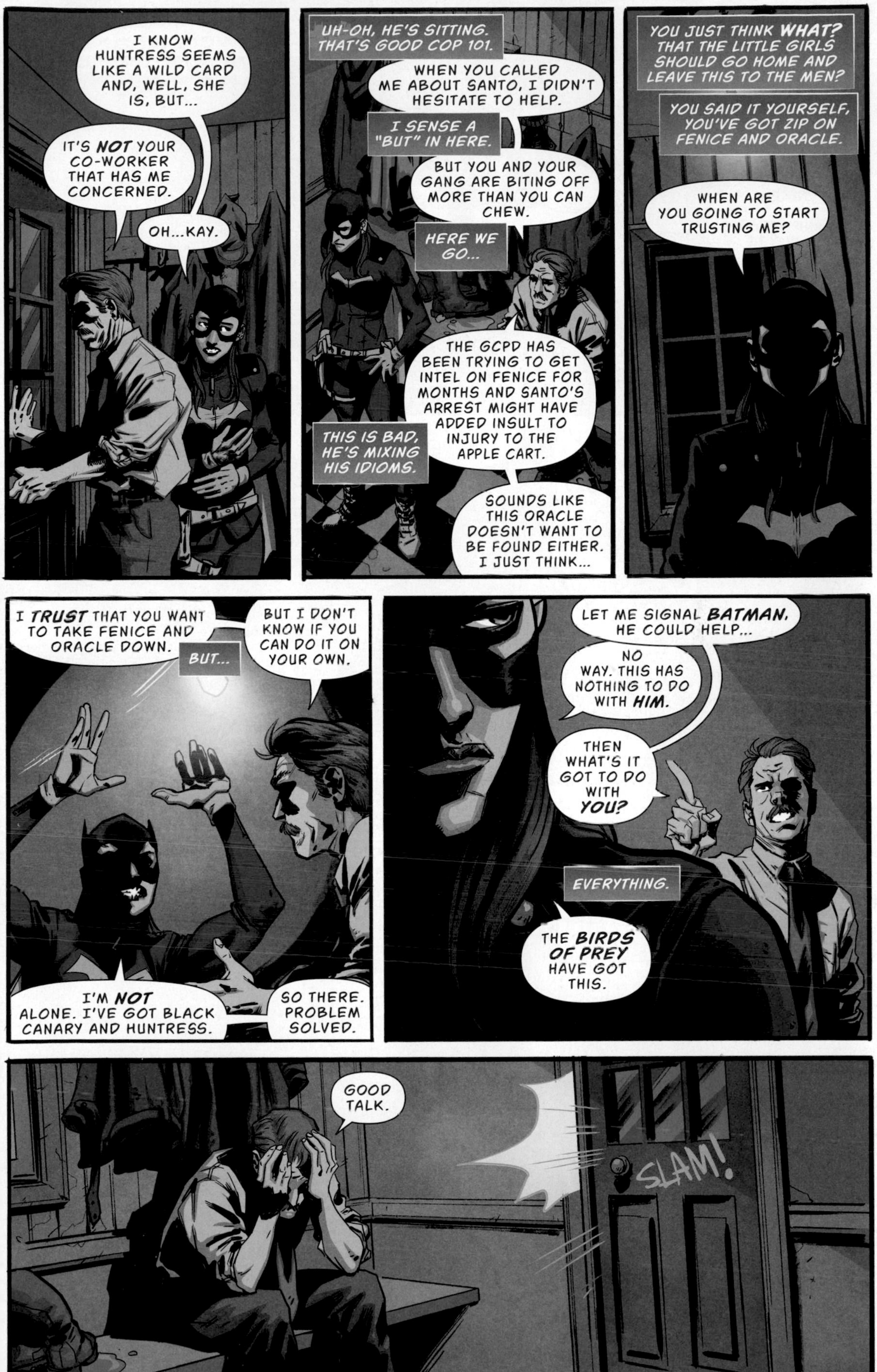

I KNOW HUNTRESS SEEMS LIKE A WILD CARD AND, WELL, SHE IS, BUT...
IT'S NOT YOUR CO-WORKER THAT HAS ME CONCERNED.
OH...KAY.
UH-OH, HE'S SITTING. THAT'S GOOD COP 101.
WHEN YOU CALLED ME ABOUT SANTO, I DIDN'T HESITATE TO HELP.
I SENSE A "BUT" IN HERE.
BUT YOU AND YOUR GANG ARE BITING OFF MORE THAN YOU CAN CHEW.
HERE WE GO...
THE GCPD HAS BEEN TRYING TO GET INTEL ON FENICE FOR MONTHS AND SANTO'S ARREST MIGHT HAVE ADDED INSULT TO INJURY TO THE APPLE CART.
THIS IS BAD, HE'S MIXING HIS IDIOMS.
SOUNDS LIKE THIS ORACLE DOESN'T WANT TO BE FOUND EITHER. I JUST THINK...
YOU JUST THINK WHAT? THAT THE LITTLE GIRLS SHOULD GO HOME AND LEAVE THIS TO THE MEN?
YOU SAID IT YOURSELF, YOU'VE GOT ZIP ON FENICE AND ORACLE.
WHEN ARE YOU GOING TO START TRUSTING ME?
I TRUST THAT YOU WANT TO TAKE FENICE AND ORACLE DOWN.
BUT...
BUT I DON'T KNOW IF YOU CAN DO IT ON YOUR OWN.
I'M NOT ALONE. I'VE GOT BLACK CANARY AND HUNTRESS.
SO THERE. PROBLEM SOLVED.
LET ME SIGNAL BATMAN. HE COULD HELP...
NO WAY. THIS HAS NOTHING TO DO WITH HIM.
THEN WHAT'S IT GOT TO DO WITH YOU?
EVERYTHING.
THE BIRDS OF PREY HAVE GOT THIS.
GOOD TALK.
SLAM!

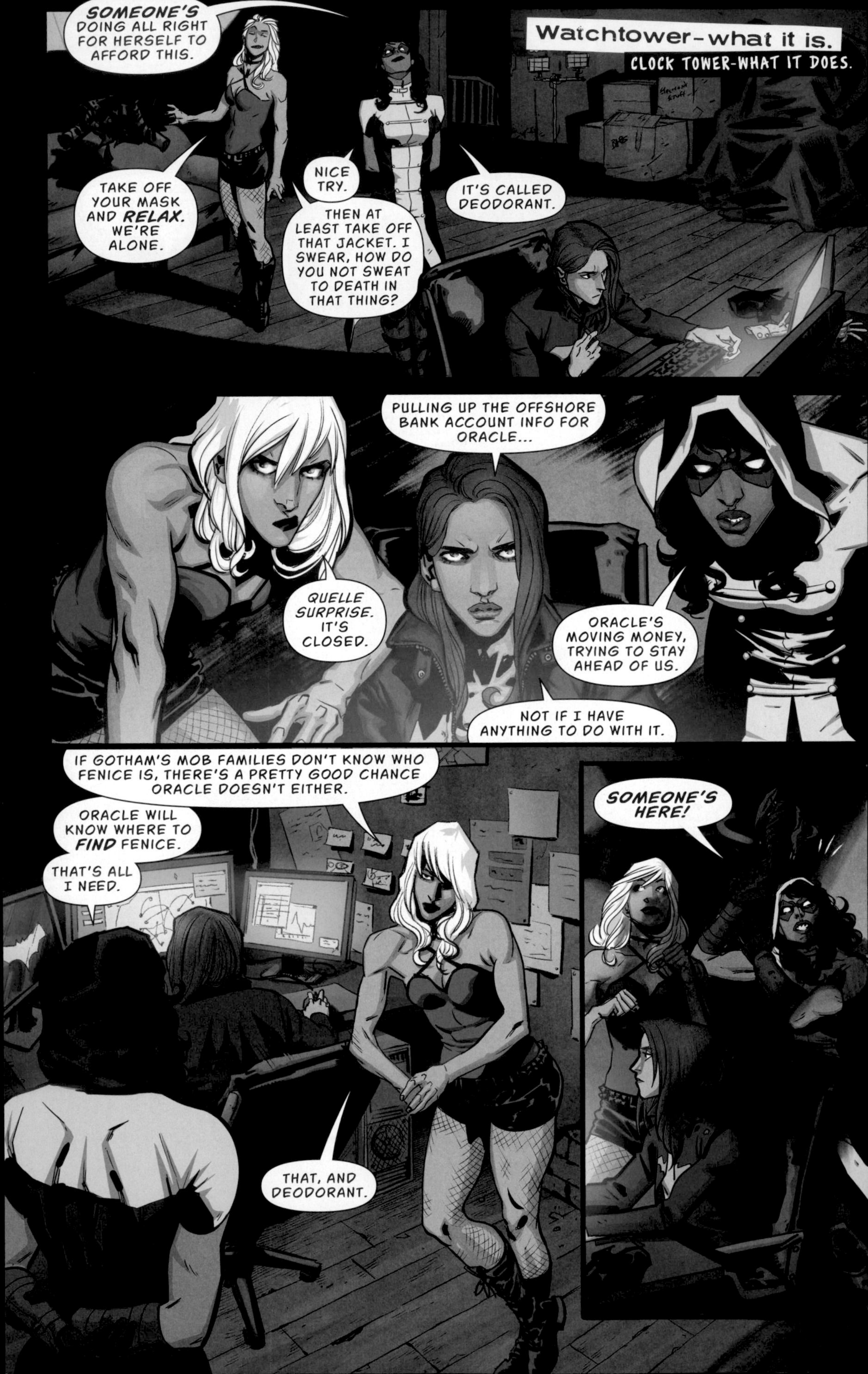
Watchtower-what it is.
CLOCK TOWER-WHAT IT DOES.
SOMEONE'S DOING ALL RIGHT FOR HERSELF TO AFFORD THIS.
TAKE OFF YOUR MASK AND RELAX. WE'RE ALONE.
NICE TRY.
THEN AT LEAST TAKE OFF THAT JACKET. I SWEAR, HOW DO YOU NOT SWEAT TO DEATH IN THAT THING?
IT'S CALLED DEODORANT.
PULLING UP THE OFFSHORE BANK ACCOUNT INFO FOR ORACLE...
QUELLE SURPRISE. IT'S CLOSED.
ORACLE'S MOVING MONEY, TRYING TO STAY AHEAD OF US.
NOT IF I HAVE ANYTHING TO DO WITH IT.
IF GOTHAM'S MOB FAMILIES DON'T KNOW WHO FENICE IS, THERE'S A PRETTY GOOD CHANCE ORACLE DOESN'T EITHER.
ORACLE WILL KNOW WHERE TO FIND FENICE.
THAT'S ALL I NEED.
THAT, AND DEODORANT.
SOMEONE'S HERE!

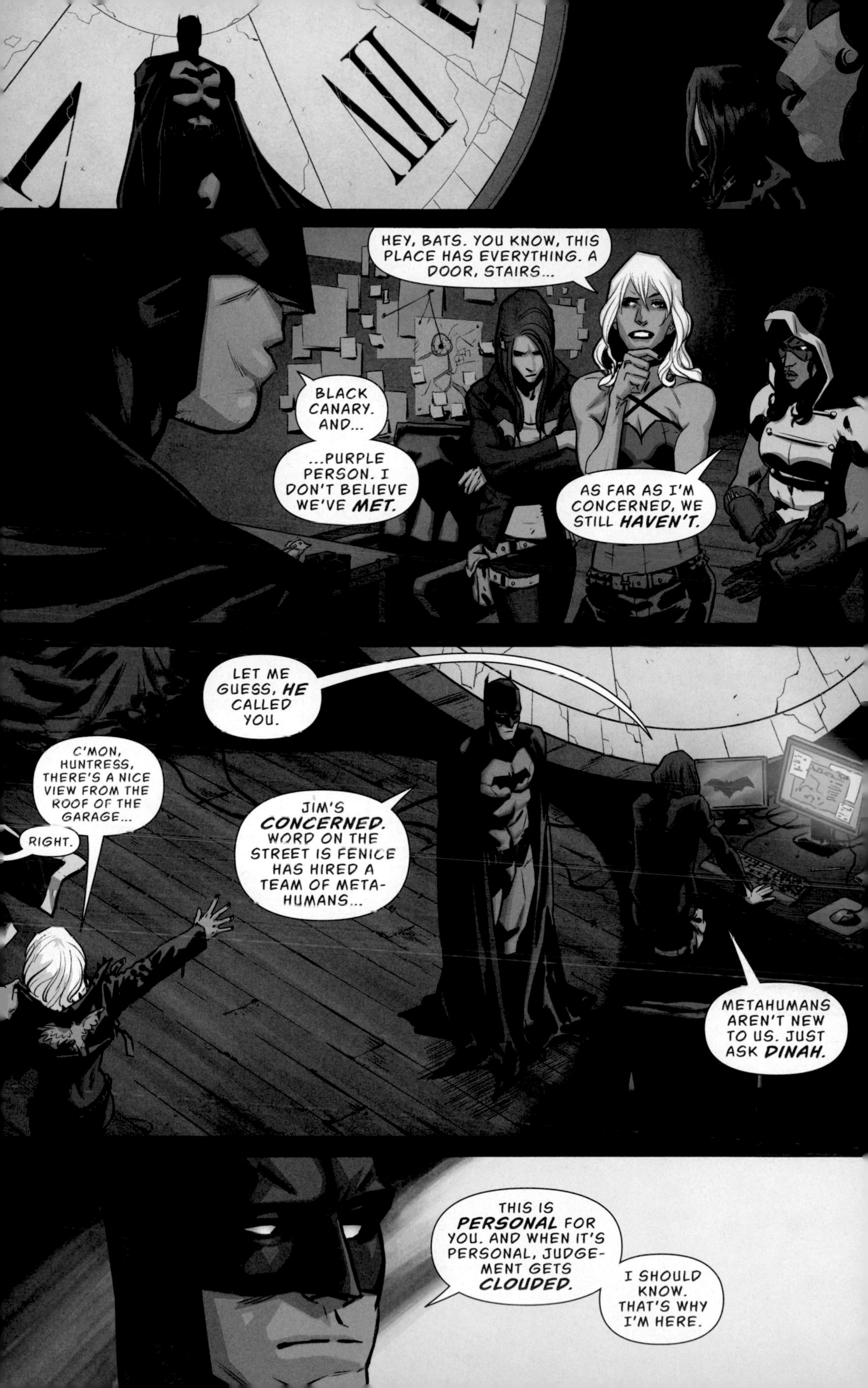
HEY, BATS. YOU KNOW, THIS PLACE HAS EVERYTHING. A DOOR, STAIRS...
BLACK CANARY. AND...
...PURPLE PERSON. I DON'T BELIEVE WE'VE MET.
AS FAR AS I'M CONCERNED, WE STILL HAVEN'T.
LET ME GUESS, HE CALLED YOU.
C'MON, HUNTRESS, THERE'S A NICE VIEW FROM THE ROOF OF THE GARAGE...
RIGHT.
JIM'S CONCERNED. WORD ON THE STREET IS FENICE HAS HIRED A TEAM OF META-HUMANS...
METAHUMANS AREN'T NEW TO US. JUST ASK DINAH.
THIS IS PERSONAL FOR YOU. AND WHEN IT'S PERSONAL, JUDGEMENT GETS CLOUDED.
I SHOULD KNOW. THAT'S WHY I'M HERE.

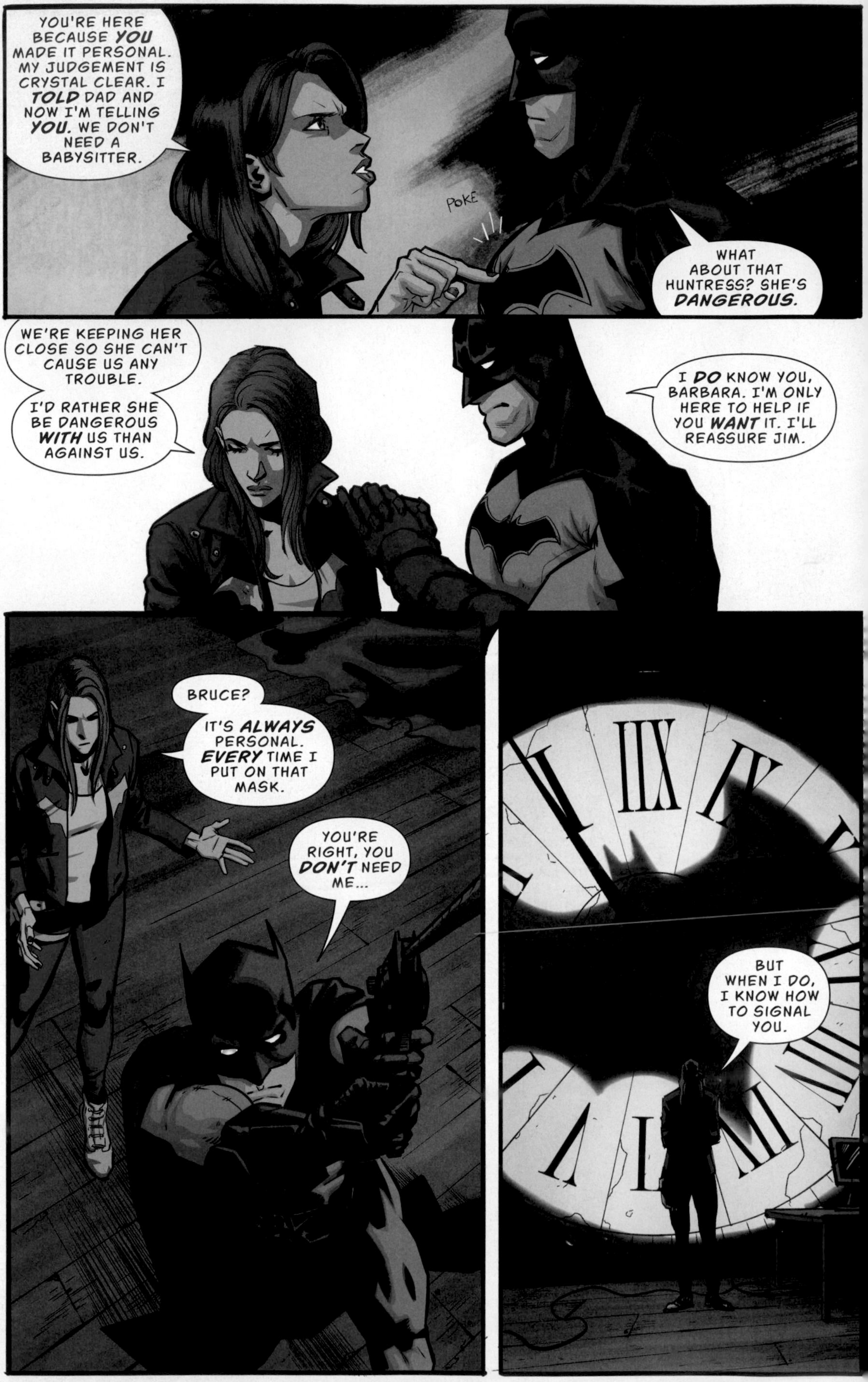
YOU'RE HERE BECAUSE YOU MADE IT PERSONAL. MY JUDGEMENT IS CRYSTAL CLEAR. I TOLD DAD AND NOW I'M TELLING YOU. WE DON'T NEED A BABYSITTER.
POKE
WHAT ABOUT THAT HUNTRESS? SHE'S DANGEROUS.
WE'RE KEEPING HER CLOSE SO SHE CAN'T CAUSE US ANY TROUBLE.
I'D RATHER SHE BE DANGEROUS WITH US THAN AGAINST US.
I DO KNOW YOU, BARBARA. I'M ONLY HERE TO HELP IF YOU WANT IT. I'LL REASSURE JIM.
BRUCE?
IT'S ALWAYS PERSONAL. EVERY TIME I PUT ON THAT MASK.
YOU'RE RIGHT, YOU DON'T NEED ME...
BUT WHEN I DO, I KNOW HOW TO SIGNAL YOU.

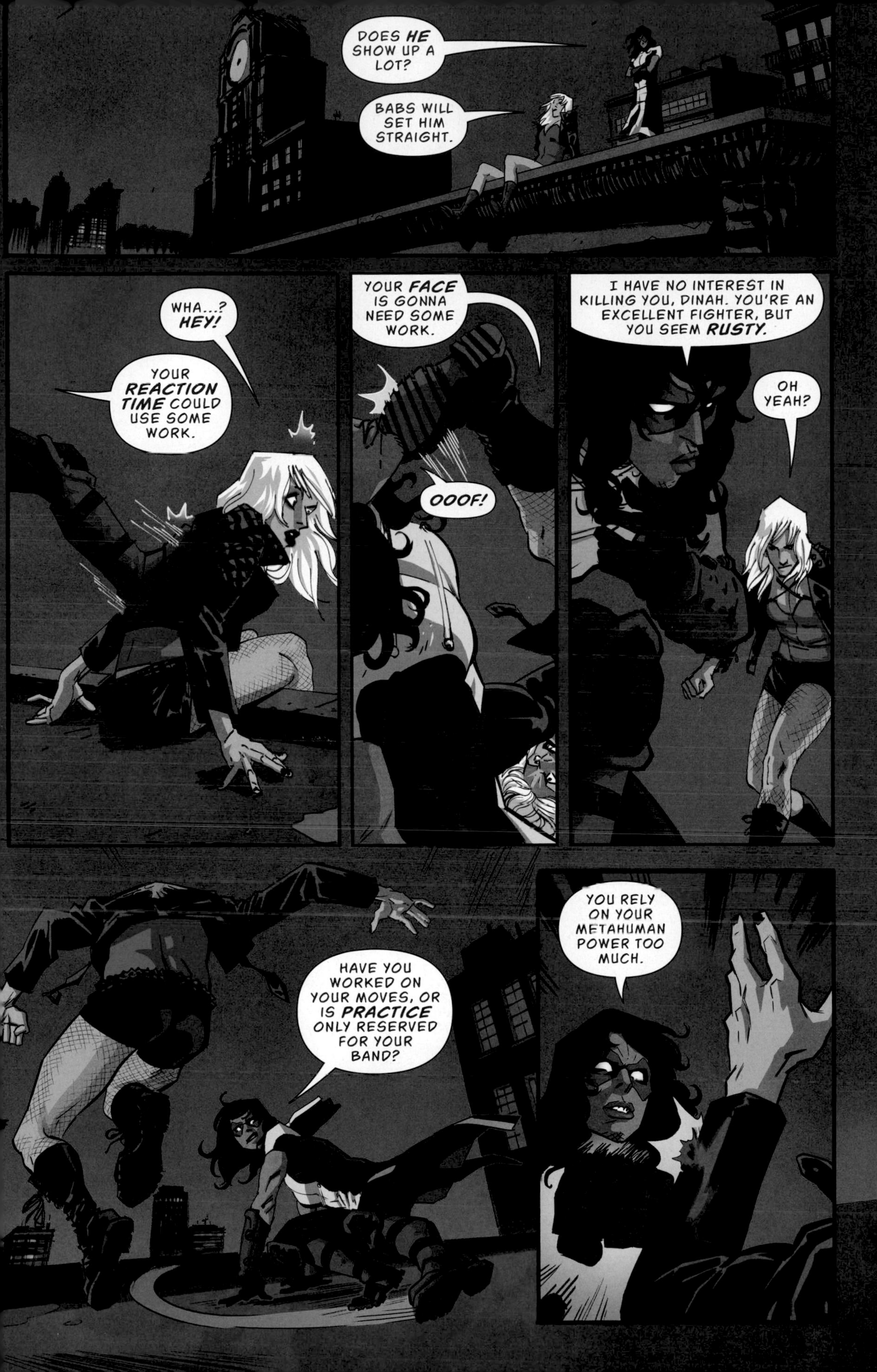
DOES HE SHOW UP A LOT?
BABS WILL SET HIM STRAIGHT.
WHA...? HEY!
YOUR REACTION TIME COULD USE SOME WORK.
YOUR FACE IS GONNA NEED SOME WORK.
OOOF!
I HAVE NO INTEREST IN KILLING YOU, DINAH. YOU'RE AN EXCELLENT FIGHTER, BUT YOU SEEM RUSTY.
OH YEAH?
HAVE YOU WORKED ON YOUR MOVES, OR IS PRACTICE ONLY RESERVED FOR YOUR BAND?
YOU RELY ON YOUR METAHUMAN POWER TOO MUCH.

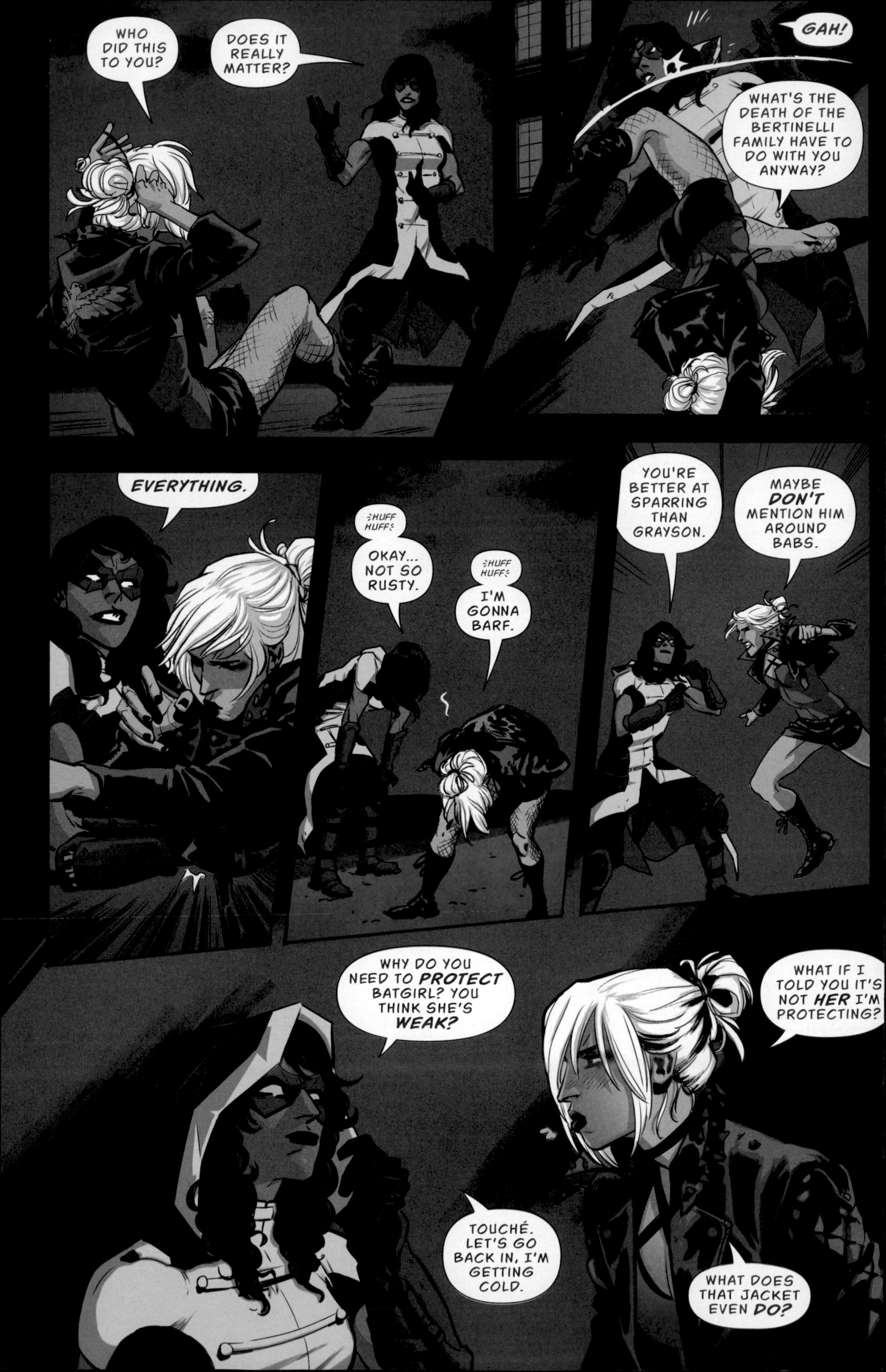
WHO DID THIS TO YOU?
DOES IT REALLY MATTER?
GAH!
WHAT'S THE DEATH OF THE BERTINELLI FAMILY HAVE TO DO WITH YOU ANYWAY?
EVERYTHING.
HUFF HUFF
OKAY... NOT SO RUSTY.
HUFF HUFF
I'M GONNA BARF.
YOU'RE BETTER AT SPARRING THAN GRAYSON.
MAYBE DON'T MENTION HIM AROUND BABS.
WHY DO YOU NEED TO PROTECT BATGIRL? YOU THINK SHE'S WEAK?
WHAT IF I TOLD YOU IT'S NOT HER I'M PROTECTING?
TOUCHÉ. LET'S GO BACK IN, I'M GETTING COLD.
WHAT DOES THAT JACKET EVEN DO?

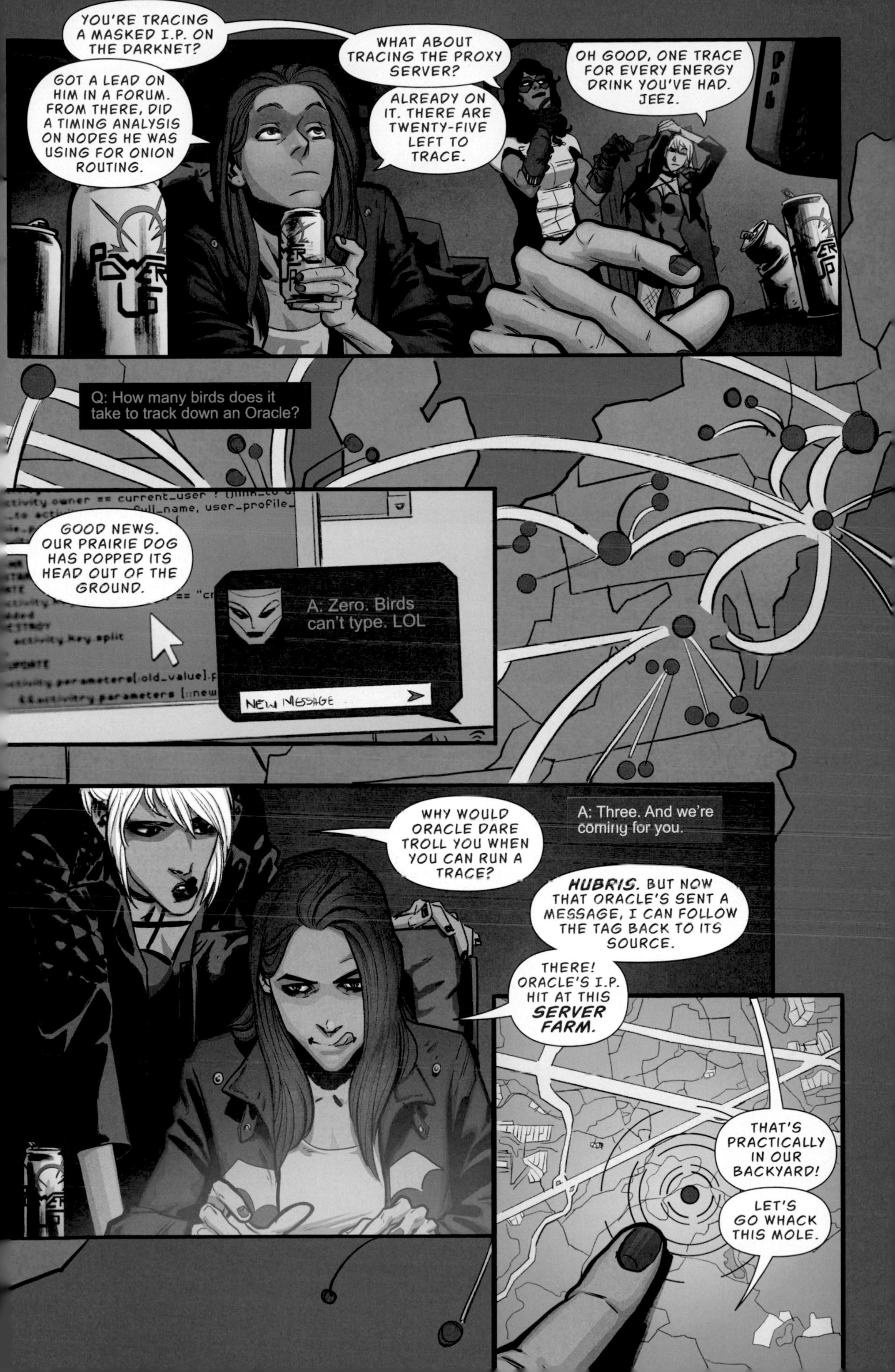
YOU'RE TRACING A MASKED I.P. ON THE DARKNET?
GOT A LEAD ON HIM IN A FORUM. FROM THERE, DID A TIMING ANALYSIS ON NODES HE WAS USING FOR ONION ROUTING.
WHAT ABOUT TRACING THE PROXY SERVER?
ALREADY ON IT. THERE ARE TWENTY-FIVE LEFT TO TRACE.
OH GOOD, ONE TRACE FOR EVERY ENERGY DRINK YOU'VE HAD. JEEZ.
POWER UP
Q: How many birds does it take to track down an Oracle?
GOOD NEWS. OUR PRAIRIE DOG HAS POPPED ITS HEAD OUT OF THE GROUND.
A: Zero. Birds can't type. LOL
NEW MESSAGE
WHY WOULD ORACLE DARE TROLL YOU WHEN YOU CAN RUN A TRACE?
A: Three. And we're coming for you.
HUBRIS. BUT NOW THAT ORACLE'S SENT A MESSAGE, I CAN FOLLOW THE TAG BACK TO ITS SOURCE.
THERE! ORACLE'S I.P. HIT AT THIS SERVER FARM.
THAT'S PRACTICALLY IN OUR BACKYARD!
LET'S GO WHACK THIS MOLE.

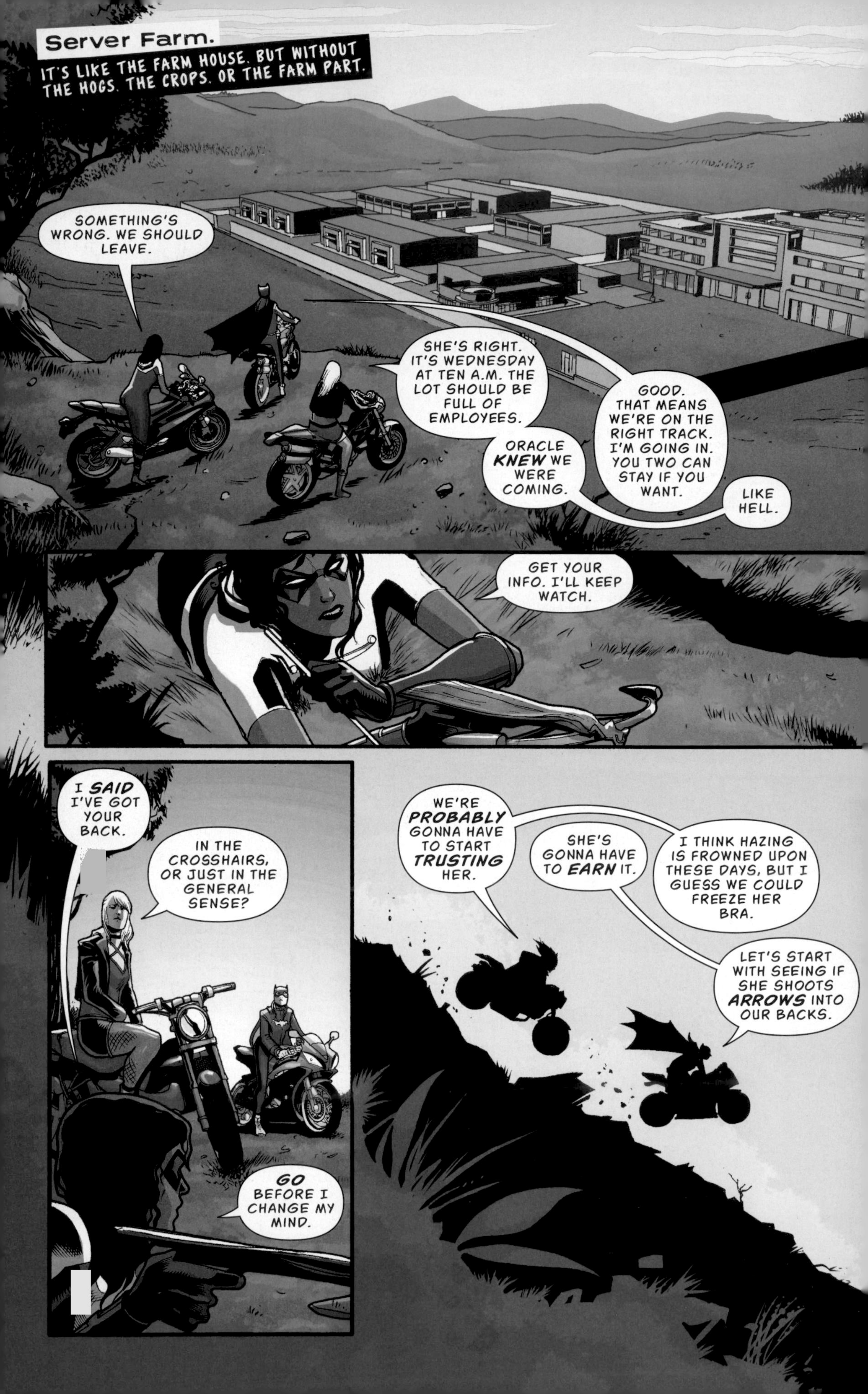
Server Farm.
IT'S LIKE THE FARM HOUSE. BUT WITHOUT THE HOGS. THE CROPS. OR THE FARM PART.
SOMETHING'S WRONG. WE SHOULD LEAVE.
SHE'S RIGHT. IT'S WEDNESDAY AT TEN A.M. THE LOT SHOULD BE FULL OF EMPLOYEES.
GOOD. THAT MEANS WE'RE ON THE RIGHT TRACK. I'M GOING IN. YOU TWO CAN STAY IF YOU WANT.
ORACLE KNEW WE WERE COMING.
LIKE HELL.
GET YOUR INFO. I'LL KEEP WATCH.
I SAID I'VE GOT YOUR BACK.
IN THE CROSSHAIRS, OR JUST IN THE GENERAL SENSE?
GO BEFORE I CHANGE MY MIND.
WE'RE PROBABLY GONNA HAVE TO START TRUSTING HER.
SHE'S GONNA HAVE TO EARN IT.
I THINK HAZING IS FROWNED UPON THESE DAYS, BUT I GUESS WE COULD FREEZE HER BRA.
LET'S START WITH SEEING IF SHE SHOOTS ARROWS INTO OUR BACKS.

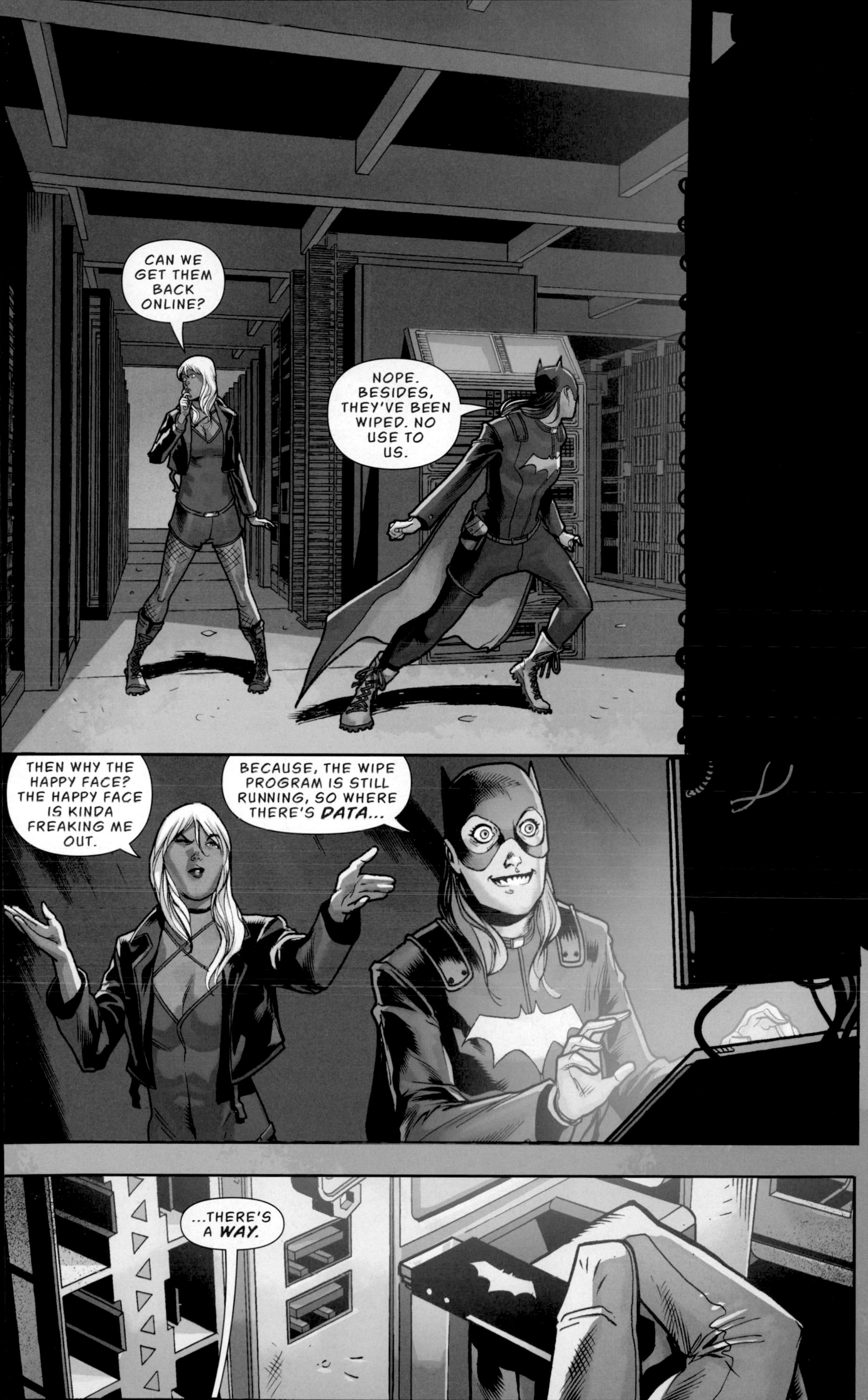
CAN WE GET THEM BACK ONLINE?
NOPE. BESIDES, THEY'VE BEEN WIPED. NO USE TO US.
THEN WHY THE HAPPY FACE? THE HAPPY FACE IS KINDA FREAKING ME OUT.
BECAUSE, THE WIPE PROGRAM IS STILL RUNNING, SO WHERE THERE'S DATA...
...THERE'S A WAY.

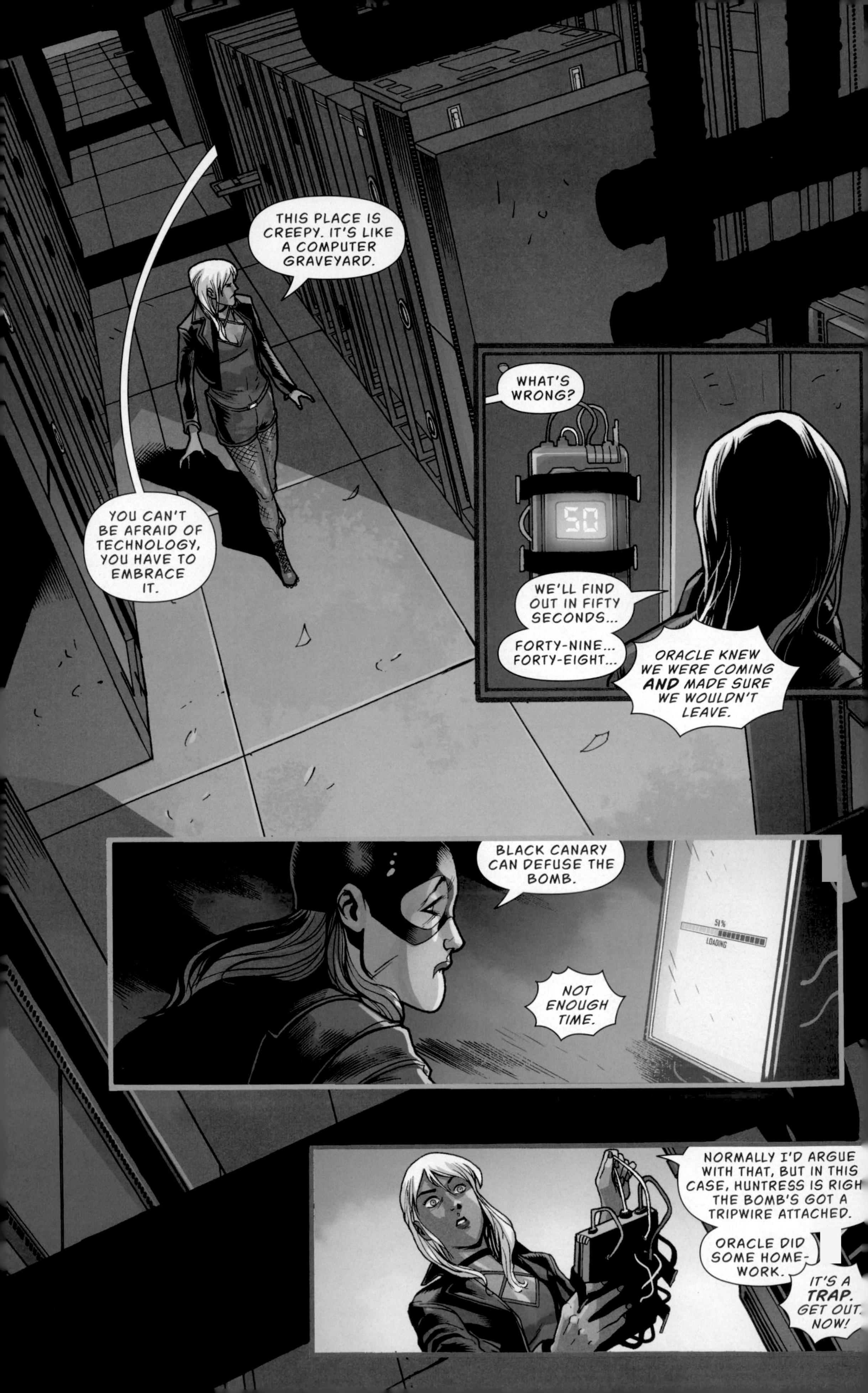
THIS PLACE IS CREEPY. IT'S LIKE A COMPUTER GRAVEYARD.
YOU CAN'T BE AFRAID OF TECHNOLOGY, YOU HAVE TO EMBRACE IT.
WHAT'S WRONG?
50
WE'LL FIND OUT IN FIFTY SECONDS...
FORTY-NINE... FORTY-EIGHT...
ORACLE KNEW WE WERE COMING AND MADE SURE WE WOULDN'T LEAVE.
BLACK CANARY CAN DEFUSE THE BOMB.
51%
LOADING
NOT ENOUGH TIME.
NORMALLY I'D ARGUE WITH THAT, BUT IN THIS CASE, HUNTRESS IS RIGH THE BOMB'S GOT A TRIPWIRE ATTACHED.
ORACLE DID SOME HOME-WORK.
IT'S A TRAP. GET OUT. NOW!

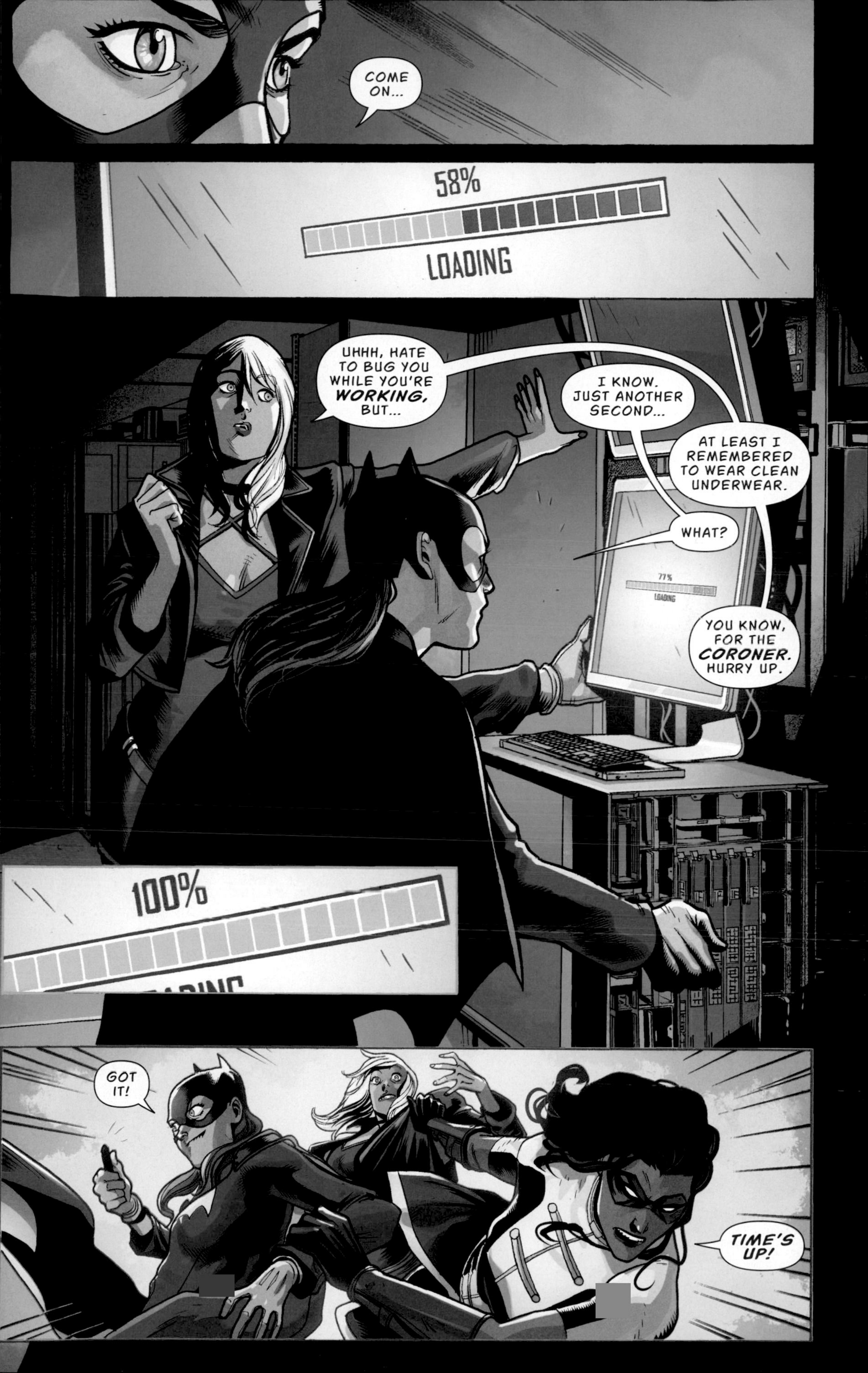
COME ON...
58%
LOADING
UHHH, HATE TO BUG YOU WHILE YOU'RE **WORKING,** BUT...
I KNOW. JUST ANOTHER SECOND...
AT LEAST I REMEMBERED TO WEAR CLEAN UNDERWEAR.
WHAT?
77%
LOADING
YOU KNOW, FOR THE **CORONER.** HURRY UP.
100%
GOT IT!
TIME'S UP!

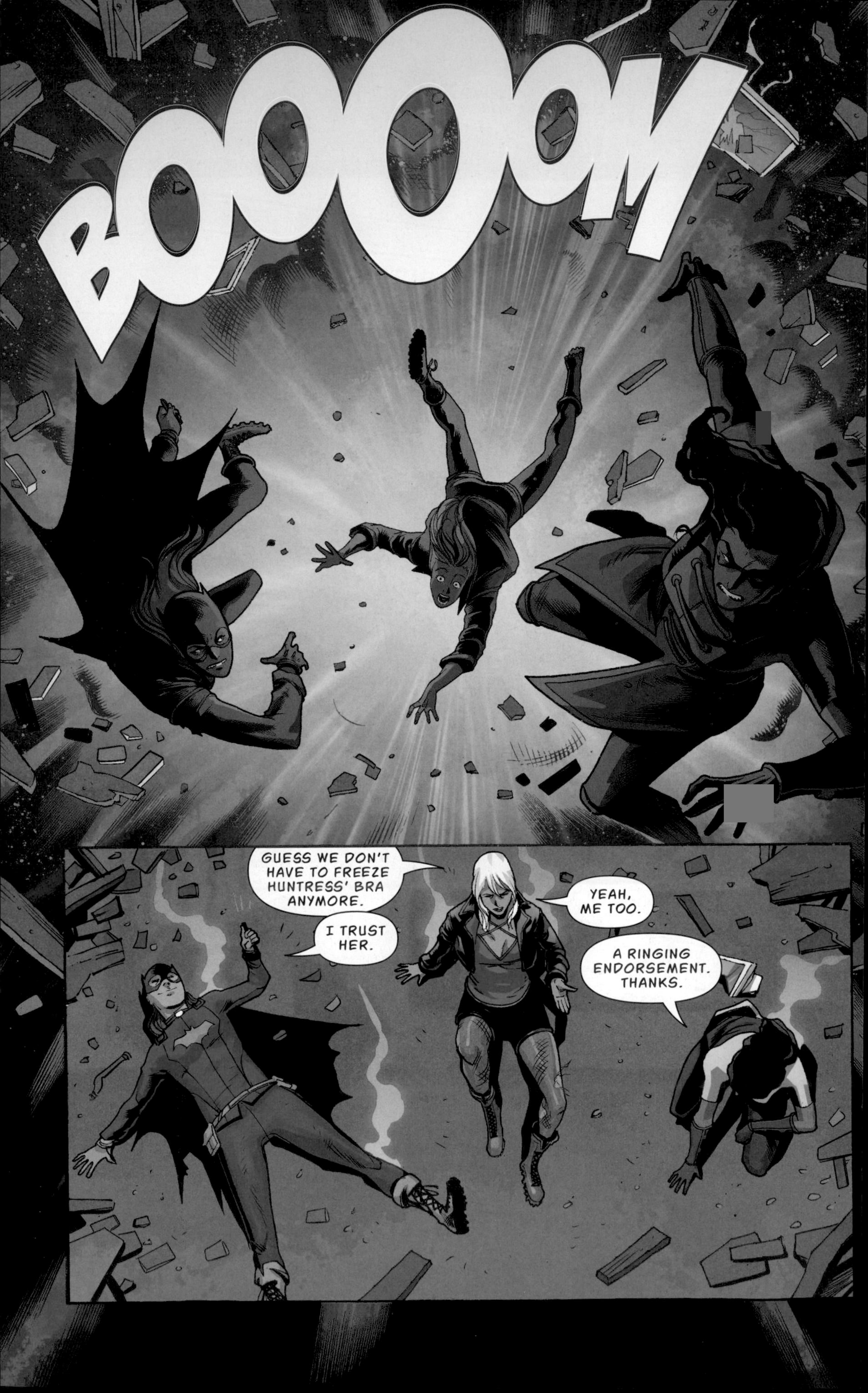
BOOOOM
GUESS WE DON'T HAVE TO FREEZE HUNTRESS' BRA ANYMORE.
I TRUST HER.
YEAH, ME TOO.
A RINGING ENDORSEMENT. THANKS.

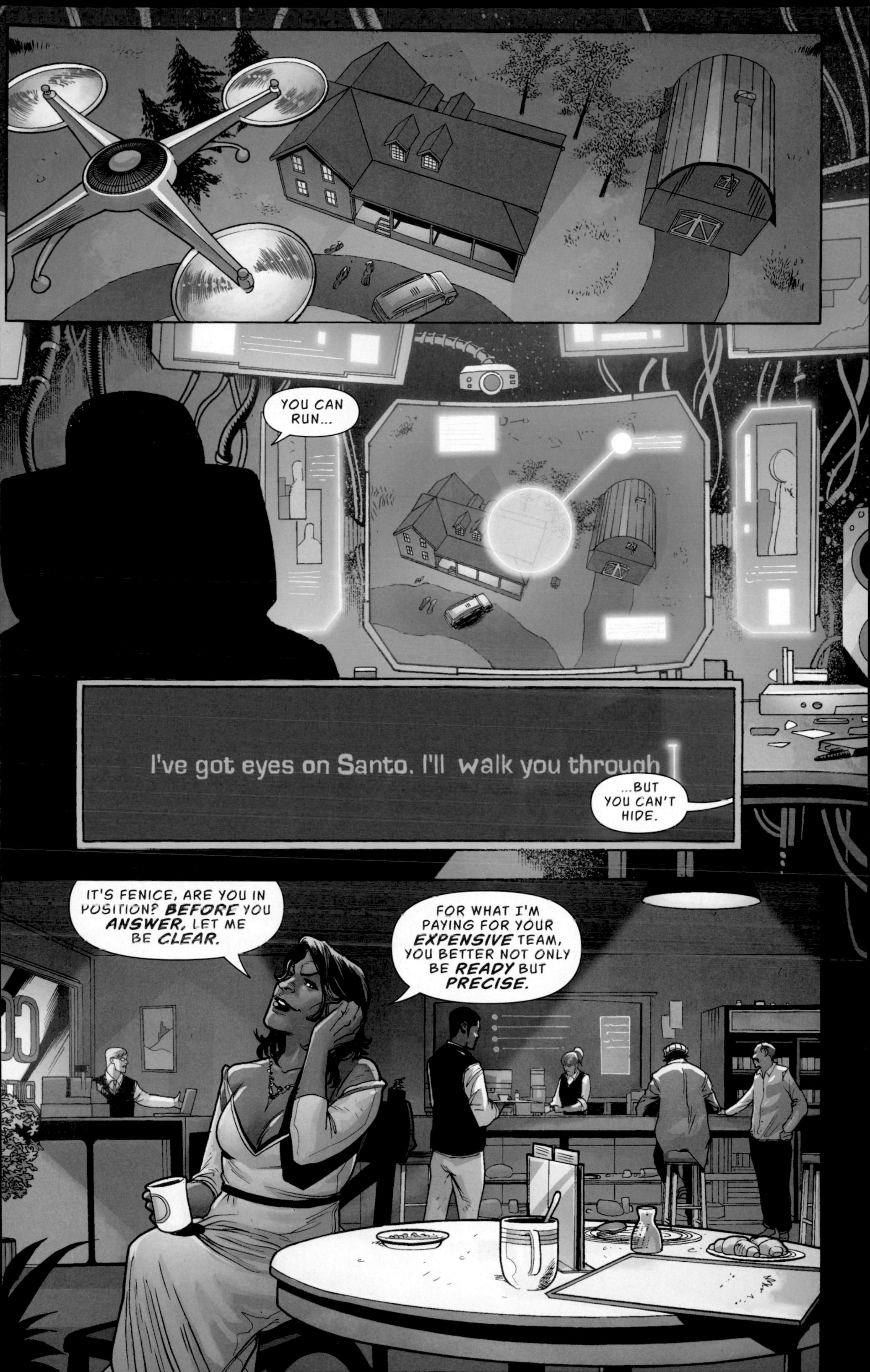

YOU CAN RUN...
I've got eyes on Santo. I'll walk you through
...BUT YOU CAN'T HIDE.
IT'S FENICE, ARE YOU IN POSITION? BEFORE YOU ANSWER, LET ME BE CLEAR.
FOR WHAT I'M PAYING FOR YOUR EXPENSIVE TEAM, YOU BETTER NOT ONLY BE READY BUT PRECISE.

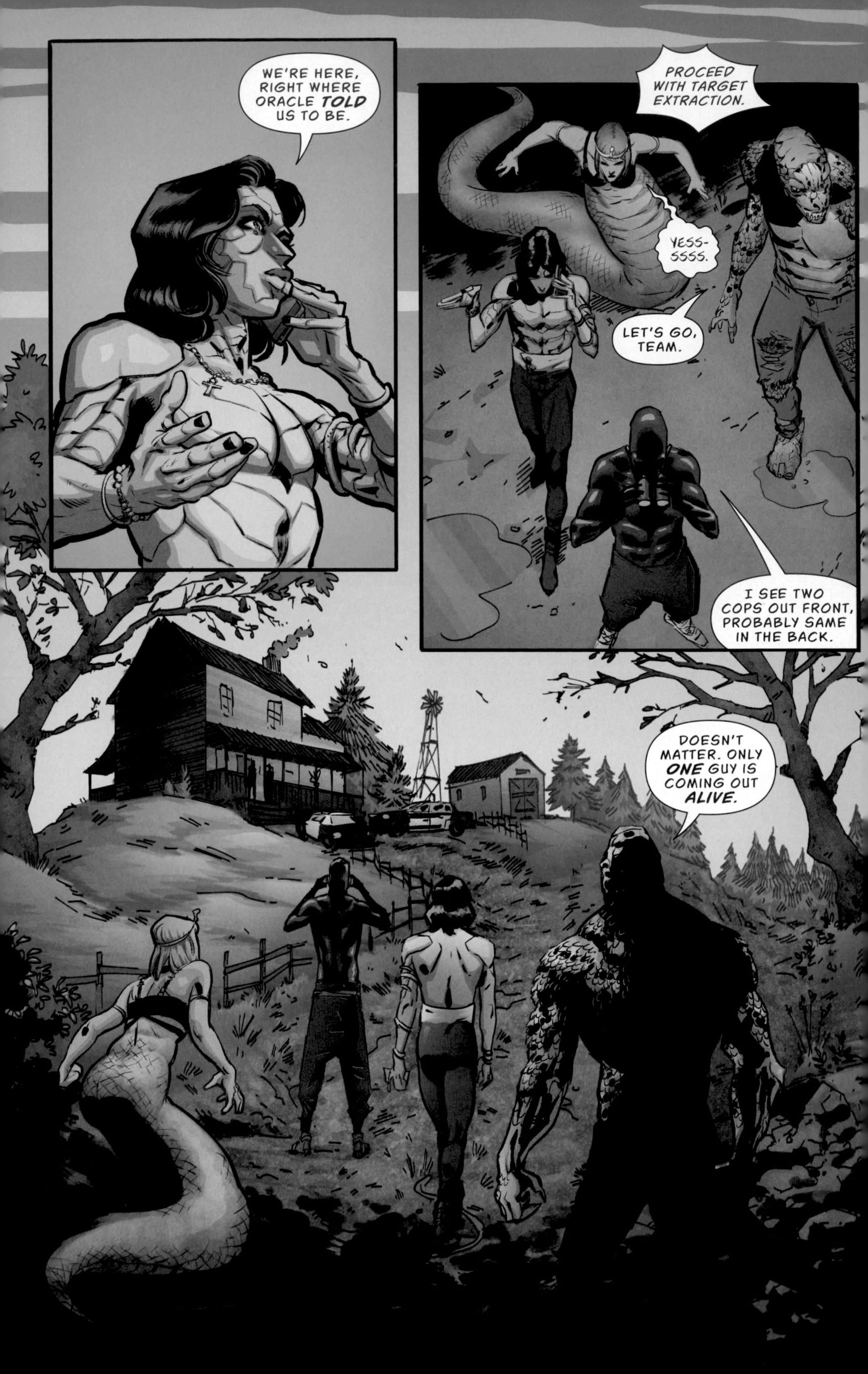
WE'RE HERE, RIGHT WHERE ORACLE TOLD US TO BE.
PROCEED WITH TARGET EXTRACTION.
YESS-SSSS.
LET'S GO, TEAM.
I SEE TWO COPS OUT FRONT, PROBABLY SAME IN THE BACK.
DOESN'T MATTER. ONLY ONE GUY IS COMING OUT ALIVE.

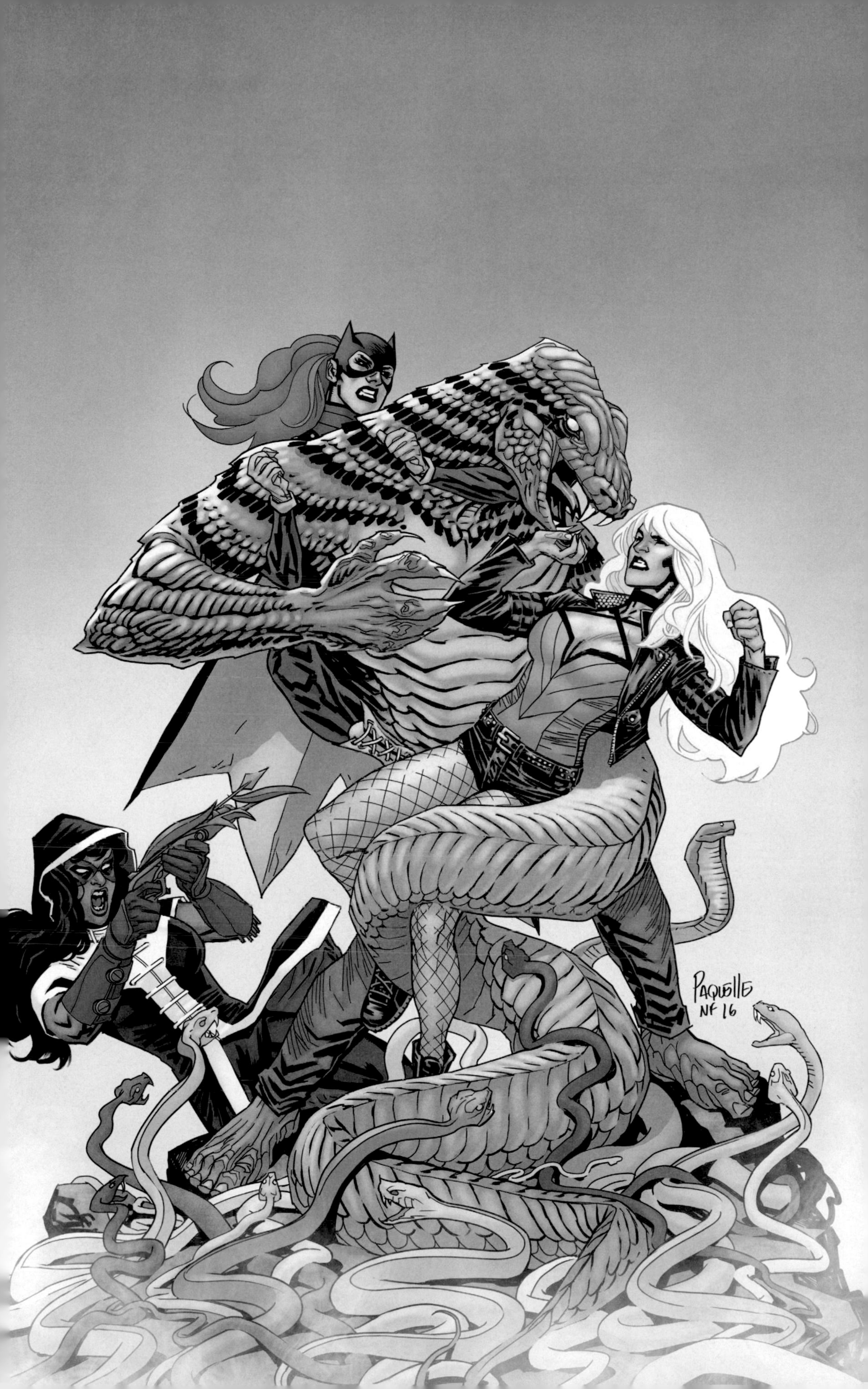
PAQUETTE
NF 16

PART THREE: ALL YOUR LIFE

JULIE and SHAWNA BENSON writers * CLAIRE ROE and ROGE ANTONIO artists
ALLEN PASSALAQUA colorist * DERON BENNETT letterer

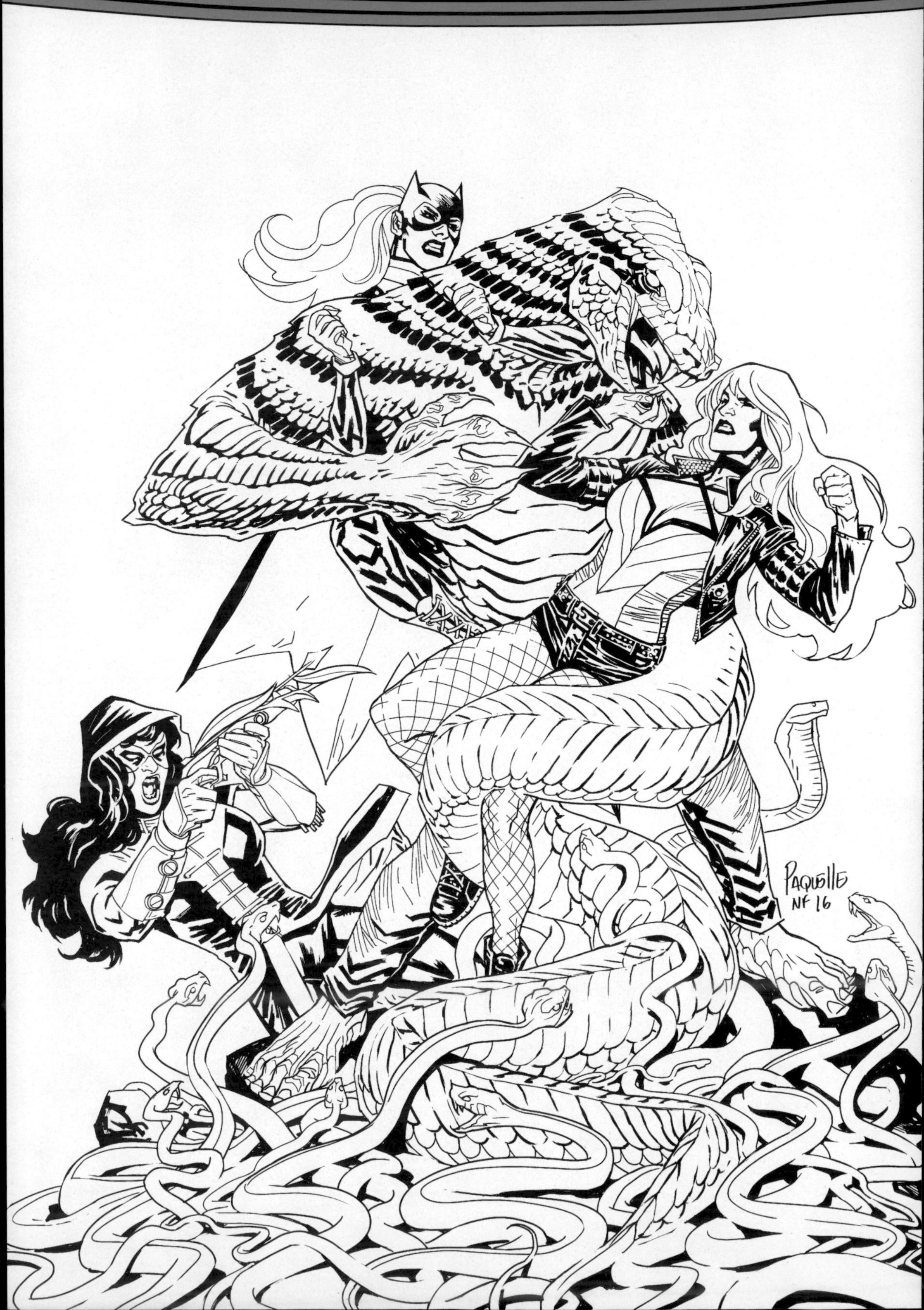

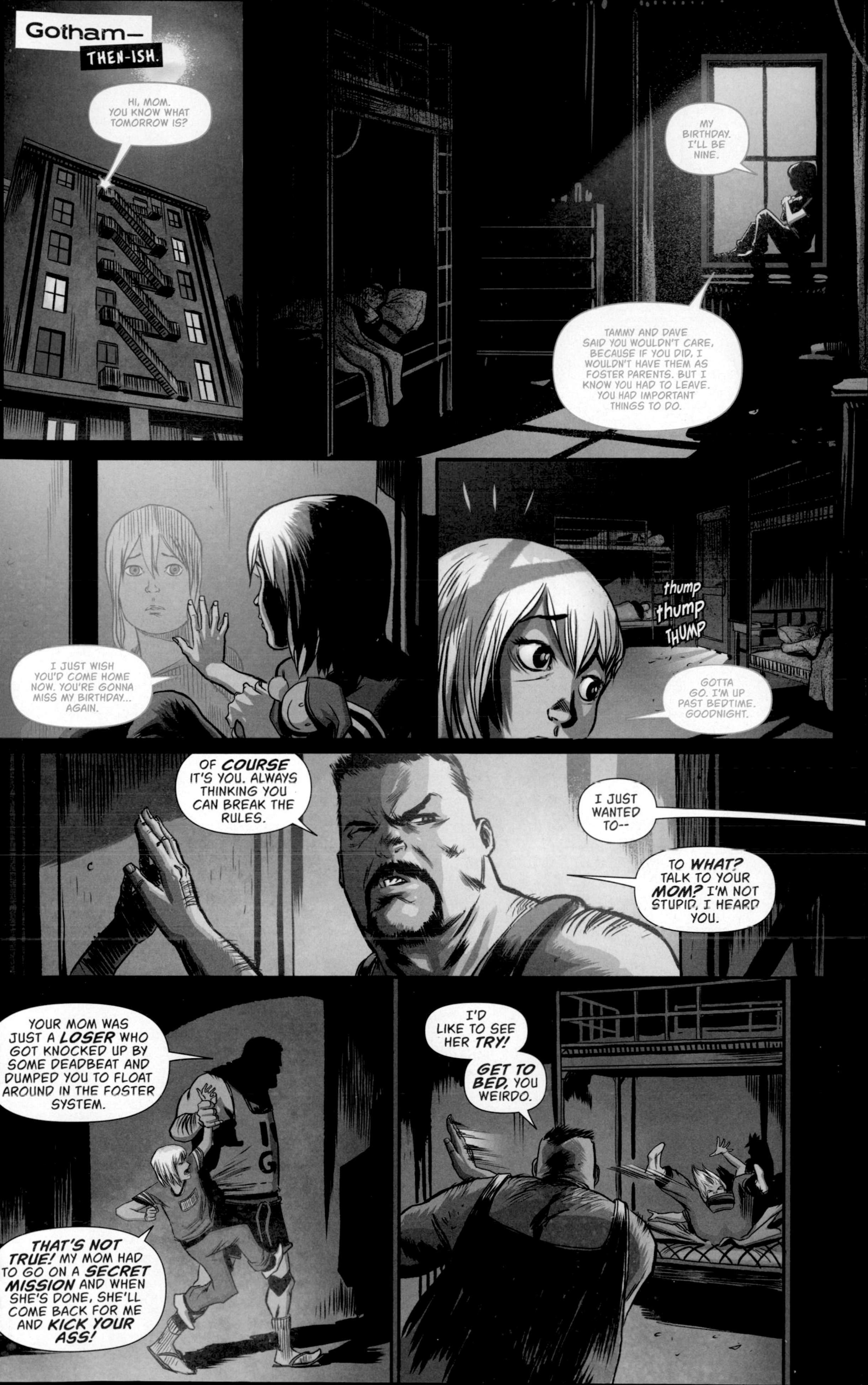
Gotham—
THEN-ISH.
HI, MOM. YOU KNOW WHAT TOMORROW IS?
MY BIRTHDAY. I'LL BE NINE.
TAMMY AND DAVE SAID YOU WOULDN'T CARE, BECAUSE IF YOU DID, I WOULDN'T HAVE THEM AS FOSTER PARENTS. BUT I KNOW YOU HAD TO LEAVE. YOU HAD IMPORTANT THINGS TO DO.
I JUST WISH YOU'D COME HOME NOW. YOU'RE GONNA MISS MY BIRTHDAY... AGAIN.
thump thump THUMP
GOTTA GO. I'M UP PAST BEDTIME. GOODNIGHT.
OF COURSE IT'S YOU. ALWAYS THINKING YOU CAN BREAK THE RULES.
I JUST WANTED TO--
TO WHAT? TALK TO YOUR MOM? I'M NOT STUPID, I HEARD YOU.
YOUR MOM WAS JUST A LOSER WHO GOT KNOCKED UP BY SOME DEADBEAT AND DUMPED YOU TO FLOAT AROUND IN THE FOSTER SYSTEM.
THAT'S NOT TRUE! MY MOM HAD TO GO ON A SECRET MISSION AND WHEN SHE'S DONE, SHE'LL COME BACK FOR ME AND KICK YOUR ASS!
I'D LIKE TO SEE HER TRY!
GET TO BED, YOU WEIRDO.

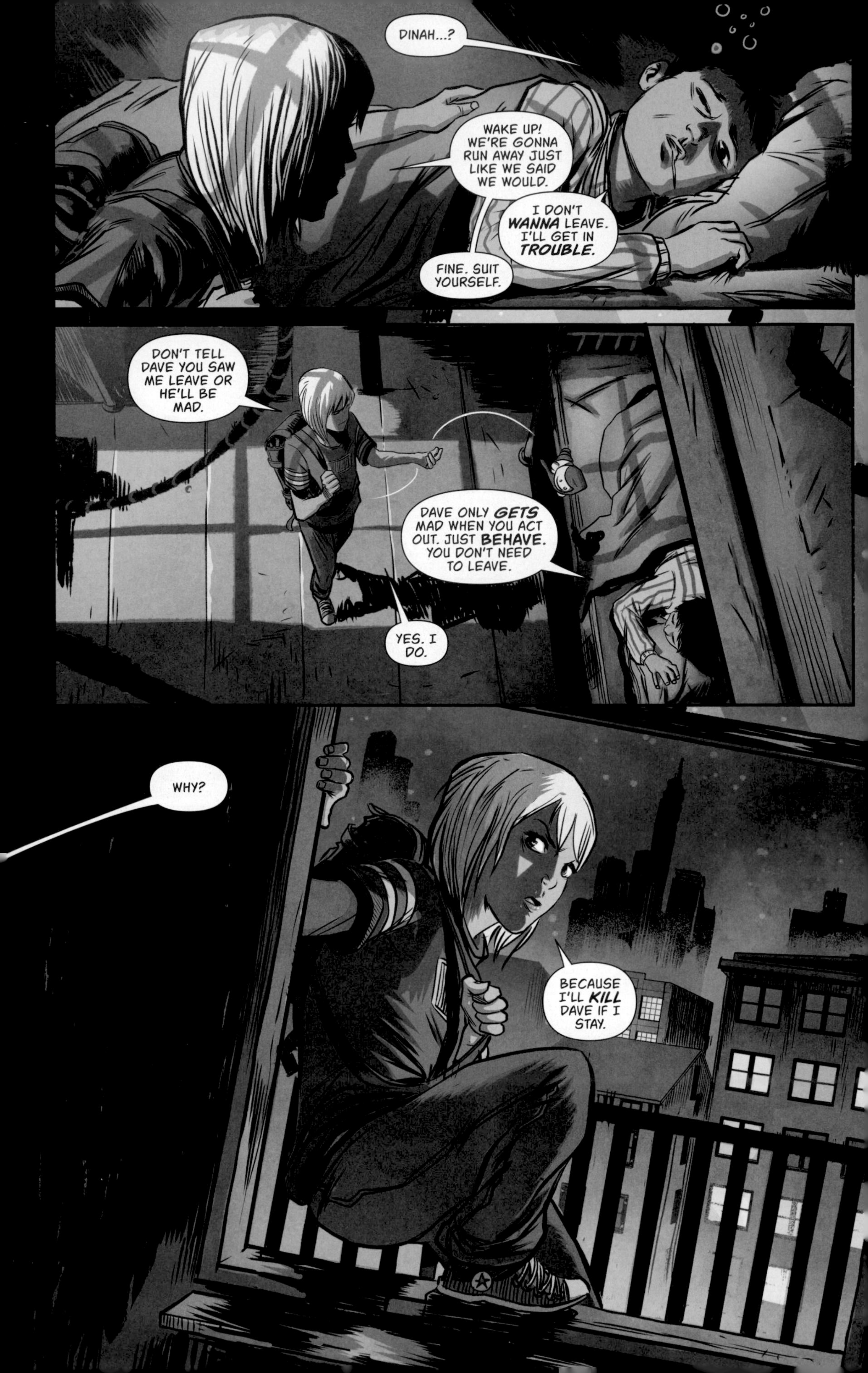
DINAH...?
WAKE UP! WE'RE GONNA RUN AWAY JUST LIKE WE SAID WE WOULD.
I DON'T WANNA LEAVE. I'LL GET IN TROUBLE.
FINE. SUIT YOURSELF.
DON'T TELL DAVE YOU SAW ME LEAVE OR HE'LL BE MAD.
DAVE ONLY GETS MAD WHEN YOU ACT OUT. JUST BEHAVE. YOU DON'T NEED TO LEAVE.
YES. I DO.
WHY?
BECAUSE I'LL KILL DAVE IF I STAY.

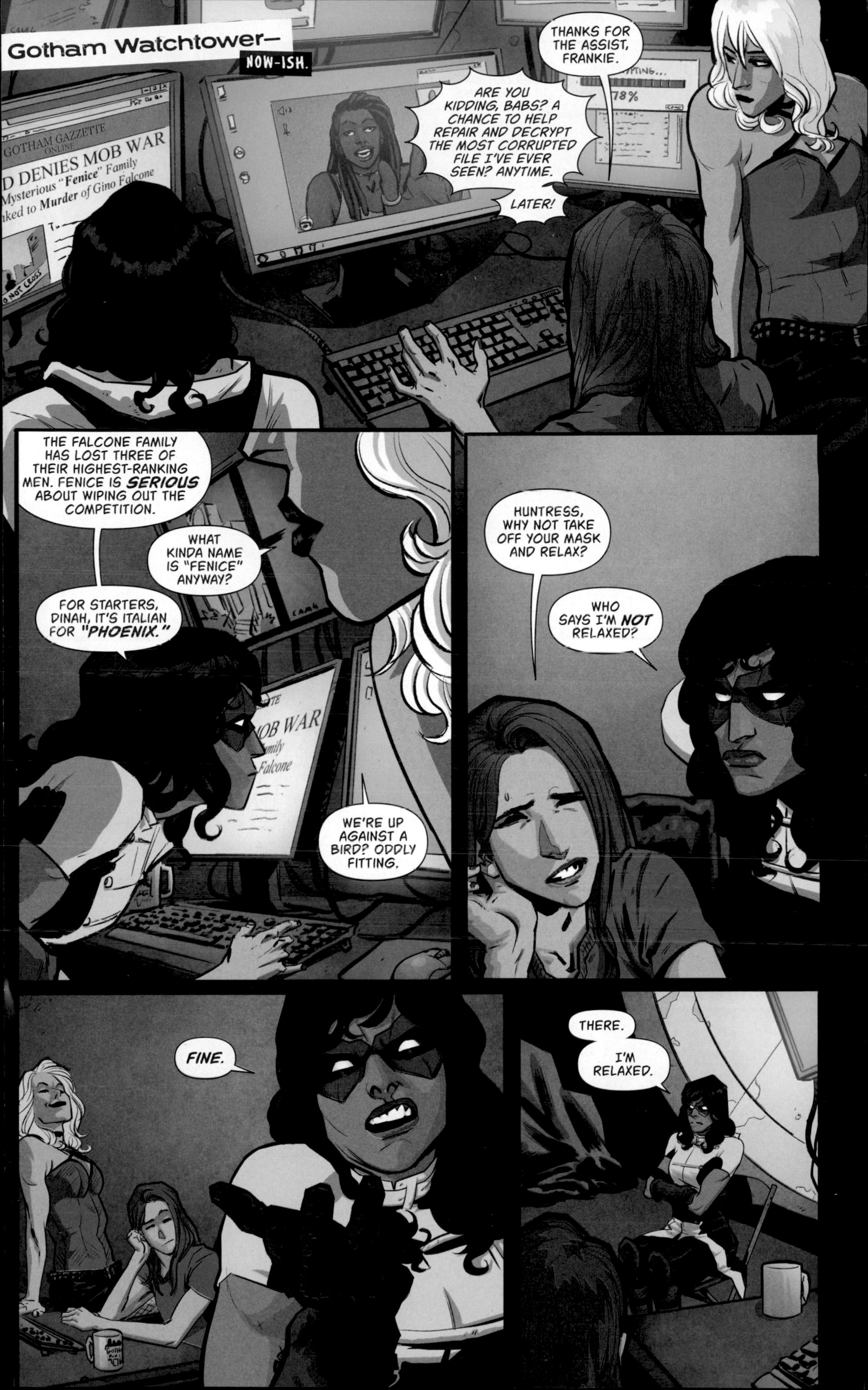
Gotham Watchtower—
NOW-ISH.
GOTHAM GAZETTE
ONLINE
D DENIES MOB WAR
Mysterious "Fenice" Family
nked to Murder of Gino Falcone
THANKS FOR THE ASSIST, FRANKIE.
ARE YOU KIDDING, BABS? A CHANCE TO HELP REPAIR AND DECRYPT THE MOST CORRUPTED FILE I'VE EVER SEEN? ANYTIME.
LATER!
THE FALCONE FAMILY HAS LOST THREE OF THEIR HIGHEST-RANKING MEN. FENICE IS SERIOUS ABOUT WIPING OUT THE COMPETITION.
WHAT KINDA NAME IS "FENICE" ANYWAY?
FOR STARTERS, DINAH, IT'S ITALIAN FOR "PHOENIX."
WE'RE UP AGAINST A BIRD? ODDLY FITTING.
HUNTRESS, WHY NOT TAKE OFF YOUR MASK AND RELAX?
WHO SAYS I'M NOT RELAXED?
FINE.
THERE.
I'M RELAXED.

BOOOOOOP BOOOOOOP

YOUR REALTOR? *AGAIN?* ARE YOU SKIPPING OUT ON BILLS OR SOMETHING?

NOPE. PAID IN FULL. I HAVE NO IDEA WHAT THEY'RE AFTER.

OR WHY THEY WON'T JUST CALL ME.

I REALLY WANT TO KNOW THE ANSWER, BUT WATCHING THEM TEST OUT YOUR NEW SECURITY SYSTEM BRINGS ME NOTHING BUT JOY.

THE ELECTRO-FENCE *MIGHT* HAVE BEEN OVERKILL.

I'M STARTING TO LIKE THE WAY YOU THINK.

FILE'S DECRYPTED! LET'S SEE WHAT ORACLE WAS SELLING FENICE.

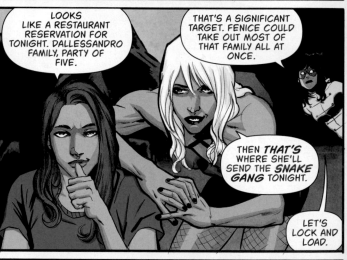

LOOKS LIKE A RESTAURANT RESERVATION FOR TONIGHT. DALLESSANDRO FAMILY, PARTY OF FIVE.

THAT'S A SIGNIFICANT TARGET. FENICE COULD TAKE OUT MOST OF THAT FAMILY ALL AT ONCE.

THEN *THAT'S* WHERE SHE'LL SEND THE *SNAKE GANG* TONIGHT.

LET'S LOCK AND LOAD.

OR, WE AVOID THE SNAKES AND *WARN* THE FAMILY SO THEY CAN LEAVE THE RESTAURANT.

AND HOW DOES *THAT* GET US TO ORACLE?

IT *DOESN'T.* BUT IT SAVES A DOZEN LIVES.

THAT DON'T *DESERVE* SAVING.

TRUST ME, I WANT TO FIND ORACLE MORE THAN ANYBODY. WE'LL FIND A WAY.

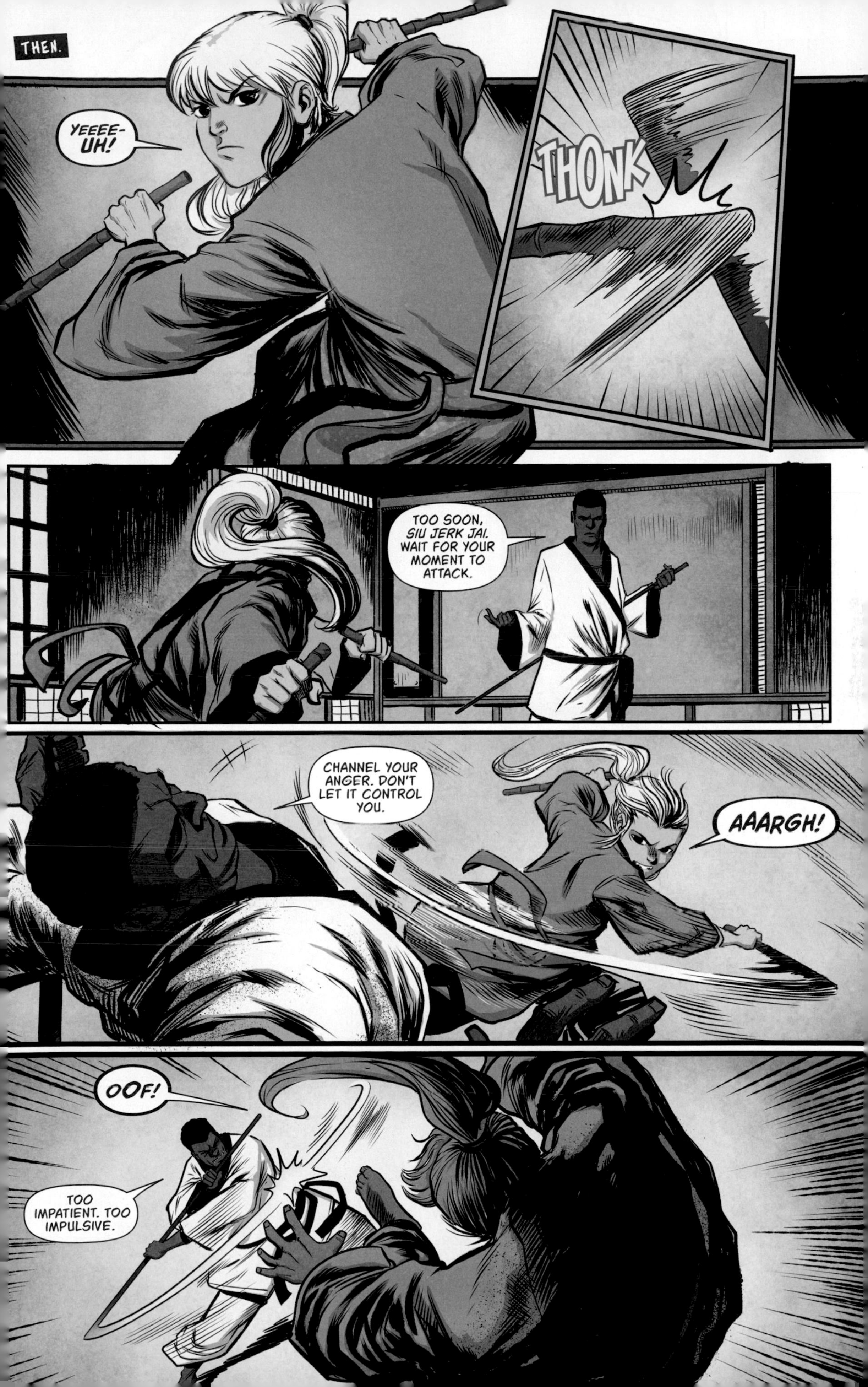
THEN.
YEEEE-UH!
THONK
TOO SOON, SIU JERK JAI. WAIT FOR YOUR MOMENT TO ATTACK.
CHANNEL YOUR ANGER. DON'T LET IT CONTROL YOU.
AAARGH!
OOF!
TOO IMPATIENT. TOO IMPULSIVE.

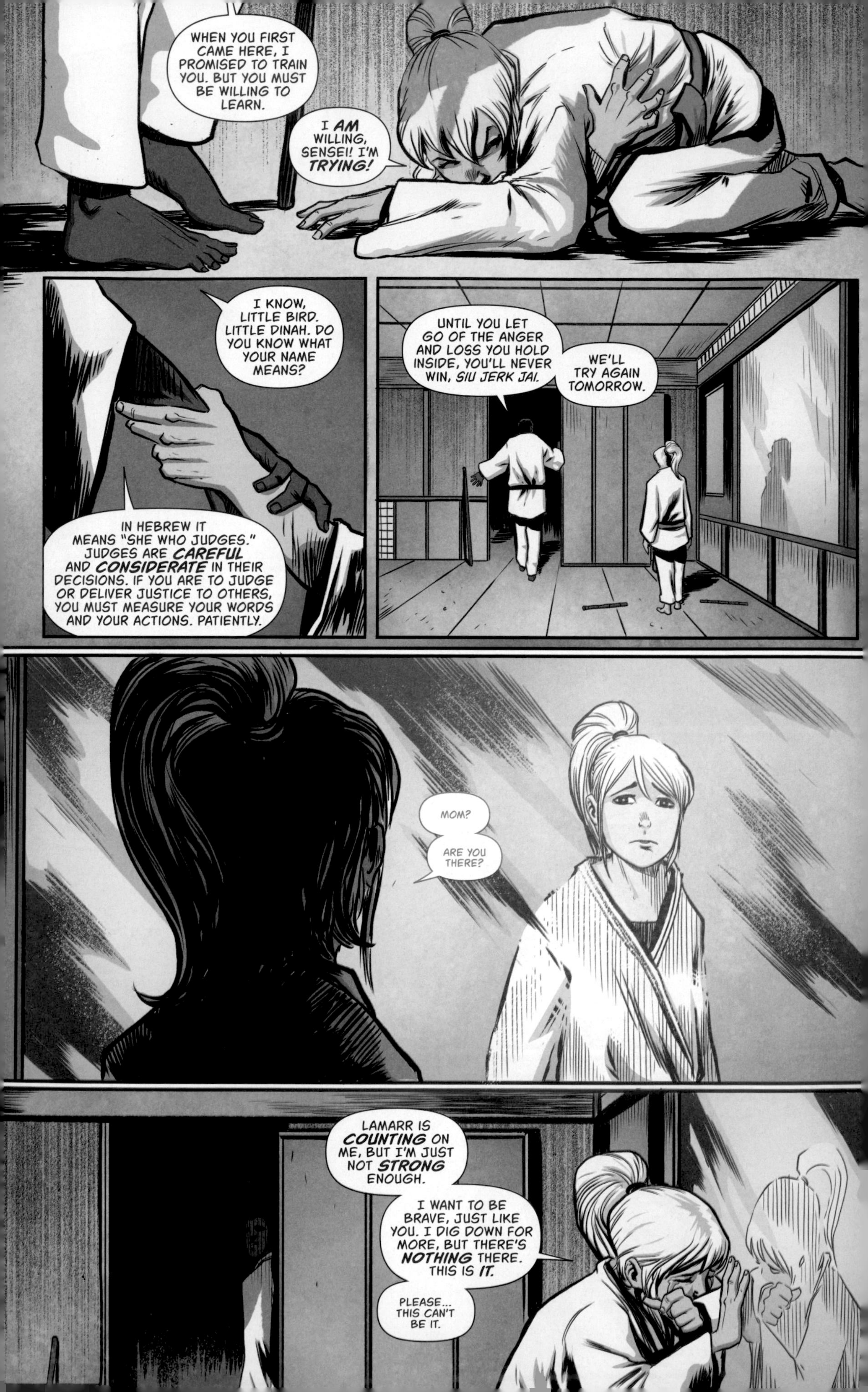
WHEN YOU FIRST CAME HERE, I PROMISED TO TRAIN YOU. BUT YOU MUST BE WILLING TO LEARN.
I *AM* WILLING, SENSEI! I'M *TRYING!*
I KNOW, LITTLE BIRD. LITTLE DINAH. DO YOU KNOW WHAT YOUR NAME MEANS?
IN HEBREW IT MEANS "SHE WHO JUDGES." JUDGES ARE *CAREFUL* AND *CONSIDERATE* IN THEIR DECISIONS. IF YOU ARE TO JUDGE OR DELIVER JUSTICE TO OTHERS, YOU MUST MEASURE YOUR WORDS AND YOUR ACTIONS. PATIENTLY.
UNTIL YOU LET GO OF THE ANGER AND LOSS YOU HOLD INSIDE, YOU'LL NEVER WIN, *SIU JERK JAI.*
WE'LL TRY AGAIN TOMORROW.
MOM?
ARE YOU THERE?
LAMARR IS *COUNTING* ON ME, BUT I'M JUST NOT *STRONG* ENOUGH.
I WANT TO BE BRAVE, JUST LIKE YOU. I DIG DOWN FOR MORE, BUT THERE'S *NOTHING* THERE. THIS IS *IT.*
PLEASE... THIS CAN'T BE IT.

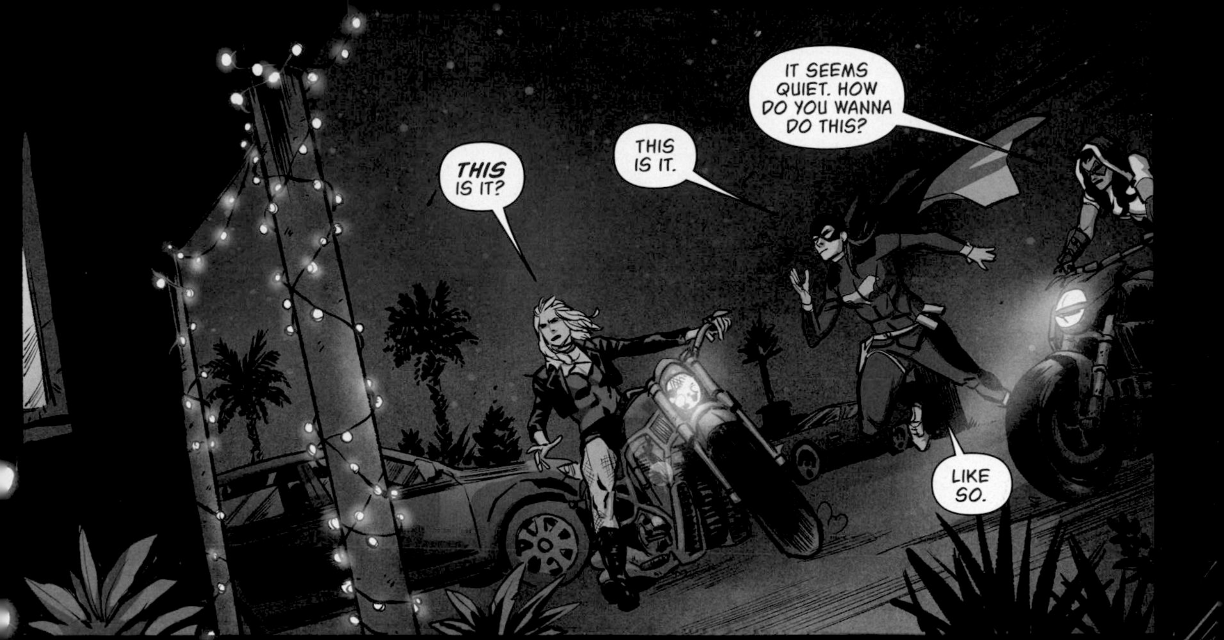
THIS IS IT?
THIS IS IT.
IT SEEMS QUIET. HOW DO YOU WANNA DO THIS?
LIKE SO.

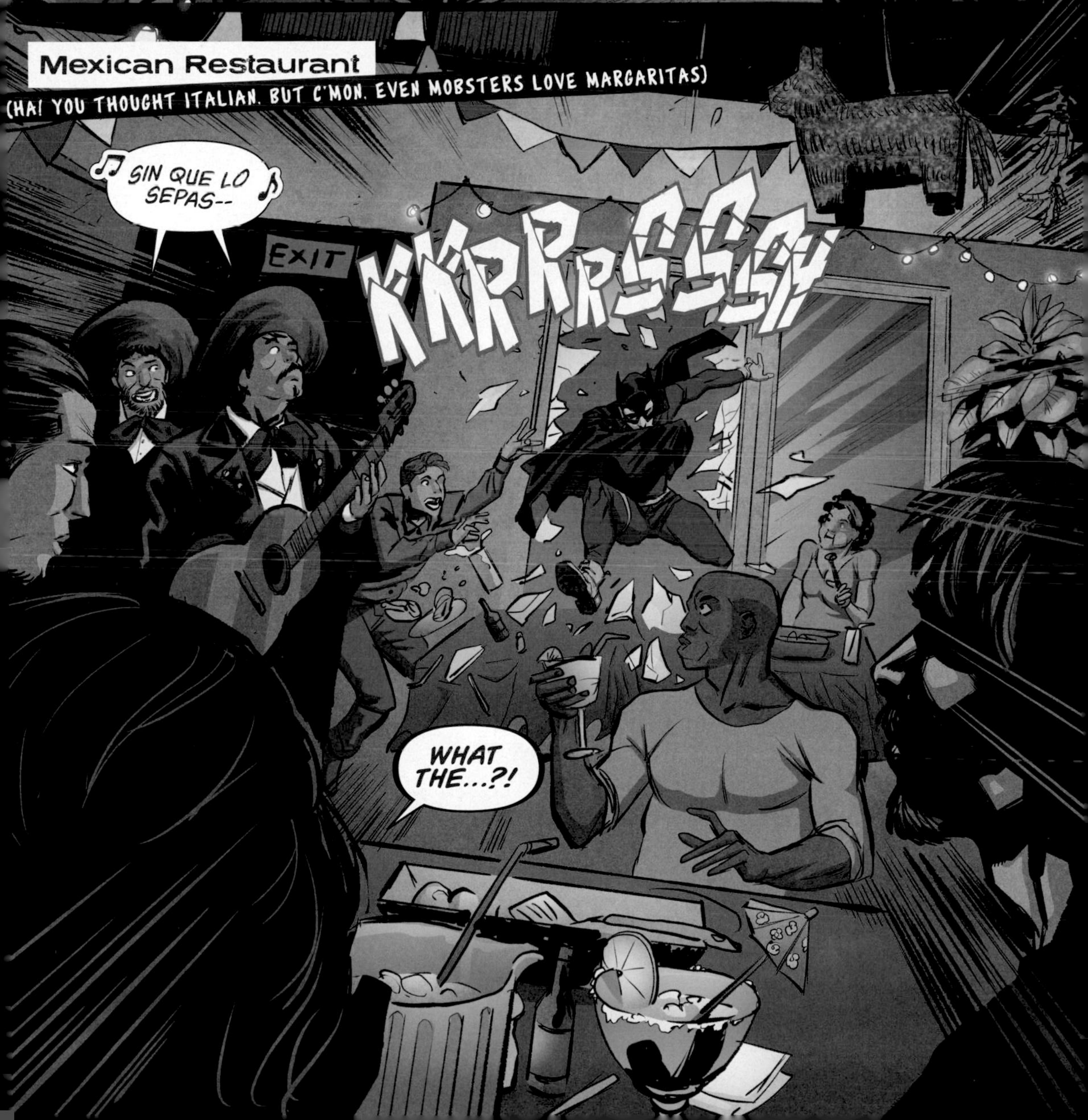
Mexican Restaurant
(HA! YOU THOUGHT ITALIAN. BUT C'MON. EVEN MOBSTERS LOVE MARGARITAS)
SIN QUE LO SEPAS--
EXIT
KKRRRSSSH
WHAT THE...?!

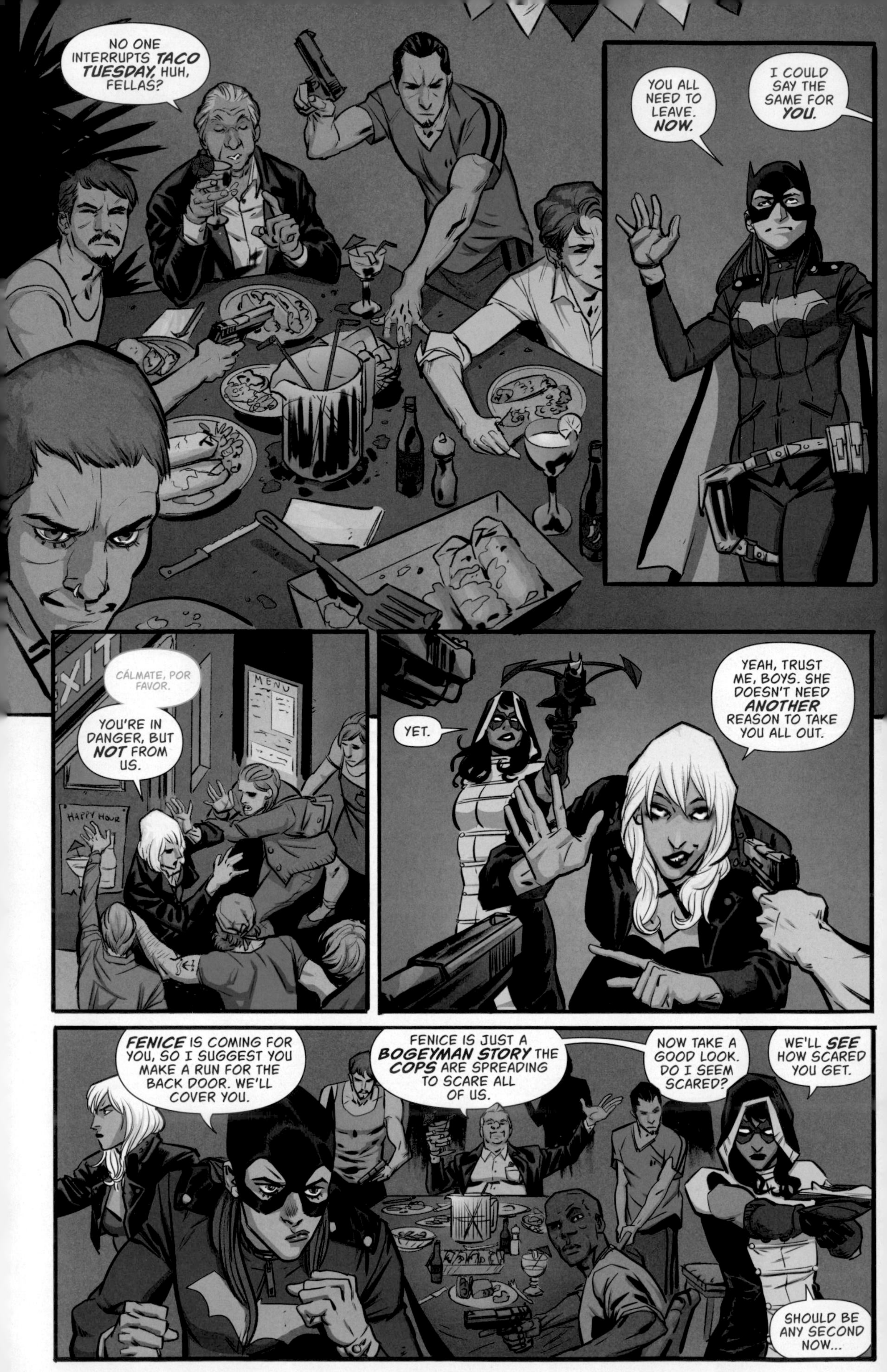
NO ONE INTERRUPTS TACO TUESDAY, HUH, FELLAS?
YOU ALL NEED TO LEAVE. NOW.
I COULD SAY THE SAME FOR YOU.
EXIT
MENU
HAPPY HOUR
CÁLMATE, POR FAVOR.
YOU'RE IN DANGER, BUT NOT FROM US.
YET.
YEAH, TRUST ME, BOYS. SHE DOESN'T NEED ANOTHER REASON TO TAKE YOU ALL OUT.
FENICE IS COMING FOR YOU, SO I SUGGEST YOU MAKE A RUN FOR THE BACK DOOR. WE'LL COVER YOU.
FENICE IS JUST A BOGEYMAN STORY THE COPS ARE SPREADING TO SCARE ALL OF US.
NOW TAKE A GOOD LOOK. DO I SEEM SCARED?
WE'LL SEE HOW SCARED YOU GET.
SHOULD BE ANY SECOND NOW...

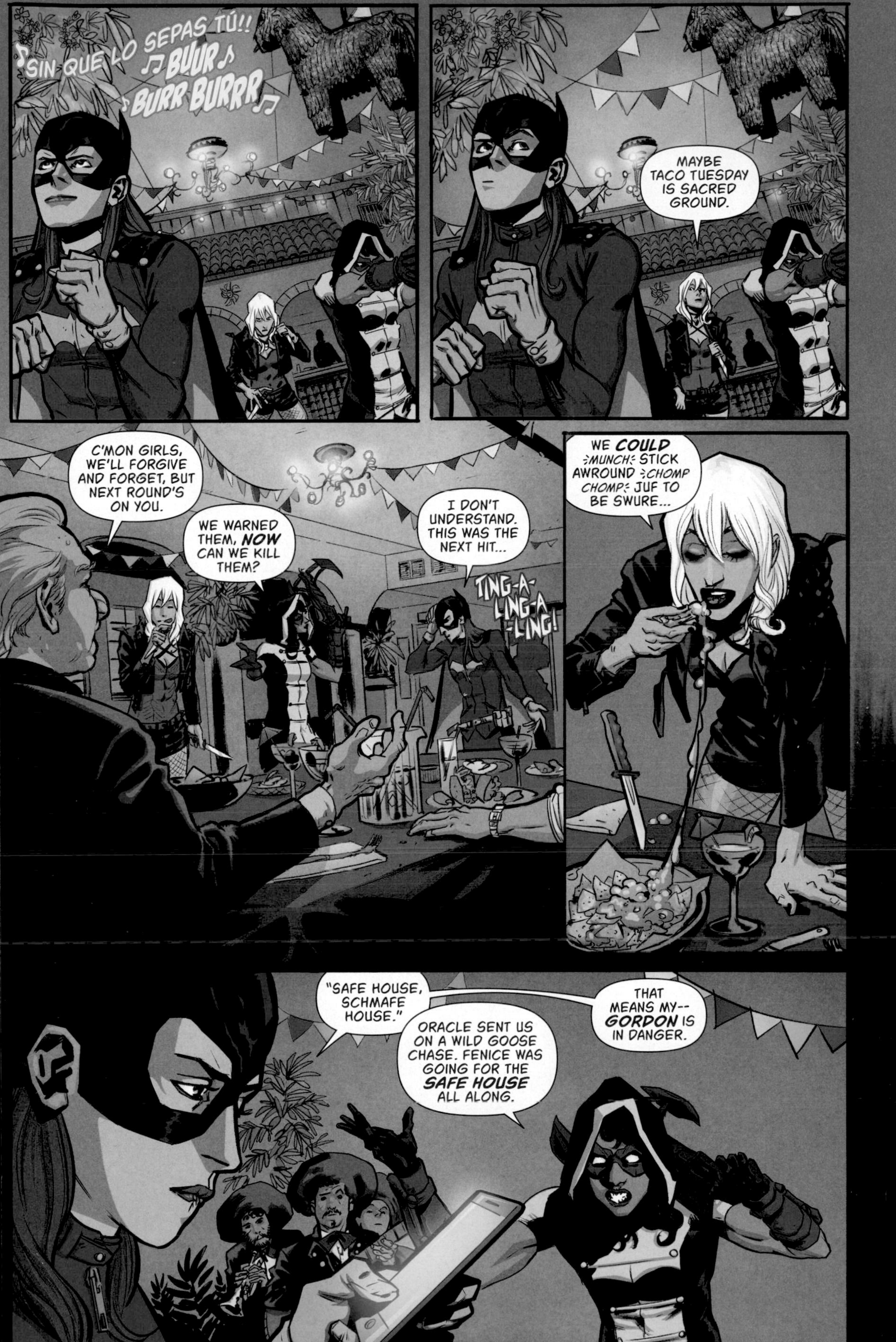
♪SIN QUE LO SEPAS TÚ!! ♫BUUR♪ ♪BURR BURRR♫
MAYBE TACO TUESDAY IS SACRED GROUND.
C'MON GIRLS, WE'LL FORGIVE AND FORGET, BUT NEXT ROUND'S ON YOU.
WE WARNED THEM, NOW CAN WE KILL THEM?
I DON'T UNDERSTAND. THIS WAS THE NEXT HIT...
TING-A-LING-A-LING!
WE COULD ⇒MUNCH⇐ STICK AWROUND ⇒CHOMP CHOMP⇐ JUF TO BE SWURE...
"SAFE HOUSE, SCHMAFE HOUSE."
ORACLE SENT US ON A WILD GOOSE CHASE. FENICE WAS GOING FOR THE SAFE HOUSE ALL ALONG.
THAT MEANS MY-- GORDON IS IN DANGER.

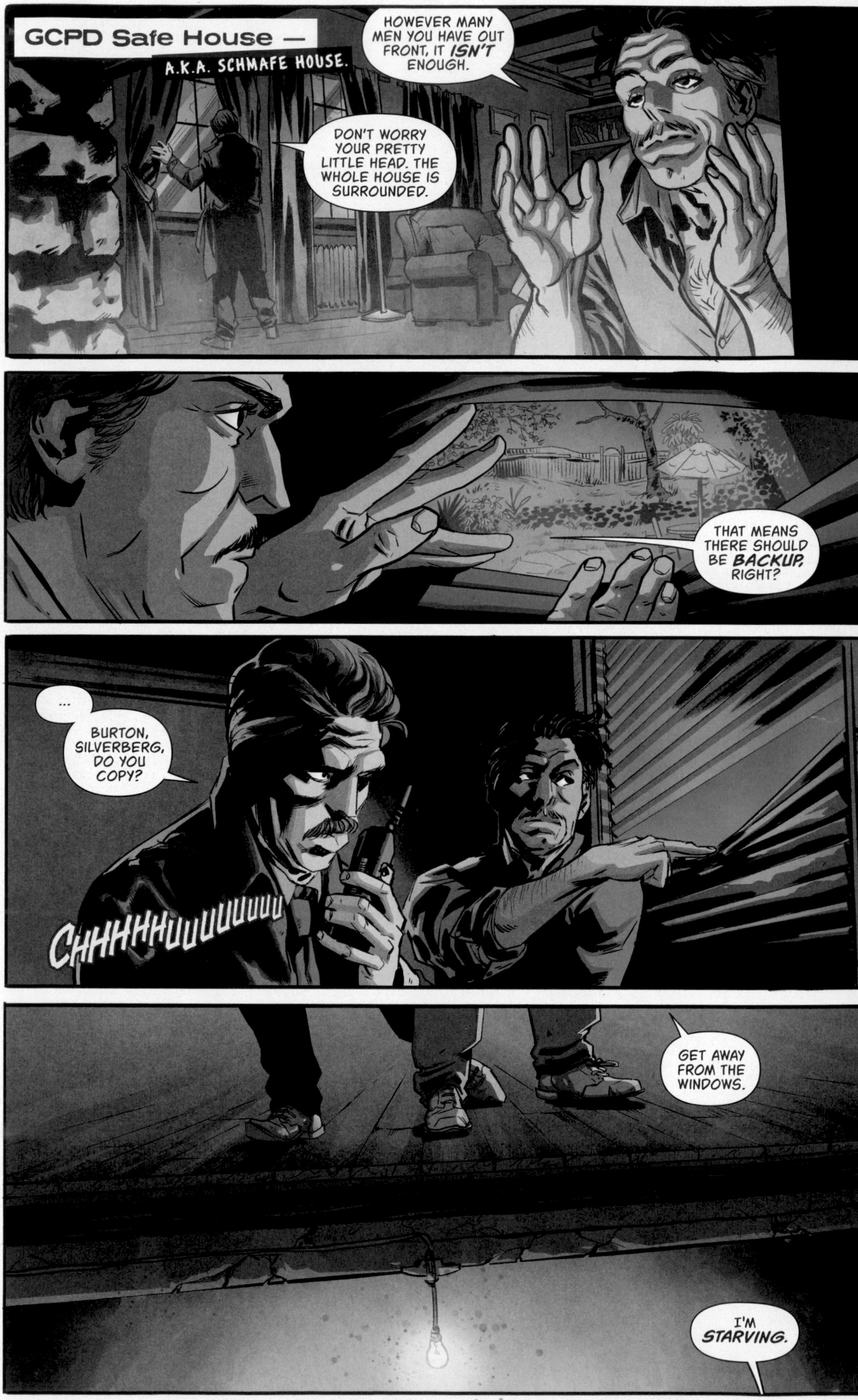
GCPD Safe House —
A.K.A. SCHMAFE HOUSE.
HOWEVER MANY MEN YOU HAVE OUT FRONT, IT ISN'T ENOUGH.
DON'T WORRY YOUR PRETTY LITTLE HEAD. THE WHOLE HOUSE IS SURROUNDED.
THAT MEANS THERE SHOULD BE BACKUP, RIGHT?
...
BURTON, SILVERBERG, DO YOU COPY?
CHHHHHUUUUUUUUU
GET AWAY FROM THE WINDOWS.
I'M STARVING.

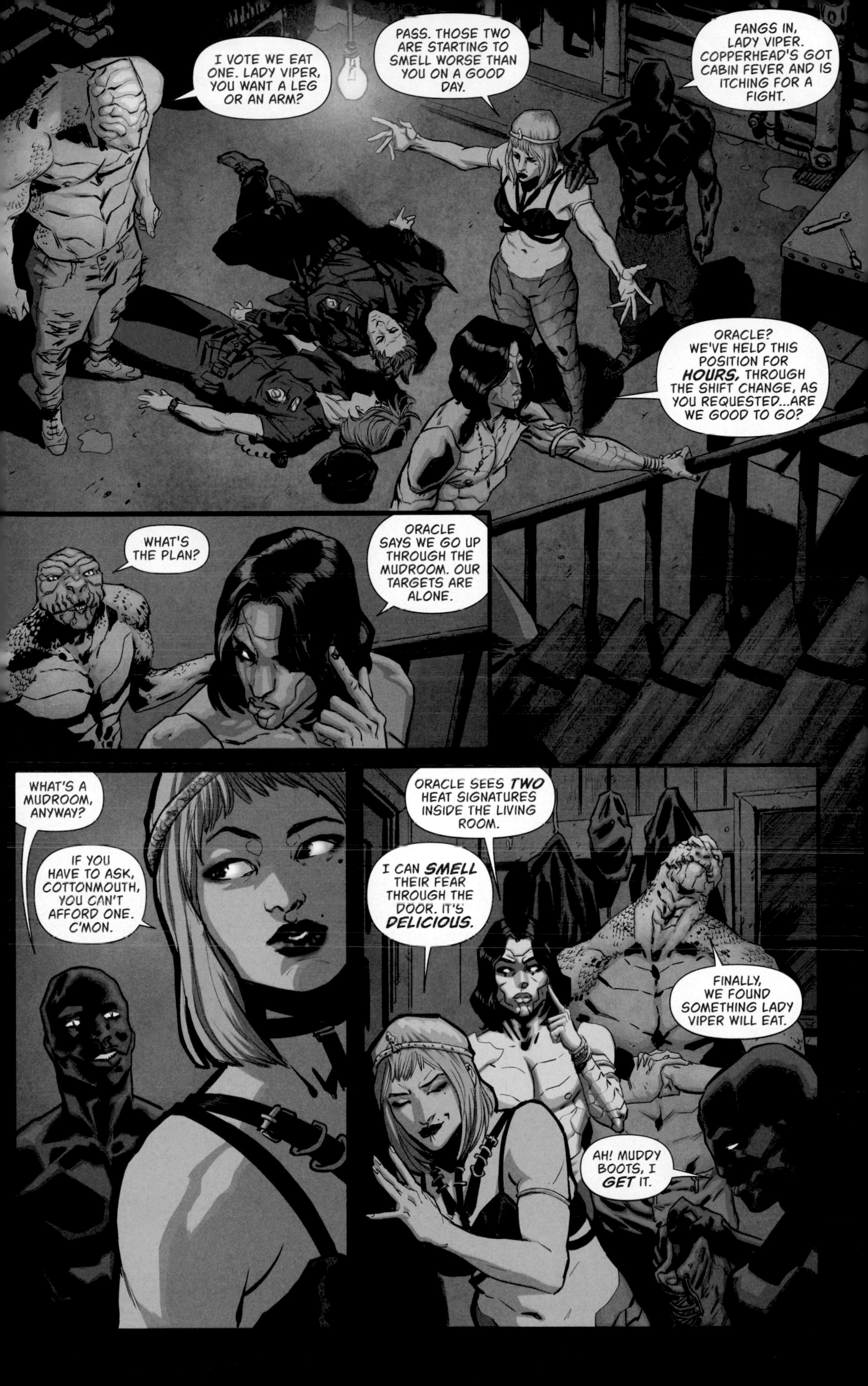
I VOTE WE EAT ONE. LADY VIPER, YOU WANT A LEG OR AN ARM?
PASS. THOSE TWO ARE STARTING TO SMELL WORSE THAN YOU ON A GOOD DAY.
FANGS IN, LADY VIPER. COPPERHEAD'S GOT CABIN FEVER AND IS ITCHING FOR A FIGHT.
ORACLE? WE'VE HELD THIS POSITION FOR HOURS, THROUGH THE SHIFT CHANGE, AS YOU REQUESTED...ARE WE GOOD TO GO?
WHAT'S THE PLAN?
ORACLE SAYS WE GO UP THROUGH THE MUDROOM. OUR TARGETS ARE ALONE.
WHAT'S A MUDROOM, ANYWAY?
IF YOU HAVE TO ASK, COTTONMOUTH, YOU CAN'T AFFORD ONE. C'MON.
ORACLE SEES TWO HEAT SIGNATURES INSIDE THE LIVING ROOM.
I CAN SMELL THEIR FEAR THROUGH THE DOOR. IT'S DELICIOUS.
FINALLY, WE FOUND SOMETHING LADY VIPER WILL EAT.
AH! MUDDY BOOTS, I GET IT.

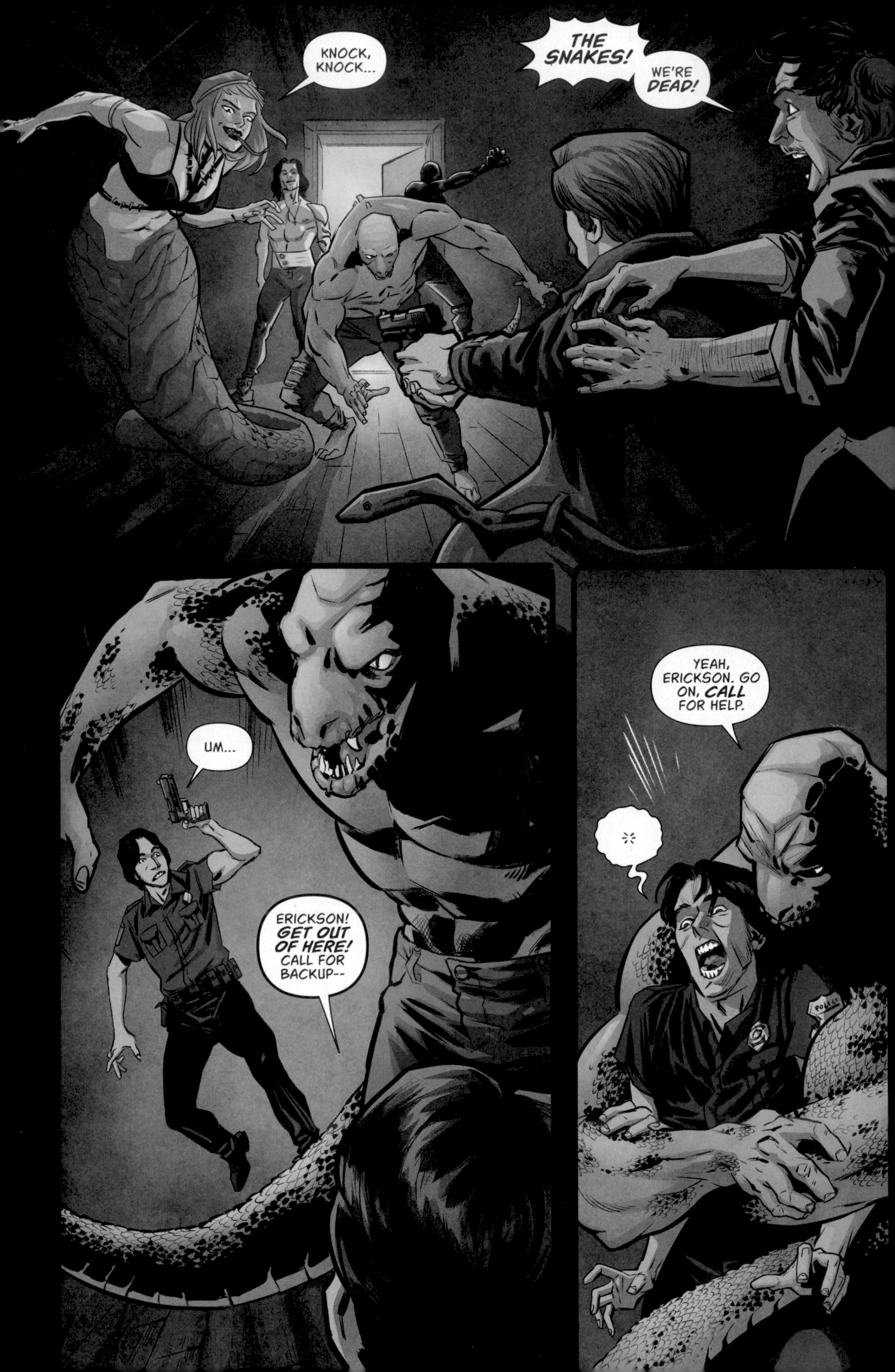
KNOCK, KNOCK...
THE SNAKES!
WE'RE DEAD!
UM...
ERICKSON! GET OUT OF HERE! CALL FOR BACKUP--
YEAH, ERICKSON. GO ON, CALL FOR HELP.

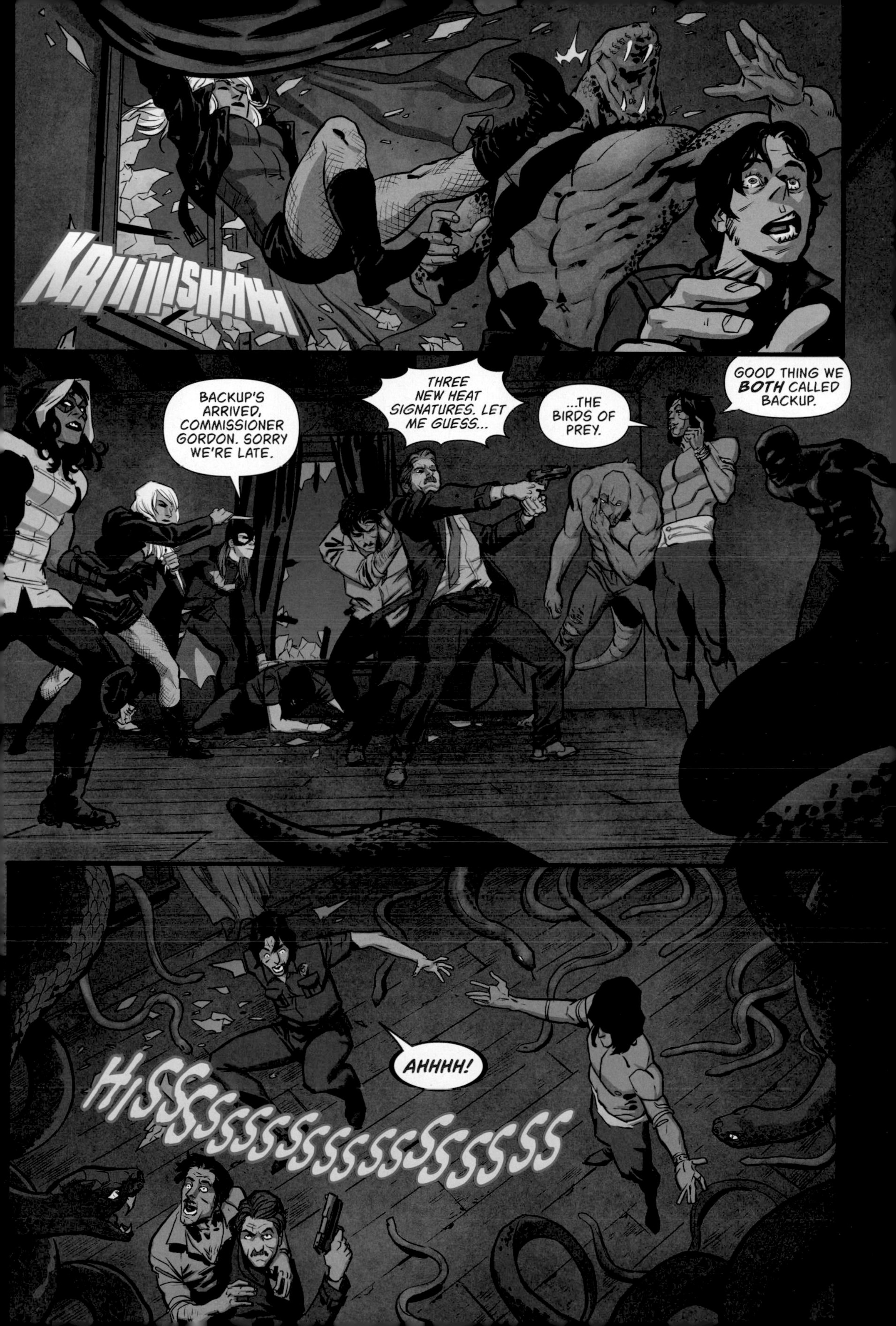

KRIIIIISHHHH
BACKUP'S ARRIVED, COMMISSIONER GORDON. SORRY WE'RE LATE.
THREE NEW HEAT SIGNATURES. LET ME GUESS...
...THE BIRDS OF PREY.
GOOD THING WE BOTH CALLED BACKUP.
AHHHH!
HISSSSSSSSSSSSSSSSSS

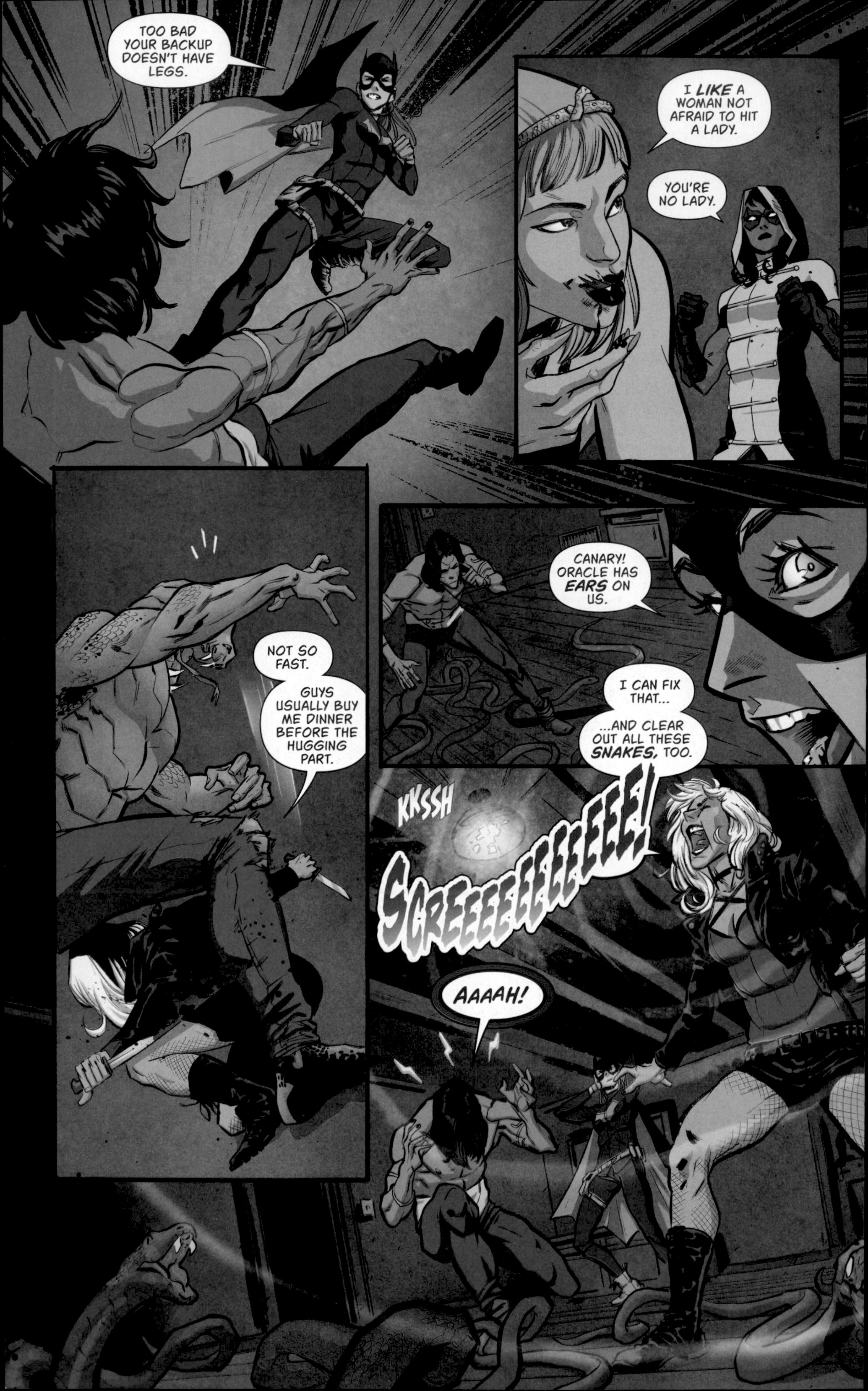
TOO BAD YOUR BACKUP DOESN'T HAVE LEGS.
I **LIKE** A WOMAN NOT AFRAID TO HIT A LADY.
YOU'RE NO LADY.
NOT SO FAST.
GUYS USUALLY BUY ME DINNER BEFORE THE HUGGING PART.
CANARY! ORACLE HAS **EARS** ON US.
I CAN FIX THAT...
...AND CLEAR OUT ALL THESE **SNAKES,** TOO.
KKSSH
SCREEEEEEEEEEEE!
AAAAH!

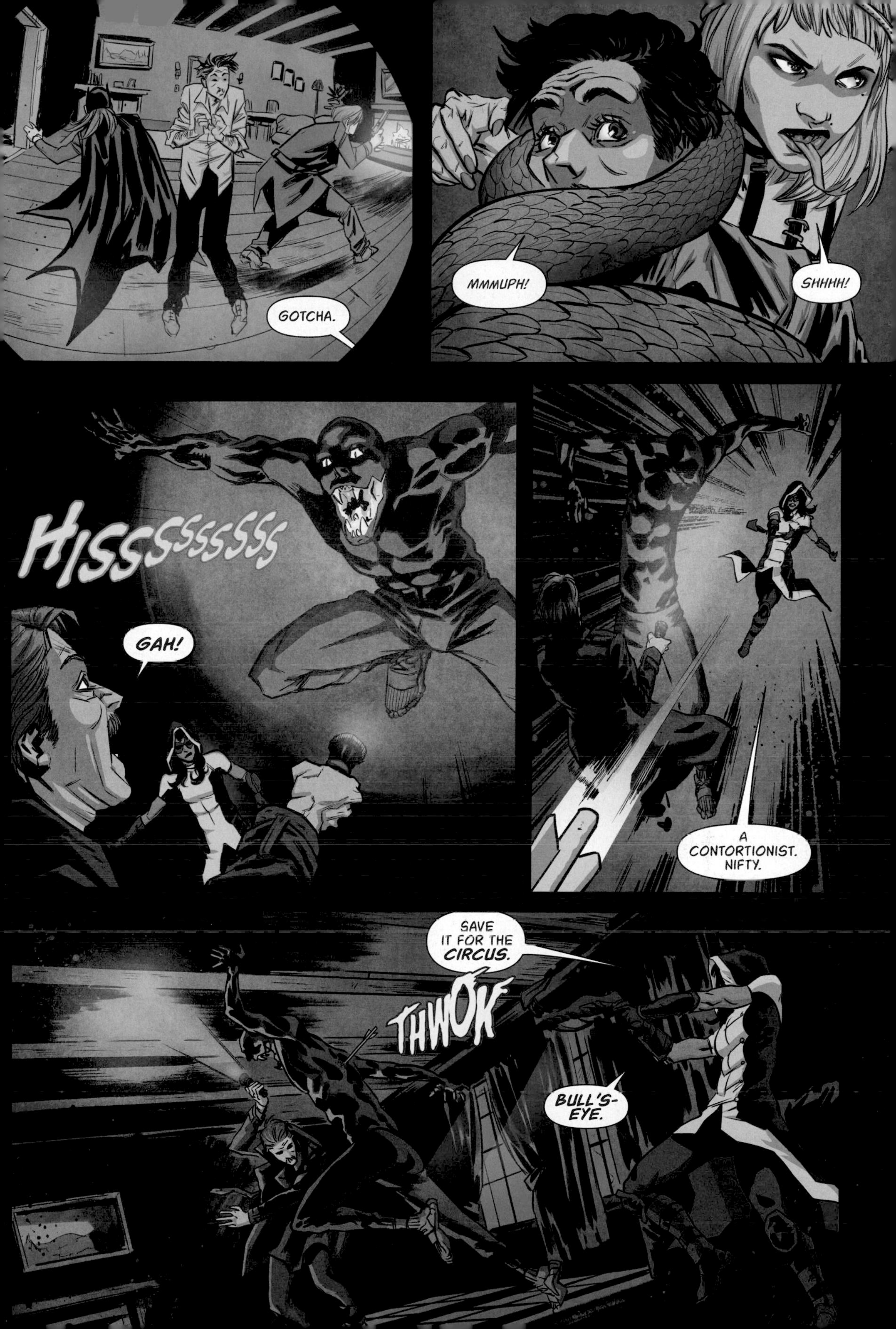
GOTCHA.
MMMUPH!
SHHHH!
HISSSSSSSSS
GAH!
A CONTORTIONIST. NIFTY.
SAVE IT FOR THE CIRCUS.
THWOK
BULL'S-EYE.

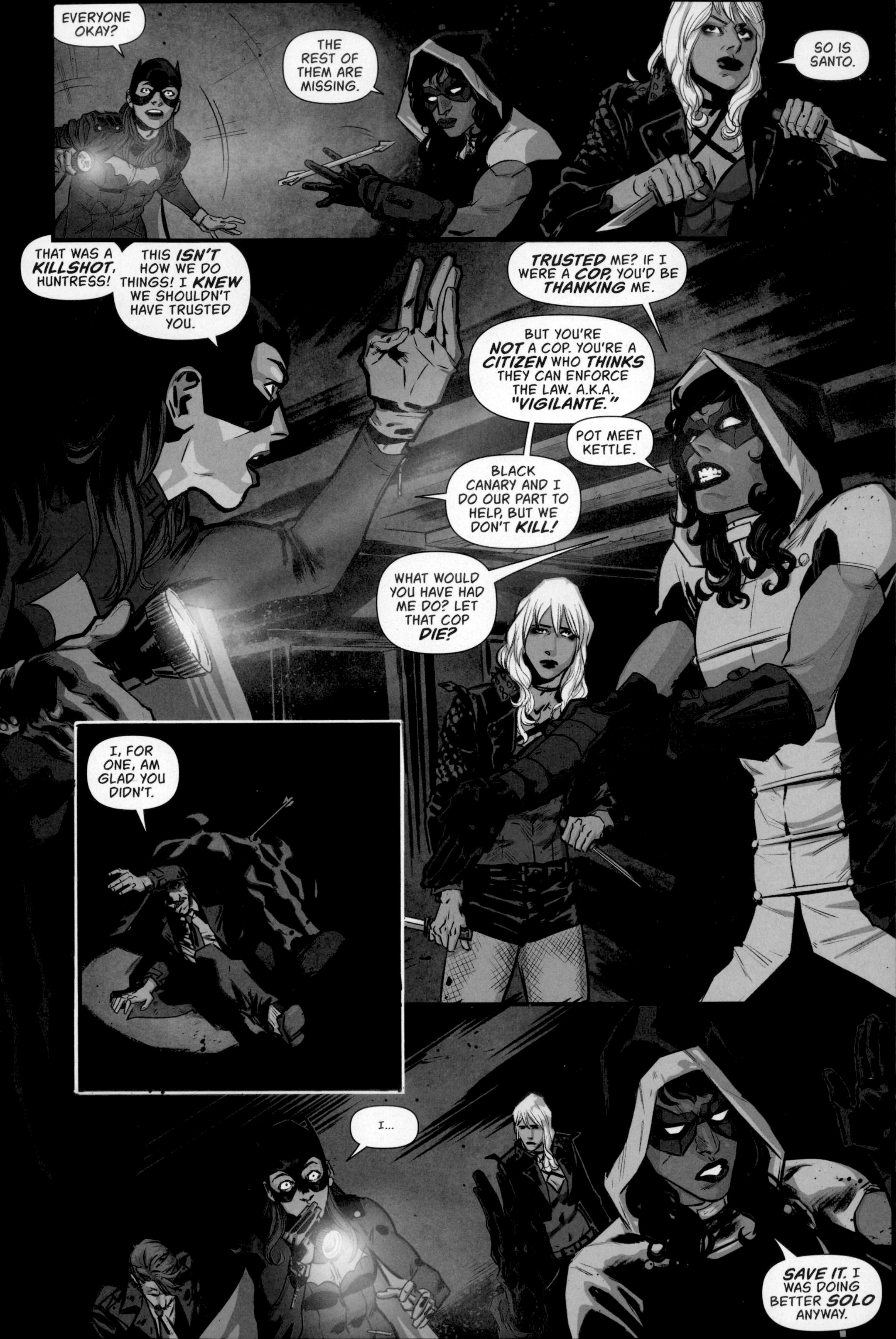
EVERYONE OKAY?
THE REST OF THEM ARE MISSING.
SO IS SANTO.
THAT WAS A KILLSHOT, HUNTRESS!
THIS ISN'T HOW WE DO THINGS! I KNEW WE SHOULDN'T HAVE TRUSTED YOU.
TRUSTED ME? IF I WERE A COP, YOU'D BE THANKING ME.
BUT YOU'RE NOT A COP. YOU'RE A CITIZEN WHO THINKS THEY CAN ENFORCE THE LAW. A.K.A. "VIGILANTE."
POT MEET KETTLE.
BLACK CANARY AND I DO OUR PART TO HELP, BUT WE DON'T KILL!
WHAT WOULD YOU HAVE HAD ME DO? LET THAT COP DIE?
I, FOR ONE, AM GLAD YOU DIDN'T.
I...
SAVE IT. I WAS DOING BETTER SOLO ANYWAY.

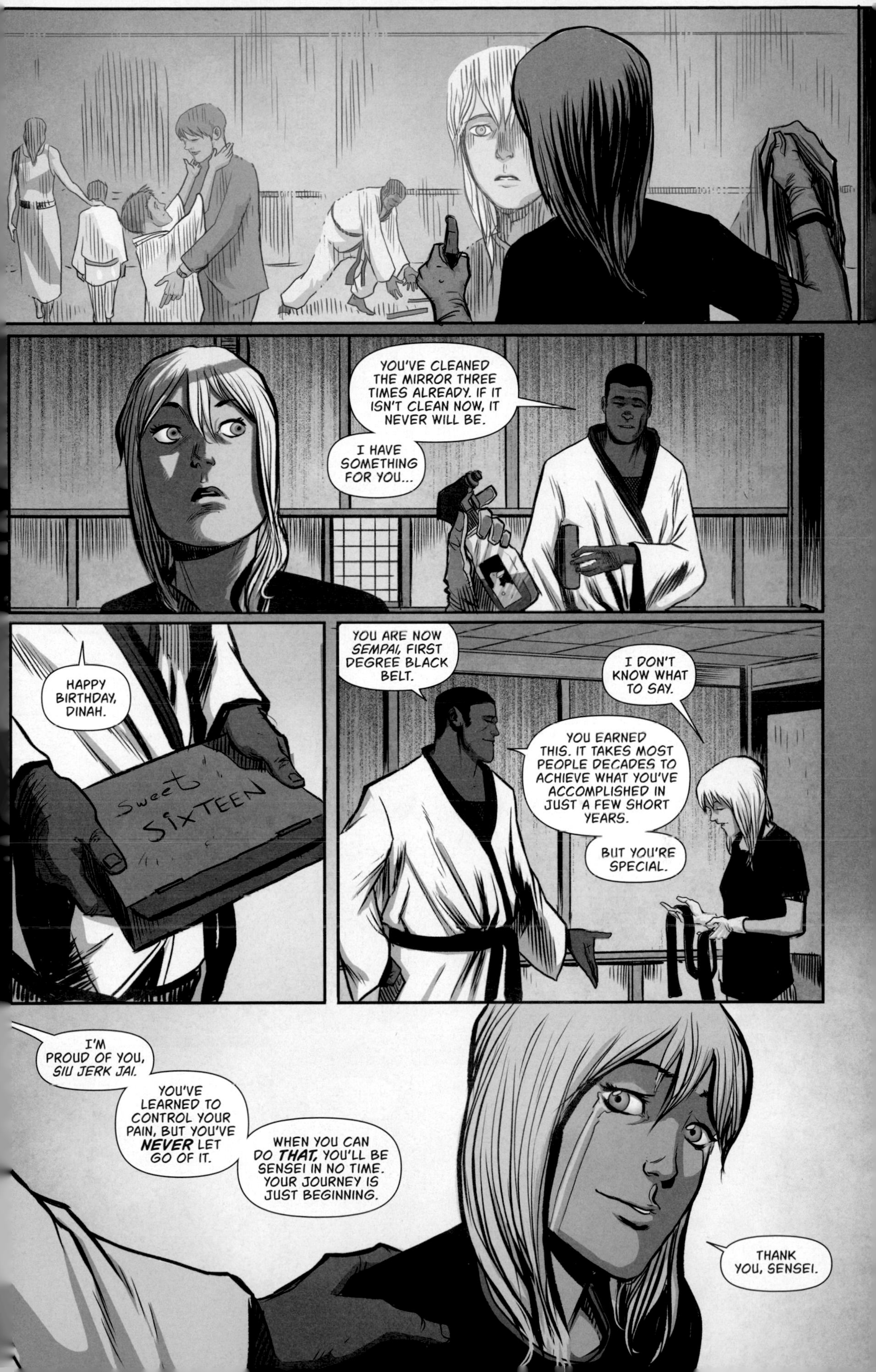
YOU'VE CLEANED THE MIRROR THREE TIMES ALREADY. IF IT ISN'T CLEAN NOW, IT NEVER WILL BE.
I HAVE SOMETHING FOR YOU...
HAPPY BIRTHDAY, DINAH.
Sweet SIXTEEN
YOU ARE NOW *SEMPAI*, FIRST DEGREE BLACK BELT.
I DON'T KNOW WHAT TO SAY.
YOU EARNED THIS. IT TAKES MOST PEOPLE DECADES TO ACHIEVE WHAT YOU'VE ACCOMPLISHED IN JUST A FEW SHORT YEARS.
BUT YOU'RE SPECIAL.
I'M PROUD OF YOU, *SIU JERK JAI.*
YOU'VE LEARNED TO CONTROL YOUR PAIN, BUT YOU'VE ***NEVER*** LET GO OF IT.
WHEN YOU CAN DO ***THAT,*** YOU'LL BE SENSEI IN NO TIME. YOUR JOURNEY IS JUST BEGINNING.
THANK YOU, SENSEI.

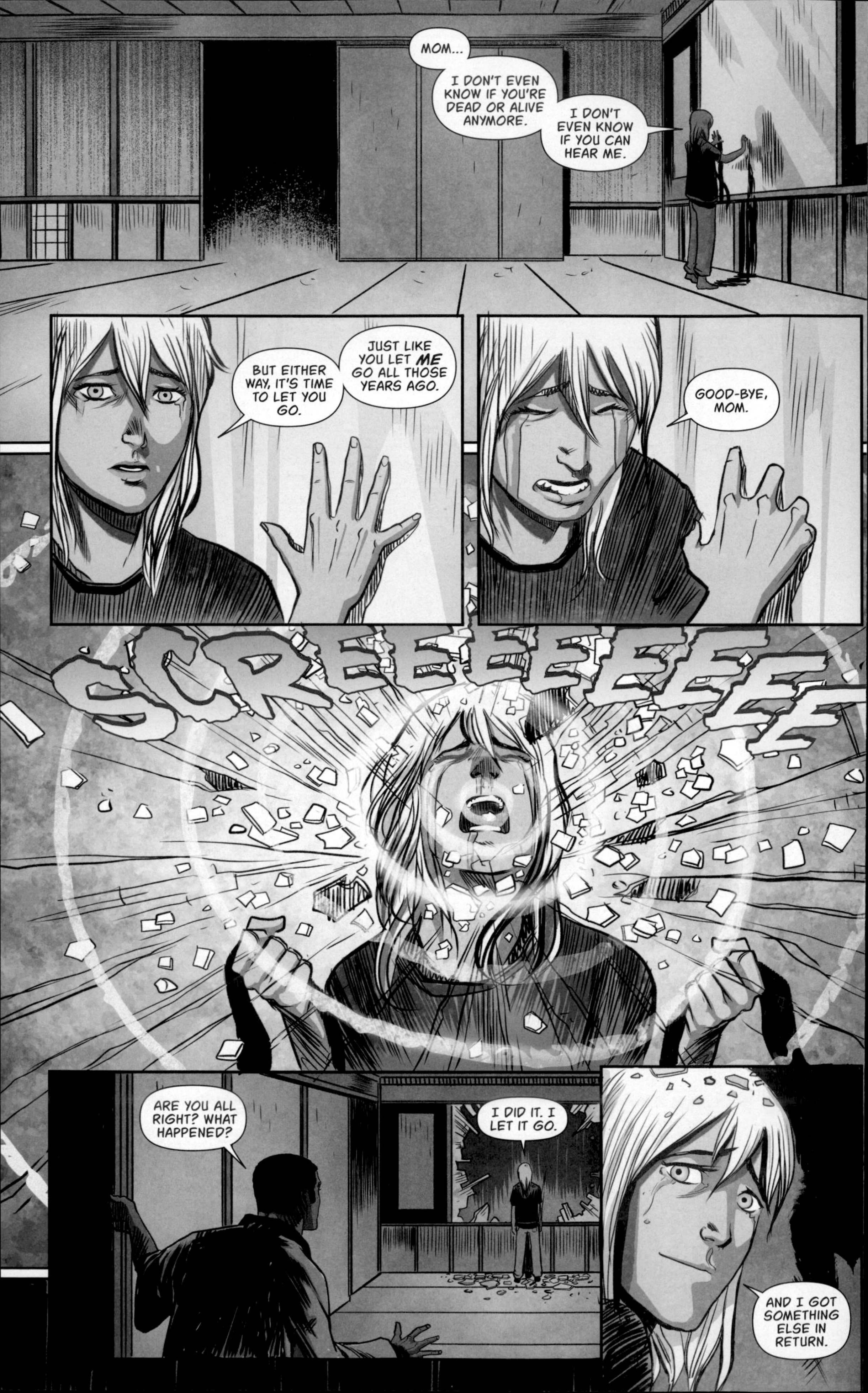
MOM...
I DON'T EVEN KNOW IF YOU'RE DEAD OR ALIVE ANYMORE.
I DON'T EVEN KNOW IF YOU CAN HEAR ME.
BUT EITHER WAY, IT'S TIME TO LET YOU GO.
JUST LIKE YOU LET ME GO ALL THOSE YEARS AGO.
GOOD-BYE, MOM.
SCREEEEEEEE
ARE YOU ALL RIGHT? WHAT HAPPENED?
I DID IT. I LET IT GO.
AND I GOT SOMETHING ELSE IN RETURN.

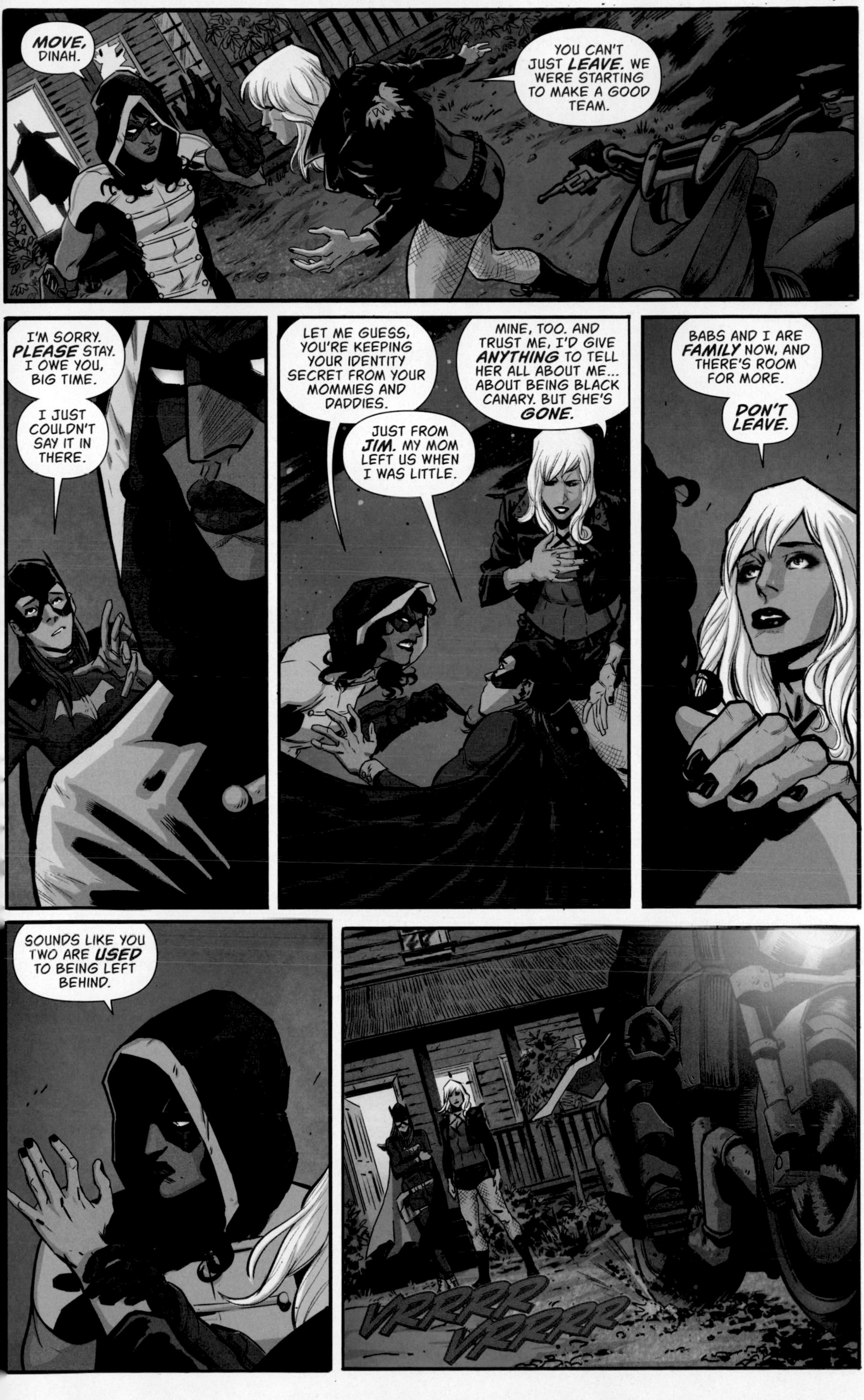
MOVE, DINAH.
YOU CAN'T JUST LEAVE. WE WERE STARTING TO MAKE A GOOD TEAM.
I'M SORRY. PLEASE STAY. I OWE YOU, BIG TIME.
I JUST COULDN'T SAY IT IN THERE.
LET ME GUESS, YOU'RE KEEPING YOUR IDENTITY SECRET FROM YOUR MOMMIES AND DADDIES.
JUST FROM JIM. MY MOM LEFT US WHEN I WAS LITTLE.
MINE, TOO. AND TRUST ME, I'D GIVE ANYTHING TO TELL HER ALL ABOUT ME... ABOUT BEING BLACK CANARY. BUT SHE'S GONE.
BABS AND I ARE FAMILY NOW, AND THERE'S ROOM FOR MORE.
DON'T LEAVE.
SOUNDS LIKE YOU TWO ARE USED TO BEING LEFT BEHIND.
VRRRRR VRRRRR

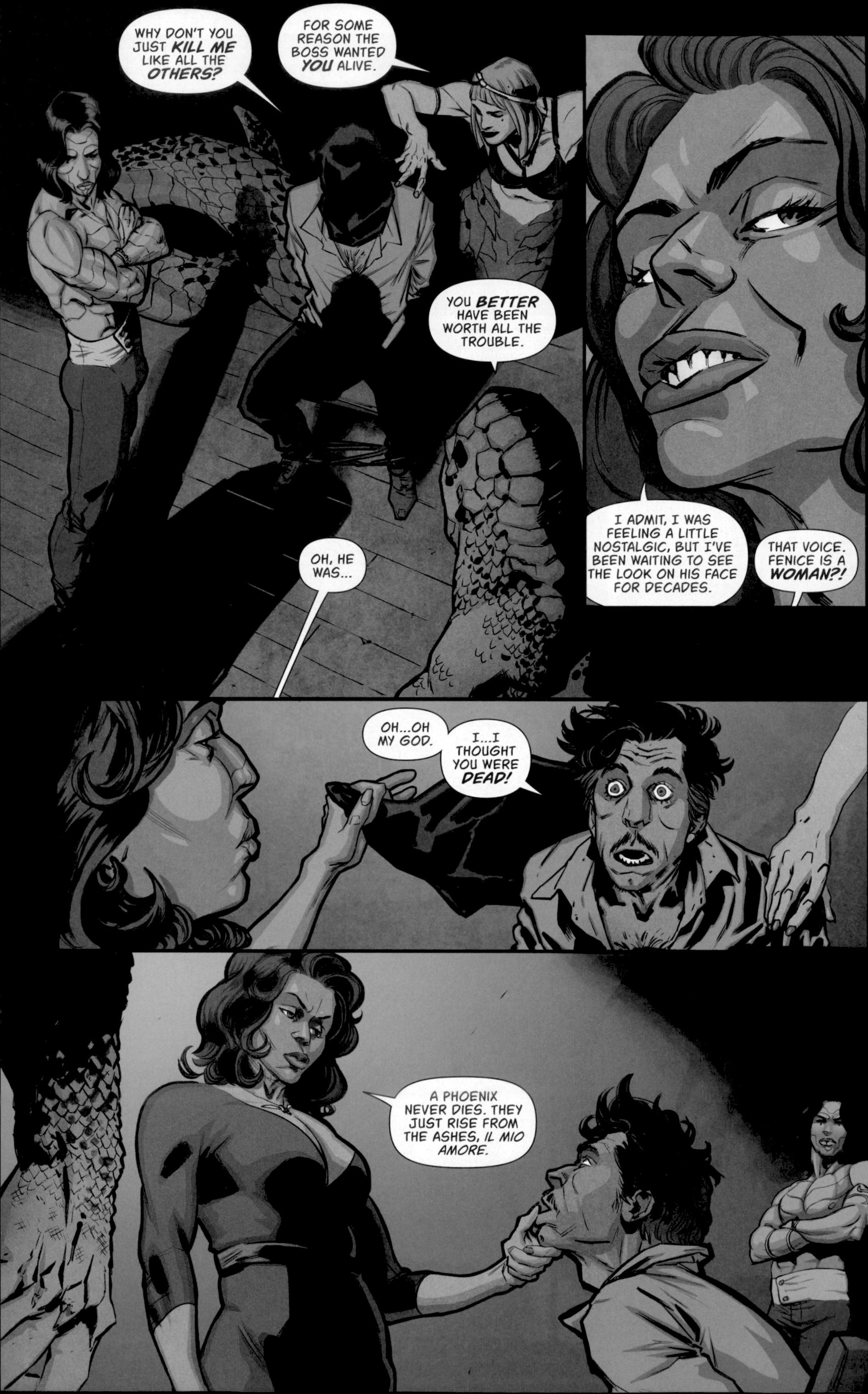
WHY DON'T YOU JUST KILL ME LIKE ALL THE OTHERS?
FOR SOME REASON THE BOSS WANTED YOU ALIVE.
YOU BETTER HAVE BEEN WORTH ALL THE TROUBLE.
OH, HE WAS...
I ADMIT, I WAS FEELING A LITTLE NOSTALGIC, BUT I'VE BEEN WAITING TO SEE THE LOOK ON HIS FACE FOR DECADES.
THAT VOICE. FENICE IS A WOMAN?!
OH...OH MY GOD.
I...I THOUGHT YOU WERE DEAD!
A PHOENIX NEVER DIES. THEY JUST RISE FROM THE ASHES, IL MIO AMORE.

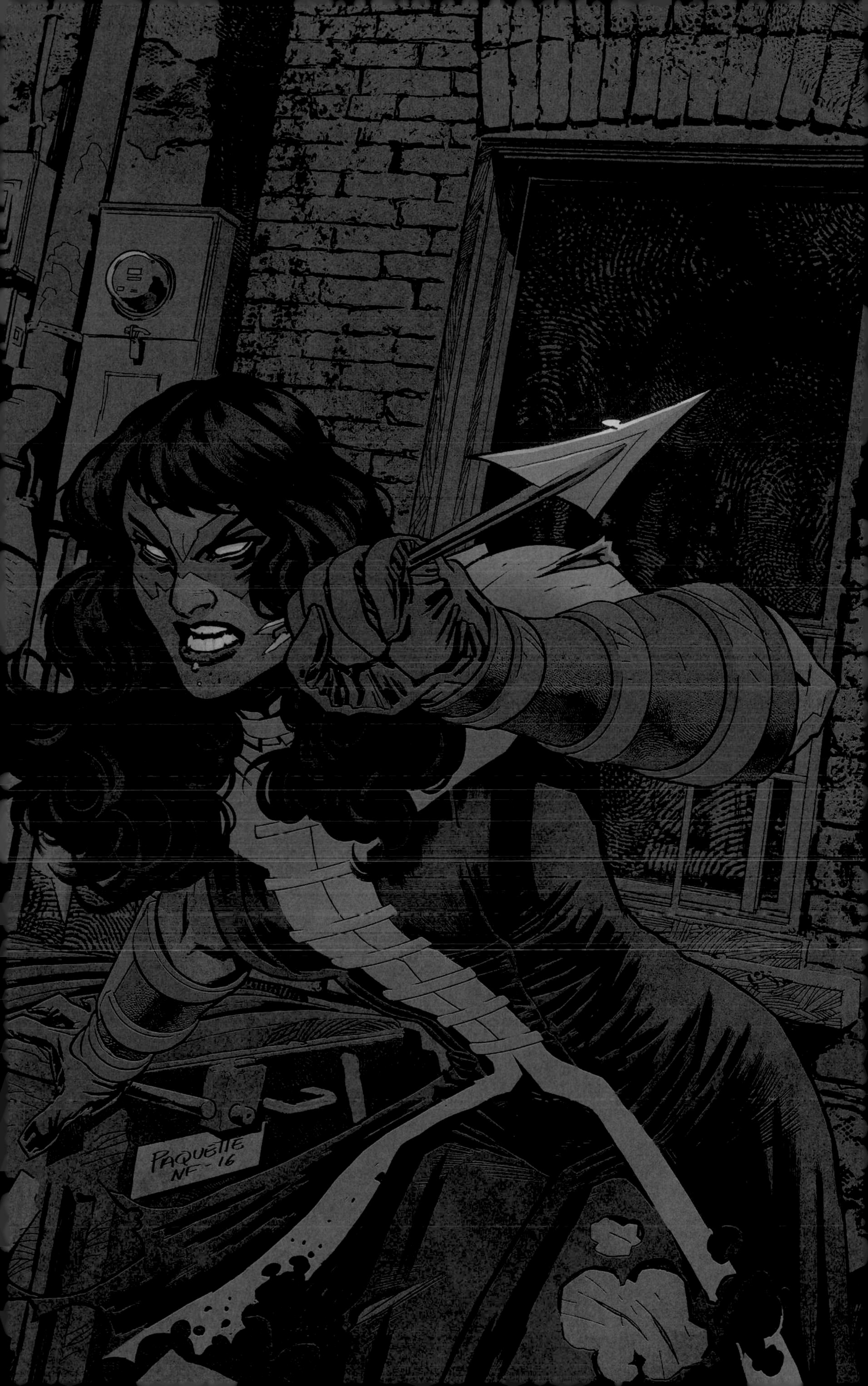
PAQUETTE
NF-16

PART FOUR: WAITING FOR THIS MOMENT

JULIE and SHAWNA BENSON writers * ROGE ANTONIO artist
ALLEN PASSALAQUA colorist * DERON BENNETT letterer

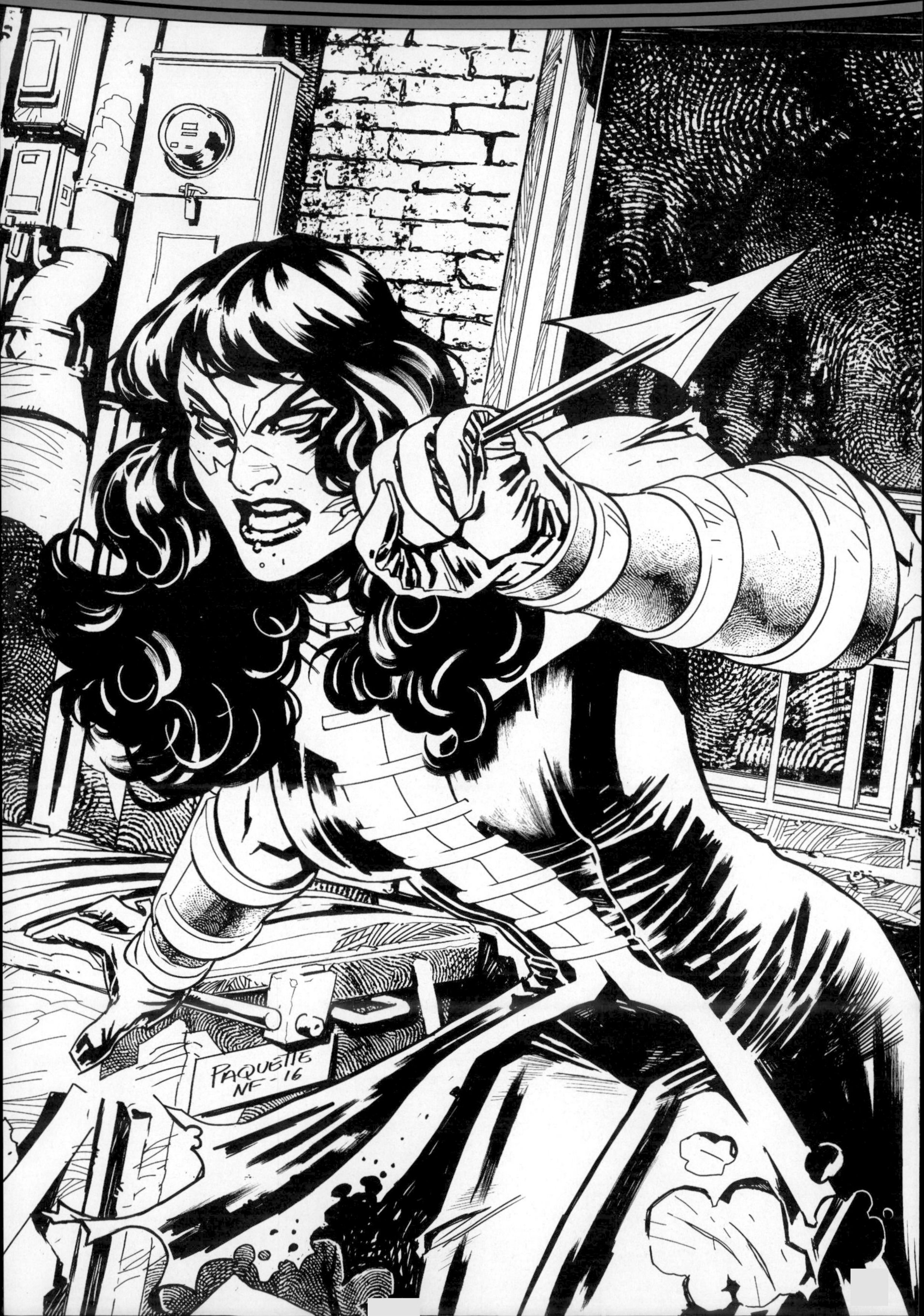
PAQUETTE
NF-16

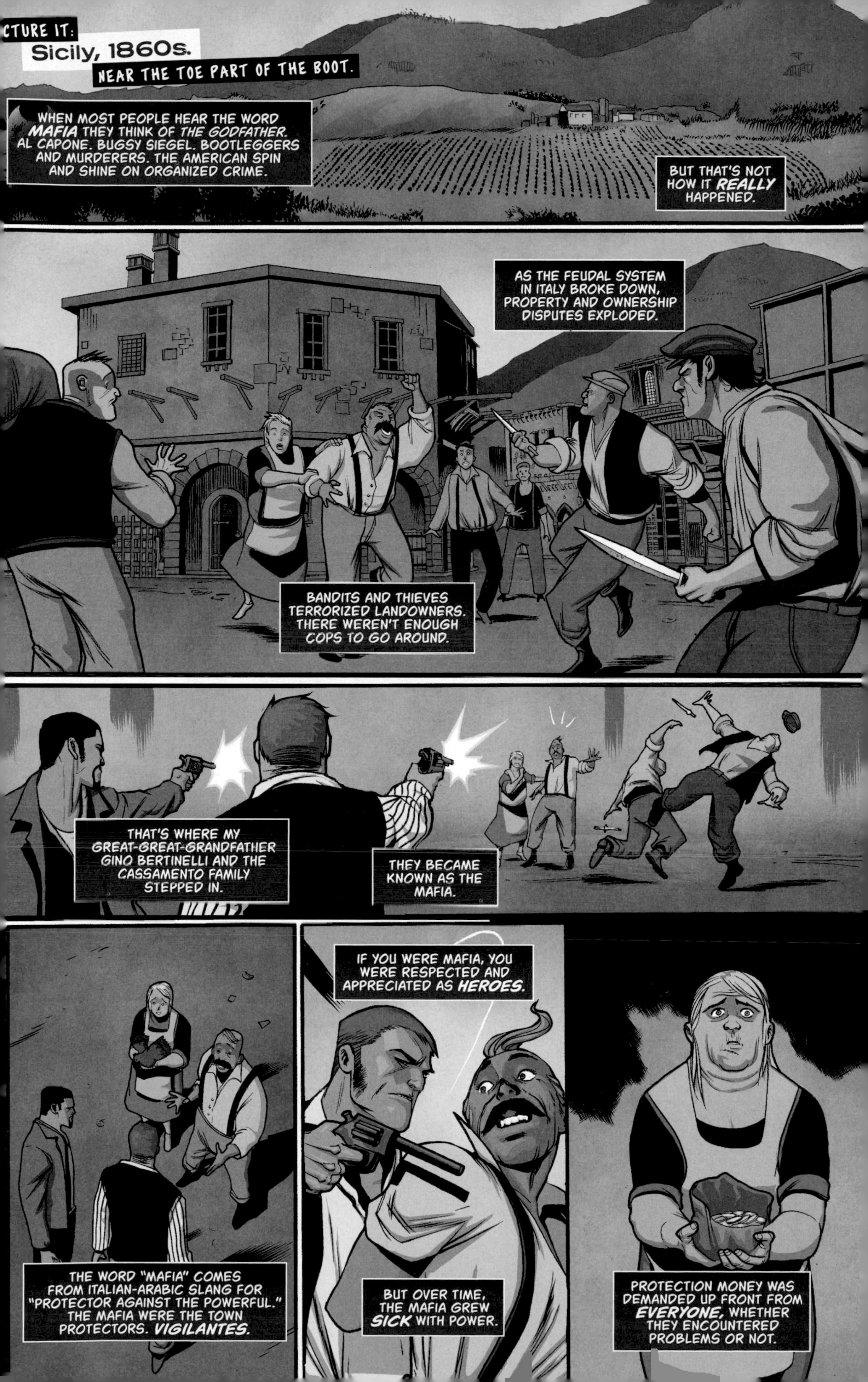
CTURE IT:
Sicily, 1860s.
NEAR THE TOE PART OF THE BOOT.
WHEN MOST PEOPLE HEAR THE WORD MAFIA THEY THINK OF THE GODFATHER. AL CAPONE. BUGSY SIEGEL. BOOTLEGGERS AND MURDERERS. THE AMERICAN SPIN AND SHINE ON ORGANIZED CRIME.
BUT THAT'S NOT HOW IT REALLY HAPPENED.
AS THE FEUDAL SYSTEM IN ITALY BROKE DOWN, PROPERTY AND OWNERSHIP DISPUTES EXPLODED.
BANDITS AND THIEVES TERRORIZED LANDOWNERS. THERE WEREN'T ENOUGH COPS TO GO AROUND.
THAT'S WHERE MY GREAT-GREAT-GRANDFATHER GINO BERTINELLI AND THE CASSAMENTO FAMILY STEPPED IN.
THEY BECAME KNOWN AS THE MAFIA.
THE WORD "MAFIA" COMES FROM ITALIAN-ARABIC SLANG FOR "PROTECTOR AGAINST THE POWERFUL." THE MAFIA WERE THE TOWN PROTECTORS. VIGILANTES.
IF YOU WERE MAFIA, YOU WERE RESPECTED AND APPRECIATED AS HEROES.
BUT OVER TIME, THE MAFIA GREW SICK WITH POWER.
PROTECTION MONEY WAS DEMANDED UP FRONT FROM EVERYONE, WHETHER THEY ENCOUNTERED PROBLEMS OR NOT.

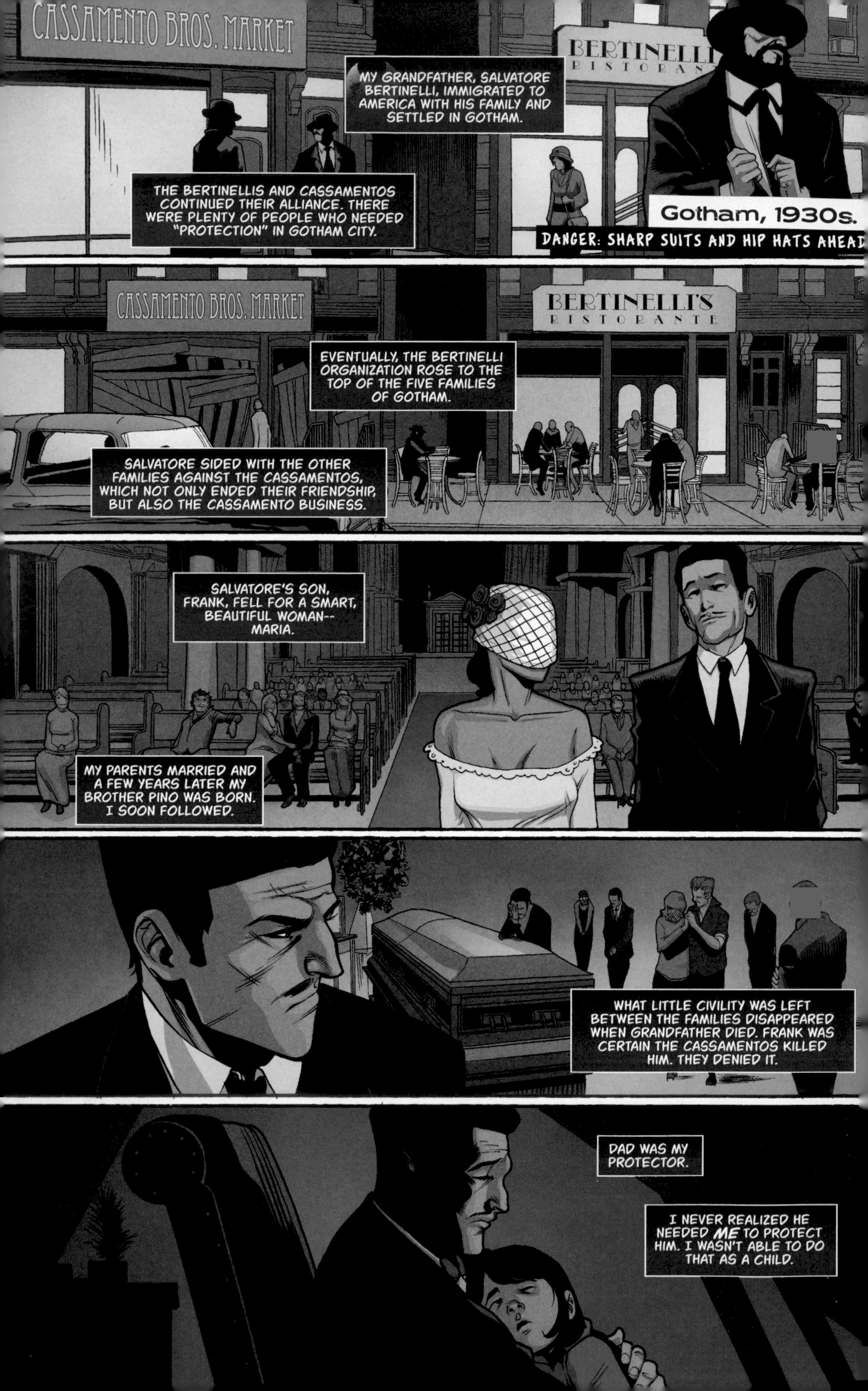
CASSAMENTO BROS. MARKET
BERTINELLI RISTORANTE
MY GRANDFATHER, SALVATORE BERTINELLI, IMMIGRATED TO AMERICA WITH HIS FAMILY AND SETTLED IN GOTHAM.
Gotham, 1930s.
DANGER: SHARP SUITS AND HIP HATS AHEAD
THE BERTINELLIS AND CASSAMENTOS CONTINUED THEIR ALLIANCE. THERE WERE PLENTY OF PEOPLE WHO NEEDED "PROTECTION" IN GOTHAM CITY.
CASSAMENTO BROS. MARKET
BERTINELLI'S RISTORANTE
EVENTUALLY, THE BERTINELLI ORGANIZATION ROSE TO THE TOP OF THE FIVE FAMILIES OF GOTHAM.
SALVATORE SIDED WITH THE OTHER FAMILIES AGAINST THE CASSAMENTOS, WHICH NOT ONLY ENDED THEIR FRIENDSHIP, BUT ALSO THE CASSAMENTO BUSINESS.
SALVATORE'S SON, FRANK, FELL FOR A SMART, BEAUTIFUL WOMAN-- MARIA.
MY PARENTS MARRIED AND A FEW YEARS LATER MY BROTHER PINO WAS BORN. I SOON FOLLOWED.
WHAT LITTLE CIVILITY WAS LEFT BETWEEN THE FAMILIES DISAPPEARED WHEN GRANDFATHER DIED. FRANK WAS CERTAIN THE CASSAMENTOS KILLED HIM. THEY DENIED IT.
DAD WAS MY PROTECTOR.
I NEVER REALIZED HE NEEDED *ME* TO PROTECT HIM. I WASN'T ABLE TO DO THAT AS A CHILD.

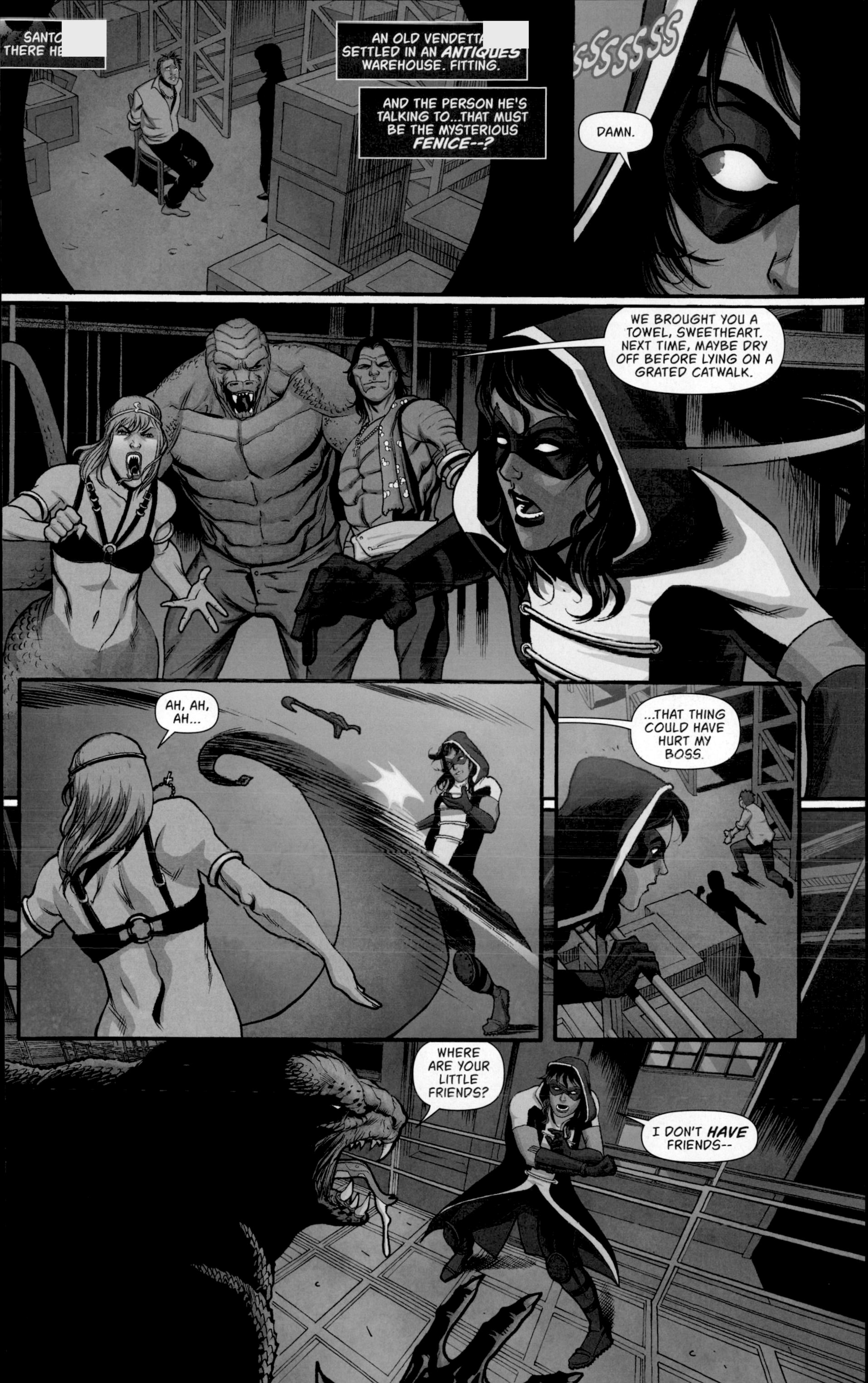

SANTO
THERE HE
AN OLD VENDETTA
SETTLED IN AN ANTIQUES WAREHOUSE. FITTING.
AND THE PERSON HE'S TALKING TO...THAT MUST BE THE MYSTERIOUS FENICE--?
SSSSSSSS
DAMN.
WE BROUGHT YOU A TOWEL, SWEETHEART. NEXT TIME, MAYBE DRY OFF BEFORE LYING ON A GRATED CATWALK.
AH, AH, AH...
...THAT THING COULD HAVE HURT MY BOSS.
WHERE ARE YOUR LITTLE FRIENDS?
I DON'T HAVE FRIENDS--

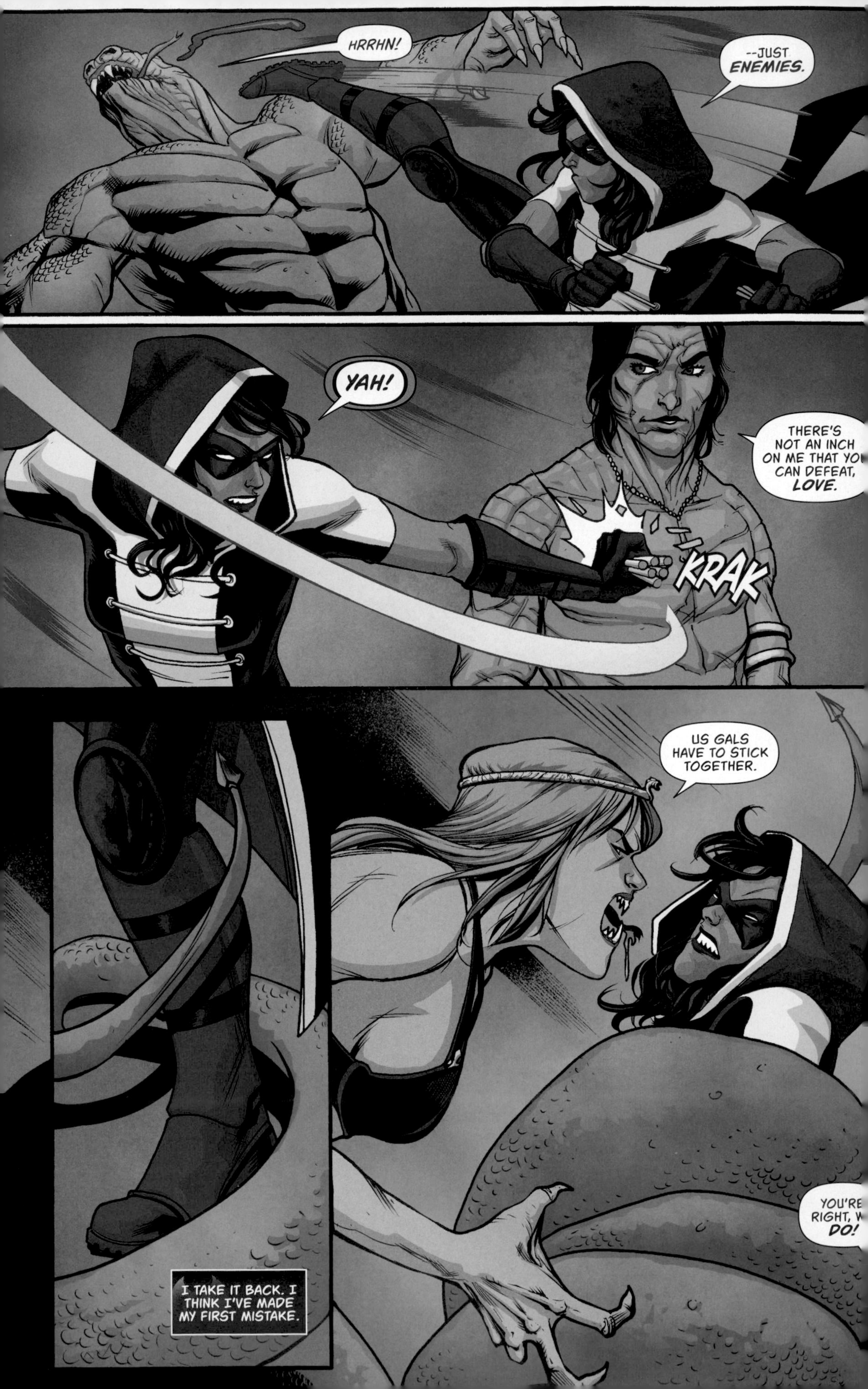
HRRHN!
--JUST ENEMIES.
YAH!
THERE'S NOT AN INCH ON ME THAT YO CAN DEFEAT, LOVE.
KRAK
US GALS HAVE TO STICK TOGETHER.
YOU'RE RIGHT, W DO!
I TAKE IT BACK. I THINK I'VE MADE MY FIRST MISTAKE.

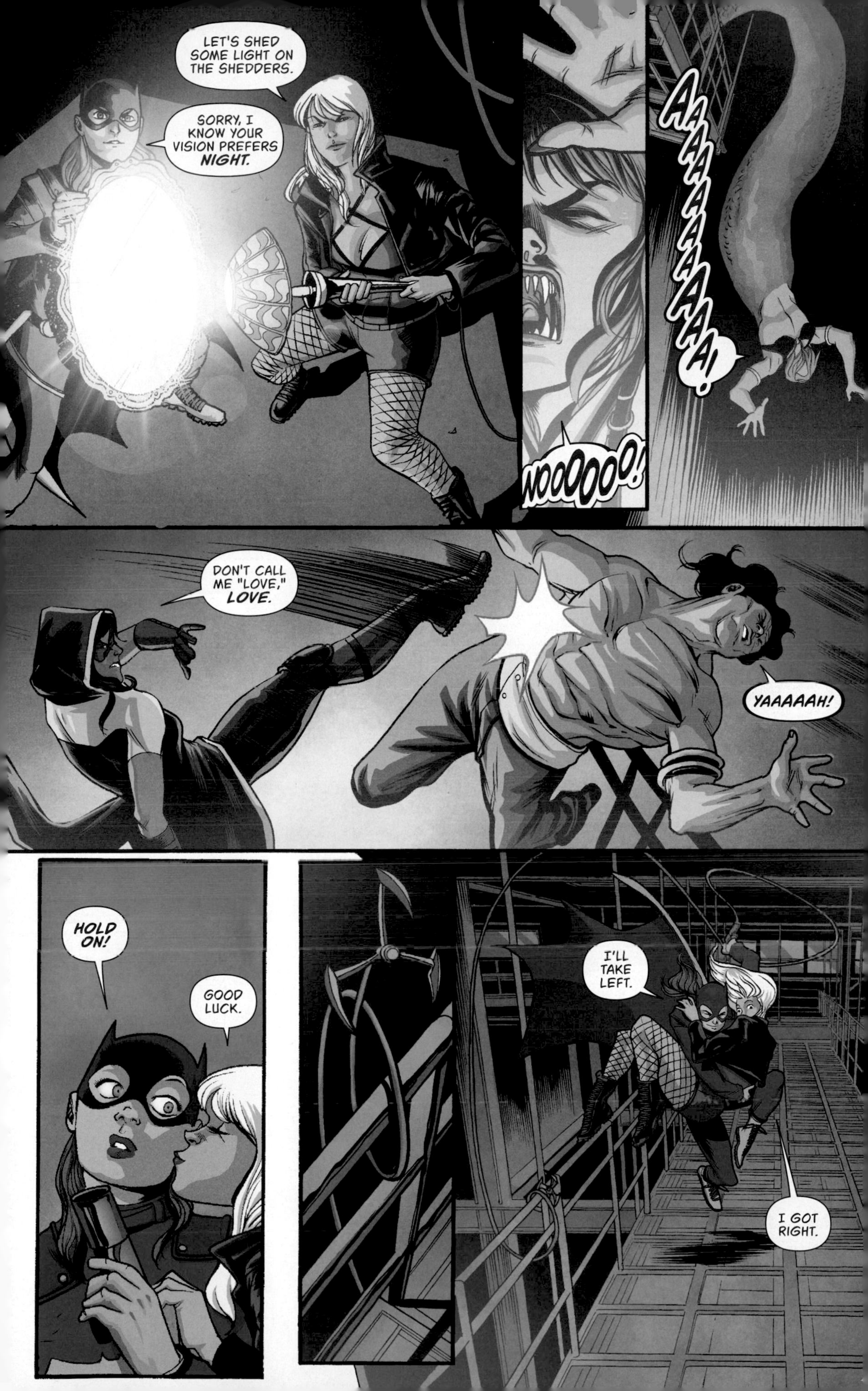
LET'S SHED SOME LIGHT ON THE SHEDDERS.
SORRY, I KNOW YOUR VISION PREFERS NIGHT.
AAAAAAAAAAAA!
NOOOOOO!
DON'T CALL ME "LOVE," LOVE.
YAAAAAH!
HOLD ON!
GOOD LUCK.
I'LL TAKE LEFT.
I GOT RIGHT.

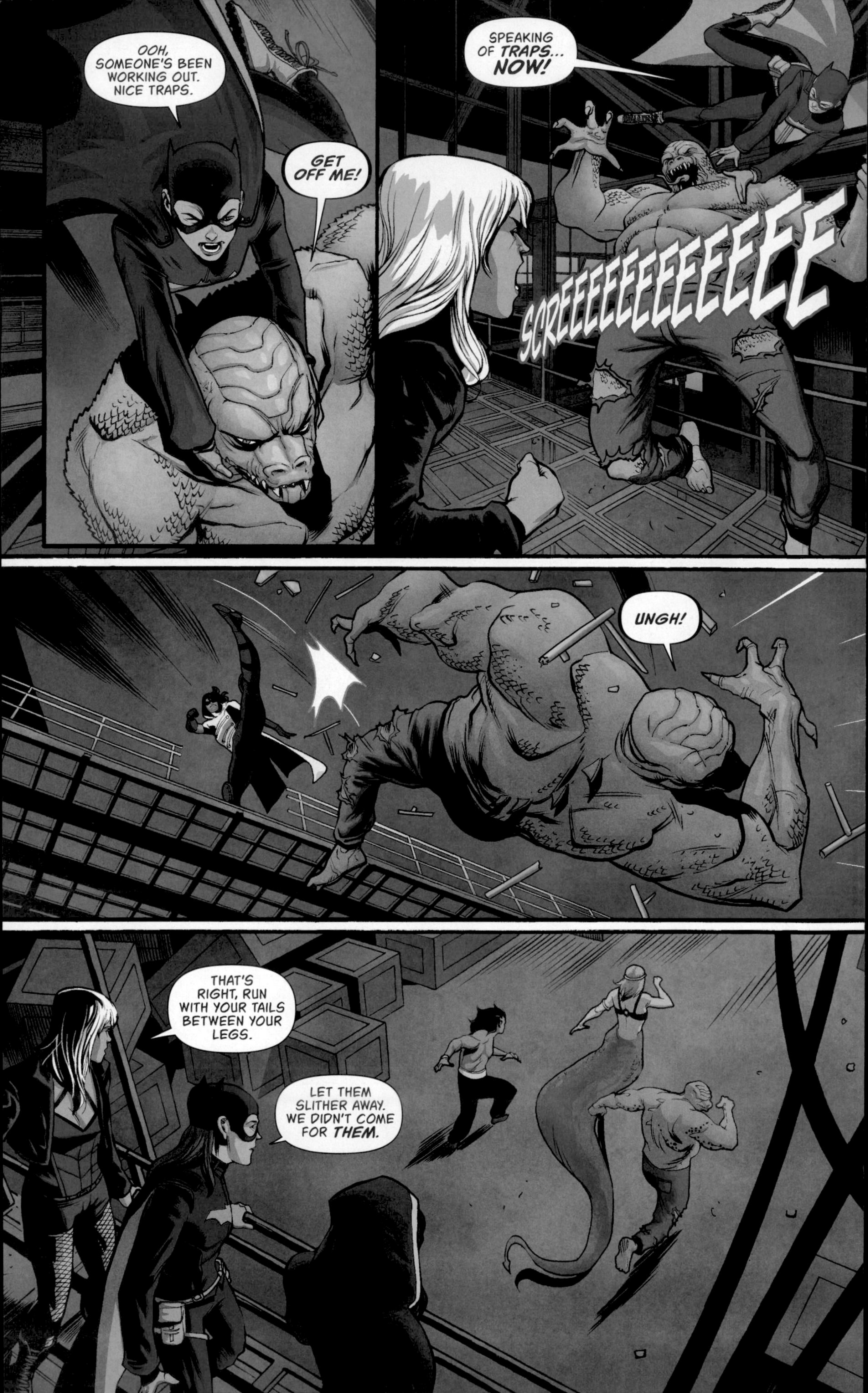

OOH, SOMEONE'S BEEN WORKING OUT. NICE TRAPS.
GET OFF ME!
SPEAKING OF TRAPS... NOW!
SCREEEEEEEEEEEEEE
UNGH!
THAT'S RIGHT, RUN WITH YOUR TAILS BETWEEN YOUR LEGS.
LET THEM SLITHER AWAY. WE DIDN'T COME FOR THEM.

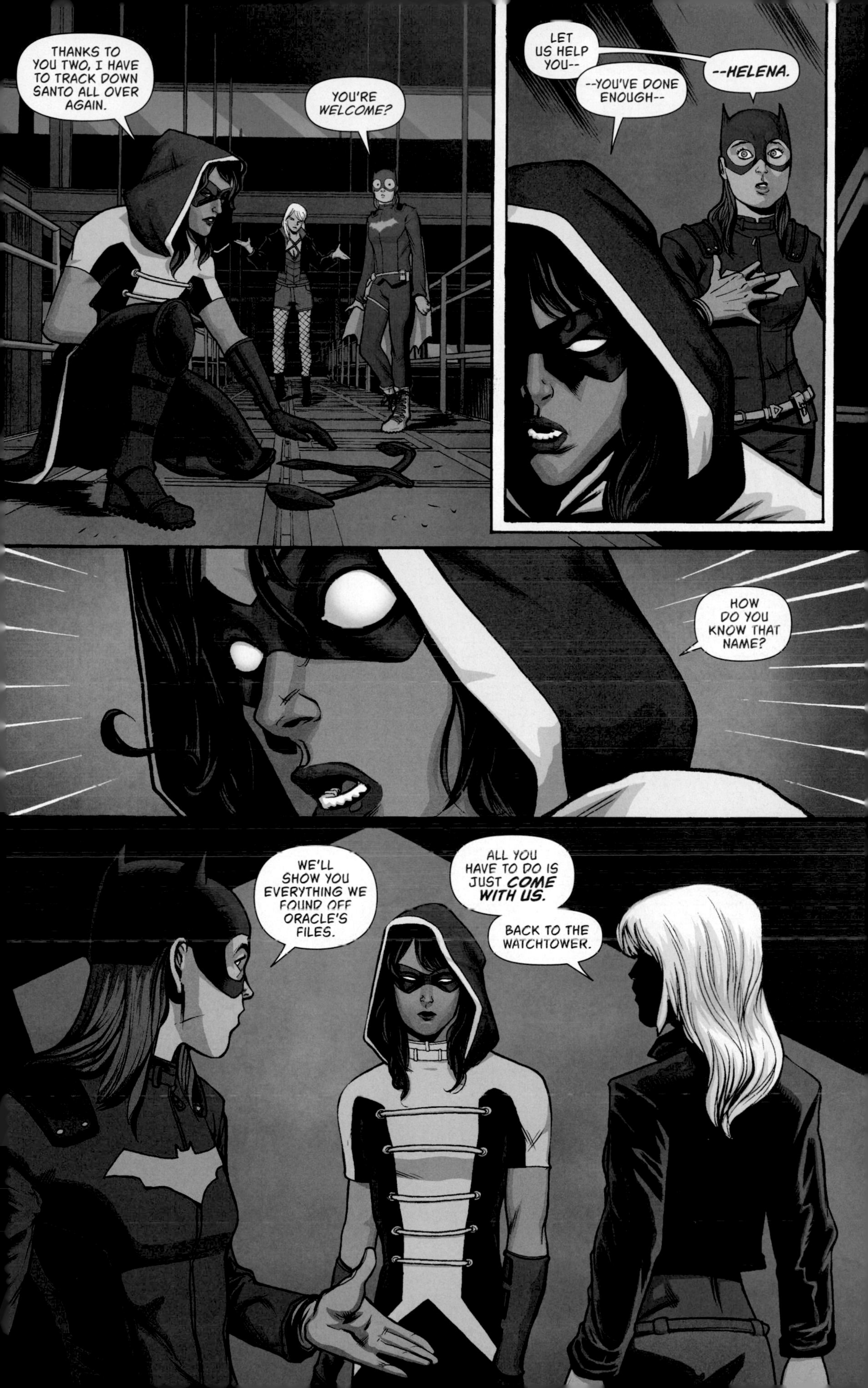

THANKS TO YOU TWO, I HAVE TO TRACK DOWN SANTO ALL OVER AGAIN.
YOU'RE WELCOME?
LET US HELP YOU--
--YOU'VE DONE ENOUGH--
--HELENA.
HOW DO YOU KNOW THAT NAME?
WE'LL SHOW YOU EVERYTHING WE FOUND OFF ORACLE'S FILES.
ALL YOU HAVE TO DO IS JUST COME WITH US.
BACK TO THE WATCHTOWER.

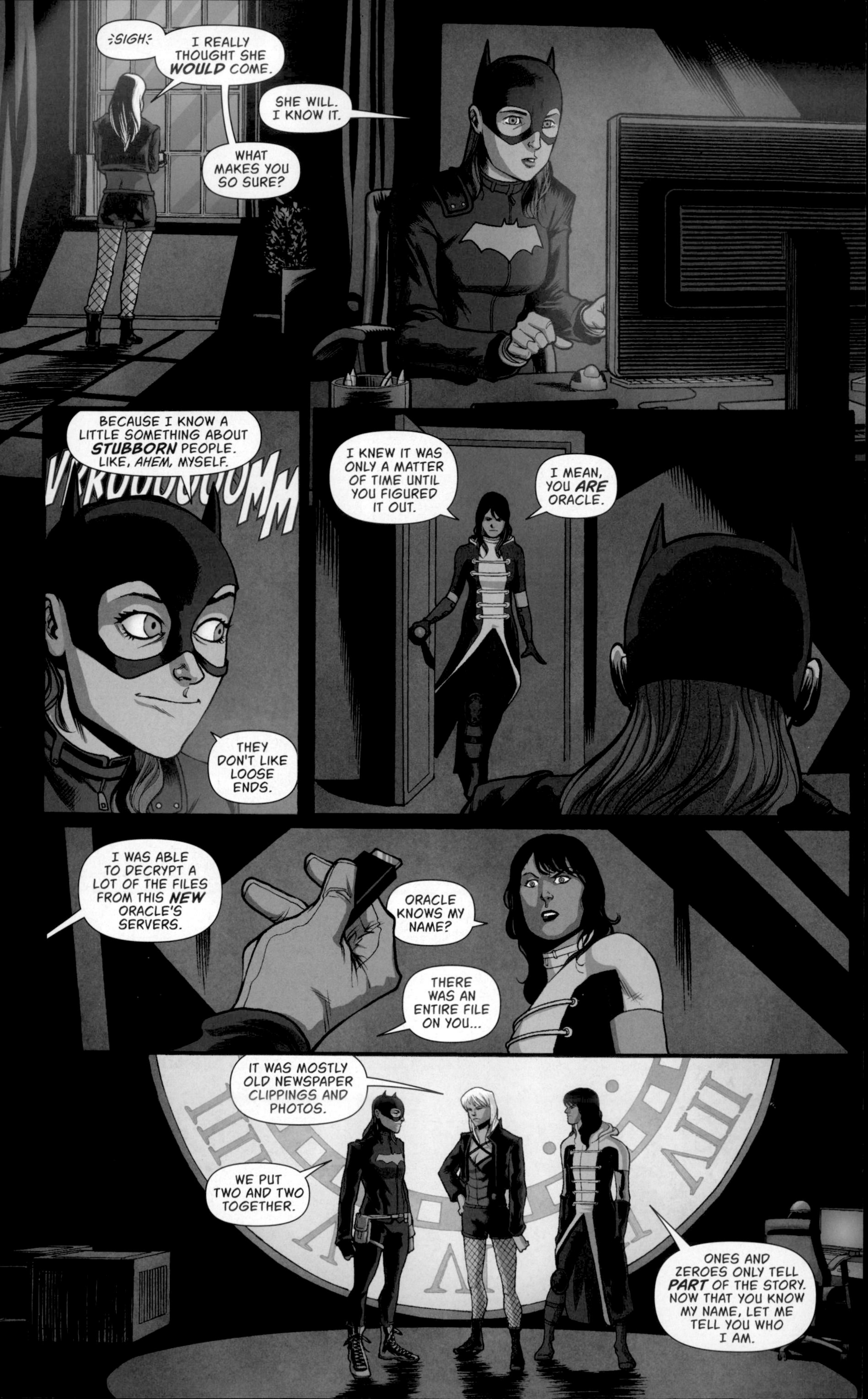

SIGH
I REALLY THOUGHT SHE WOULD COME.
SHE WILL. I KNOW IT.
WHAT MAKES YOU SO SURE?
BECAUSE I KNOW A LITTLE SOMETHING ABOUT STUBBORN PEOPLE. LIKE, AHEM, MYSELF.
VRROOOOOOMM
THEY DON'T LIKE LOOSE ENDS.
I KNEW IT WAS ONLY A MATTER OF TIME UNTIL YOU FIGURED IT OUT.
I MEAN, YOU ARE ORACLE.
I WAS ABLE TO DECRYPT A LOT OF THE FILES FROM THIS NEW ORACLE'S SERVERS.
ORACLE KNOWS MY NAME?
THERE WAS AN ENTIRE FILE ON YOU...
IT WAS MOSTLY OLD NEWSPAPER CLIPPINGS AND PHOTOS.
WE PUT TWO AND TWO TOGETHER.
ONES AND ZEROES ONLY TELL PART OF THE STORY. NOW THAT YOU KNOW MY NAME, LET ME TELL YOU WHO I AM.

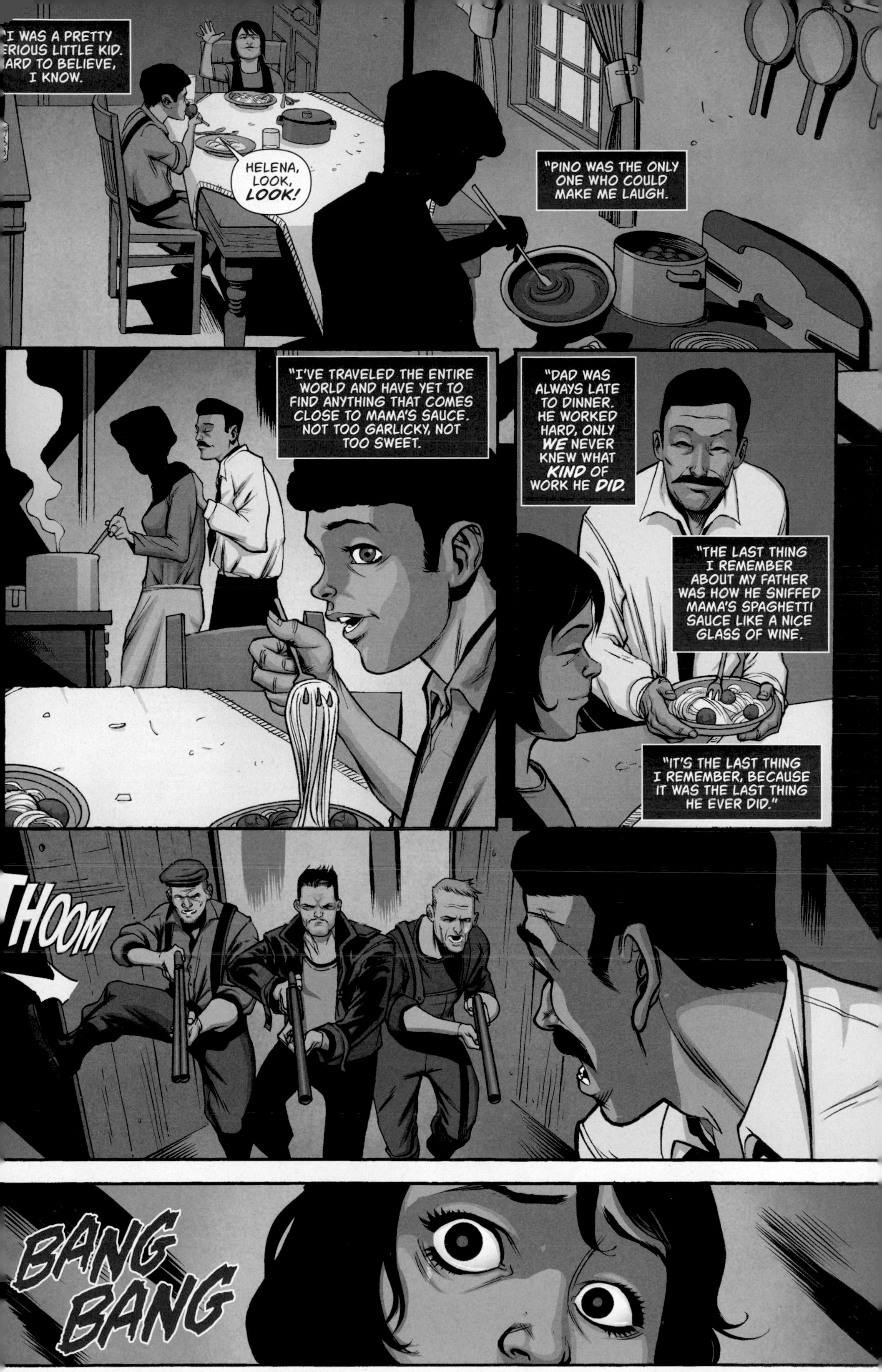
"I WAS A PRETTY
SERIOUS LITTLE KID.
HARD TO BELIEVE,
I KNOW.
HELENA, LOOK, LOOK!
"PINO WAS THE ONLY ONE WHO COULD MAKE ME LAUGH.
"I'VE TRAVELED THE ENTIRE WORLD AND HAVE YET TO FIND ANYTHING THAT COMES CLOSE TO MAMA'S SAUCE. NOT TOO GARLICKY, NOT TOO SWEET.
"DAD WAS ALWAYS LATE TO DINNER. HE WORKED HARD, ONLY WE NEVER KNEW WHAT KIND OF WORK HE DID.
"THE LAST THING I REMEMBER ABOUT MY FATHER WAS HOW HE SNIFFED MAMA'S SPAGHETTI SAUCE LIKE A NICE GLASS OF WINE.
"IT'S THE LAST THING I REMEMBER, BECAUSE IT WAS THE LAST THING HE EVER DID."
THOOM
BANG
BANG

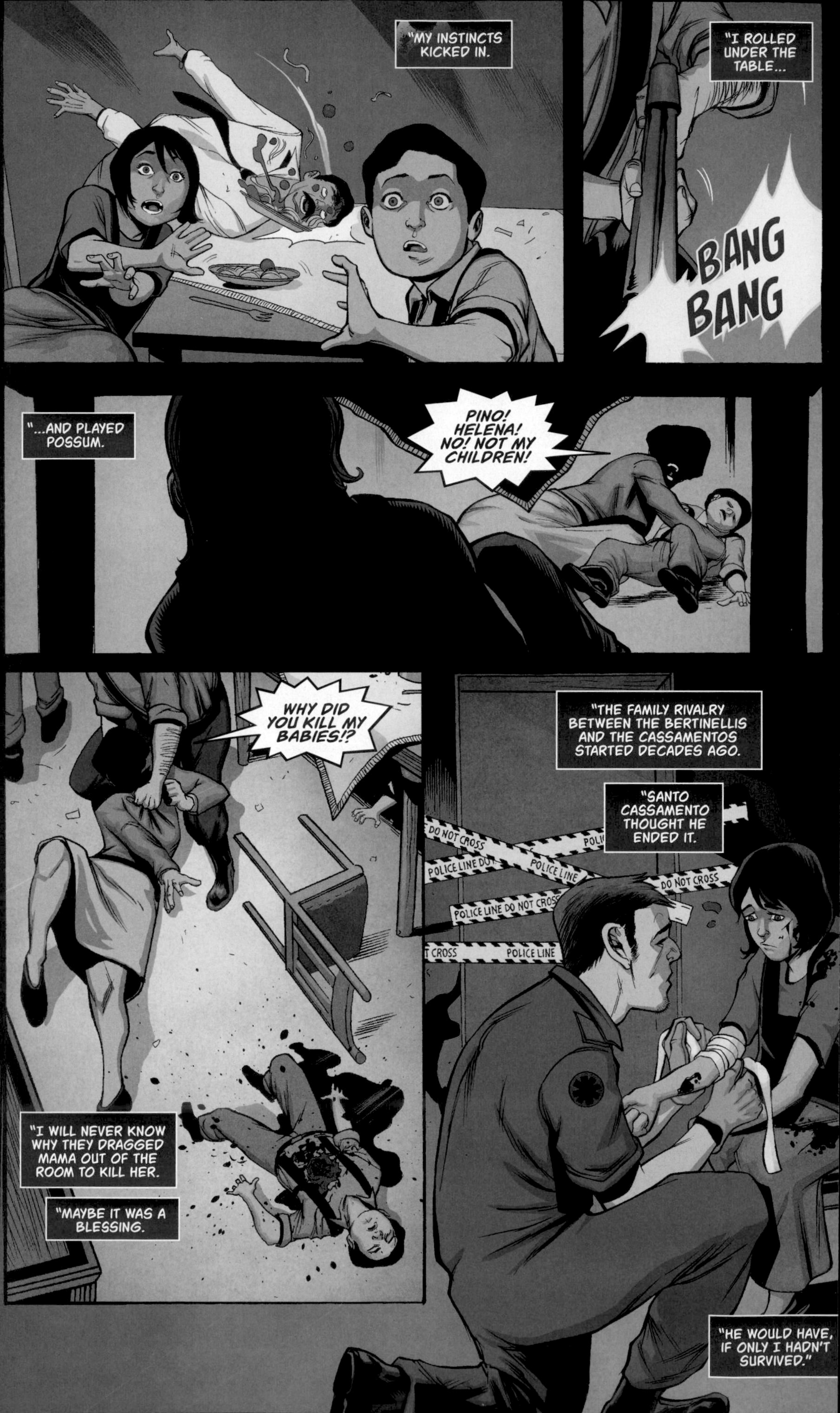
"MY INSTINCTS KICKED IN.
"I ROLLED UNDER THE TABLE...
BANG BANG
"...AND PLAYED POSSUM.
PINO! HELENA! NO! NOT MY CHILDREN!
WHY DID YOU KILL MY BABIES!?
"I WILL NEVER KNOW WHY THEY DRAGGED MAMA OUT OF THE ROOM TO KILL HER.
"MAYBE IT WAS A BLESSING.
"THE FAMILY RIVALRY BETWEEN THE BERTINELLIS AND THE CASSAMENTOS STARTED DECADES AGO.
"SANTO CASSAMENTO THOUGHT HE ENDED IT.
DO NOT CROSS
POLICE LINE
"HE WOULD HAVE, IF ONLY I HADN'T SURVIVED."

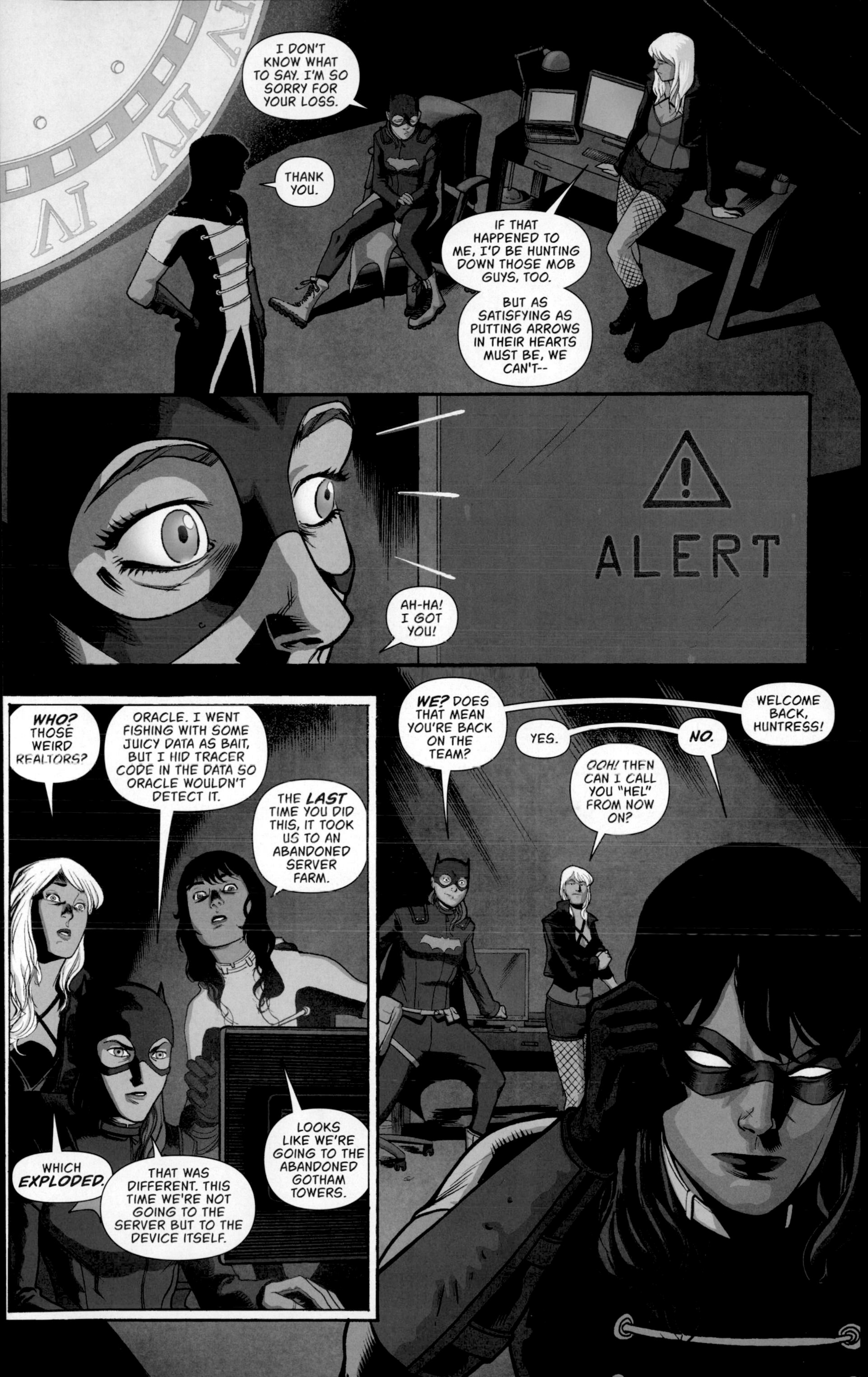
I DON'T KNOW WHAT TO SAY. I'M SO SORRY FOR YOUR LOSS.
THANK YOU.
IF THAT HAPPENED TO ME, I'D BE HUNTING DOWN THOSE MOB GUYS, TOO.
BUT AS SATISFYING AS PUTTING ARROWS IN THEIR HEARTS MUST BE, WE CAN'T--
ALERT
AH-HA! I GOT YOU!
WHO? THOSE WEIRD REALTORS?
ORACLE. I WENT FISHING WITH SOME JUICY DATA AS BAIT, BUT I HID TRACER CODE IN THE DATA SO ORACLE WOULDN'T DETECT IT.
THE LAST TIME YOU DID THIS, IT TOOK US TO AN ABANDONED SERVER FARM.
WHICH EXPLODED.
THAT WAS DIFFERENT. THIS TIME WE'RE NOT GOING TO THE SERVER BUT TO THE DEVICE ITSELF.
LOOKS LIKE WE'RE GOING TO THE ABANDONED GOTHAM TOWERS.
WE? DOES THAT MEAN YOU'RE BACK ON THE TEAM?
YES.
NO.
WELCOME BACK, HUNTRESS!
OOH! THEN CAN I CALL YOU "HEL" FROM NOW ON?

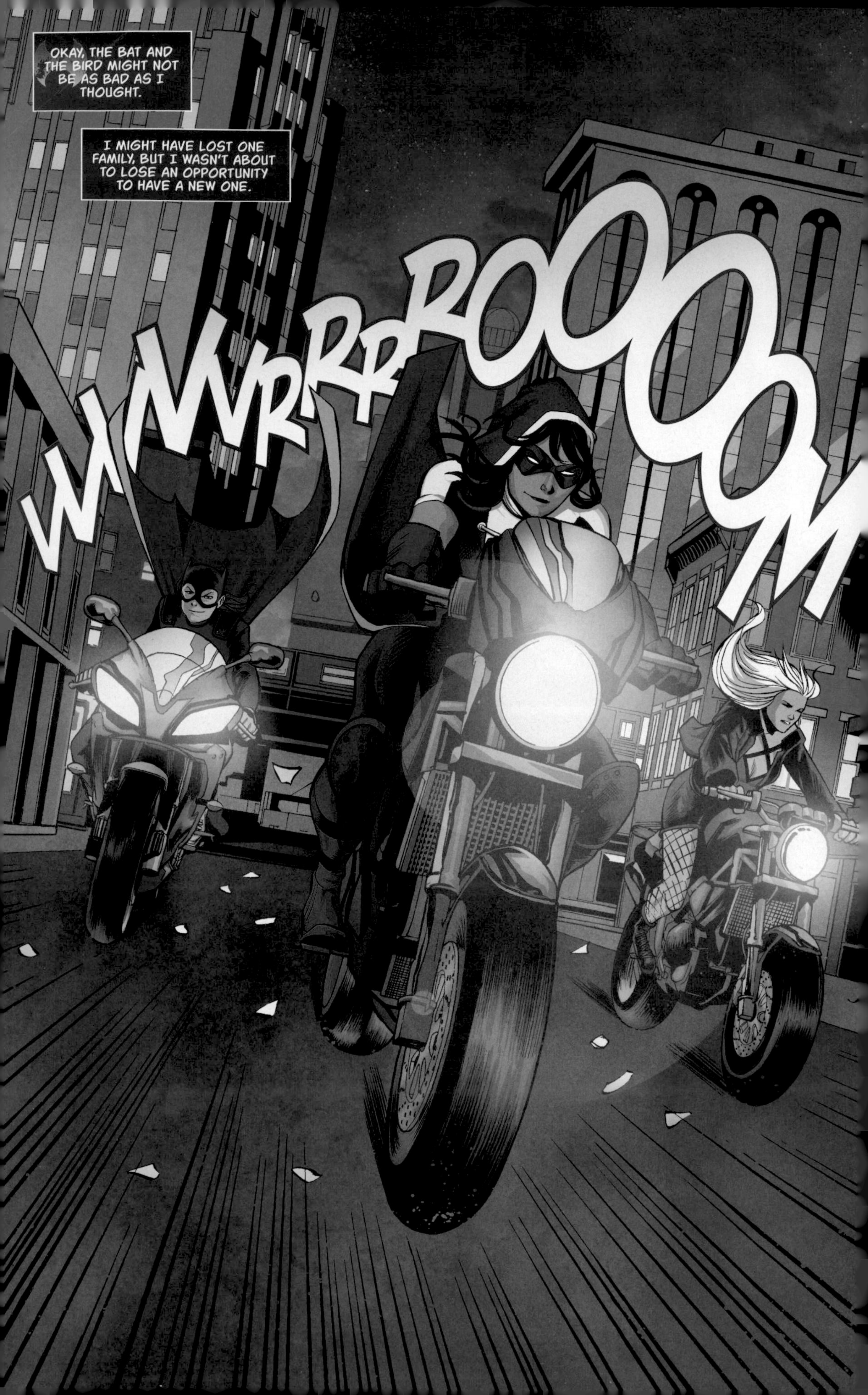
OKAY, THE BAT AND THE BIRD MIGHT NOT BE AS BAD AS I THOUGHT.
I MIGHT HAVE LOST ONE FAMILY, BUT I WASN'T ABOUT TO LOSE AN OPPORTUNITY TO HAVE A NEW ONE.
WWWRRRROOOOOM

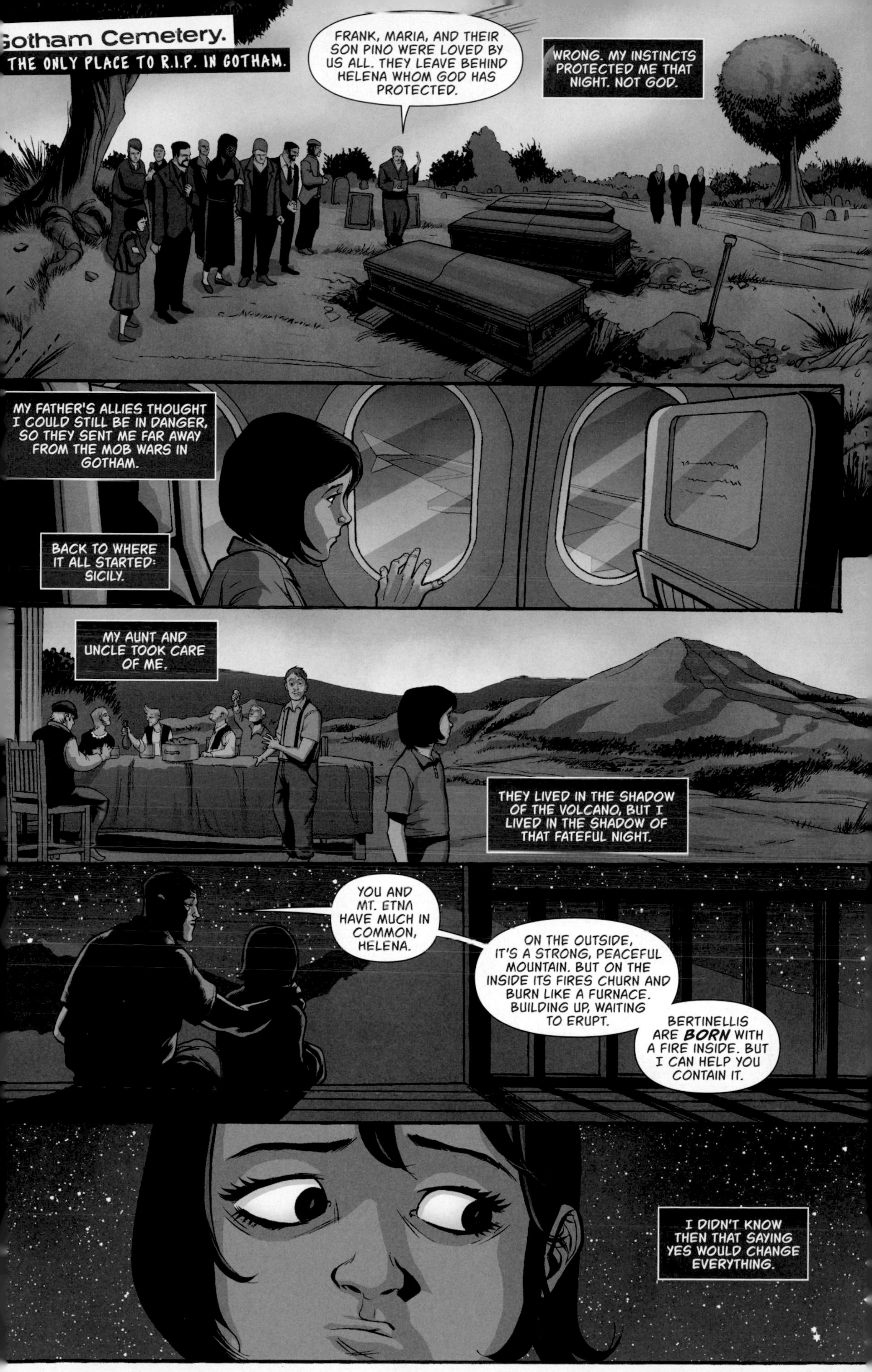
Gotham Cemetery.
THE ONLY PLACE TO R.I.P. IN GOTHAM.
FRANK, MARIA, AND THEIR SON PINO WERE LOVED BY US ALL. THEY LEAVE BEHIND HELENA WHOM GOD HAS PROTECTED.
WRONG. MY INSTINCTS PROTECTED ME THAT NIGHT. NOT GOD.
MY FATHER'S ALLIES THOUGHT I COULD STILL BE IN DANGER, SO THEY SENT ME FAR AWAY FROM THE MOB WARS IN GOTHAM.
BACK TO WHERE IT ALL STARTED: SICILY.
MY AUNT AND UNCLE TOOK CARE OF ME.
THEY LIVED IN THE SHADOW OF THE VOLCANO, BUT I LIVED IN THE SHADOW OF THAT FATEFUL NIGHT.
YOU AND MT. ETNA HAVE MUCH IN COMMON, HELENA.
ON THE OUTSIDE, IT'S A STRONG, PEACEFUL MOUNTAIN. BUT ON THE INSIDE ITS FIRES CHURN AND BURN LIKE A FURNACE. BUILDING UP, WAITING TO ERUPT.
BERTINELLIS ARE BORN WITH A FIRE INSIDE. BUT I CAN HELP YOU CONTAIN IT.
I DIDN'T KNOW THEN THAT SAYING YES WOULD CHANGE EVERYTHING.

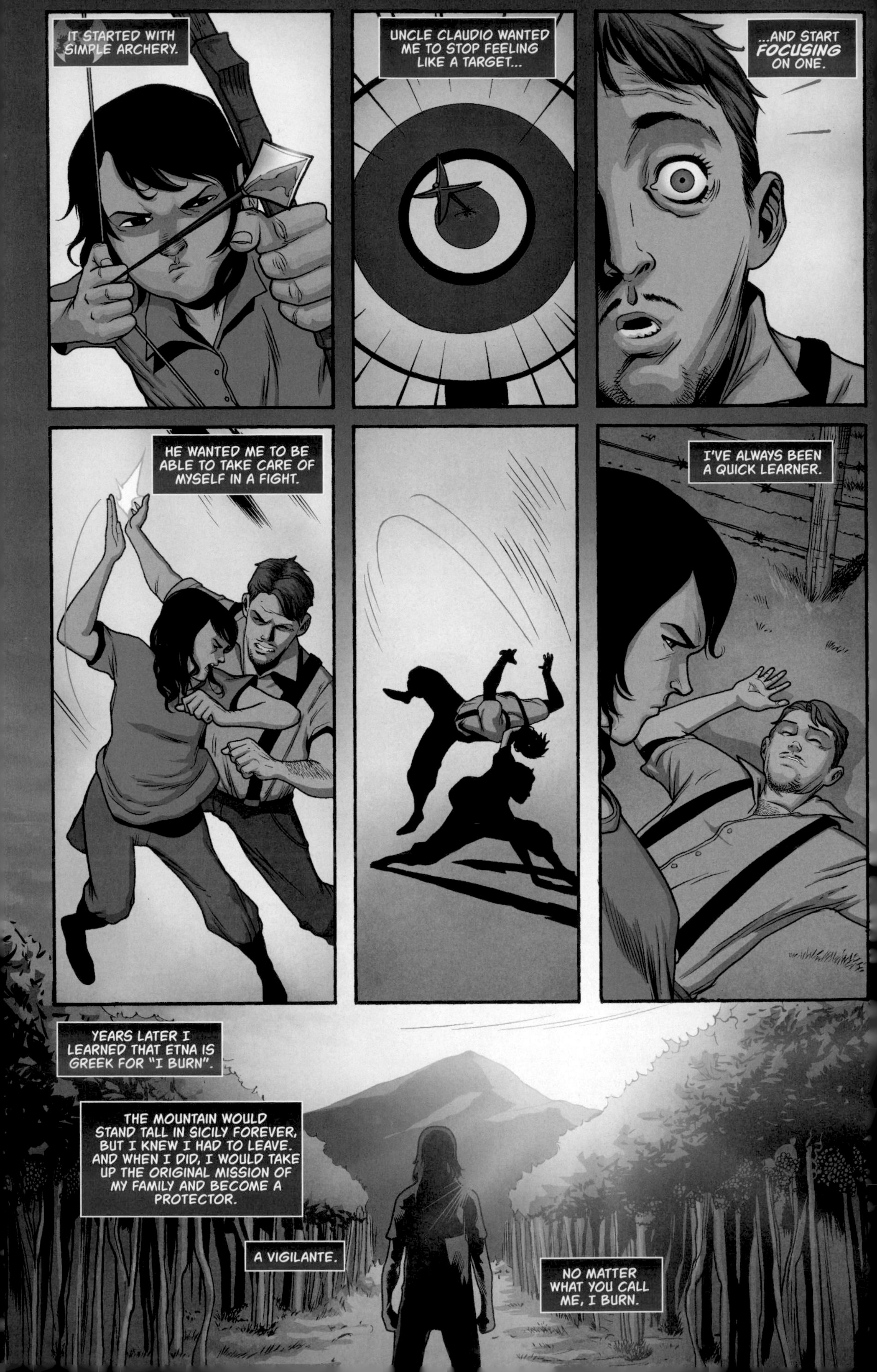
IT STARTED WITH SIMPLE ARCHERY.
UNCLE CLAUDIO WANTED ME TO STOP FEELING LIKE A TARGET...
...AND START *FOCUSING* ON ONE.
HE WANTED ME TO BE ABLE TO TAKE CARE OF MYSELF IN A FIGHT.
I'VE ALWAYS BEEN A QUICK LEARNER.
YEARS LATER I LEARNED THAT ETNA IS GREEK FOR "I BURN".
THE MOUNTAIN WOULD STAND TALL IN SICILY FOREVER, BUT I KNEW I HAD TO LEAVE. AND WHEN I DID, I WOULD TAKE UP THE ORIGINAL MISSION OF MY FAMILY AND BECOME A PROTECTOR.
A VIGILANTE.
NO MATTER WHAT YOU CALL ME, I BURN.

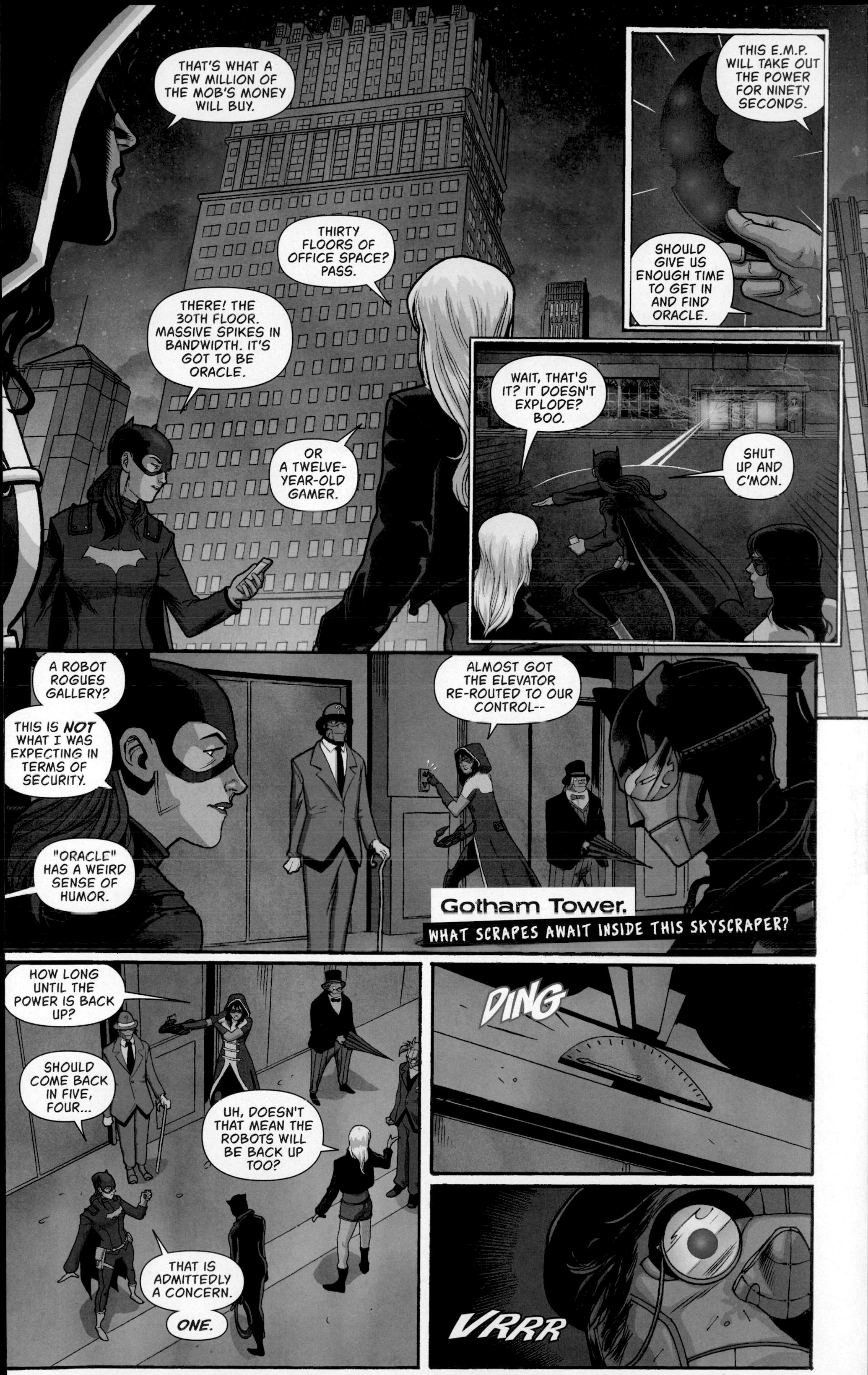
THAT'S WHAT A FEW MILLION OF THE MOB'S MONEY WILL BUY.
THIRTY FLOORS OF OFFICE SPACE? PASS.
THERE! THE 30TH FLOOR. MASSIVE SPIKES IN BANDWIDTH. IT'S GOT TO BE ORACLE.
OR A TWELVE-YEAR-OLD GAMER.
THIS E.M.P. WILL TAKE OUT THE POWER FOR NINETY SECONDS.
SHOULD GIVE US ENOUGH TIME TO GET IN AND FIND ORACLE.
WAIT, THAT'S IT? IT DOESN'T EXPLODE? BOO.
SHUT UP AND C'MON.
A ROBOT ROGUES GALLERY?
THIS IS NOT WHAT I WAS EXPECTING IN TERMS OF SECURITY.
"ORACLE" HAS A WEIRD SENSE OF HUMOR.
ALMOST GOT THE ELEVATOR RE-ROUTED TO OUR CONTROL--
Gotham Tower.
WHAT SCRAPES AWAIT INSIDE THIS SKYSCRAPER?
HOW LONG UNTIL THE POWER IS BACK UP?
SHOULD COME BACK IN FIVE, FOUR...
UH, DOESN'T THAT MEAN THE ROBOTS WILL BE BACK UP TOO?
THAT IS ADMITTEDLY A CONCERN.
ONE.
DING
VRRR

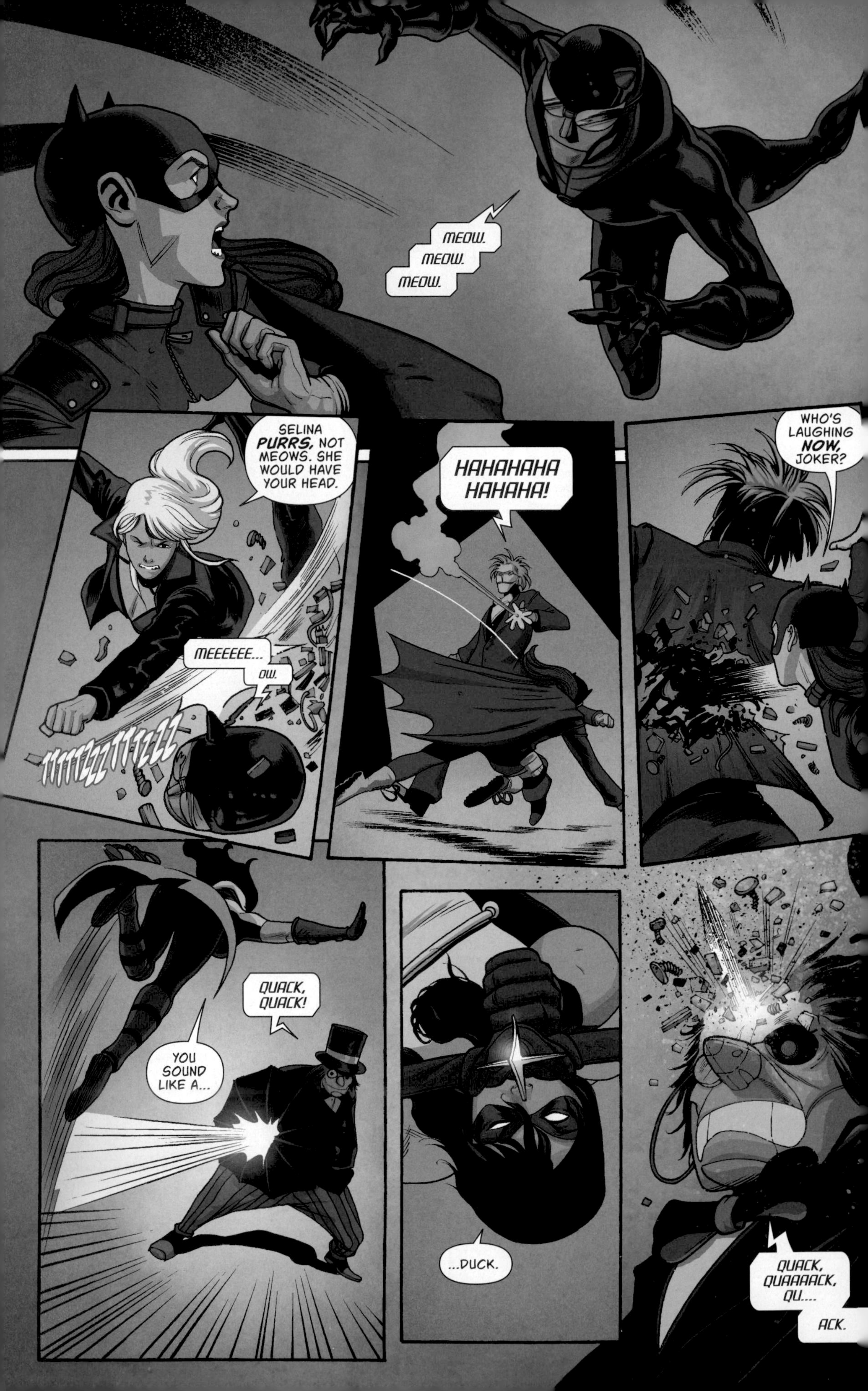
MEOW.
MEOW.
MEOW.
SELINA PURRS, NOT MEOWS. SHE WOULD HAVE YOUR HEAD.
MEEEEEE...
OW.
TTTTTZZZ TTTZZZ
HAHAHAHA HAHAHA!
WHO'S LAUGHING NOW, JOKER?
YOU SOUND LIKE A...
QUACK, QUACK!
...DUCK.
QUACK, QUAAAACK, QU....
ACK.

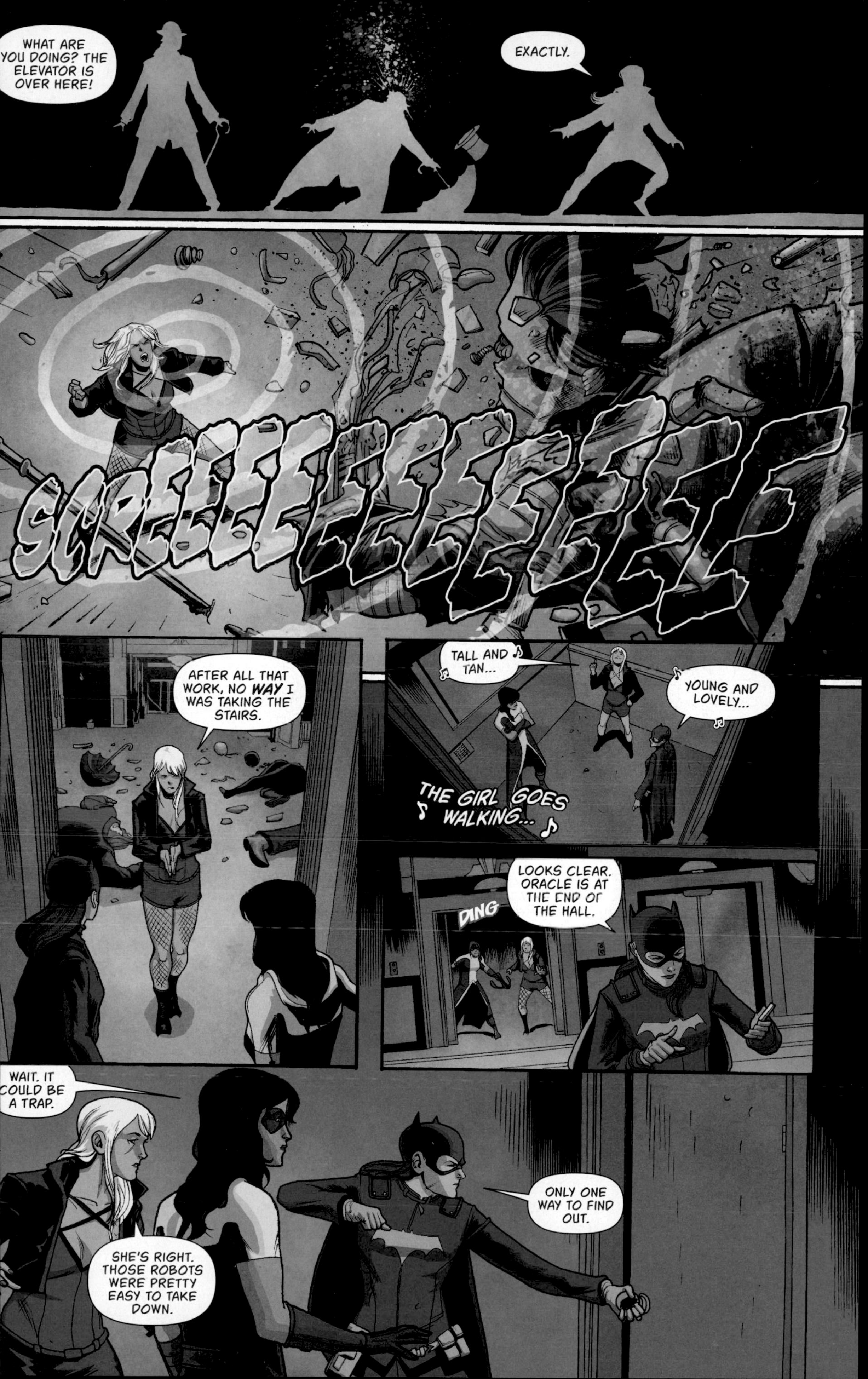
WHAT ARE YOU DOING? THE ELEVATOR IS OVER HERE!
EXACTLY.
SCREEEEEEEEEEEEE
AFTER ALL THAT WORK, NO WAY I WAS TAKING THE STAIRS.
TALL AND TAN...
YOUNG AND LOVELY...
THE GIRL GOES WALKING...
DING
LOOKS CLEAR. ORACLE IS AT THE END OF THE HALL.
WAIT. IT COULD BE A TRAP.
SHE'S RIGHT. THOSE ROBOTS WERE PRETTY EASY TO TAKE DOWN.
ONLY ONE WAY TO FIND OUT.

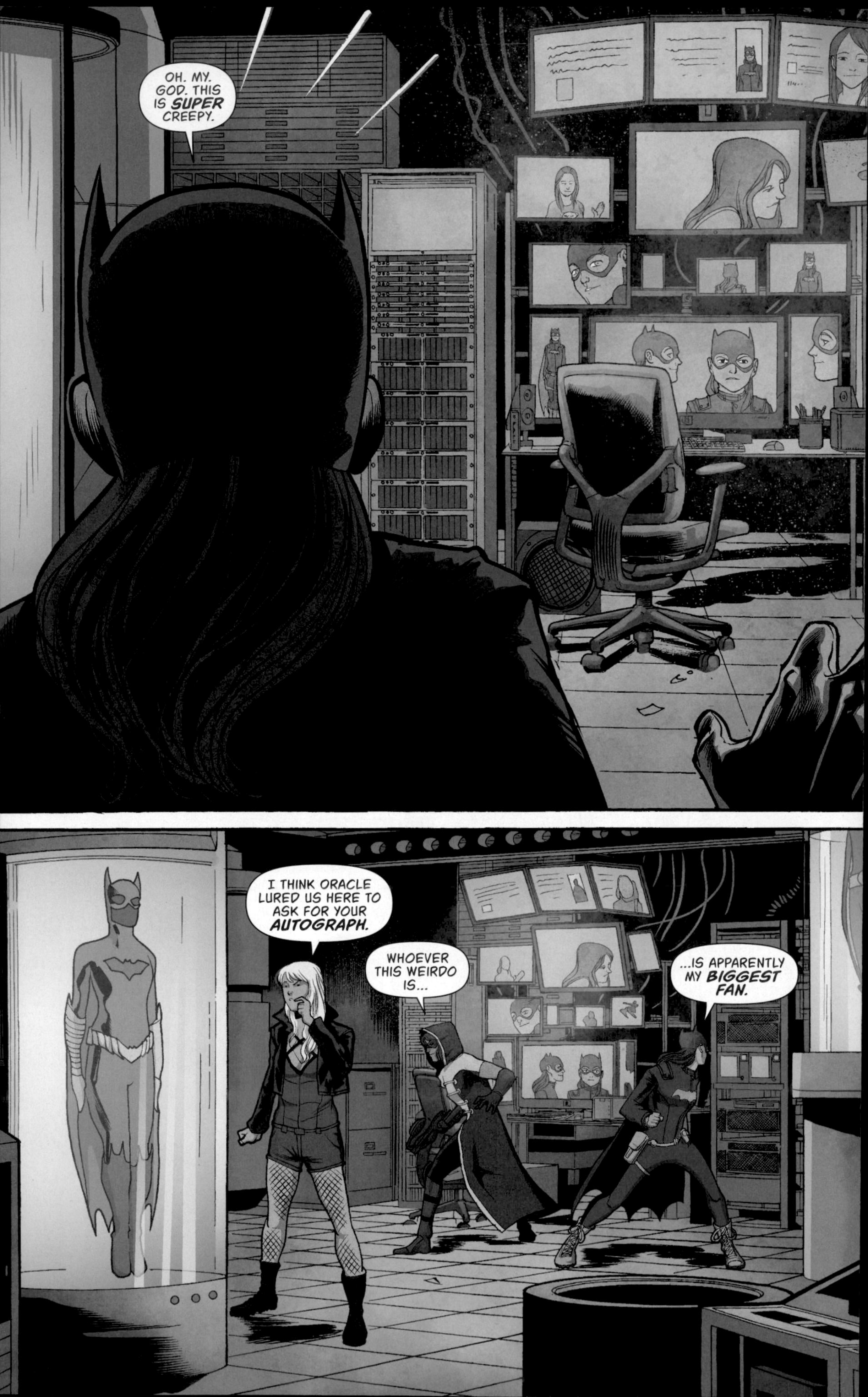

OH. MY. GOD. THIS IS SUPER CREEPY.
I THINK ORACLE LURED US HERE TO ASK FOR YOUR AUTOGRAPH.
WHOEVER THIS WEIRDO IS...
...IS APPARENTLY MY BIGGEST FAN.

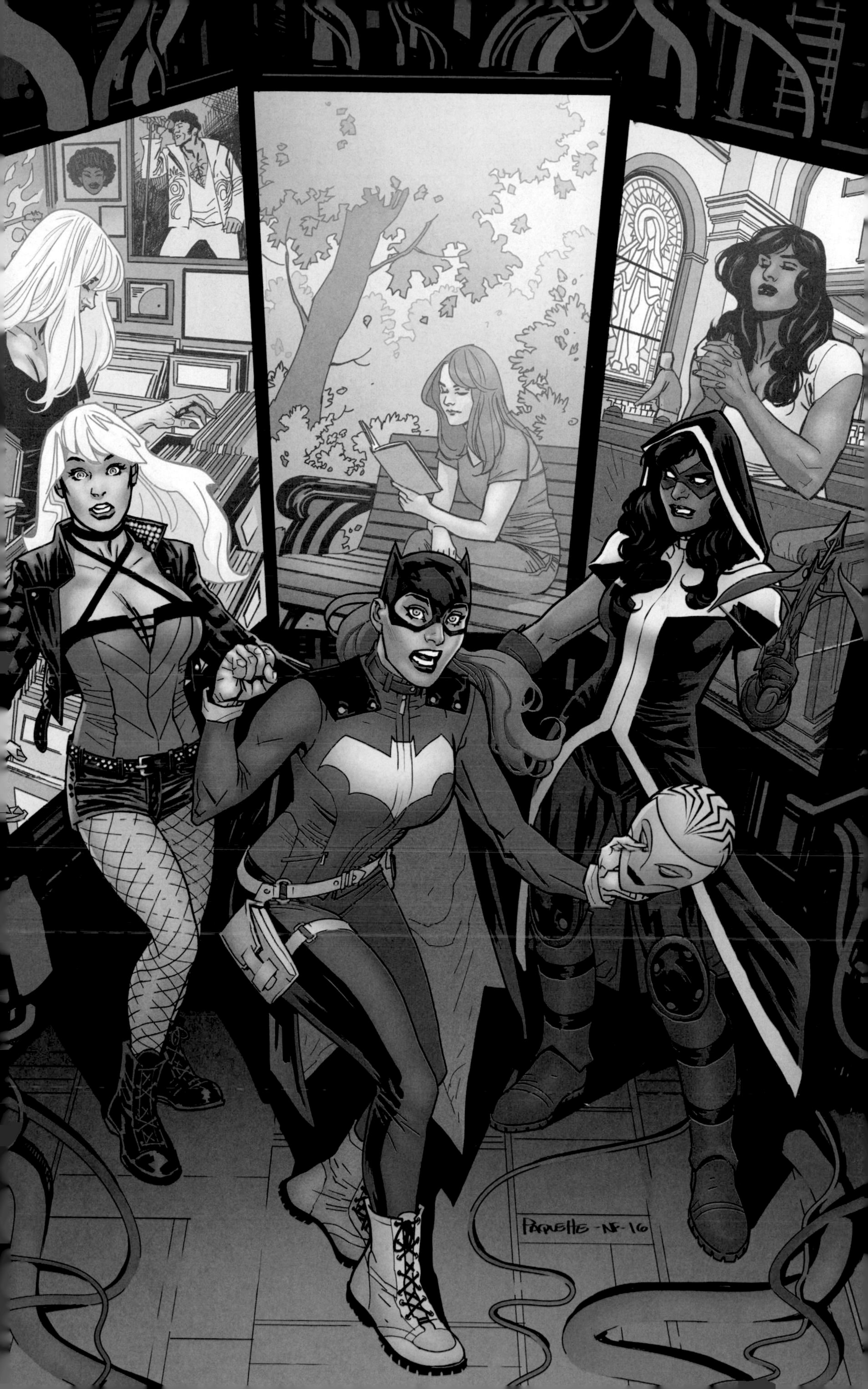
PAQUETTE -NF-16

PART FIVE: INTO THE LIGHT

JULIE and SHAWNA BENSON writers ∗ ROGE ANTONIO artist
ALLEN PASSALAQUA colorist ∗ DERON BENNETT letterer

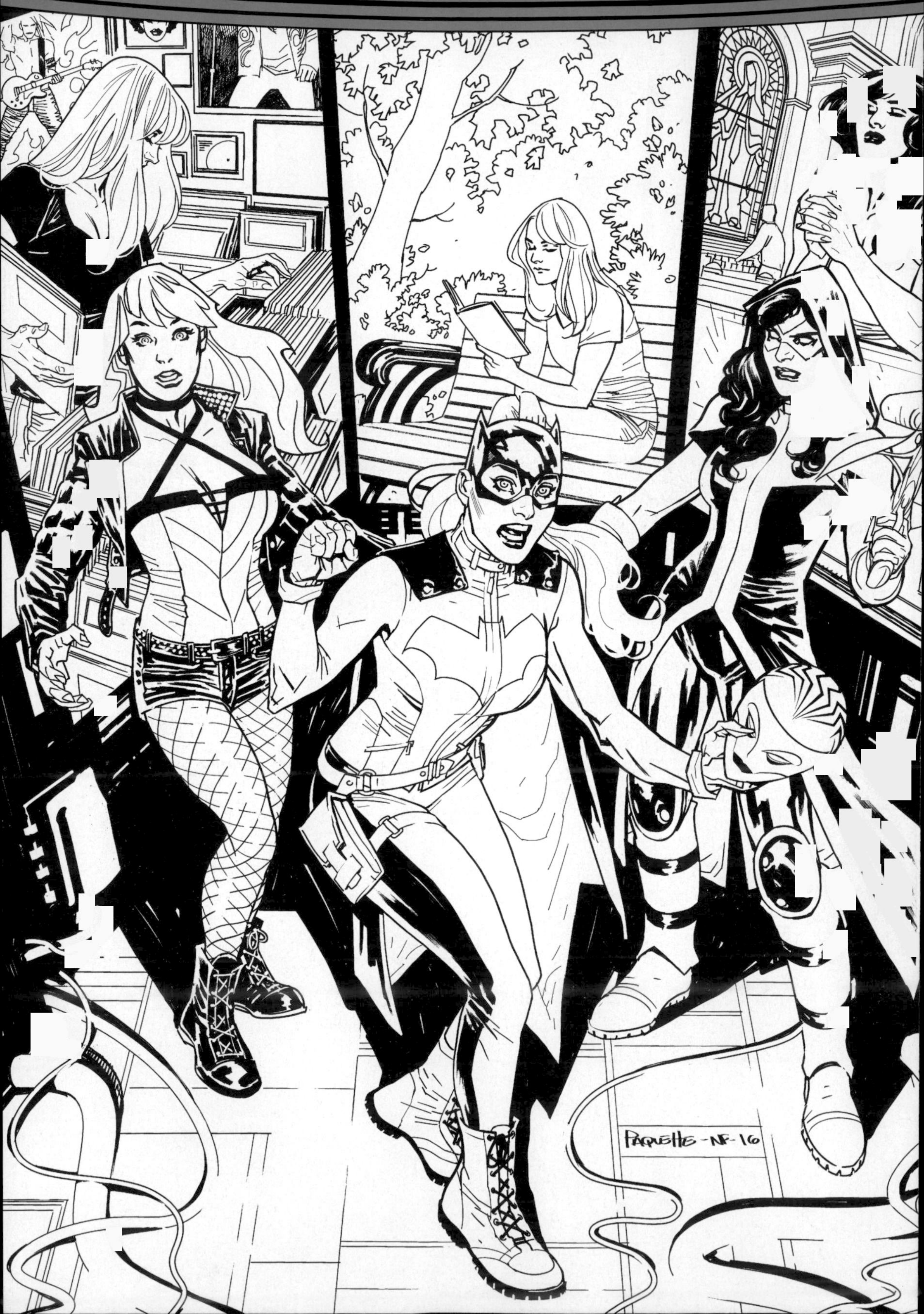
PAQUETTE -NF- 16

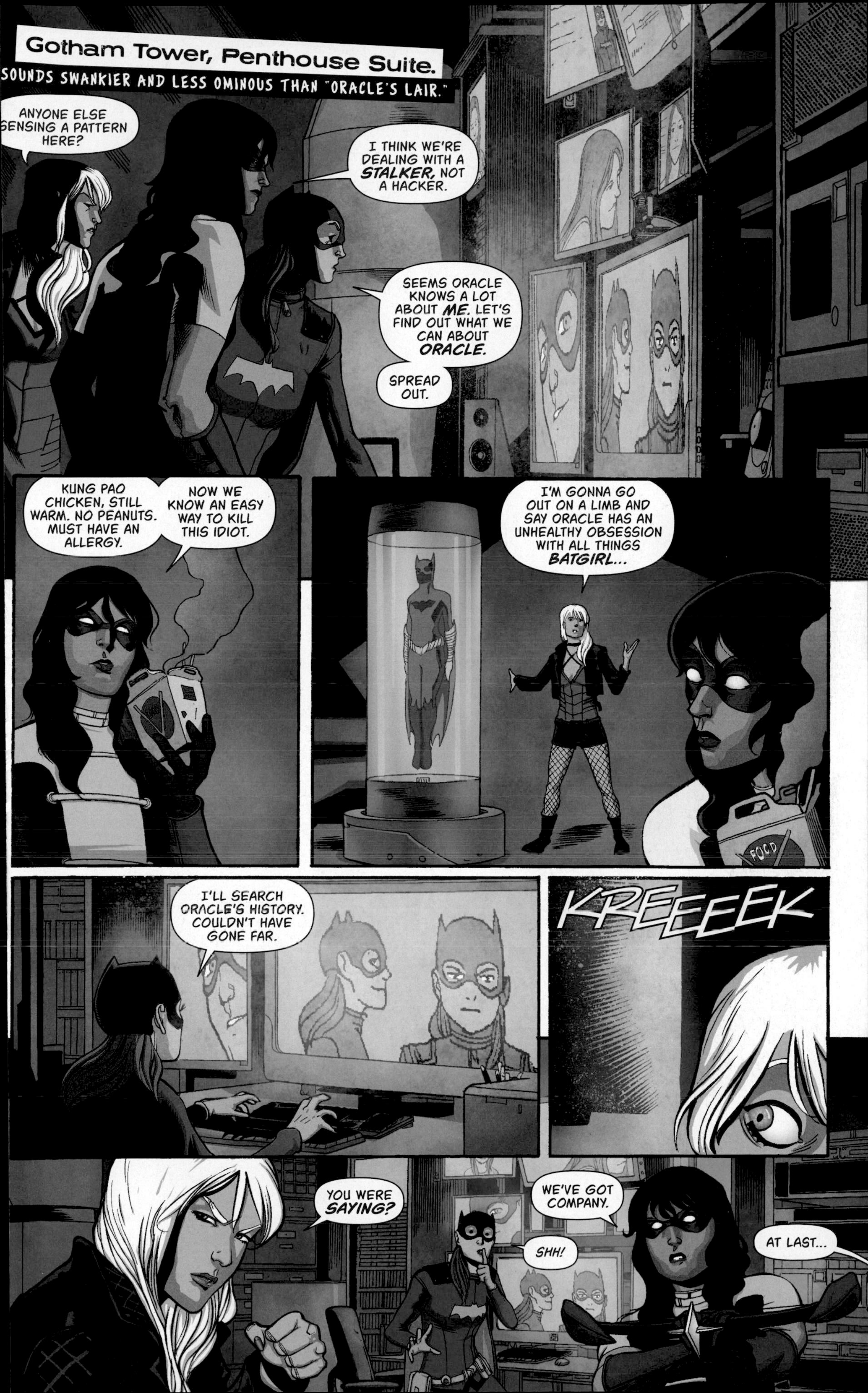
Gotham Tower, Penthouse Suite.
SOUNDS SWANKIER AND LESS OMINOUS THAN "ORACLE'S LAIR."
ANYONE ELSE SENSING A PATTERN HERE?
I THINK WE'RE DEALING WITH A STALKER, NOT A HACKER.
SEEMS ORACLE KNOWS A LOT ABOUT ME. LET'S FIND OUT WHAT WE CAN ABOUT ORACLE.
SPREAD OUT.
KUNG PAO CHICKEN, STILL WARM. NO PEANUTS. MUST HAVE AN ALLERGY.
NOW WE KNOW AN EASY WAY TO KILL THIS IDIOT.
I'M GONNA GO OUT ON A LIMB AND SAY ORACLE HAS AN UNHEALTHY OBSESSION WITH ALL THINGS BATGIRL...
FOOD
I'LL SEARCH ORACLE'S HISTORY. COULDN'T HAVE GONE FAR.
KREEEEEK
YOU WERE SAYING?
WE'VE GOT COMPANY.
SHH!
AT LAST...

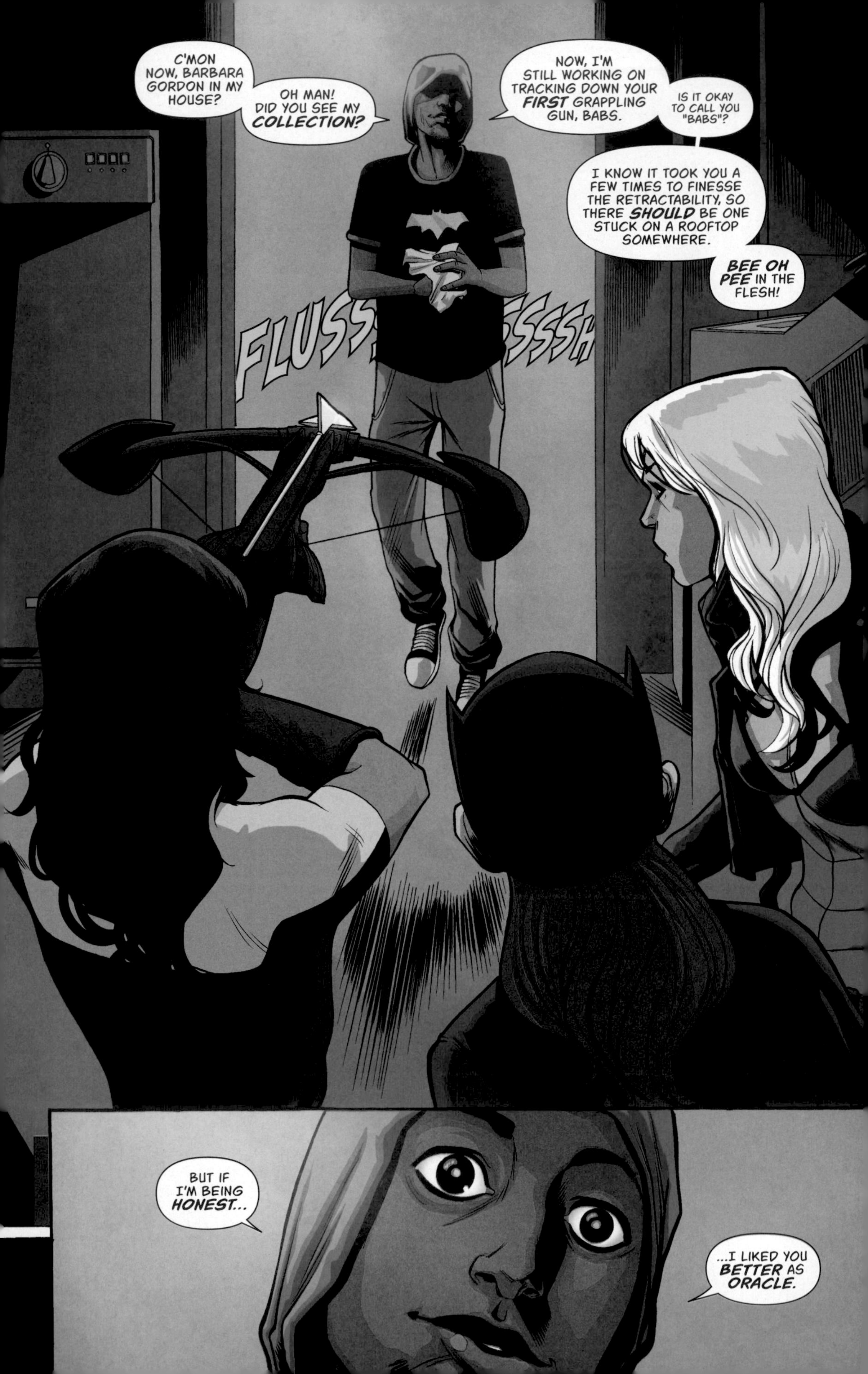
C'MON NOW, BARBARA GORDON IN MY HOUSE?
OH MAN! DID YOU SEE MY COLLECTION?
NOW, I'M STILL WORKING ON TRACKING DOWN YOUR FIRST GRAPPLING GUN, BABS.
IS IT OKAY TO CALL YOU "BABS"?
I KNOW IT TOOK YOU A FEW TIMES TO FINESSE THE RETRACTABILITY, SO THERE SHOULD BE ONE STUCK ON A ROOFTOP SOMEWHERE.
BEE OH PEE IN THE FLESH!
FLUSS...SSSSH
BUT IF I'M BEING HONEST...
...I LIKED YOU BETTER AS ORACLE.

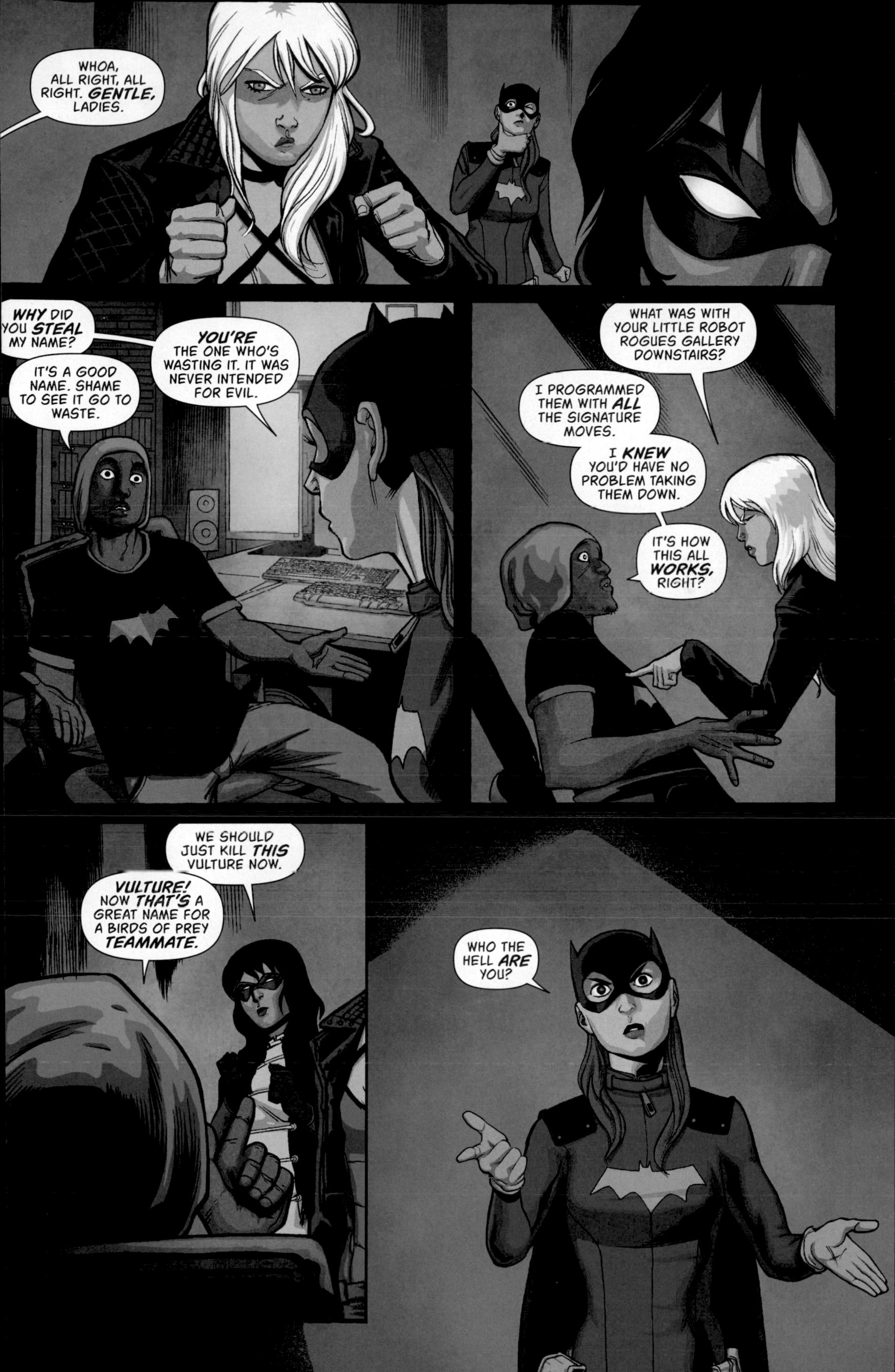
WHOA, ALL RIGHT, ALL RIGHT. GENTLE, LADIES.
WHY DID YOU STEAL MY NAME?
IT'S A GOOD NAME. SHAME TO SEE IT GO TO WASTE.
YOU'RE THE ONE WHO'S WASTING IT. IT WAS NEVER INTENDED FOR EVIL.
WHAT WAS WITH YOUR LITTLE ROBOT ROGUES GALLERY DOWNSTAIRS?
I PROGRAMMED THEM WITH ALL THE SIGNATURE MOVES.
I KNEW YOU'D HAVE NO PROBLEM TAKING THEM DOWN.
IT'S HOW THIS ALL WORKS, RIGHT?
WE SHOULD JUST KILL THIS VULTURE NOW.
VULTURE! NOW THAT'S A GREAT NAME FOR A BIRDS OF PREY TEAMMATE.
WHO THE HELL ARE YOU?

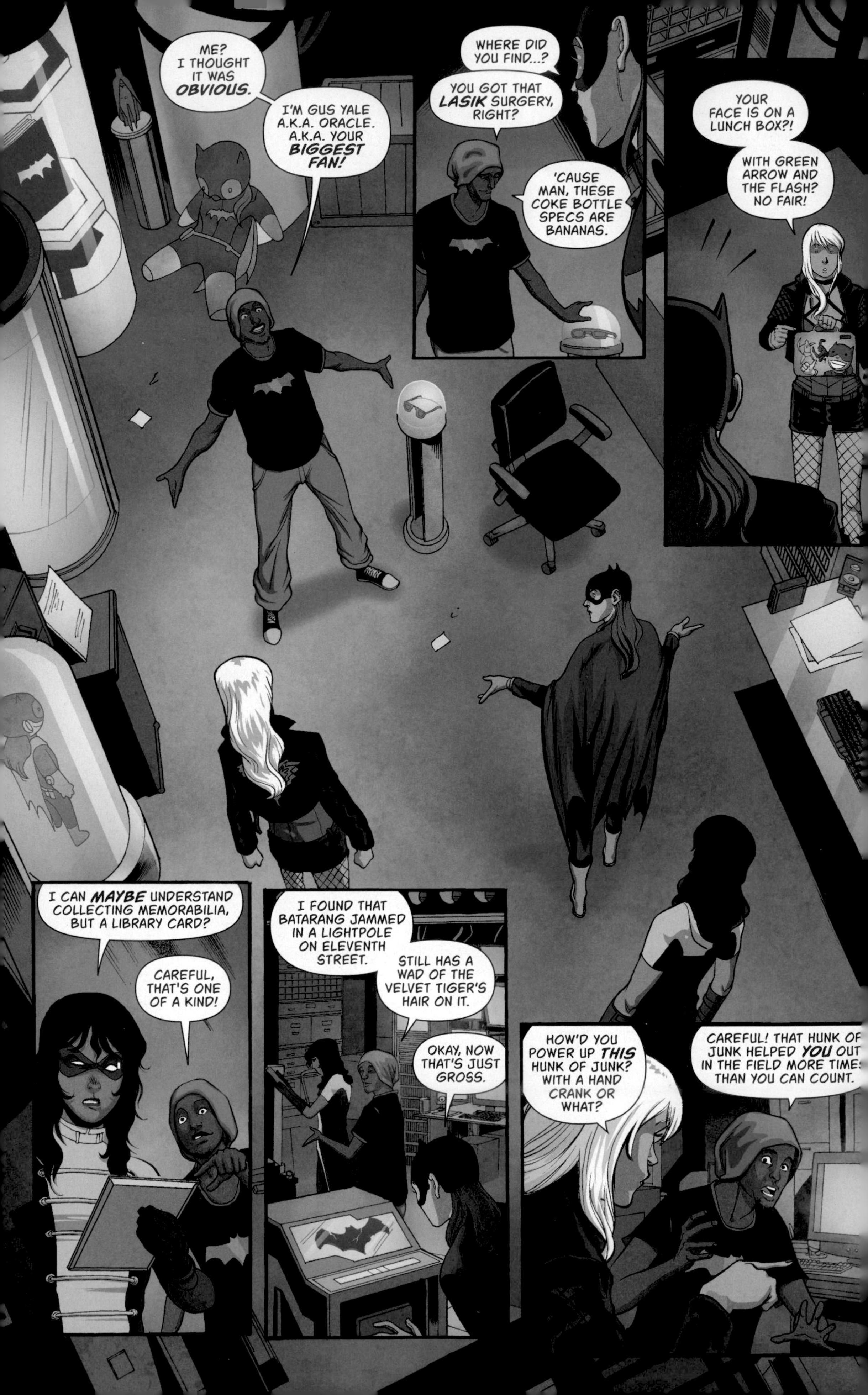

ME? I THOUGHT IT WAS OBVIOUS.
I'M GUS YALE A.K.A. ORACLE. A.K.A. YOUR BIGGEST FAN!
WHERE DID YOU FIND...?
YOU GOT THAT LASIK SURGERY, RIGHT?
'CAUSE MAN, THESE COKE BOTTLE SPECS ARE BANANAS.
YOUR FACE IS ON A LUNCH BOX?!
WITH GREEN ARROW AND THE FLASH? NO FAIR!
I CAN MAYBE UNDERSTAND COLLECTING MEMORABILIA, BUT A LIBRARY CARD?
CAREFUL, THAT'S ONE OF A KIND!
I FOUND THAT BATARANG JAMMED IN A LIGHTPOLE ON ELEVENTH STREET.
STILL HAS A WAD OF THE VELVET TIGER'S HAIR ON IT.
OKAY, NOW THAT'S JUST GROSS.
HOW'D YOU POWER UP THIS HUNK OF JUNK? WITH A HAND CRANK OR WHAT?
CAREFUL! THAT HUNK OF JUNK HELPED YOU OUT IN THE FIELD MORE TIMES THAN YOU CAN COUNT.

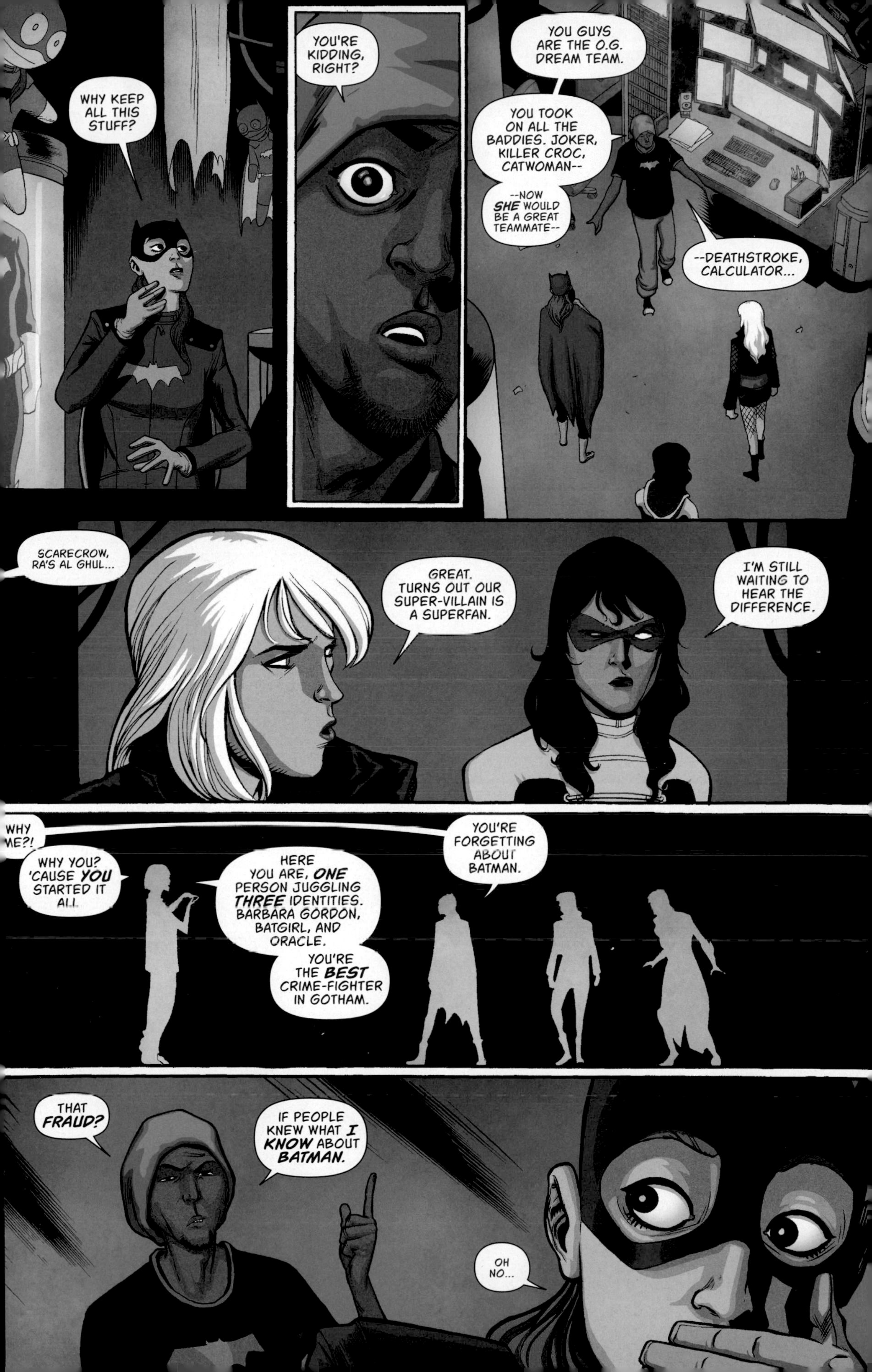

WHY KEEP ALL THIS STUFF?
YOU'RE KIDDING, RIGHT?
YOU GUYS ARE THE O.G. DREAM TEAM.
YOU TOOK ON ALL THE BADDIES. JOKER, KILLER CROC, CATWOMAN--
--NOW SHE WOULD BE A GREAT TEAMMATE--
--DEATHSTROKE, CALCULATOR...
SCARECROW, RA'S AL GHUL...
GREAT. TURNS OUT OUR SUPER-VILLAIN IS A SUPERFAN.
I'M STILL WAITING TO HEAR THE DIFFERENCE.
WHY ME?!
WHY YOU? 'CAUSE YOU STARTED IT ALL.
HERE YOU ARE, ONE PERSON JUGGLING THREE IDENTITIES. BARBARA GORDON, BATGIRL, AND ORACLE.
YOU'RE THE BEST CRIME-FIGHTER IN GOTHAM.
YOU'RE FORGETTING ABOUT BATMAN.
THAT FRAUD?
IF PEOPLE KNEW WHAT I KNOW ABOUT BATMAN.
OH NO...

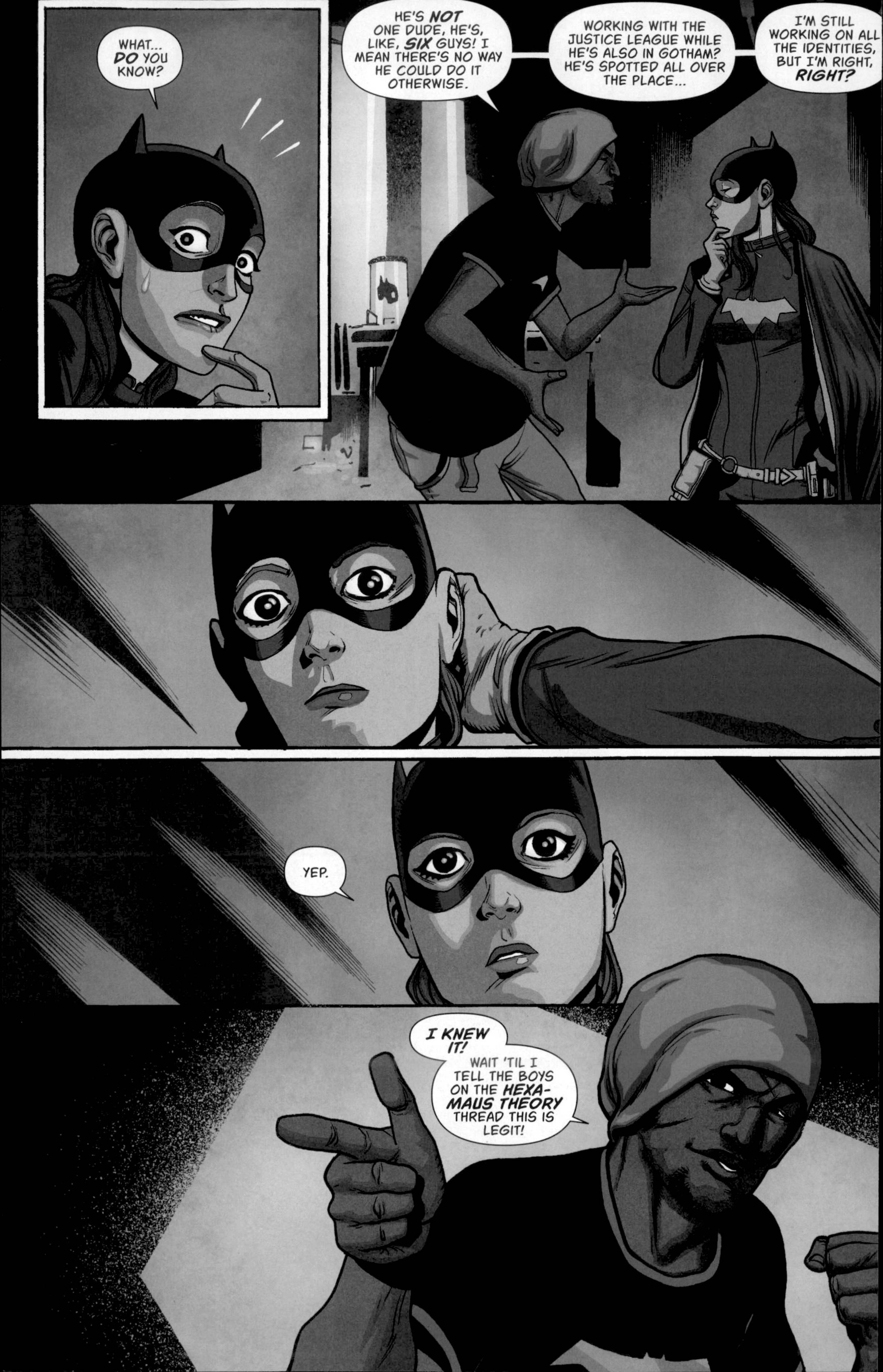
WHAT... **DO** YOU KNOW?
HE'S **NOT** ONE DUDE, HE'S, LIKE, **SIX** GUYS! I MEAN THERE'S NO WAY HE COULD DO IT OTHERWISE.
WORKING WITH THE JUSTICE LEAGUE WHILE HE'S ALSO IN GOTHAM? HE'S SPOTTED ALL OVER THE PLACE...
I'M STILL WORKING ON ALL THE IDENTITIES, BUT I'M RIGHT, **RIGHT?**
YEP.
I KNEW IT!
WAIT 'TIL I TELL THE BOYS ON THE **HEXA-MAUS THEORY** THREAD THIS IS LEGIT!

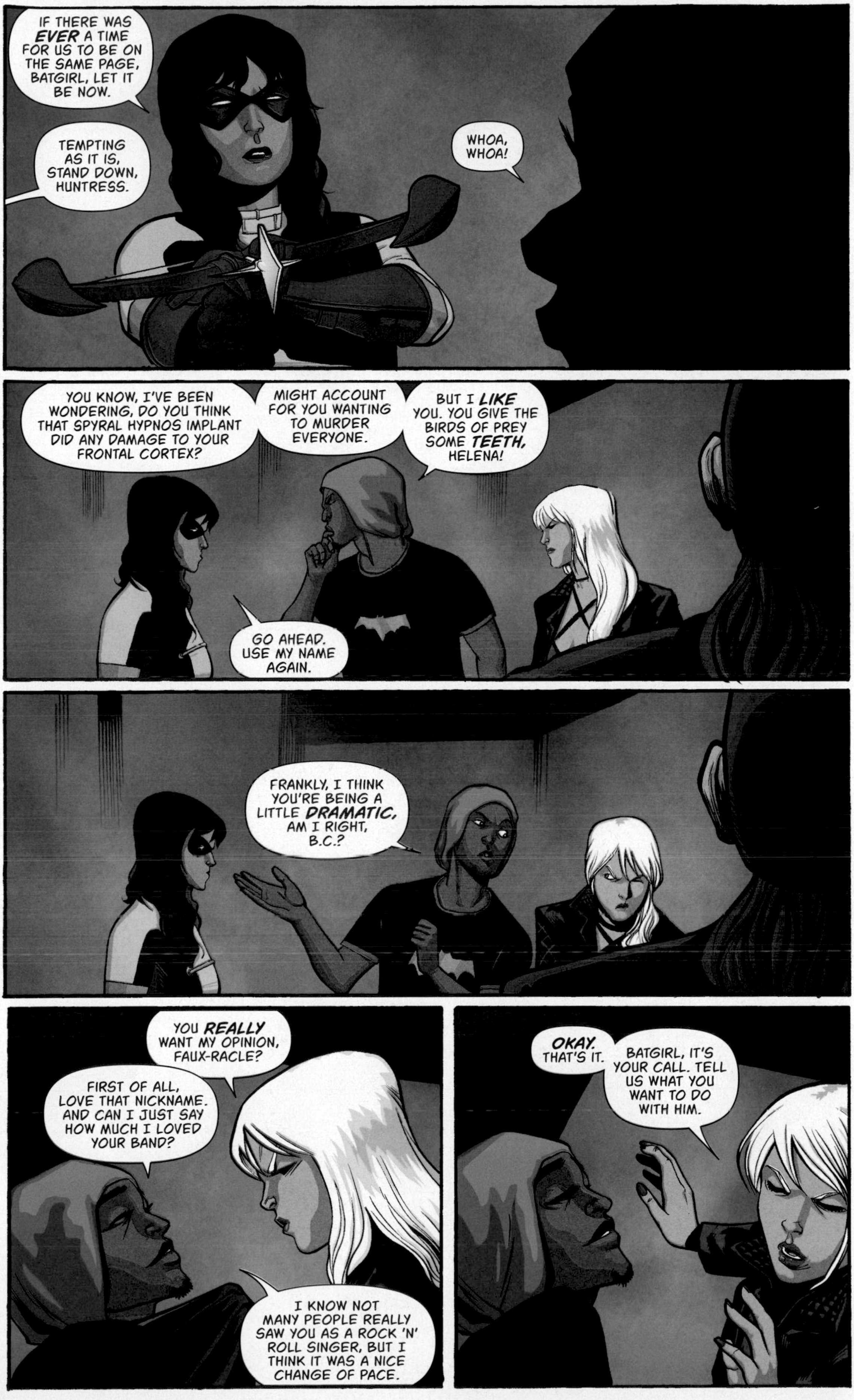
IF THERE WAS EVER A TIME FOR US TO BE ON THE SAME PAGE, BATGIRL, LET IT BE NOW.
TEMPTING AS IT IS, STAND DOWN, HUNTRESS.
WHOA, WHOA!
YOU KNOW, I'VE BEEN WONDERING, DO YOU THINK THAT SPYRAL HYPNOS IMPLANT DID ANY DAMAGE TO YOUR FRONTAL CORTEX?
MIGHT ACCOUNT FOR YOU WANTING TO MURDER EVERYONE.
BUT I LIKE YOU. YOU GIVE THE BIRDS OF PREY SOME TEETH, HELENA!
GO AHEAD. USE MY NAME AGAIN.
FRANKLY, I THINK YOU'RE BEING A LITTLE DRAMATIC, AM I RIGHT, B.C.?
YOU REALLY WANT MY OPINION, FAUX-RACLE?
FIRST OF ALL, LOVE THAT NICKNAME. AND CAN I JUST SAY HOW MUCH I LOVED YOUR BAND?
I KNOW NOT MANY PEOPLE REALLY SAW YOU AS A ROCK 'N' ROLL SINGER, BUT I THINK IT WAS A NICE CHANGE OF PACE.
OKAY. THAT'S IT.
BATGIRL, IT'S YOUR CALL. TELL US WHAT YOU WANT TO DO WITH HIM.

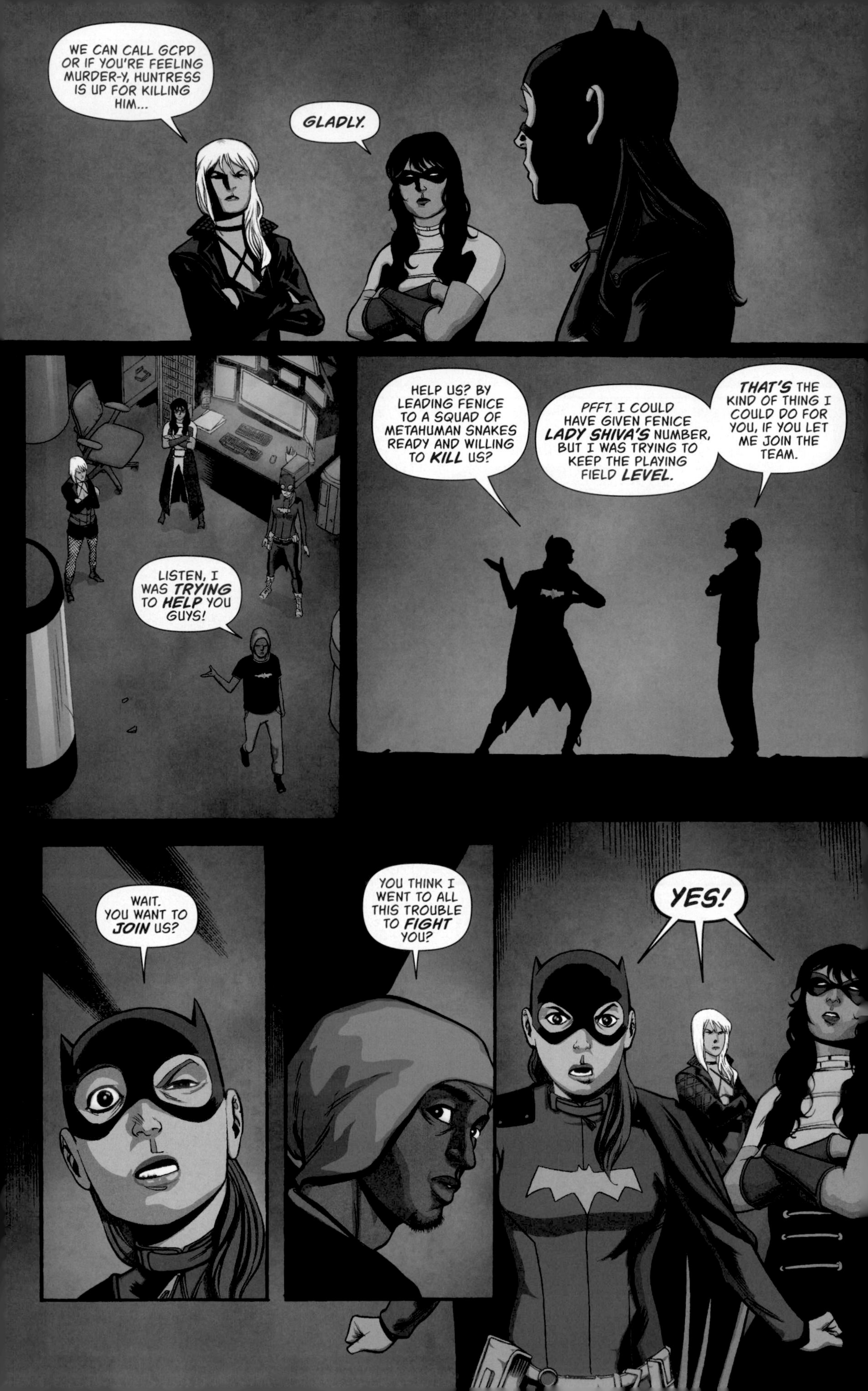
WE CAN CALL GCPD OR IF YOU'RE FEELING MURDER-Y, HUNTRESS IS UP FOR KILLING HIM...
GLADLY.
LISTEN, I WAS TRYING TO HELP YOU GUYS!
HELP US? BY LEADING FENICE TO A SQUAD OF METAHUMAN SNAKES READY AND WILLING TO KILL US?
PFFT. I COULD HAVE GIVEN FENICE LADY SHIVA'S NUMBER, BUT I WAS TRYING TO KEEP THE PLAYING FIELD LEVEL.
THAT'S THE KIND OF THING I COULD DO FOR YOU, IF YOU LET ME JOIN THE TEAM.
WAIT. YOU WANT TO JOIN US?
YOU THINK I WENT TO ALL THIS TROUBLE TO FIGHT YOU?
YES!

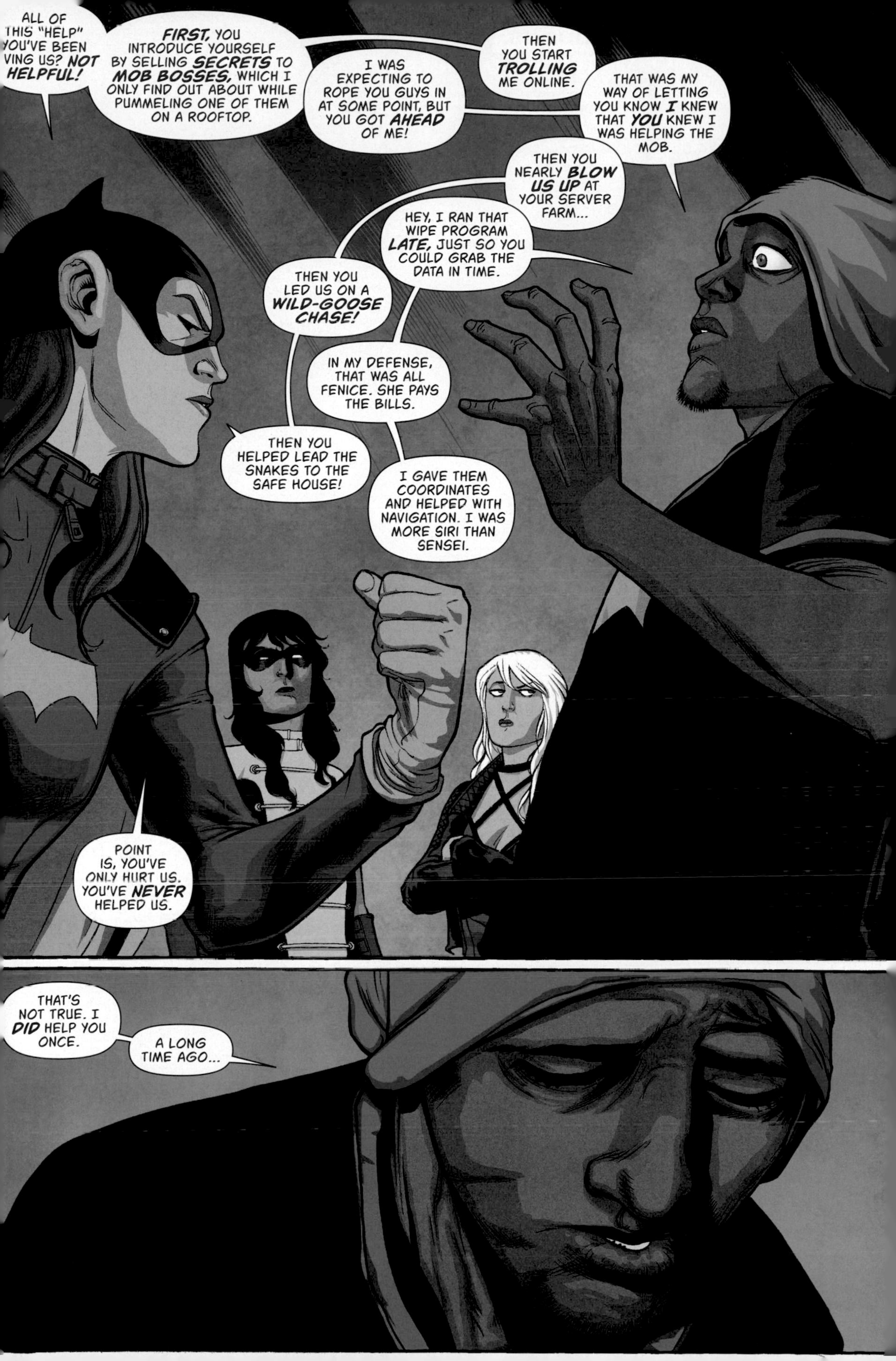

ALL OF THIS "HELP" YOU'VE BEEN GIVING US? NOT HELPFUL!
FIRST, YOU INTRODUCE YOURSELF BY SELLING SECRETS TO MOB BOSSES, WHICH I ONLY FIND OUT ABOUT WHILE PUMMELING ONE OF THEM ON A ROOFTOP.
I WAS EXPECTING TO ROPE YOU GUYS IN AT SOME POINT, BUT YOU GOT AHEAD OF ME!
THEN YOU START TROLLING ME ONLINE.
THAT WAS MY WAY OF LETTING YOU KNOW I KNEW THAT YOU KNEW I WAS HELPING THE MOB.
THEN YOU NEARLY BLOW US UP AT YOUR SERVER FARM...
HEY, I RAN THAT WIPE PROGRAM LATE, JUST SO YOU COULD GRAB THE DATA IN TIME.
THEN YOU LED US ON A WILD-GOOSE CHASE!
IN MY DEFENSE, THAT WAS ALL FENICE. SHE PAYS THE BILLS.
THEN YOU HELPED LEAD THE SNAKES TO THE SAFE HOUSE!
I GAVE THEM COORDINATES AND HELPED WITH NAVIGATION. I WAS MORE SIRI THAN SENSEI.
POINT IS, YOU'VE ONLY HURT US. YOU'VE NEVER HELPED US.
THAT'S NOT TRUE. I DID HELP YOU ONCE.
A LONG TIME AGO...

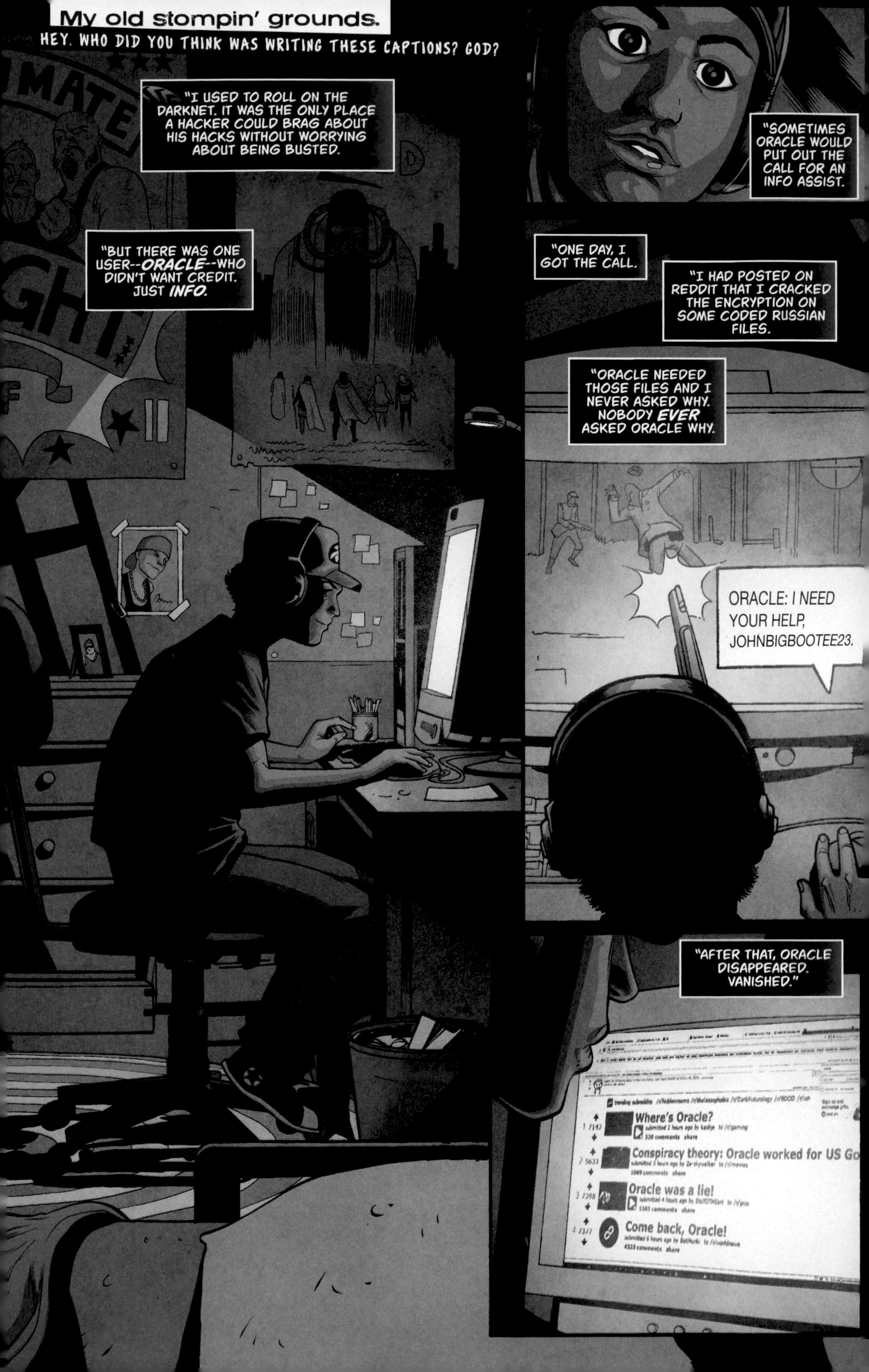

My old stompin' grounds.
HEY. WHO DID YOU THINK WAS WRITING THESE CAPTIONS? GOD?
"I USED TO ROLL ON THE DARKNET. IT WAS THE ONLY PLACE A HACKER COULD BRAG ABOUT HIS HACKS WITHOUT WORRYING ABOUT BEING BUSTED.
"BUT THERE WAS ONE USER--*ORACLE*--WHO DIDN'T WANT CREDIT. JUST *INFO.*
"SOMETIMES ORACLE WOULD PUT OUT THE CALL FOR AN INFO ASSIST.
"ONE DAY, I GOT THE CALL.
"I HAD POSTED ON REDDIT THAT I CRACKED THE ENCRYPTION ON SOME CODED RUSSIAN FILES.
"ORACLE NEEDED THOSE FILES AND I NEVER ASKED WHY. NOBODY *EVER* ASKED ORACLE WHY.
ORACLE: *I NEED* YOUR HELP, JOHNBIGBOOTEE23.
"AFTER THAT, ORACLE DISAPPEARED. VANISHED."
Where's Oracle?
Conspiracy theory: Oracle worked for US Go
Oracle was a lie!
Come back, Oracle!

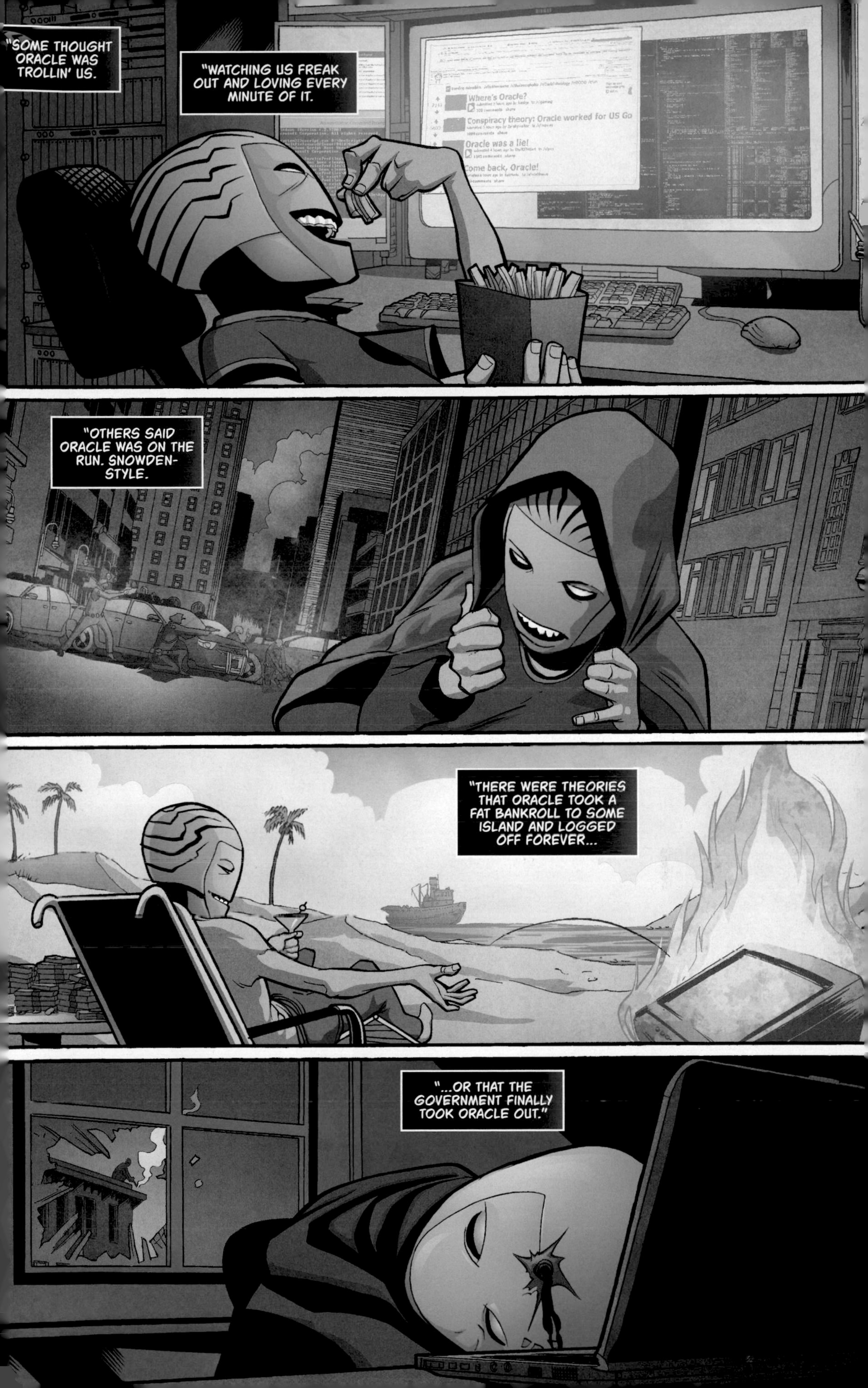
"SOME THOUGHT ORACLE WAS TROLLIN' US.
"WATCHING US FREAK OUT AND LOVING EVERY MINUTE OF IT.
Where's Oracle?
Conspiracy theory: Oracle worked for US Go
Oracle was a lie!
Come back, Oracle!
"OTHERS SAID ORACLE WAS ON THE RUN. SNOWDEN-STYLE.
"THERE WERE THEORIES THAT ORACLE TOOK A FAT BANKROLL TO SOME ISLAND AND LOGGED OFF FOREVER...
"...OR THAT THE GOVERNMENT FINALLY TOOK ORACLE OUT."

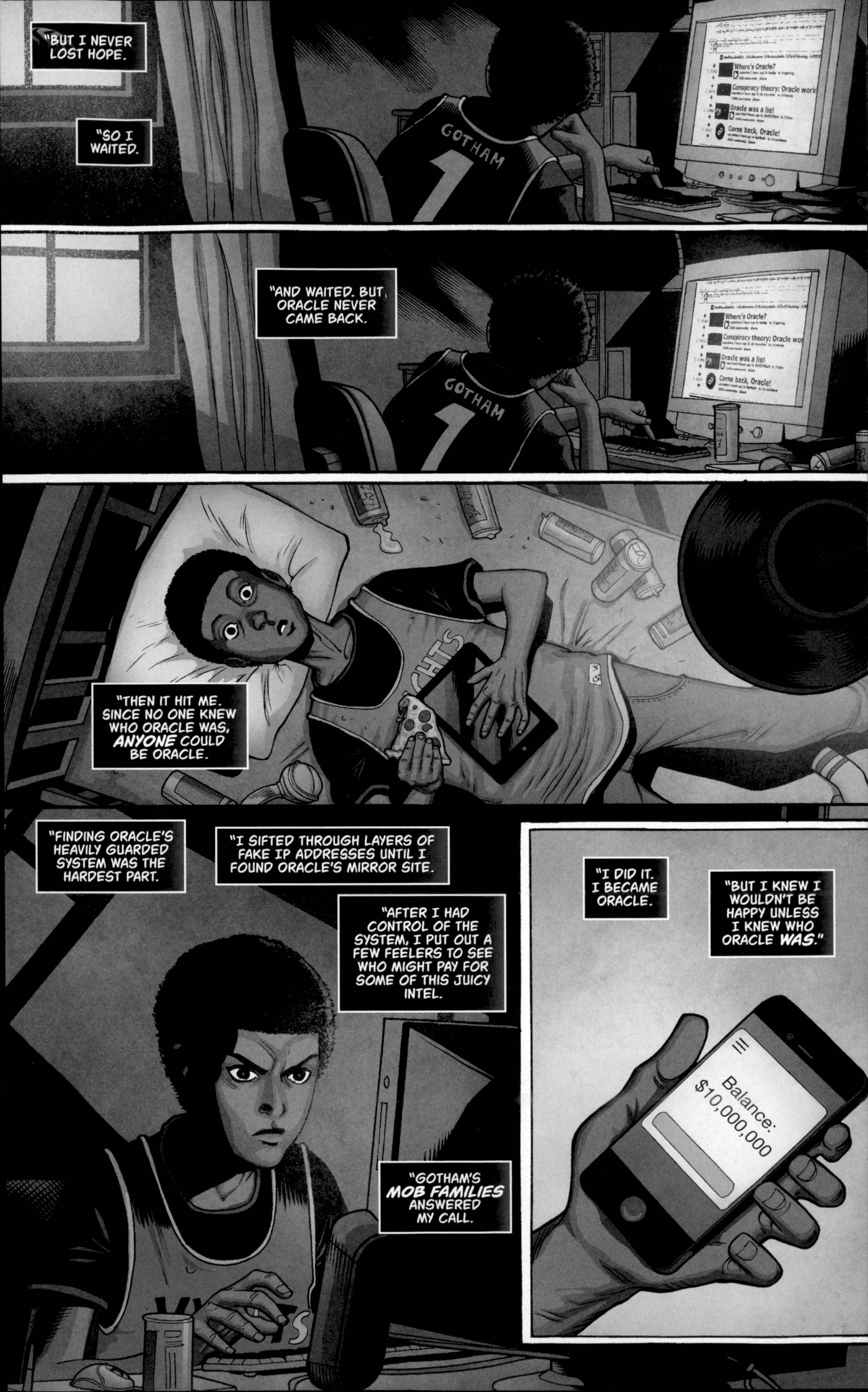
"BUT I NEVER LOST HOPE.
"SO I WAITED.
Where's Oracle?
Conspiracy theory: Oracle work
Oracle was a lie!
Come back, Oracle!
GOTHAM
"AND WAITED. BUT ORACLE NEVER CAME BACK.
Where's Oracle?
Conspiracy theory: Oracle wor
Oracle was a lie!
Come back, Oracle!
GOTHAM
"THEN IT HIT ME. SINCE NO ONE KNEW WHO ORACLE WAS, ***ANYONE*** COULD BE ORACLE.
"FINDING ORACLE'S HEAVILY GUARDED SYSTEM WAS THE HARDEST PART.
"I SIFTED THROUGH LAYERS OF FAKE IP ADDRESSES UNTIL I FOUND ORACLE'S MIRROR SITE.
"AFTER I HAD CONTROL OF THE SYSTEM, I PUT OUT A FEW FEELERS TO SEE WHO MIGHT PAY FOR SOME OF THIS JUICY INTEL.
"GOTHAM'S ***MOB FAMILIES*** ANSWERED MY CALL.
"I DID IT. I BECAME ORACLE.
"BUT I KNEW I WOULDN'T BE HAPPY UNLESS I KNEW WHO ORACLE ***WAS***."
Balance:
$10,000,000

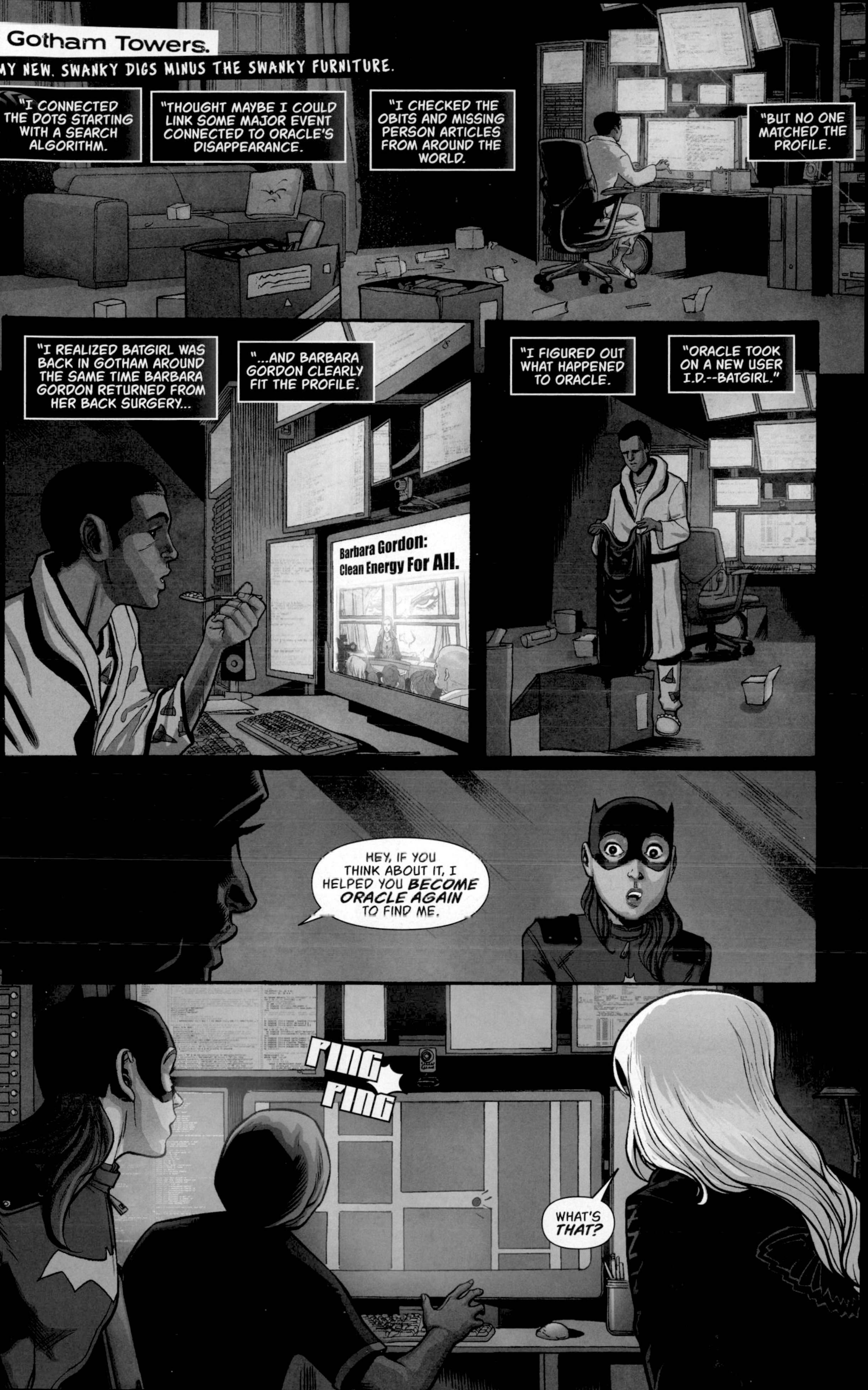
Gotham Towers.
MY NEW, SWANKY DIGS MINUS THE SWANKY FURNITURE.
"I CONNECTED THE DOTS STARTING WITH A SEARCH ALGORITHM.
"THOUGHT MAYBE I COULD LINK SOME MAJOR EVENT CONNECTED TO ORACLE'S DISAPPEARANCE.
"I CHECKED THE OBITS AND MISSING PERSON ARTICLES FROM AROUND THE WORLD.
"BUT NO ONE MATCHED THE PROFILE.
"I REALIZED BATGIRL WAS BACK IN GOTHAM AROUND THE SAME TIME BARBARA GORDON RETURNED FROM HER BACK SURGERY...
"...AND BARBARA GORDON CLEARLY FIT THE PROFILE.
Barbara Gordon: Clean Energy For All.
"I FIGURED OUT WHAT HAPPENED TO ORACLE.
"ORACLE TOOK ON A NEW USER I.D.--BATGIRL."
HEY, IF YOU THINK ABOUT IT, I HELPED YOU BECOME ORACLE AGAIN TO FIND ME.
PING PING
WHAT'S THAT?

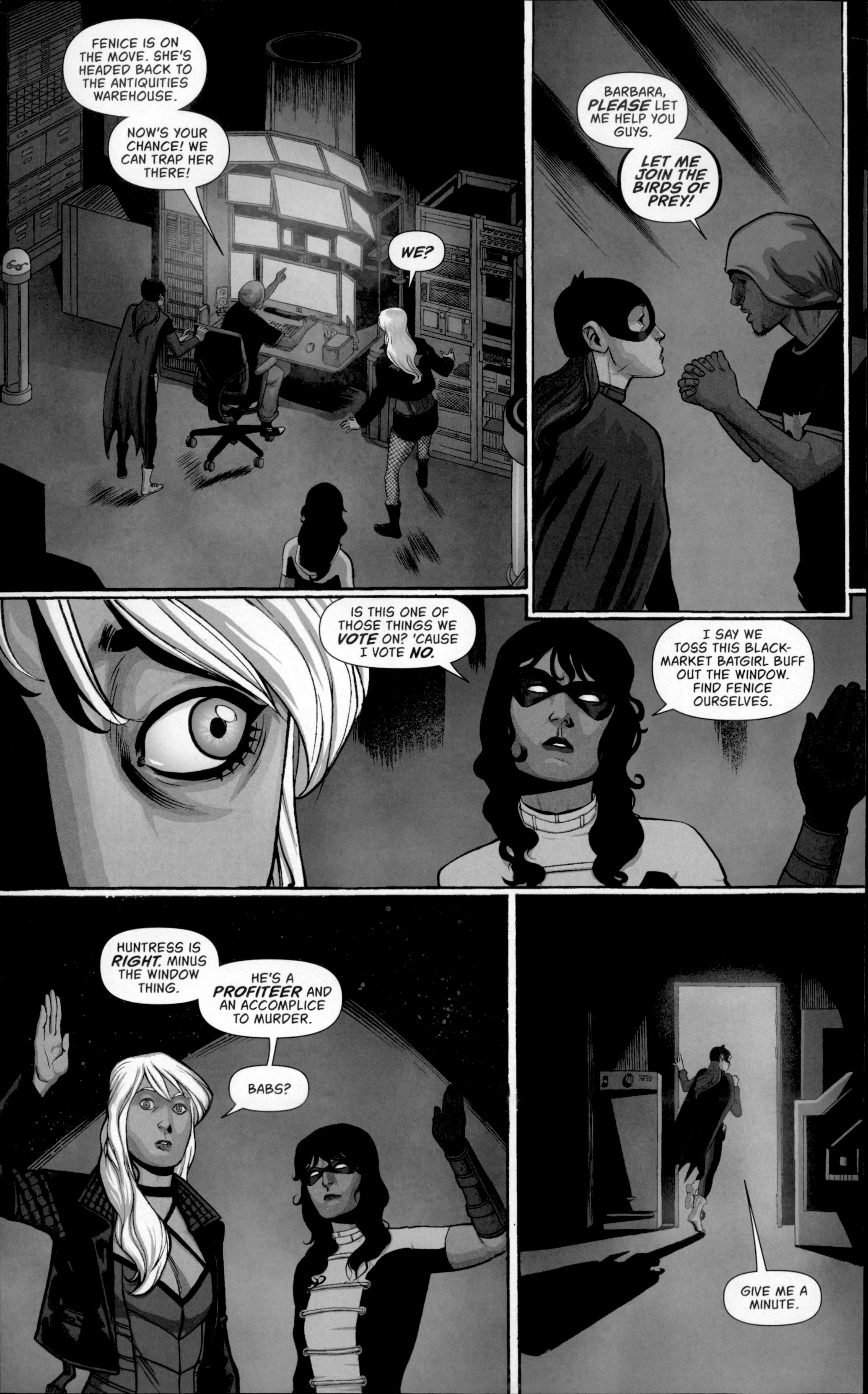
FENICE IS ON THE MOVE. SHE'S HEADED BACK TO THE ANTIQUITIES WAREHOUSE.
NOW'S YOUR CHANCE! WE CAN TRAP HER THERE!
WE?
BARBARA, PLEASE LET ME HELP YOU GUYS.
LET ME JOIN THE BIRDS OF PREY!
IS THIS ONE OF THOSE THINGS WE VOTE ON? 'CAUSE I VOTE NO.
I SAY WE TOSS THIS BLACK-MARKET BATGIRL BUFF OUT THE WINDOW. FIND FENICE OURSELVES.
HUNTRESS IS RIGHT. MINUS THE WINDOW THING.
HE'S A PROFITEER AND AN ACCOMPLICE TO MURDER.
BABS?
GIVE ME A MINUTE.

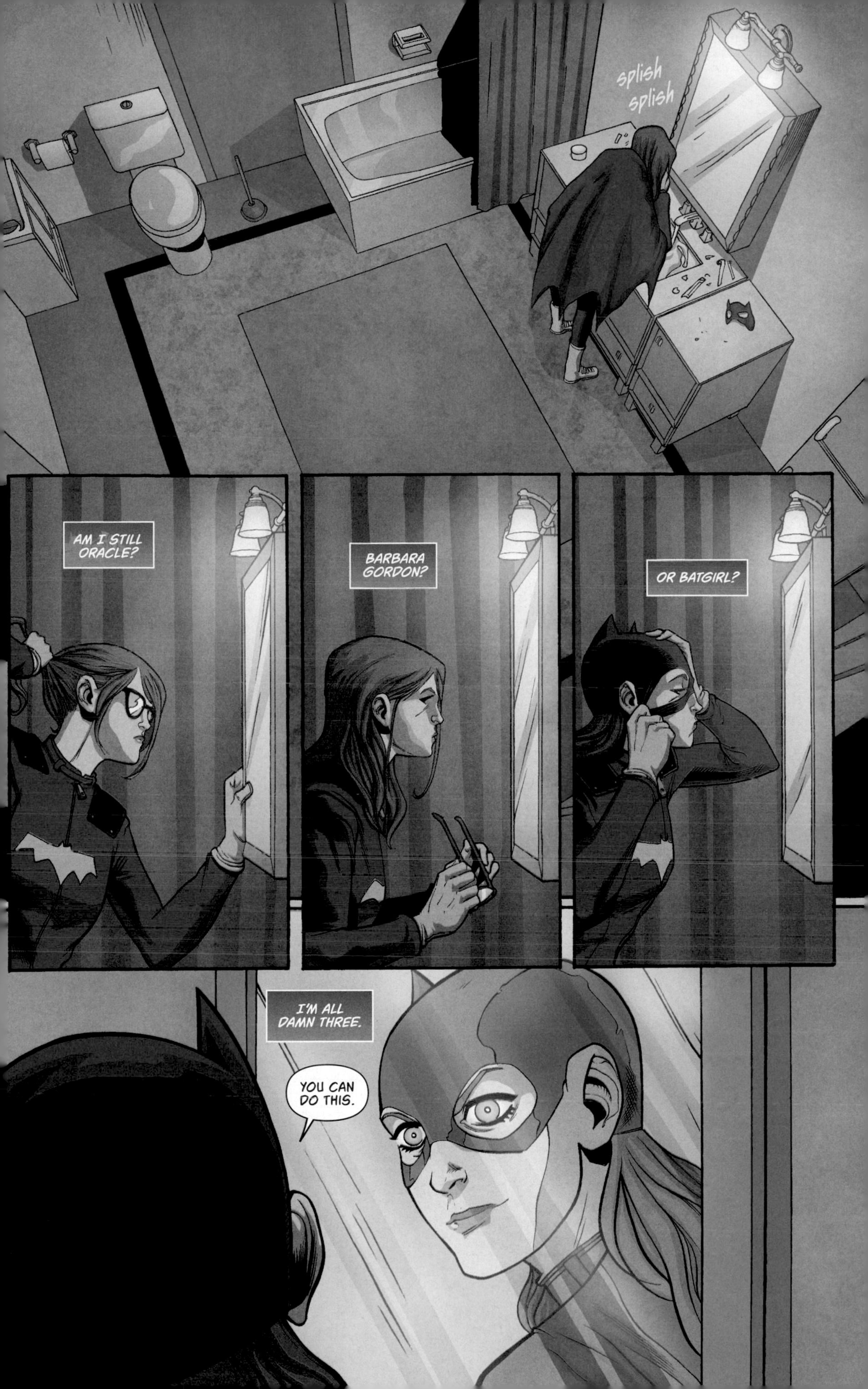
splish
splish
AM I STILL ORACLE?
BARBARA GORDON?
OR BATGIRL?
I'M ALL DAMN THREE.
YOU CAN DO THIS.

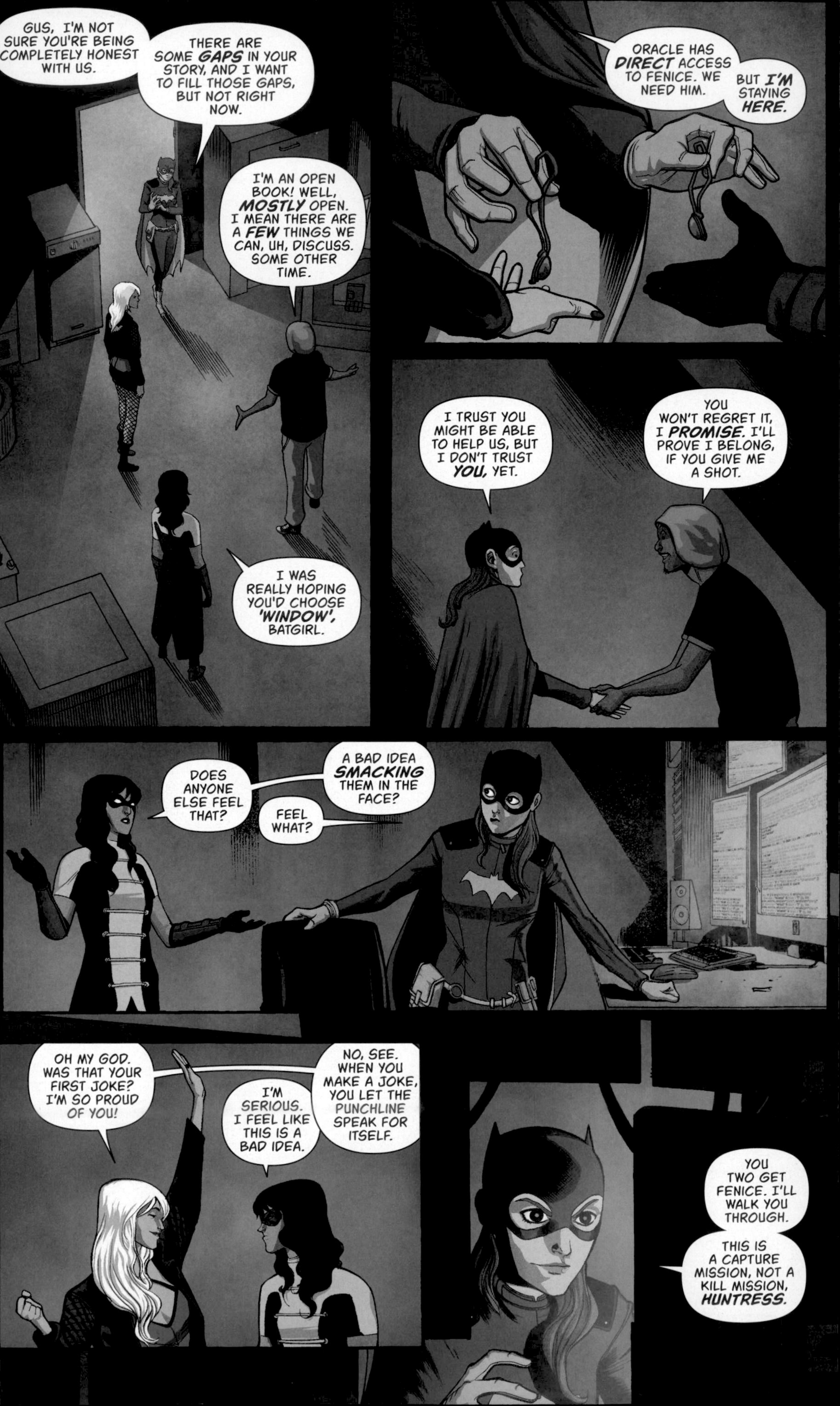

GUS, I'M NOT SURE YOU'RE BEING COMPLETELY HONEST WITH US.
THERE ARE SOME GAPS IN YOUR STORY, AND I WANT TO FILL THOSE GAPS, BUT NOT RIGHT NOW.
I'M AN OPEN BOOK! WELL, MOSTLY OPEN. I MEAN THERE ARE A FEW THINGS WE CAN, UH, DISCUSS. SOME OTHER TIME.
I WAS REALLY HOPING YOU'D CHOOSE 'WINDOW', BATGIRL.
ORACLE HAS DIRECT ACCESS TO FENICE. WE NEED HIM.
BUT I'M STAYING HERE.
I TRUST YOU MIGHT BE ABLE TO HELP US, BUT I DON'T TRUST YOU, YET.
YOU WON'T REGRET IT, I PROMISE. I'LL PROVE I BELONG, IF YOU GIVE ME A SHOT.
DOES ANYONE ELSE FEEL THAT?
FEEL WHAT?
A BAD IDEA SMACKING THEM IN THE FACE?
OH MY GOD. WAS THAT YOUR FIRST JOKE? I'M SO PROUD OF YOU!
I'M SERIOUS. I FEEL LIKE THIS IS A BAD IDEA.
NO, SEE. WHEN YOU MAKE A JOKE, YOU LET THE PUNCHLINE SPEAK FOR ITSELF.
YOU TWO GET FENICE. I'LL WALK YOU THROUGH.
THIS IS A CAPTURE MISSION, NOT A KILL MISSION, HUNTRESS.

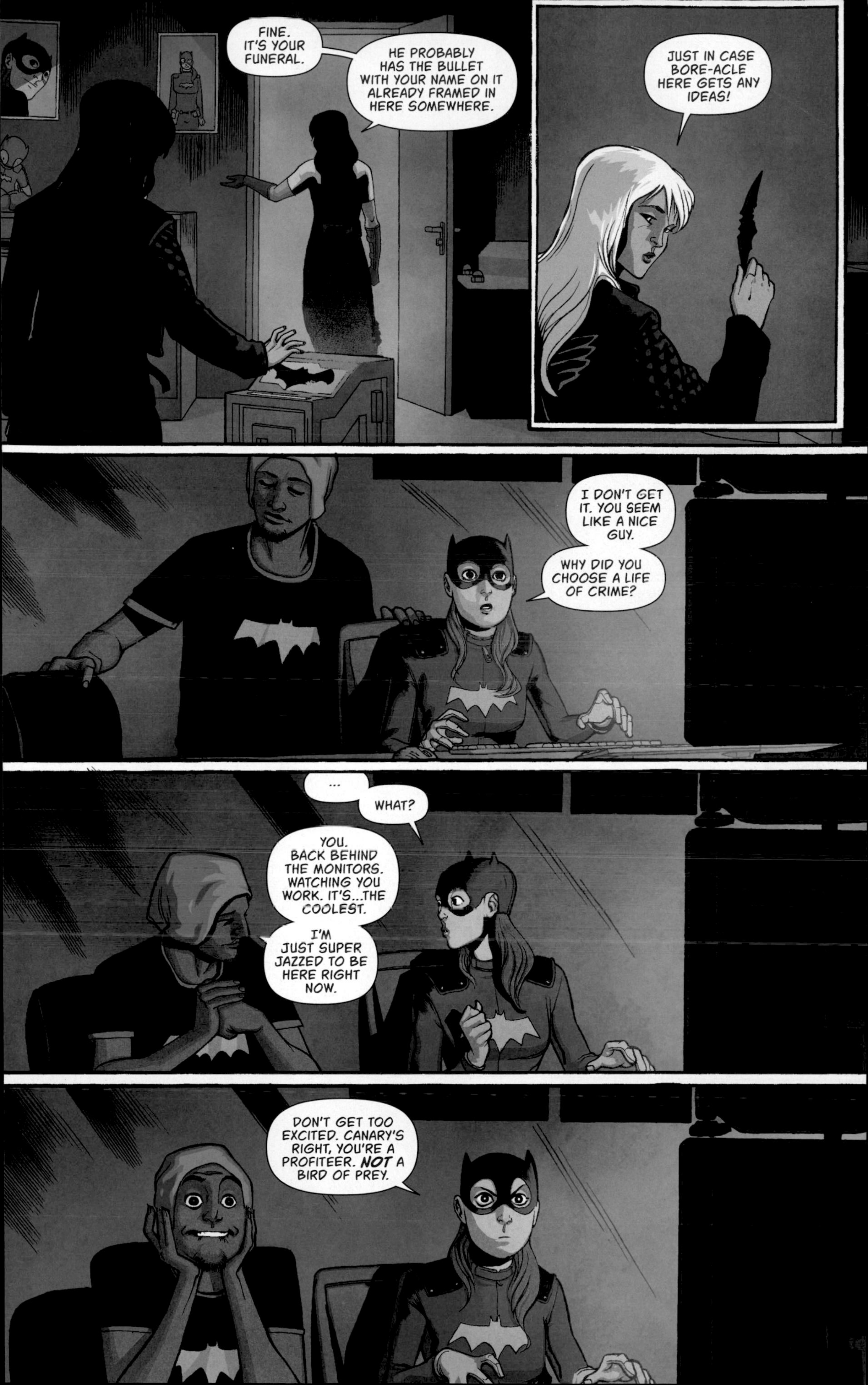
FINE. IT'S YOUR FUNERAL.
HE PROBABLY HAS THE BULLET WITH YOUR NAME ON IT ALREADY FRAMED IN HERE SOMEWHERE.
JUST IN CASE BORE-ACLE HERE GETS ANY IDEAS!
I DON'T GET IT. YOU SEEM LIKE A NICE GUY.
WHY DID YOU CHOOSE A LIFE OF CRIME?
...
WHAT?
YOU. BACK BEHIND THE MONITORS. WATCHING YOU WORK. IT'S...THE COOLEST.
I'M JUST SUPER JAZZED TO BE HERE RIGHT NOW.
DON'T GET TOO EXCITED. CANARY'S RIGHT, YOU'RE A PROFITEER. NOT A BIRD OF PREY.

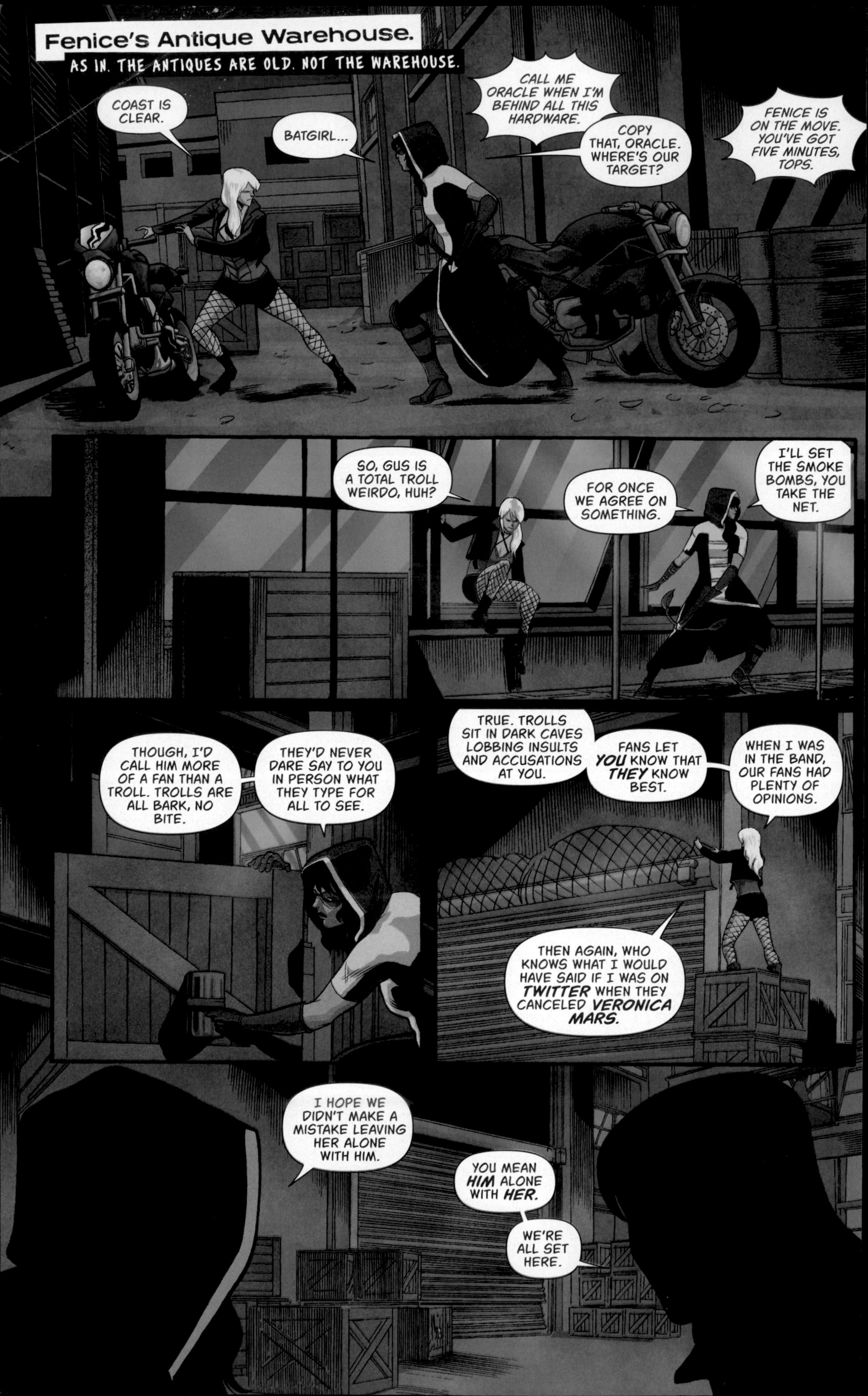
Fenice's Antique Warehouse.
AS IN. THE ANTIQUES ARE OLD. NOT THE WAREHOUSE.
COAST IS CLEAR.
BATGIRL...
CALL ME ORACLE WHEN I'M BEHIND ALL THIS HARDWARE.
COPY THAT, ORACLE. WHERE'S OUR TARGET?
FENICE IS ON THE MOVE. YOU'VE GOT FIVE MINUTES, TOPS.
SO, GUS IS A TOTAL TROLL WEIRDO, HUH?
FOR ONCE WE AGREE ON SOMETHING.
I'LL SET THE SMOKE BOMBS, YOU TAKE THE NET.
THOUGH, I'D CALL HIM MORE OF A FAN THAN A TROLL. TROLLS ARE ALL BARK, NO BITE.
THEY'D NEVER DARE SAY TO YOU IN PERSON WHAT THEY TYPE FOR ALL TO SEE.
TRUE. TROLLS SIT IN DARK CAVES LOBBING INSULTS AND ACCUSATIONS AT YOU.
FANS LET YOU KNOW THAT THEY KNOW BEST.
WHEN I WAS IN THE BAND, OUR FANS HAD PLENTY OF OPINIONS.
THEN AGAIN, WHO KNOWS WHAT I WOULD HAVE SAID IF I WAS ON TWITTER WHEN THEY CANCELED VERONICA MARS.
I HOPE WE DIDN'T MAKE A MISTAKE LEAVING HER ALONE WITH HIM.
YOU MEAN HIM ALONE WITH HER.
WE'RE ALL SET HERE.

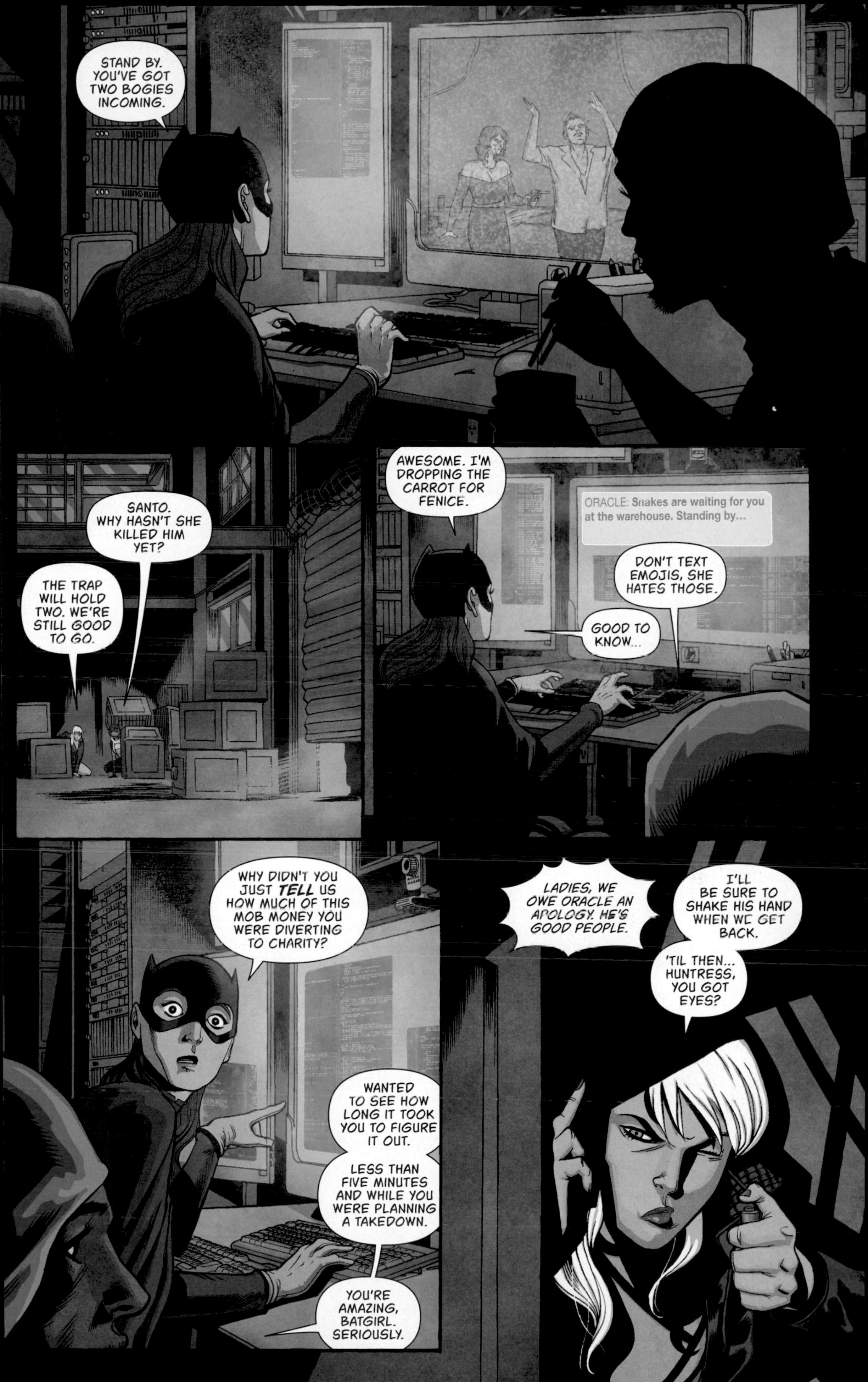
STAND BY. YOU'VE GOT TWO BOGIES INCOMING.
SANTO. WHY HASN'T SHE KILLED HIM YET?
THE TRAP WILL HOLD TWO. WE'RE STILL GOOD TO GO.
AWESOME. I'M DROPPING THE CARROT FOR FENICE.
ORACLE: Snakes are waiting for you at the warehouse. Standing by...
DON'T TEXT EMOJIS, SHE HATES THOSE.
GOOD TO KNOW...
WHY DIDN'T YOU JUST TELL US HOW MUCH OF THIS MOB MONEY YOU WERE DIVERTING TO CHARITY?
WANTED TO SEE HOW LONG IT TOOK YOU TO FIGURE IT OUT.
LESS THAN FIVE MINUTES AND WHILE YOU WERE PLANNING A TAKEDOWN.
YOU'RE AMAZING, BATGIRL. SERIOUSLY.
LADIES, WE OWE ORACLE AN APOLOGY. HE'S GOOD PEOPLE.
I'LL BE SURE TO SHAKE HIS HAND WHEN WE GET BACK.
'TIL THEN... HUNTRESS, YOU GOT EYES?

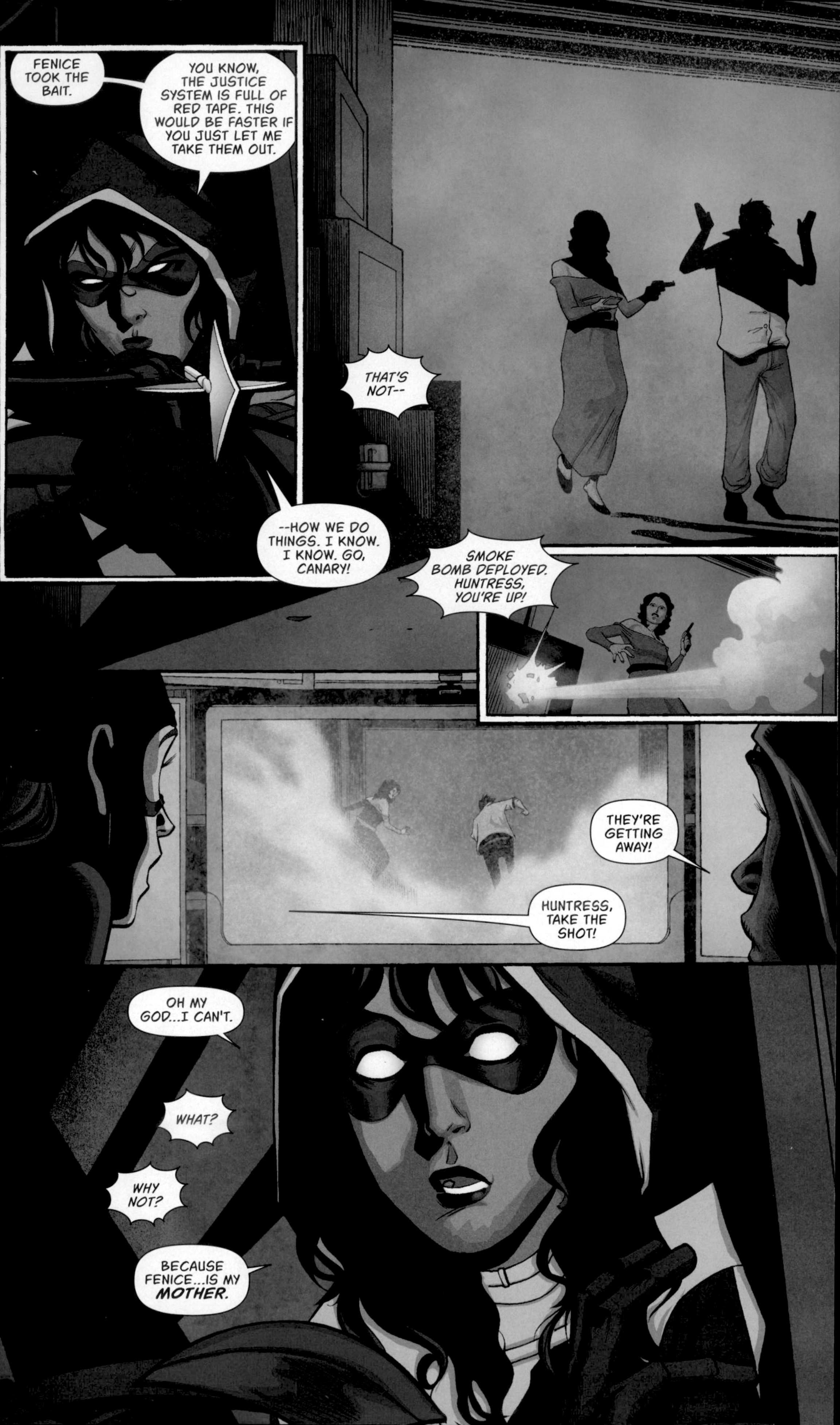
FENICE TOOK THE BAIT.
YOU KNOW, THE JUSTICE SYSTEM IS FULL OF RED TAPE. THIS WOULD BE FASTER IF YOU JUST LET ME TAKE THEM OUT.
THAT'S NOT--
--HOW WE DO THINGS. I KNOW. I KNOW. GO, CANARY!
SMOKE BOMB DEPLOYED. HUNTRESS, YOU'RE UP!
THEY'RE GETTING AWAY!
HUNTRESS, TAKE THE SHOT!
OH MY GOD...I CAN'T.
WHAT?
WHY NOT?
BECAUSE FENICE...IS MY MOTHER.

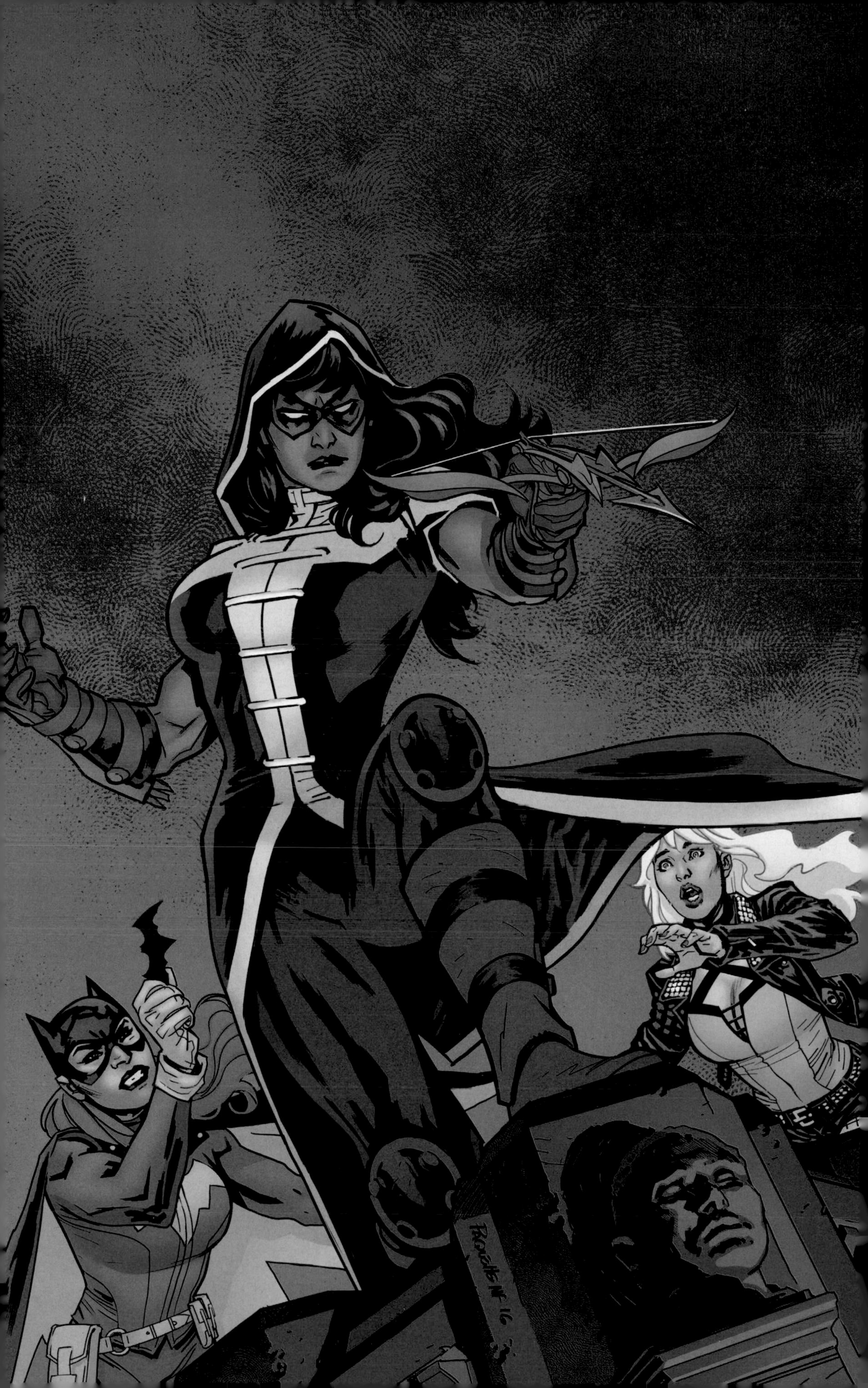

FINALE: ARISE

JULIE and SHAWNA BENSON writers * ROGE ANTONIO artist
ALLEN PASSALAQUA colorist * DERON BENNETT letterer

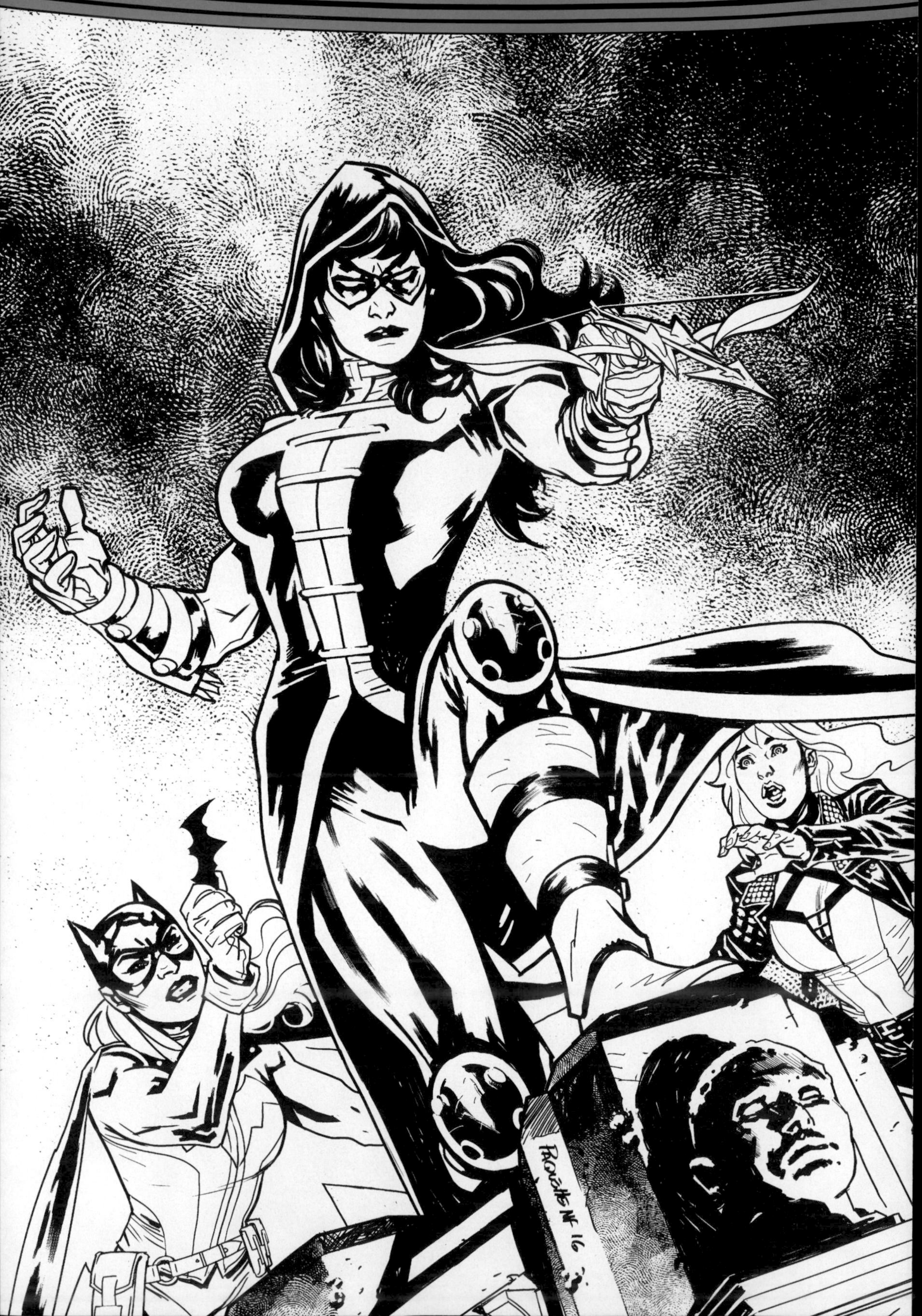

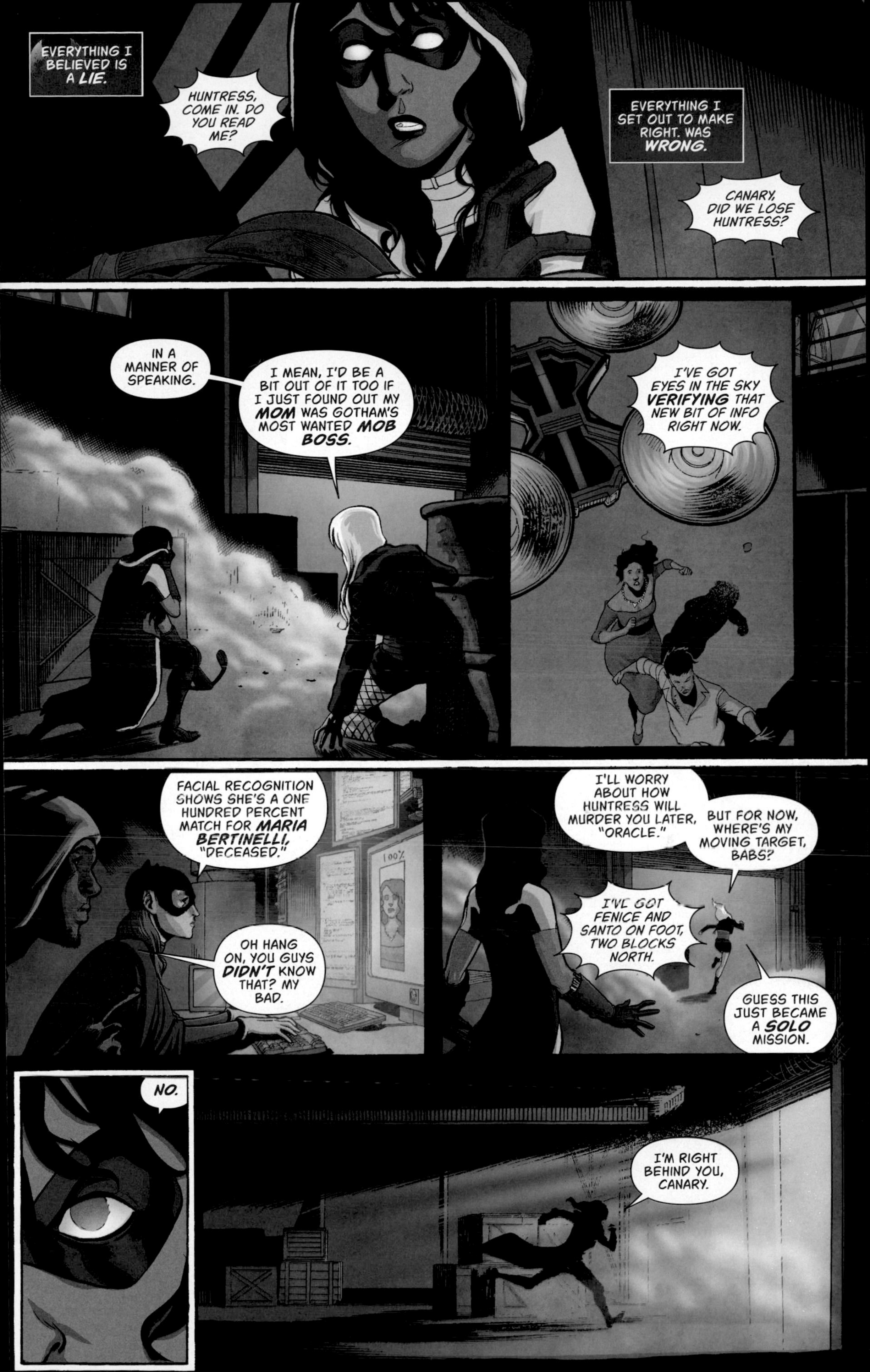
EVERYTHING I BELIEVED IS A LIE.
HUNTRESS, COME IN. DO YOU READ ME?
EVERYTHING I SET OUT TO MAKE RIGHT. WAS WRONG.
CANARY, DID WE LOSE HUNTRESS?
IN A MANNER OF SPEAKING.
I MEAN, I'D BE A BIT OUT OF IT TOO IF I JUST FOUND OUT MY MOM WAS GOTHAM'S MOST WANTED MOB BOSS.
I'VE GOT EYES IN THE SKY VERIFYING THAT NEW BIT OF INFO RIGHT NOW.
FACIAL RECOGNITION SHOWS SHE'S A ONE HUNDRED PERCENT MATCH FOR MARIA BERTINELLI, "DECEASED."
100%
OH HANG ON, YOU GUYS DIDN'T KNOW THAT? MY BAD.
I'LL WORRY ABOUT HOW HUNTRESS WILL MURDER YOU LATER, "ORACLE."
BUT FOR NOW, WHERE'S MY MOVING TARGET, BABS?
I'VE GOT FENICE AND SANTO ON FOOT, TWO BLOCKS NORTH.
GUESS THIS JUST BECAME A SOLO MISSION.
NO.
I'M RIGHT BEHIND YOU, CANARY.

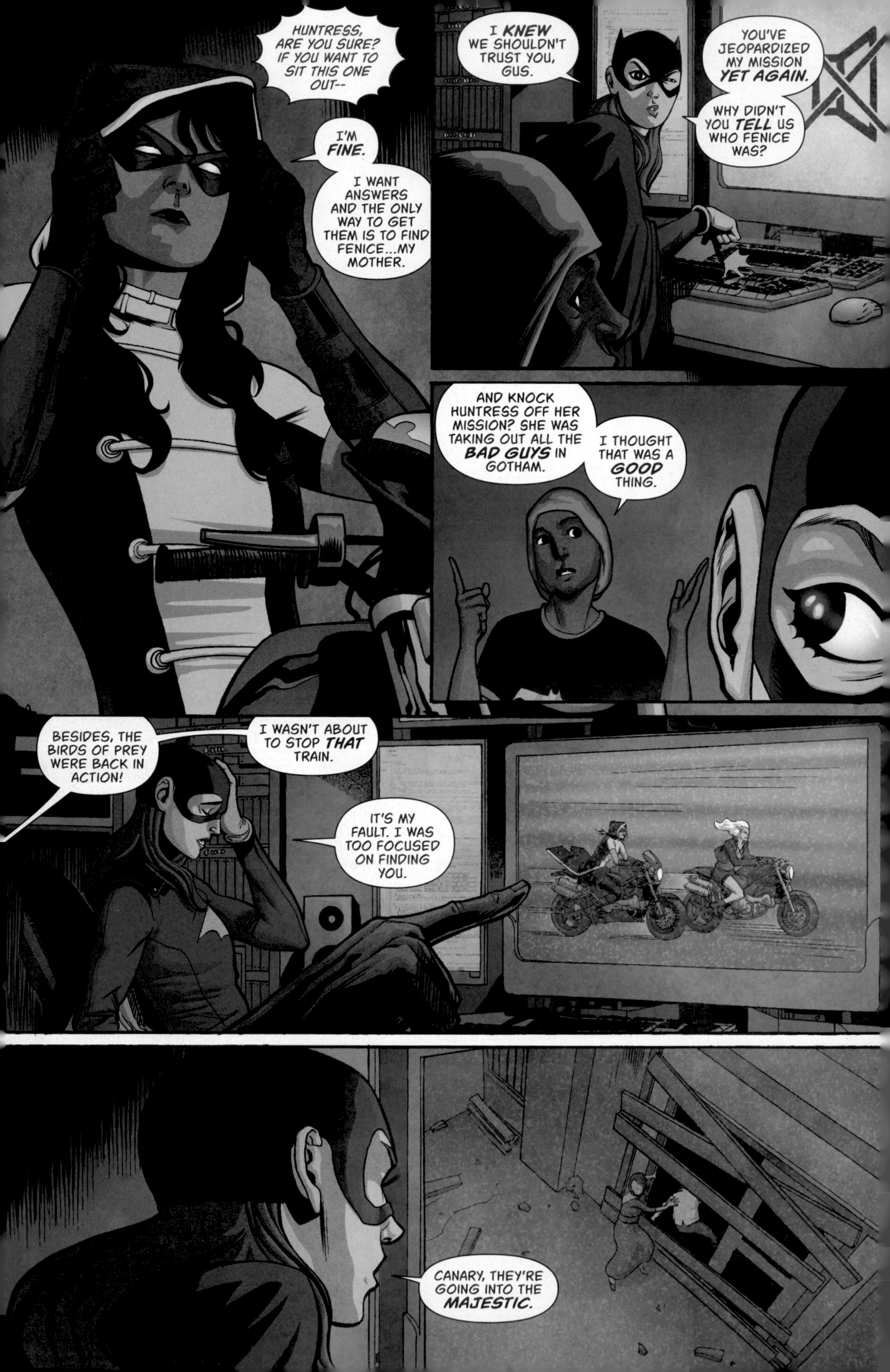
HUNTRESS, ARE YOU SURE? IF YOU WANT TO SIT THIS ONE OUT--
I'M FINE.
I WANT ANSWERS AND THE ONLY WAY TO GET THEM IS TO FIND FENICE...MY MOTHER.
I KNEW WE SHOULDN'T TRUST YOU, GUS.
YOU'VE JEOPARDIZED MY MISSION YET AGAIN.
WHY DIDN'T YOU TELL US WHO FENICE WAS?
AND KNOCK HUNTRESS OFF HER MISSION? SHE WAS TAKING OUT ALL THE BAD GUYS IN GOTHAM.
I THOUGHT THAT WAS A GOOD THING.
BESIDES, THE BIRDS OF PREY WERE BACK IN ACTION!
I WASN'T ABOUT TO STOP THAT TRAIN.
IT'S MY FAULT. I WAS TOO FOCUSED ON FINDING YOU.
CANARY, THEY'RE GOING INTO THE MAJESTIC.

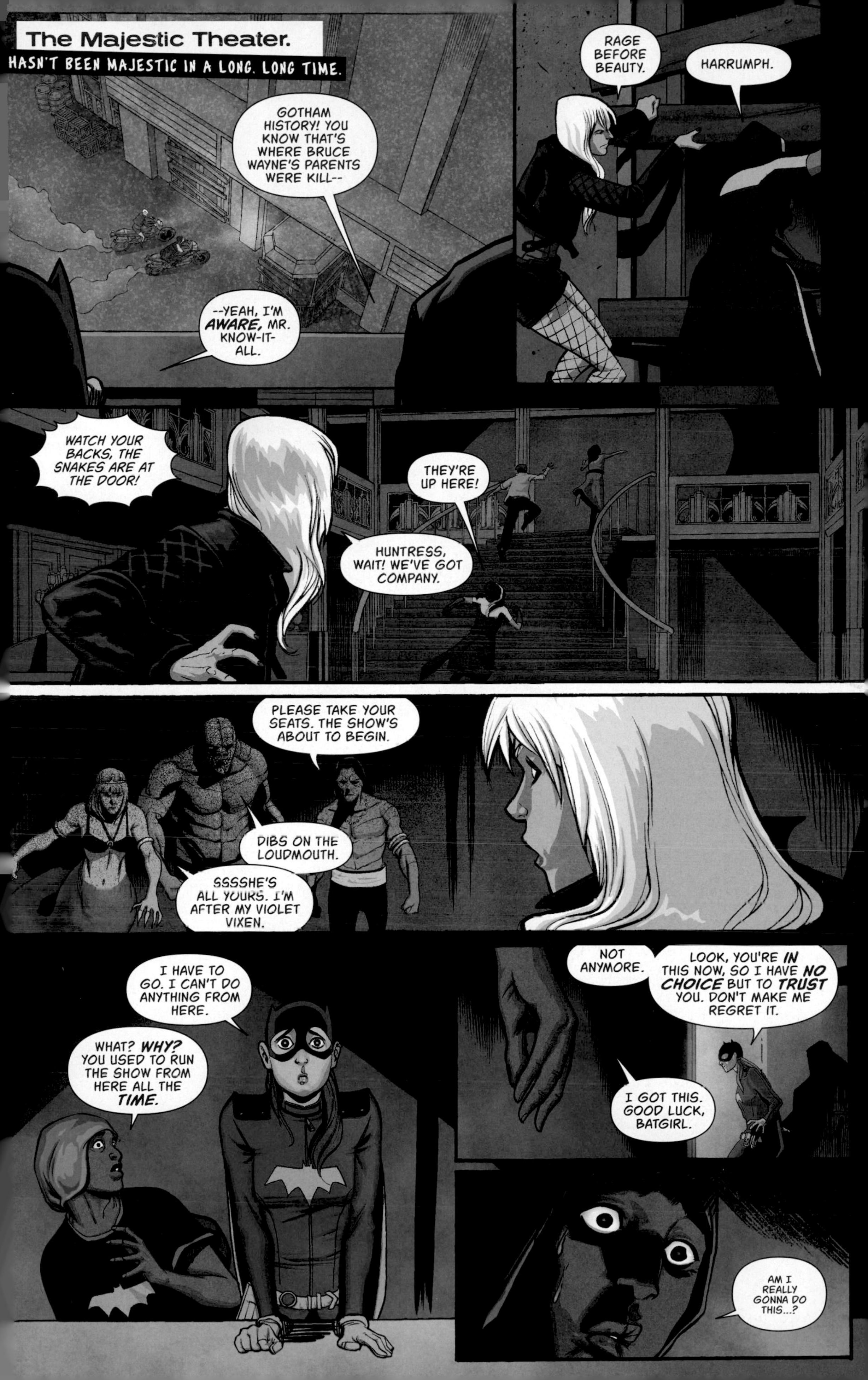
The Majestic Theater.
HASN'T BEEN MAJESTIC IN A LONG. LONG TIME.
GOTHAM HISTORY! YOU KNOW THAT'S WHERE BRUCE WAYNE'S PARENTS WERE KILL--
--YEAH, I'M AWARE, MR. KNOW-IT-ALL.
RAGE BEFORE BEAUTY.
HARRUMPH.
WATCH YOUR BACKS, THE SNAKES ARE AT THE DOOR!
THEY'RE UP HERE!
HUNTRESS, WAIT! WE'VE GOT COMPANY.
PLEASE TAKE YOUR SEATS. THE SHOW'S ABOUT TO BEGIN.
DIBS ON THE LOUDMOUTH.
SSSSHE'S ALL YOURS. I'M AFTER MY VIOLET VIXEN.
I HAVE TO GO. I CAN'T DO ANYTHING FROM HERE.
WHAT? WHY? YOU USED TO RUN THE SHOW FROM HERE ALL THE TIME.
NOT ANYMORE.
LOOK, YOU'RE IN THIS NOW, SO I HAVE NO CHOICE BUT TO TRUST YOU. DON'T MAKE ME REGRET IT.
I GOT THIS. GOOD LUCK, BATGIRL.
AM I REALLY GONNA DO THIS...?

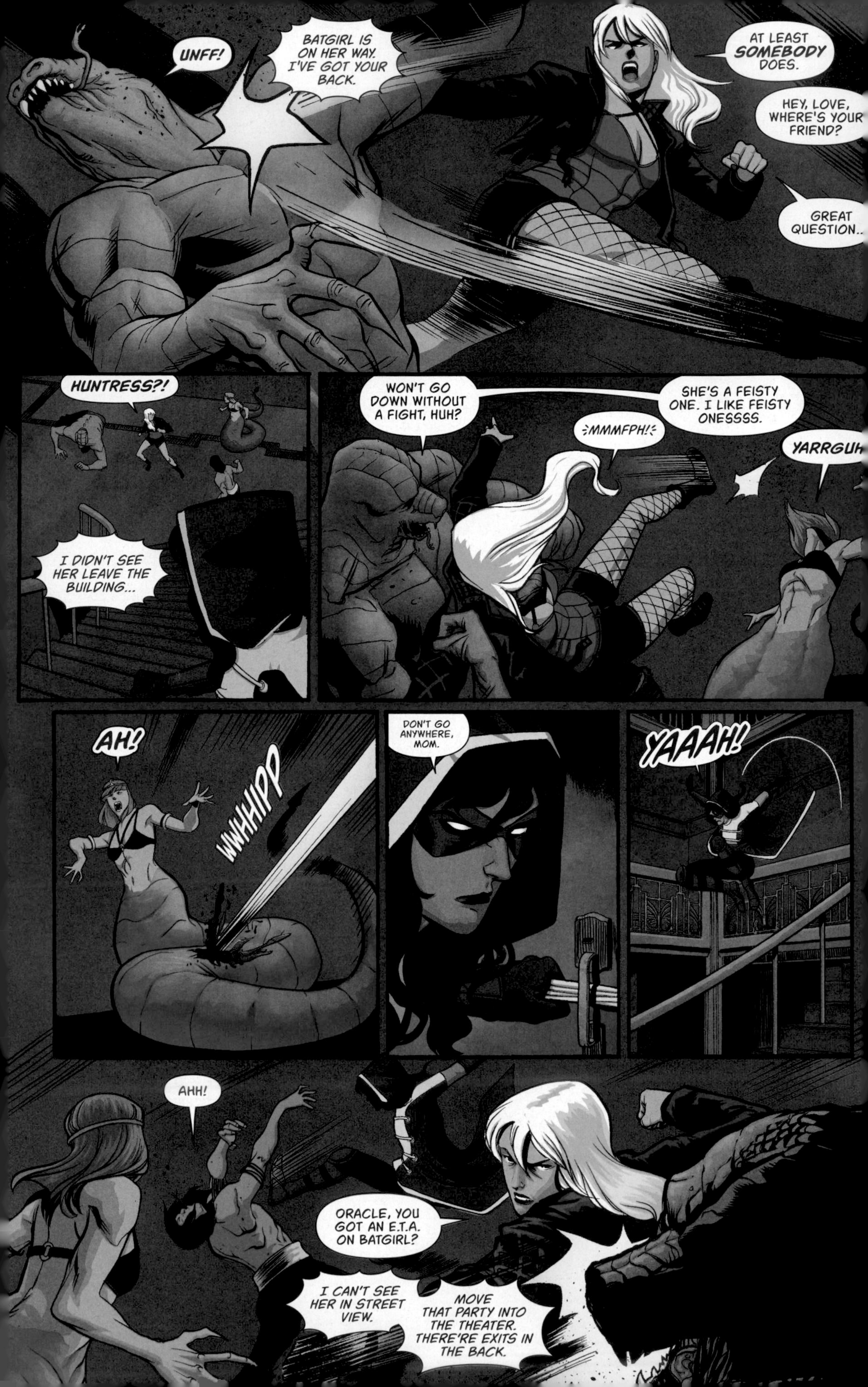
UNFF!
BATGIRL IS ON HER WAY. I'VE GOT YOUR BACK.
AT LEAST SOMEBODY DOES.
HEY, LOVE, WHERE'S YOUR FRIEND?
GREAT QUESTION...
HUNTRESS?!
I DIDN'T SEE HER LEAVE THE BUILDING...
WON'T GO DOWN WITHOUT A FIGHT, HUH?
SHE'S A FEISTY ONE. I LIKE FEISTY ONESSSS.
MMMFPH!
YARRGUH
AH!
WWHIPP
DON'T GO ANYWHERE, MOM.
YAAAH!
AHH!
ORACLE, YOU GOT AN E.T.A. ON BATGIRL?
I CAN'T SEE HER IN STREET VIEW.
MOVE THAT PARTY INTO THE THEATER. THERE'RE EXITS IN THE BACK.

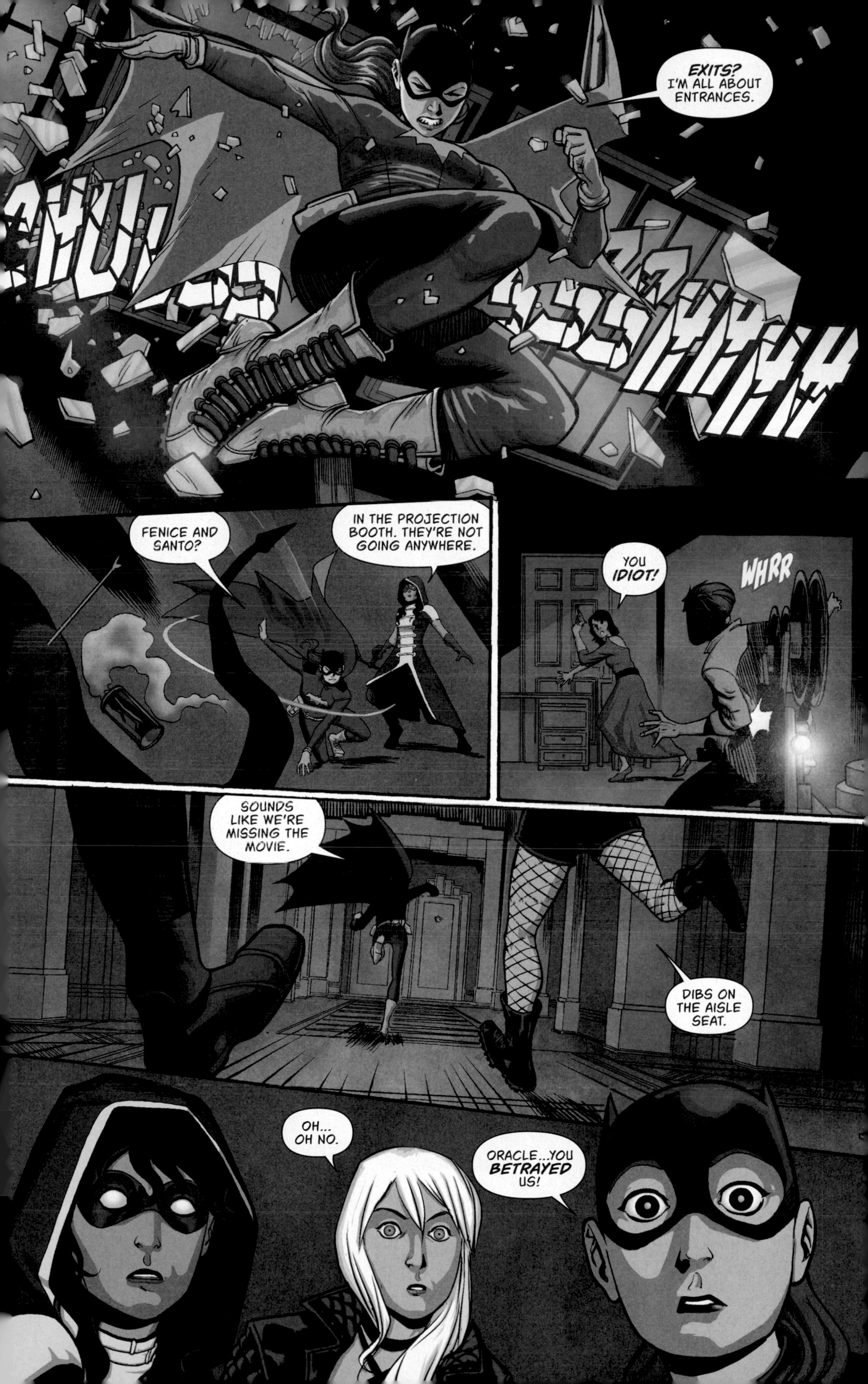
EXITS? I'M ALL ABOUT ENTRANCES.
FENICE AND SANTO?
IN THE PROJECTION BOOTH. THEY'RE NOT GOING ANYWHERE.
YOU IDIOT!
WHRR
SOUNDS LIKE WE'RE MISSING THE MOVIE.
DIBS ON THE AISLE SEAT.
OH... OH NO.
ORACLE...YOU BETRAYED US!

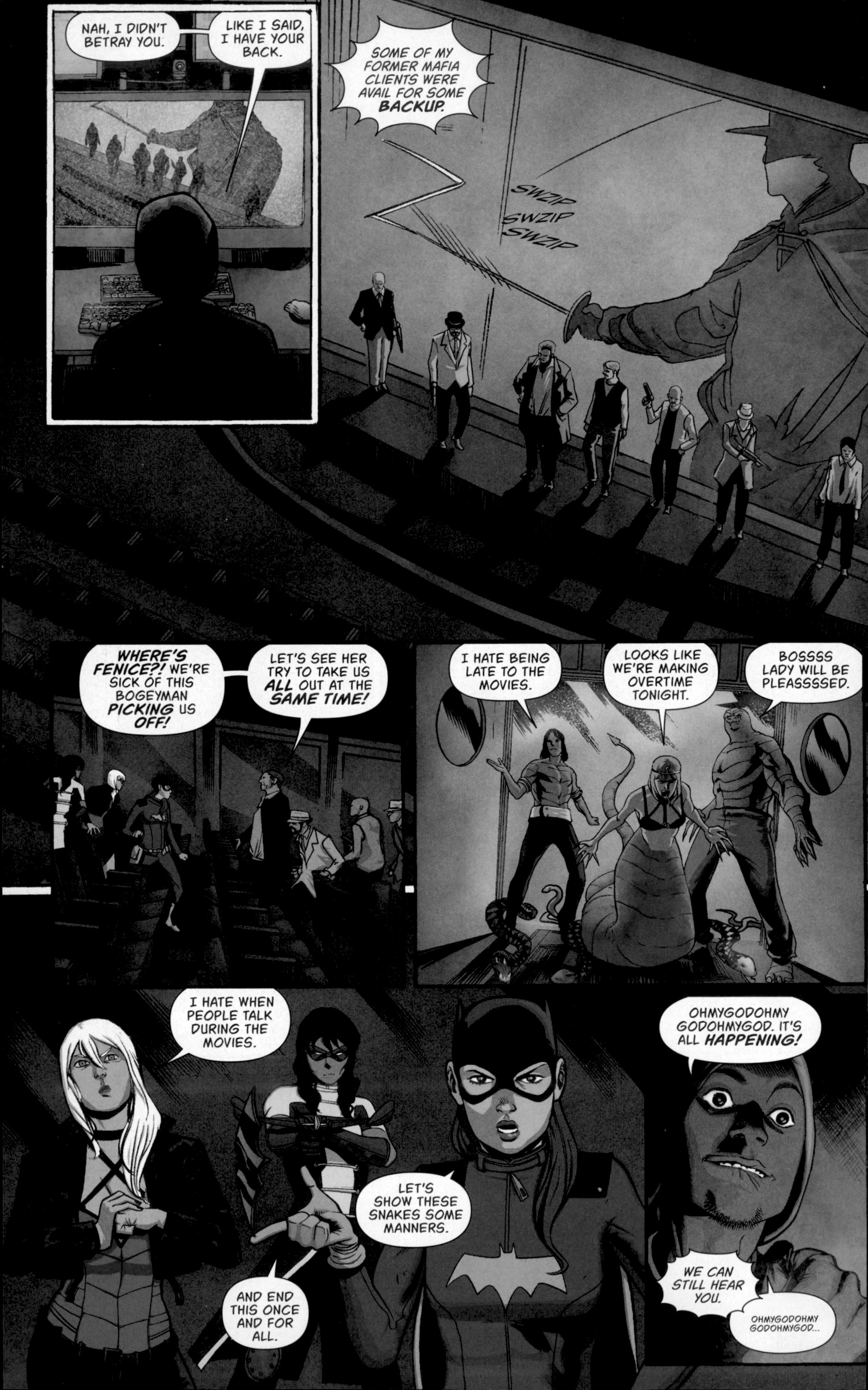
NAH, I DIDN'T BETRAY YOU.
LIKE I SAID, I HAVE YOUR BACK.
SOME OF MY FORMER MAFIA CLIENTS WERE AVAIL FOR SOME BACKUP.
SWZIP
SWZIP
SWZIP
WHERE'S FENICE?! WE'RE SICK OF THIS BOGEYMAN PICKING US OFF!
LET'S SEE HER TRY TO TAKE US ALL OUT AT THE SAME TIME!
I HATE BEING LATE TO THE MOVIES.
LOOKS LIKE WE'RE MAKING OVERTIME TONIGHT.
BOSSSS LADY WILL BE PLEASSSSED.
I HATE WHEN PEOPLE TALK DURING THE MOVIES.
OHMYGODOHMY GODOHMYGOD. IT'S ALL HAPPENING!
LET'S SHOW THESE SNAKES SOME MANNERS.
AND END THIS ONCE AND FOR ALL.
WE CAN STILL HEAR YOU.
OHMYGODOHMY GODOHMYGOD...

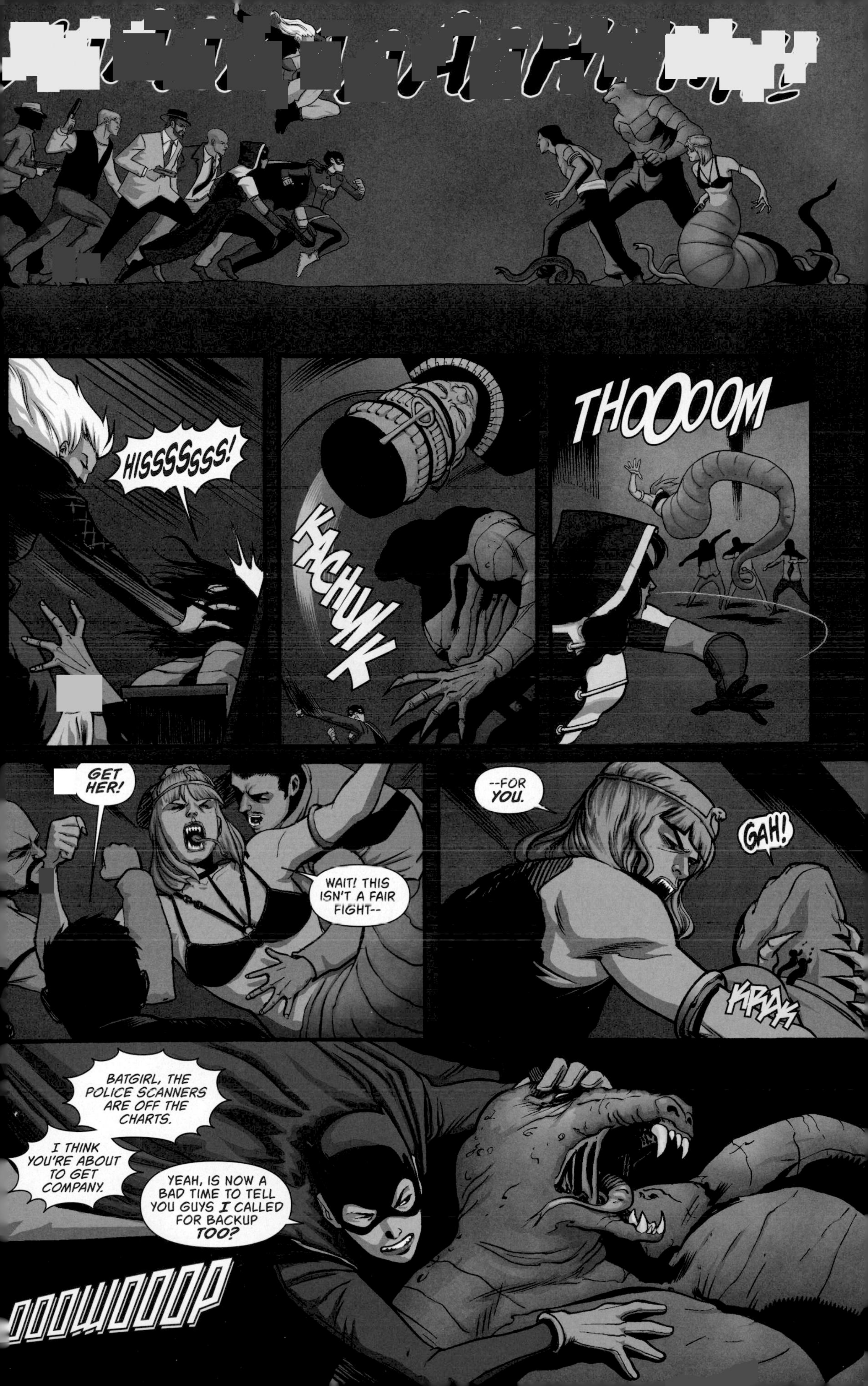
[redacted]
HISSSSsss!
KACHUNK
THOOOOM
GET HER!
WAIT! THIS ISN'T A FAIR FIGHT--
--FOR YOU.
GAH!
KRAK
BATGIRL, THE POLICE SCANNERS ARE OFF THE CHARTS.
I THINK YOU'RE ABOUT TO GET COMPANY.
YEAH, IS NOW A BAD TIME TO TELL YOU GUYS I CALLED FOR BACKUP TOO?
OOOWOOOP

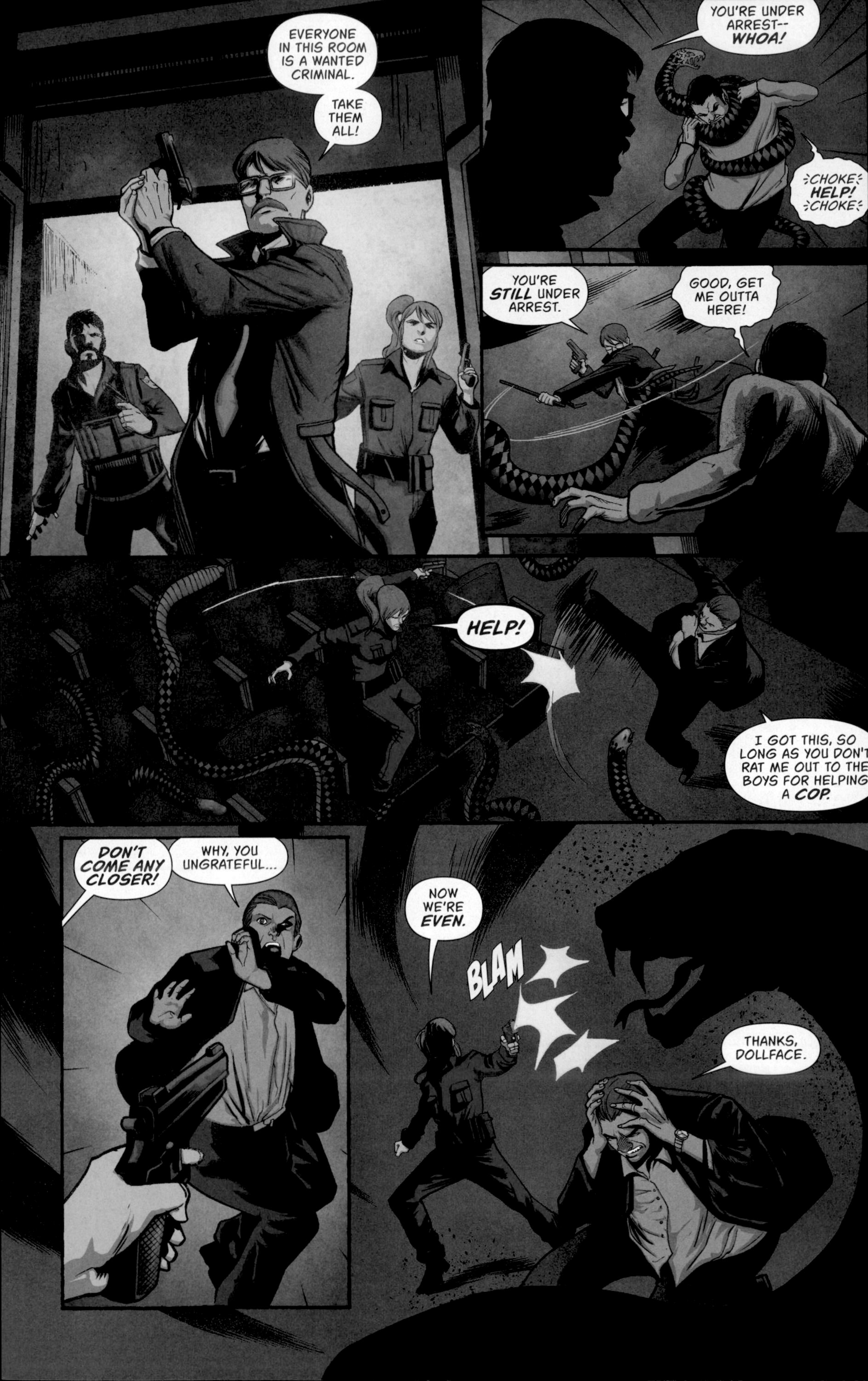

EVERYONE IN THIS ROOM IS A WANTED CRIMINAL.
TAKE THEM ALL!
YOU'RE UNDER ARREST-- **WHOA!**
CHOKE **HELP!** CHOKE
YOU'RE **STILL** UNDER ARREST.
GOOD, GET ME OUTTA HERE!
HELP!
I GOT THIS, SO LONG AS YOU DON'T RAT ME OUT TO THE BOYS FOR HELPING A **COP.**
DON'T COME ANY CLOSER!
WHY, YOU UNGRATEFUL...
NOW WE'RE **EVEN.**
BLAM
THANKS, DOLLFACE.

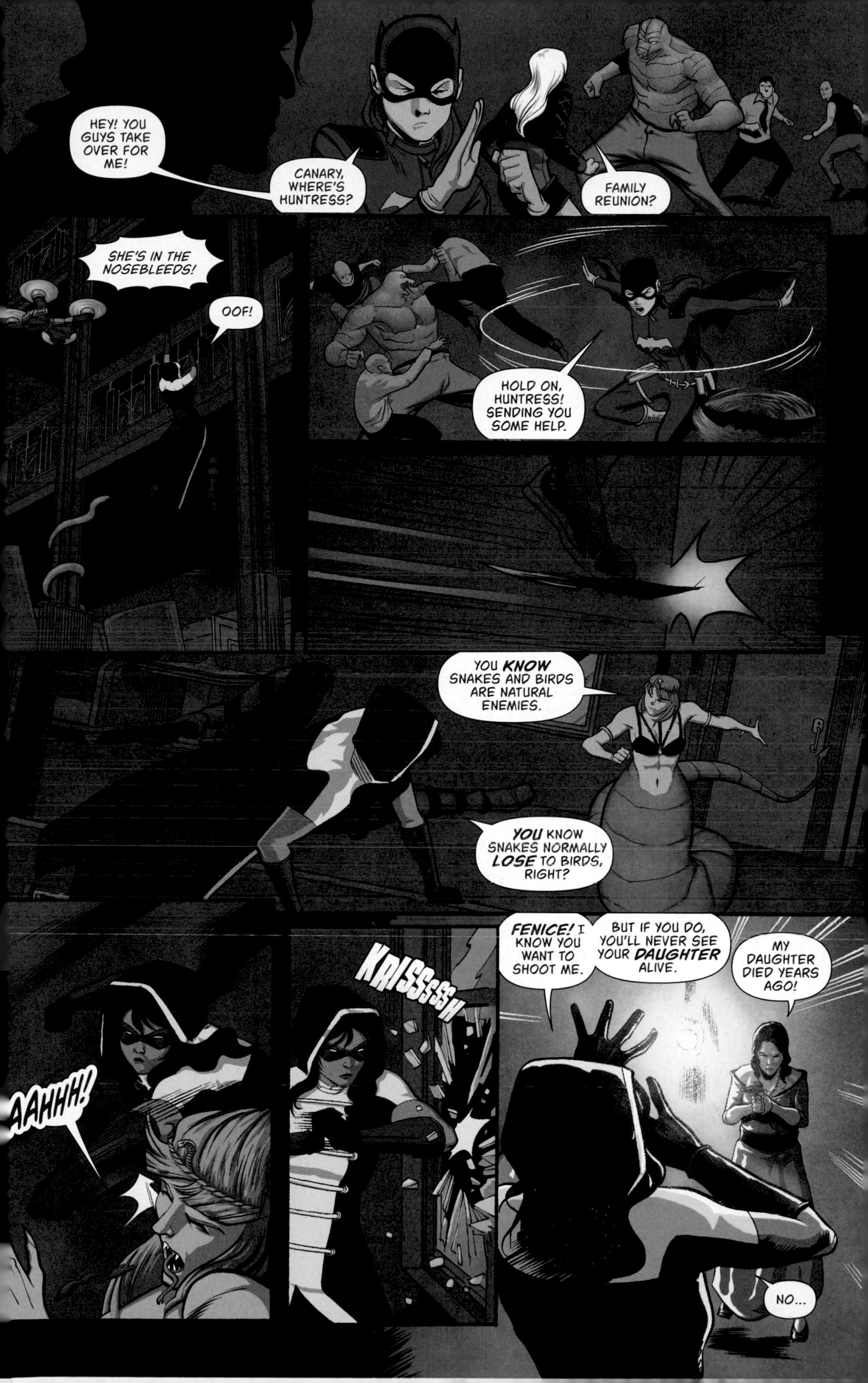
HEY! YOU GUYS TAKE OVER FOR ME!
CANARY, WHERE'S HUNTRESS?
FAMILY REUNION?
SHE'S IN THE NOSEBLEEDS!
OOF!
HOLD ON, HUNTRESS! SENDING YOU SOME HELP.
YOU KNOW SNAKES AND BIRDS ARE NATURAL ENEMIES.
YOU KNOW SNAKES NORMALLY LOSE TO BIRDS, RIGHT?
AAHHH!
KRISSSSSH
FENICE! I KNOW YOU WANT TO SHOOT ME.
BUT IF YOU DO, YOU'LL NEVER SEE YOUR DAUGHTER ALIVE.
MY DAUGHTER DIED YEARS AGO!
NO...

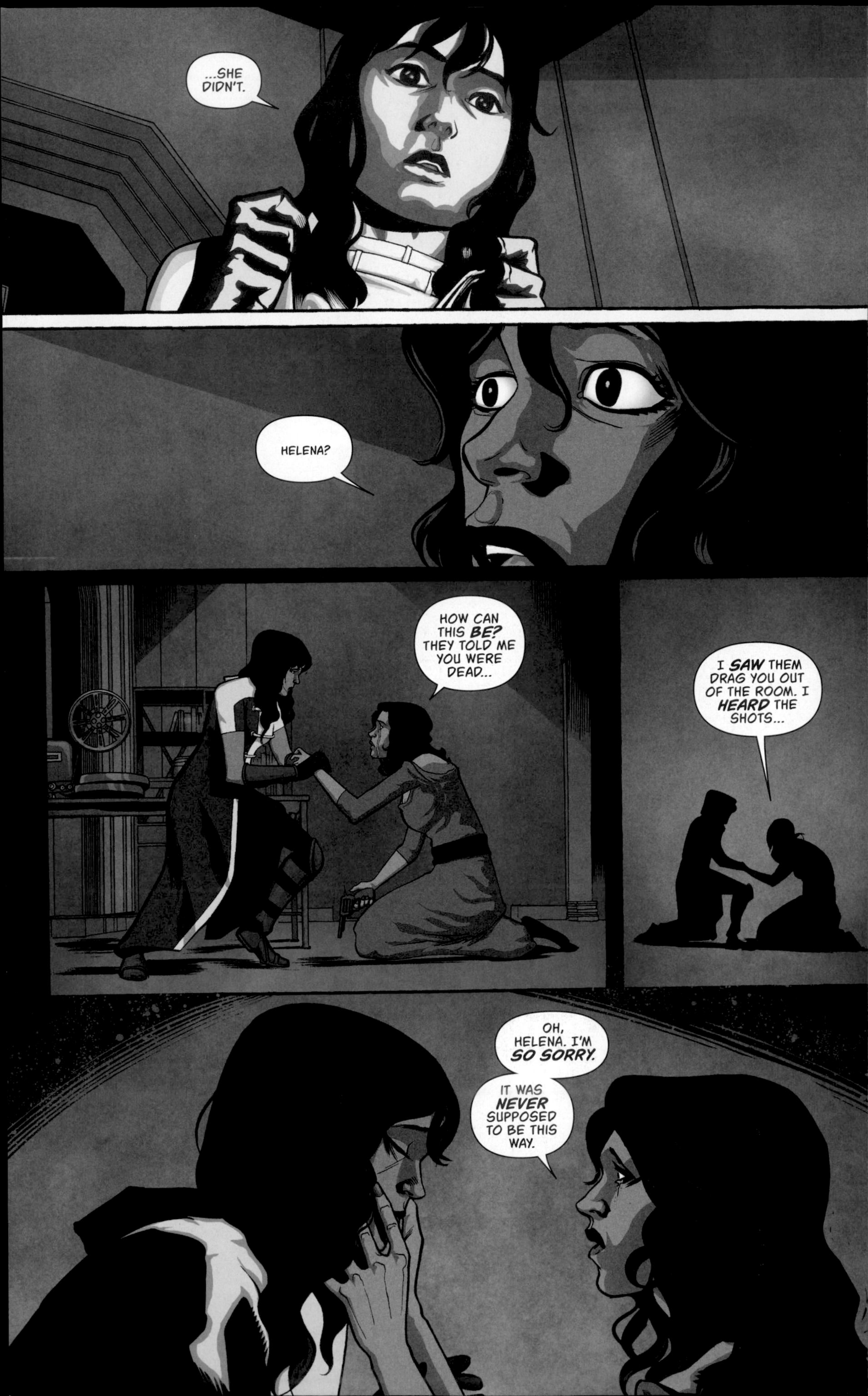
...SHE DIDN'T.
HELENA?
HOW CAN THIS **BE?** THEY TOLD ME YOU WERE DEAD...
I **SAW** THEM DRAG YOU OUT OF THE ROOM. I **HEARD** THE SHOTS...
OH, HELENA. I'M **SO SORRY.**
IT WAS **NEVER** SUPPOSED TO BE THIS WAY.

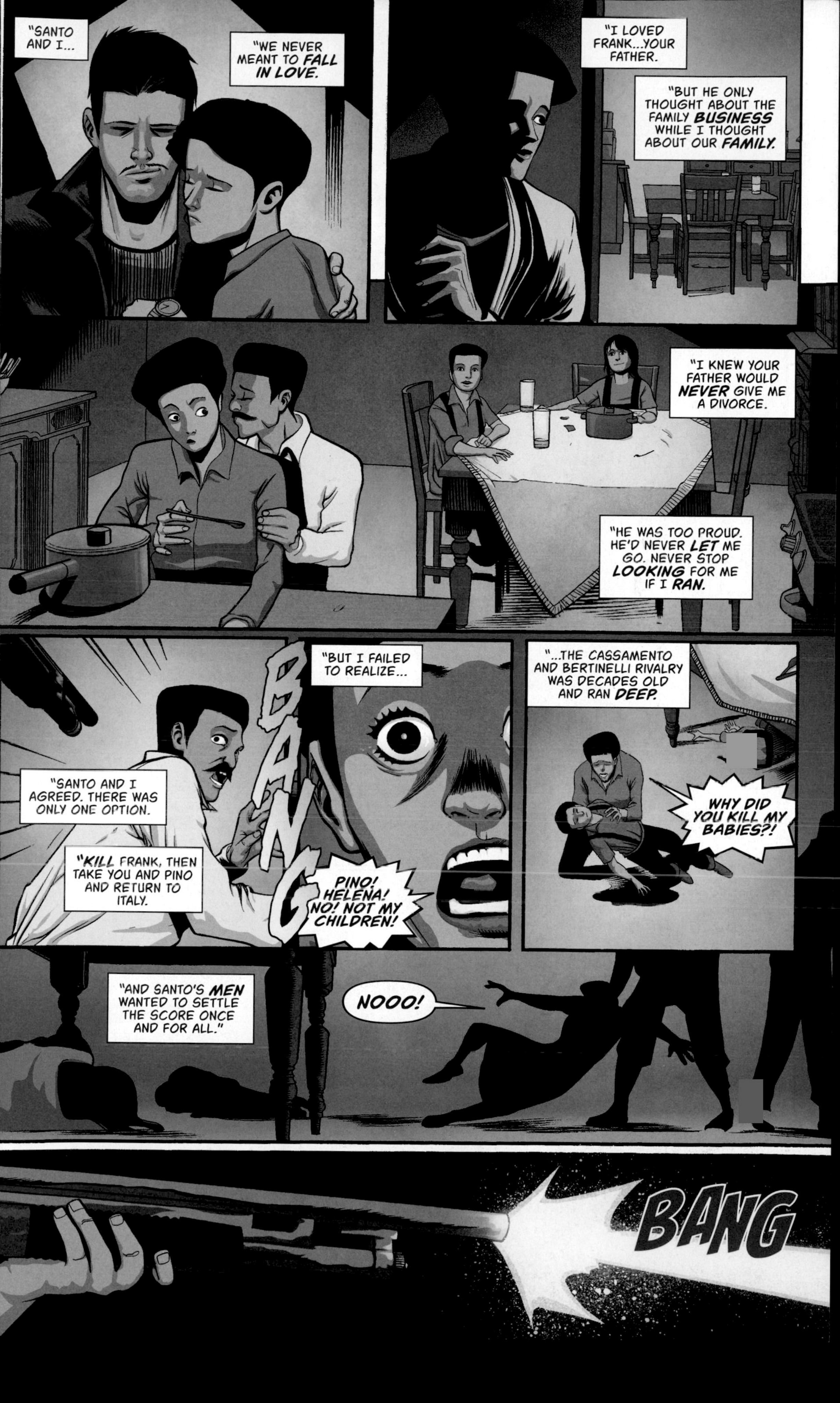
"SANTO AND I...
"WE NEVER MEANT TO FALL IN LOVE.
"I LOVED FRANK...YOUR FATHER.
"BUT HE ONLY THOUGHT ABOUT THE FAMILY BUSINESS WHILE I THOUGHT ABOUT OUR FAMILY.
"I KNEW YOUR FATHER WOULD NEVER GIVE ME A DIVORCE.
"HE WAS TOO PROUD. HE'D NEVER LET ME GO. NEVER STOP LOOKING FOR ME IF I RAN.
"SANTO AND I AGREED. THERE WAS ONLY ONE OPTION.
"KILL FRANK, THEN TAKE YOU AND PINO AND RETURN TO ITALY.
BANG
"BUT I FAILED TO REALIZE...
PINO! HELENA! NO! NOT MY CHILDREN!
"...THE CASSAMENTO AND BERTINELLI RIVALRY WAS DECADES OLD AND RAN DEEP.
WHY DID YOU KILL MY BABIES?!
"AND SANTO'S MEN WANTED TO SETTLE THE SCORE ONCE AND FOR ALL."
NOOO!
BANG

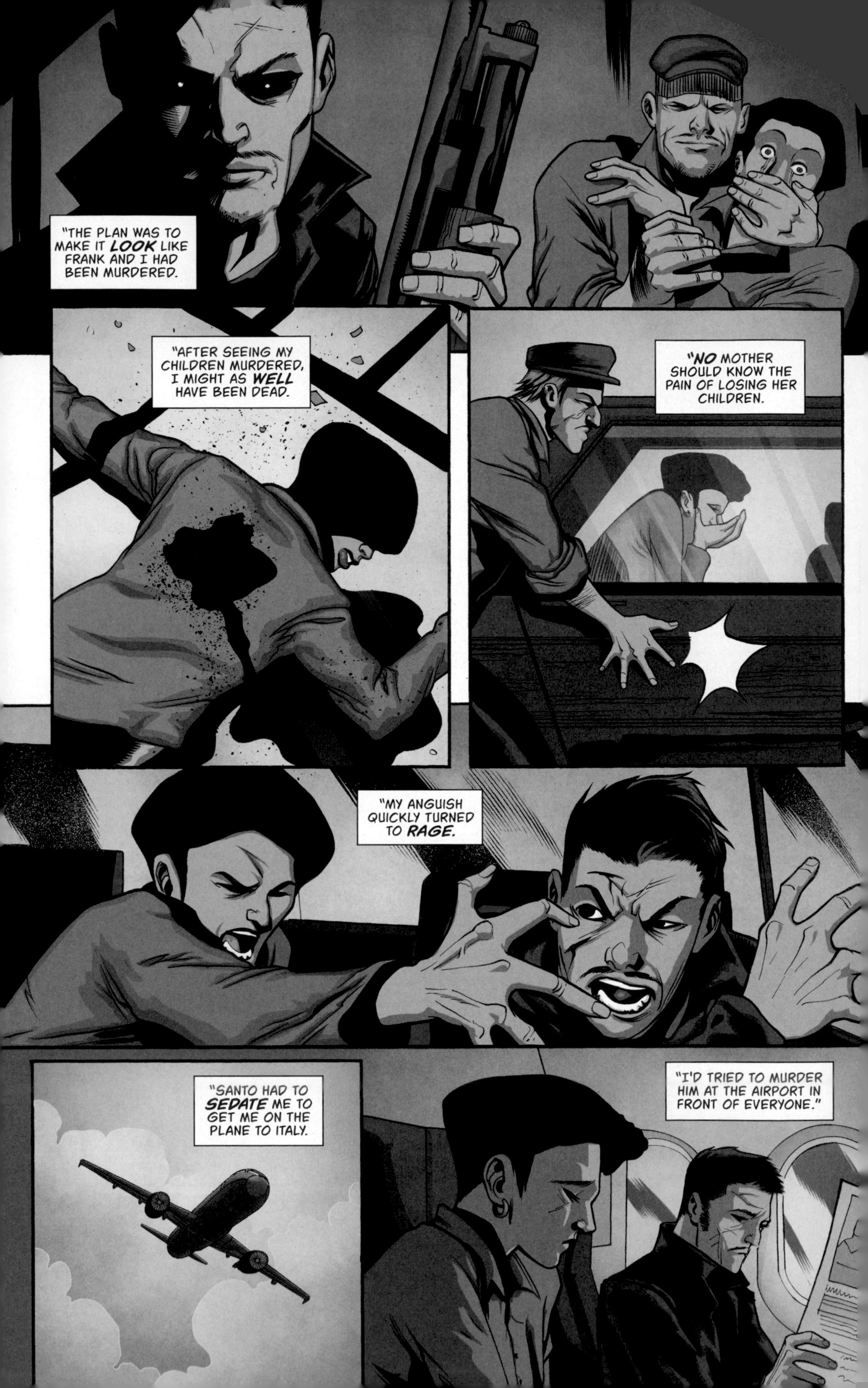
"THE PLAN WAS TO MAKE IT LOOK LIKE FRANK AND I HAD BEEN MURDERED.
"AFTER SEEING MY CHILDREN MURDERED, I MIGHT AS WELL HAVE BEEN DEAD.
"NO MOTHER SHOULD KNOW THE PAIN OF LOSING HER CHILDREN.
"MY ANGUISH QUICKLY TURNED TO RAGE.
"SANTO HAD TO SEDATE ME TO GET ME ON THE PLANE TO ITALY.
"I'D TRIED TO MURDER HIM AT THE AIRPORT IN FRONT OF EVERYONE."

"I SAID I COULDN'T LIVE WITH THE MAN WHO STOOD BY AS MY CHILDREN WERE MURDERED.

"BUT REALLY, I COULDN'T LIVE WITH *MYSELF.*

"I WELCOMED HELL BY WAY OF THE SEA, BUT GOD WOULDN'T *LET* ME KILL MYSELF.

"I HAD TO MAKE THINGS *RIGHT* BEFORE HE'D ALLOW ME INTO HEAVEN WITH MY CHILDREN.

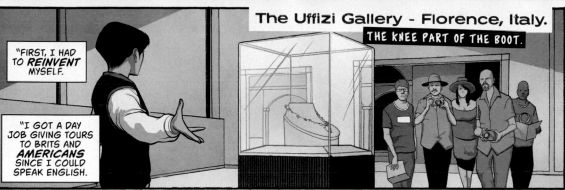

The Uffizi Gallery - Florence, Italy.

THE KNEE PART OF THE BOOT.

"FIRST, I HAD TO *REINVENT* MYSELF.

"I GOT A DAY JOB GIVING TOURS TO BRITS AND *AMERICANS* SINCE I COULD SPEAK ENGLISH.

"MY *NIGHT* JOB WAS BUILDING MY *BUSINESS* FROM THE GROUND UP.

"IT TOOK ME *YEARS* TO BUILD MY EMPIRE.

"BUT LIKE A *PHOENIX,* I ROSE FROM THE ASHES TO GET MY REVENGE."

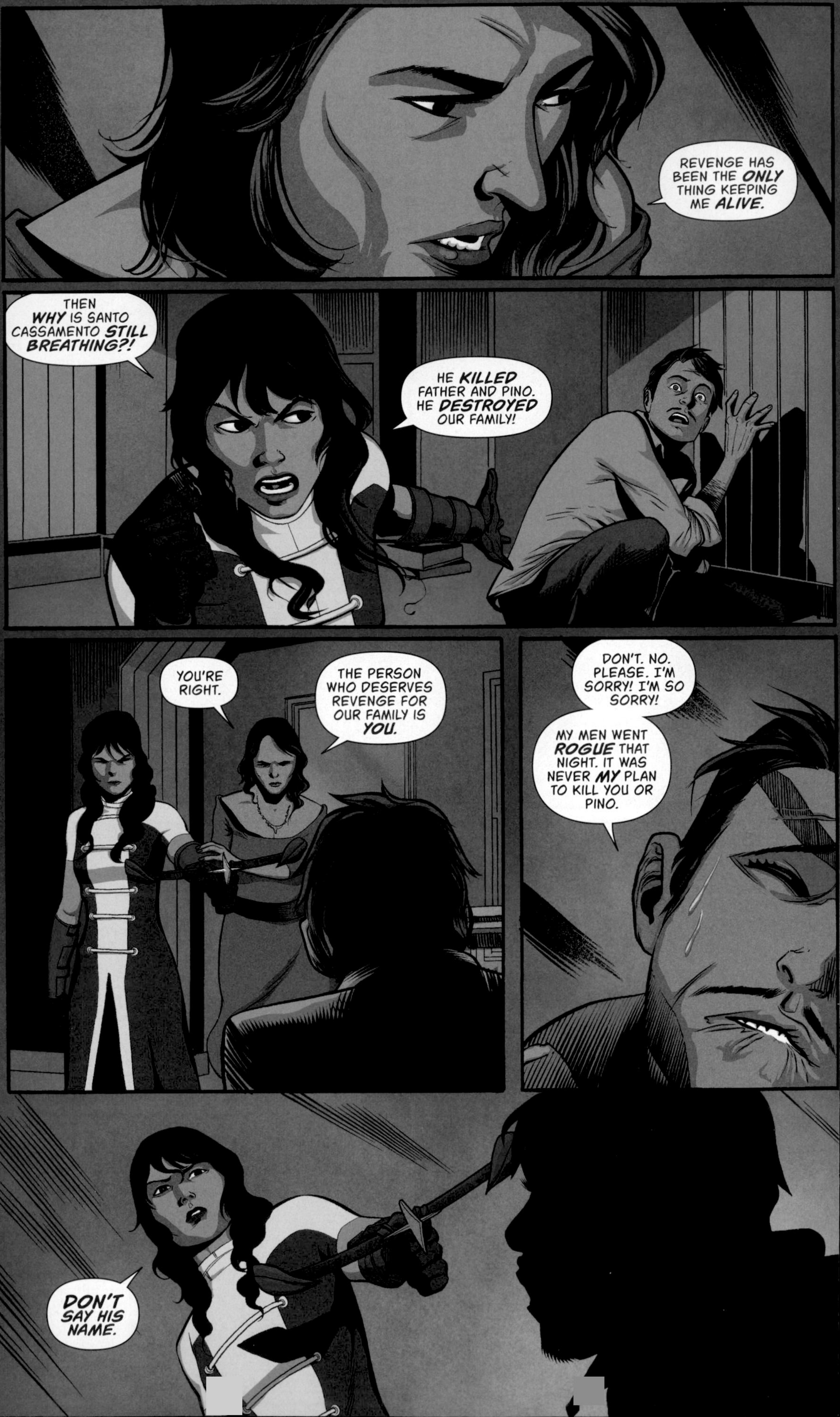
REVENGE HAS BEEN THE ONLY THING KEEPING ME ALIVE.
THEN WHY IS SANTO CASSAMENTO STILL BREATHING?!
HE KILLED FATHER AND PINO. HE DESTROYED OUR FAMILY!
YOU'RE RIGHT.
THE PERSON WHO DESERVES REVENGE FOR OUR FAMILY IS YOU.
DON'T. NO. PLEASE. I'M SORRY! I'M SO SORRY!
MY MEN WENT ROGUE THAT NIGHT. IT WAS NEVER MY PLAN TO KILL YOU OR PINO.
DON'T SAY HIS NAME.

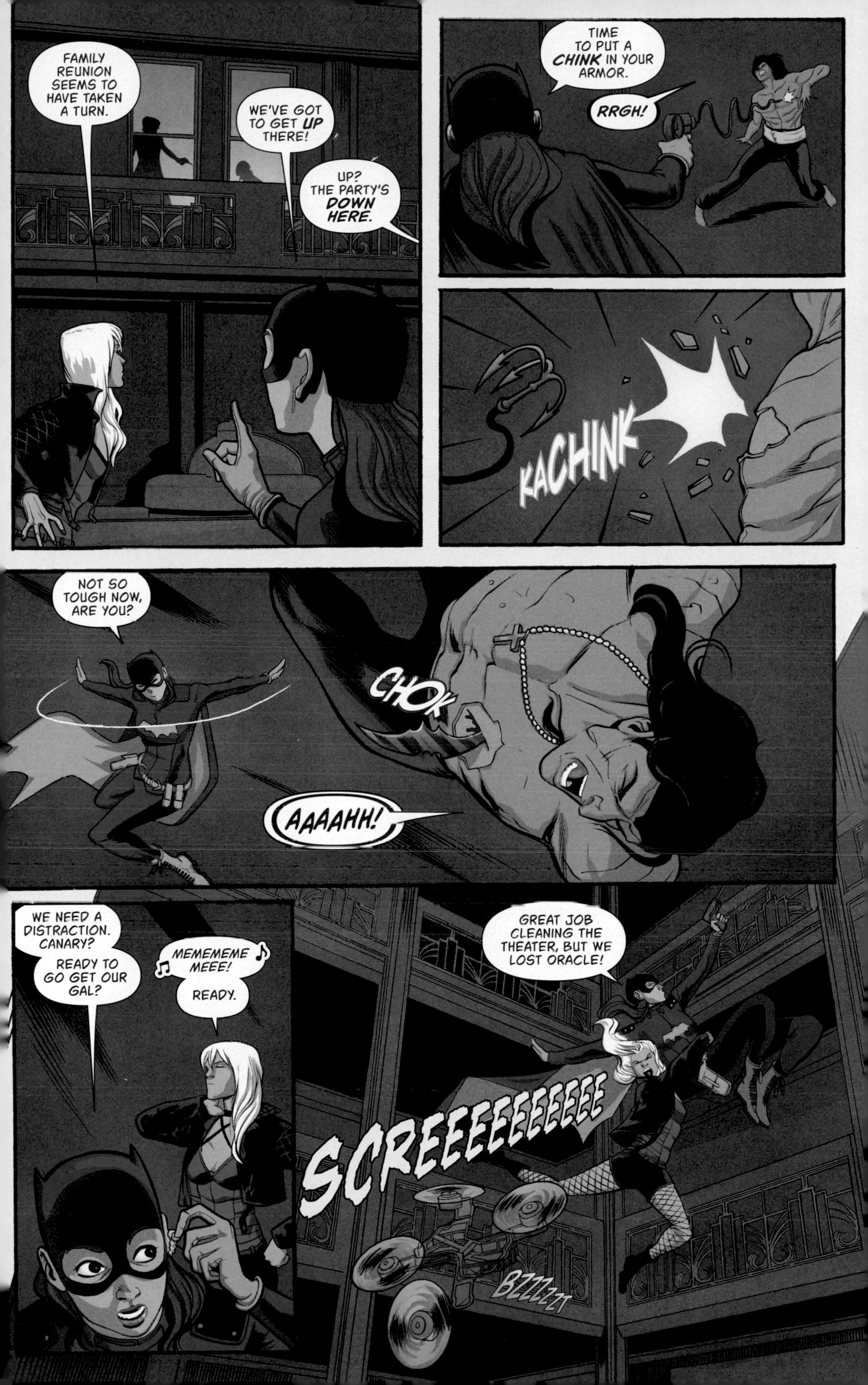
FAMILY REUNION SEEMS TO HAVE TAKEN A TURN.
WE'VE GOT TO GET UP THERE!
UP? THE PARTY'S DOWN HERE.
TIME TO PUT A CHINK IN YOUR ARMOR.
RRGH!
KACHINK
NOT SO TOUGH NOW, ARE YOU?
CHOK
AAAAHH!
WE NEED A DISTRACTION. CANARY?
READY TO GO GET OUR GAL?
MEMEMEME MEEE!
READY.
GREAT JOB CLEANING THE THEATER, BUT WE LOST ORACLE!
SCREEEEEEEEEEE
BZZZZZT

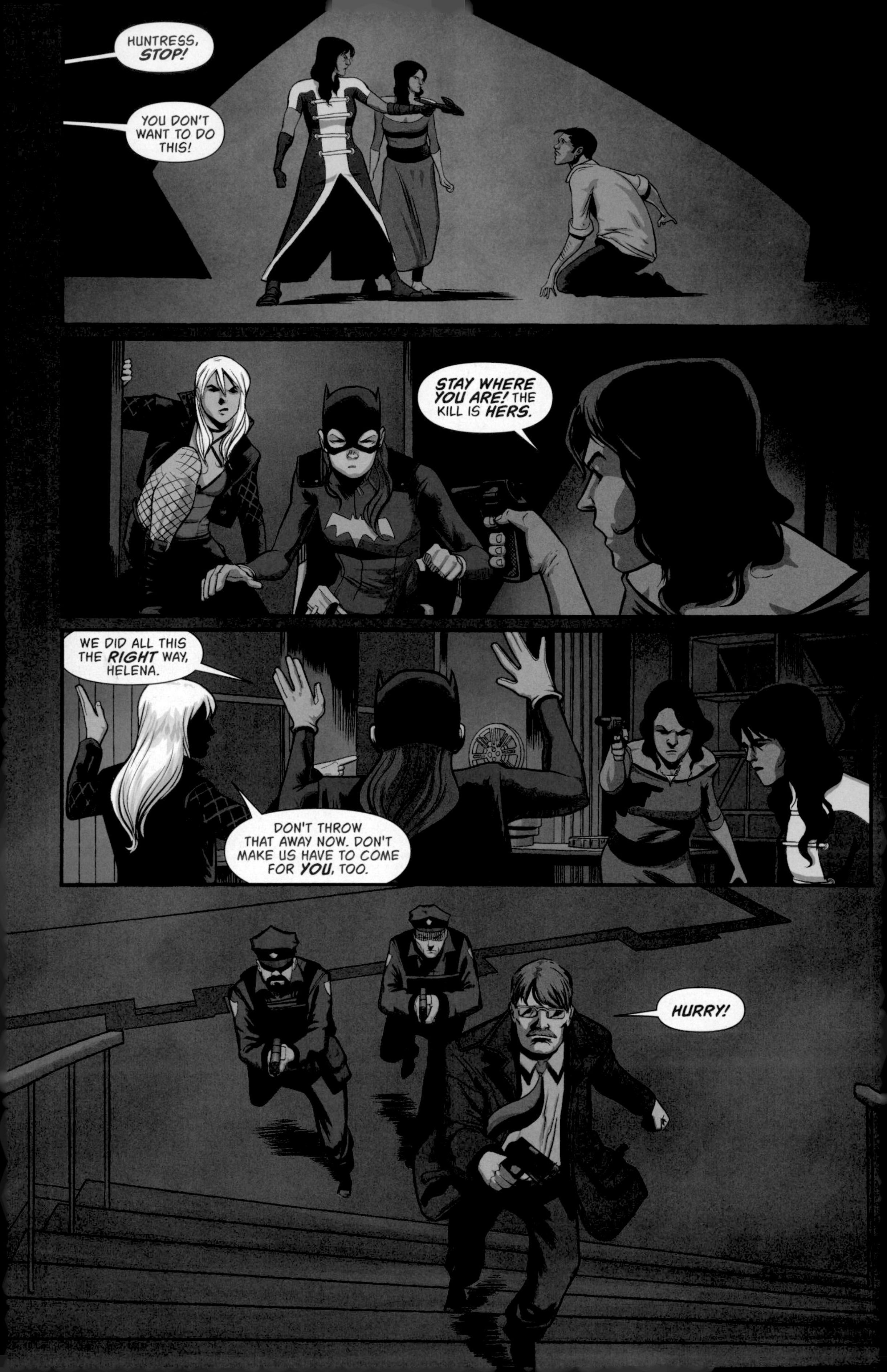
HUNTRESS, STOP!
YOU DON'T WANT TO DO THIS!
STAY WHERE YOU ARE! THE KILL IS HERS.
WE DID ALL THIS THE RIGHT WAY, HELENA.
DON'T THROW THAT AWAY NOW. DON'T MAKE US HAVE TO COME FOR YOU, TOO.
HURRY!

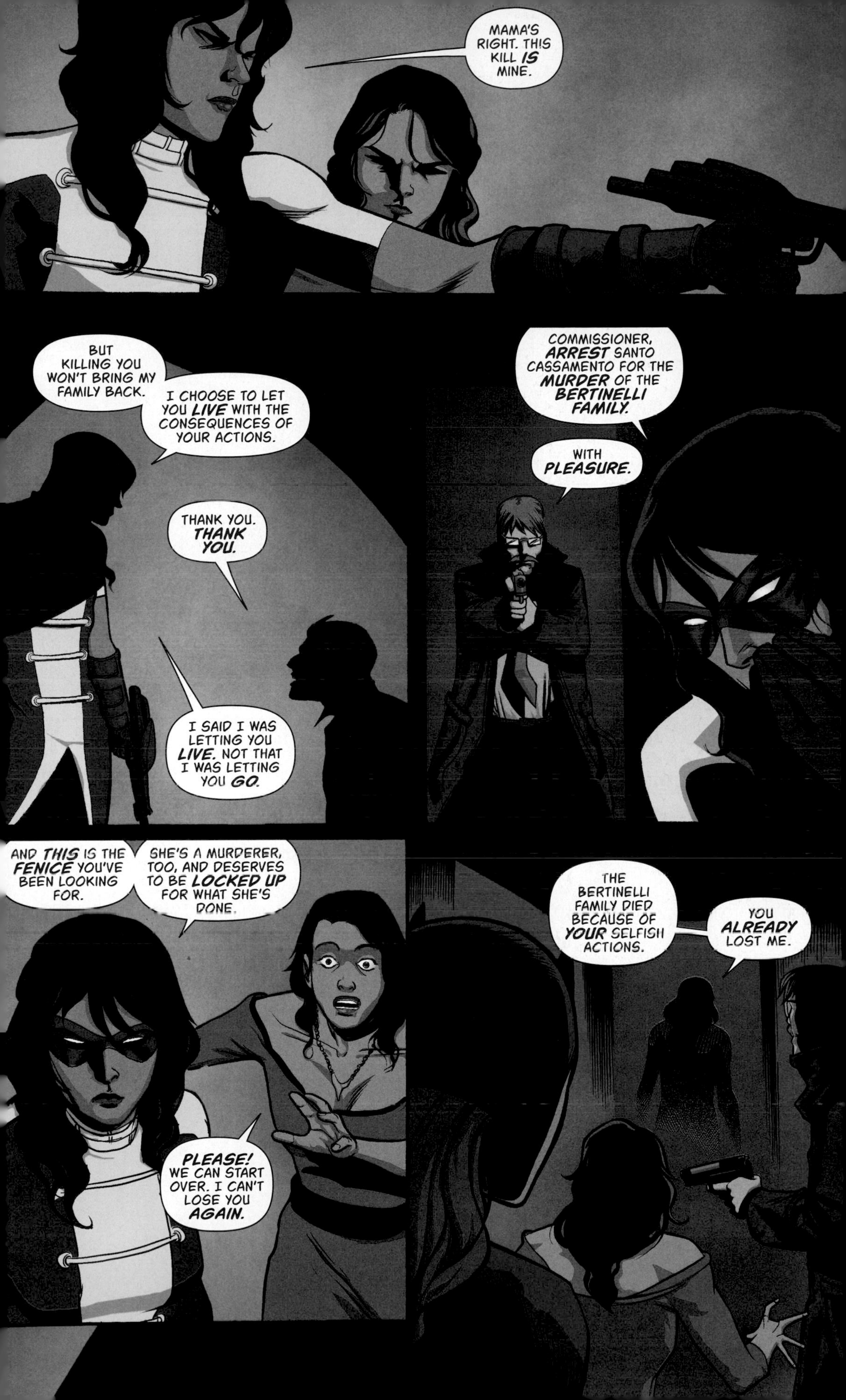
MAMA'S RIGHT. THIS KILL IS MINE.
BUT KILLING YOU WON'T BRING MY FAMILY BACK.
I CHOOSE TO LET YOU LIVE WITH THE CONSEQUENCES OF YOUR ACTIONS.
THANK YOU. THANK YOU.
I SAID I WAS LETTING YOU LIVE. NOT THAT I WAS LETTING YOU GO.
COMMISSIONER, ARREST SANTO CASSAMENTO FOR THE MURDER OF THE BERTINELLI FAMILY.
WITH PLEASURE.
AND THIS IS THE FENICE YOU'VE BEEN LOOKING FOR.
SHE'S A MURDERER, TOO, AND DESERVES TO BE LOCKED UP FOR WHAT SHE'S DONE.
PLEASE! WE CAN START OVER. I CAN'T LOSE YOU AGAIN.
THE BERTINELLI FAMILY DIED BECAUSE OF YOUR SELFISH ACTIONS.
YOU ALREADY LOST ME.

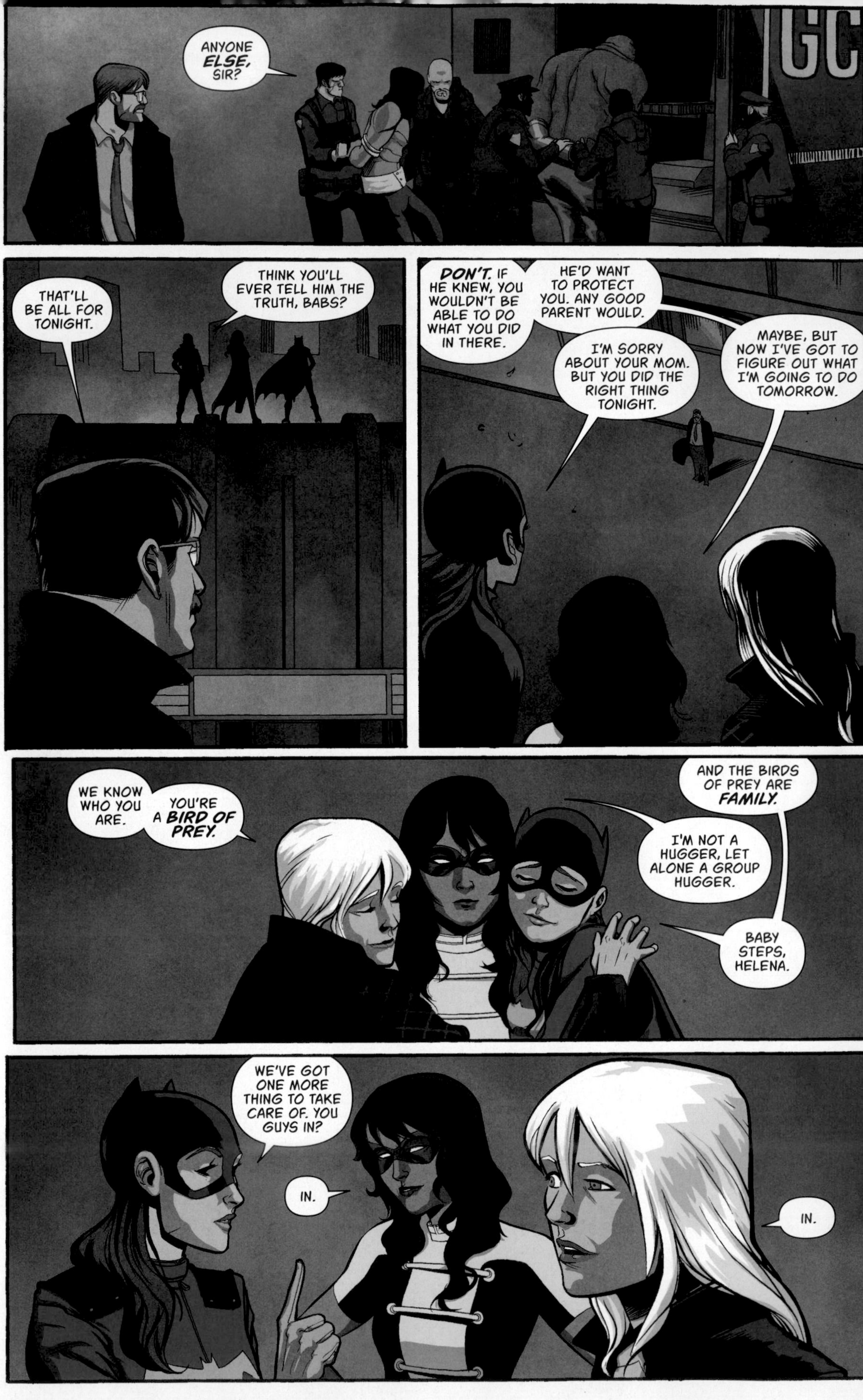
ANYONE ELSE, SIR?
THAT'LL BE ALL FOR TONIGHT.
THINK YOU'LL EVER TELL HIM THE TRUTH, BABS?
DON'T. IF HE KNEW, YOU WOULDN'T BE ABLE TO DO WHAT YOU DID IN THERE.
HE'D WANT TO PROTECT YOU. ANY GOOD PARENT WOULD.
I'M SORRY ABOUT YOUR MOM. BUT YOU DID THE RIGHT THING TONIGHT.
MAYBE, BUT NOW I'VE GOT TO FIGURE OUT WHAT I'M GOING TO DO TOMORROW.
WE KNOW WHO YOU ARE.
YOU'RE A BIRD OF PREY.
AND THE BIRDS OF PREY ARE FAMILY.
I'M NOT A HUGGER, LET ALONE A GROUP HUGGER.
BABY STEPS, HELENA.
WE'VE GOT ONE MORE THING TO TAKE CARE OF. YOU GUYS IN?
IN.
IN.

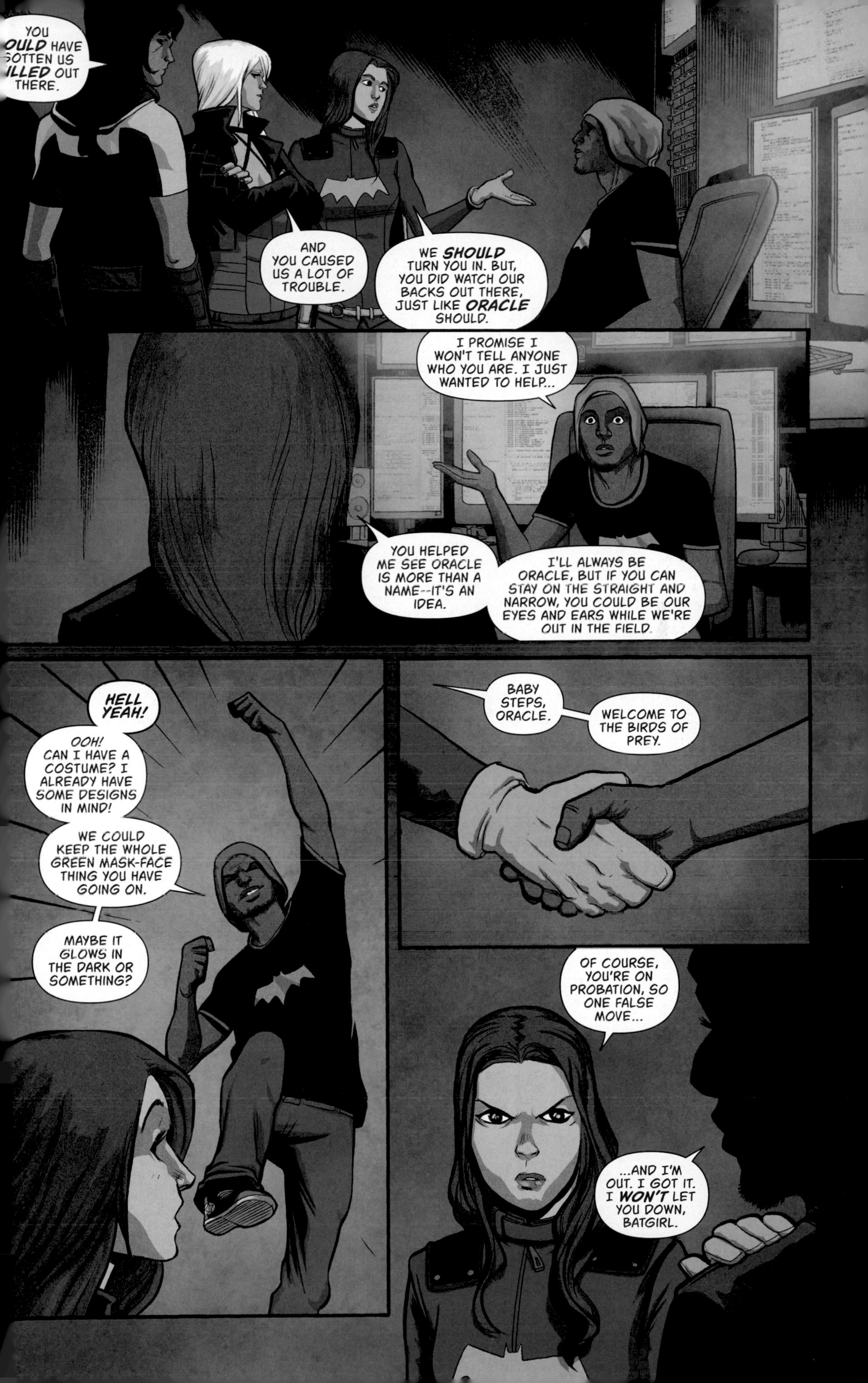
YOU OULD HAVE OTTEN US ILLED OUT THERE.
AND YOU CAUSED US A LOT OF TROUBLE.
WE SHOULD TURN YOU IN. BUT, YOU DID WATCH OUR BACKS OUT THERE, JUST LIKE ORACLE SHOULD.
I PROMISE I WON'T TELL ANYONE WHO YOU ARE. I JUST WANTED TO HELP...
YOU HELPED ME SEE ORACLE IS MORE THAN A NAME--IT'S AN IDEA.
I'LL ALWAYS BE ORACLE, BUT IF YOU CAN STAY ON THE STRAIGHT AND NARROW, YOU COULD BE OUR EYES AND EARS WHILE WE'RE OUT IN THE FIELD.
HELL YEAH!
OOH! CAN I HAVE A COSTUME? I ALREADY HAVE SOME DESIGNS IN MIND!
WE COULD KEEP THE WHOLE GREEN MASK-FACE THING YOU HAVE GOING ON.
MAYBE IT GLOWS IN THE DARK OR SOMETHING?
BABY STEPS, ORACLE.
WELCOME TO THE BIRDS OF PREY.
OF COURSE, YOU'RE ON PROBATION, SO ONE FALSE MOVE...
...AND I'M OUT. I GOT IT. I WON'T LET YOU DOWN, BATGIRL.

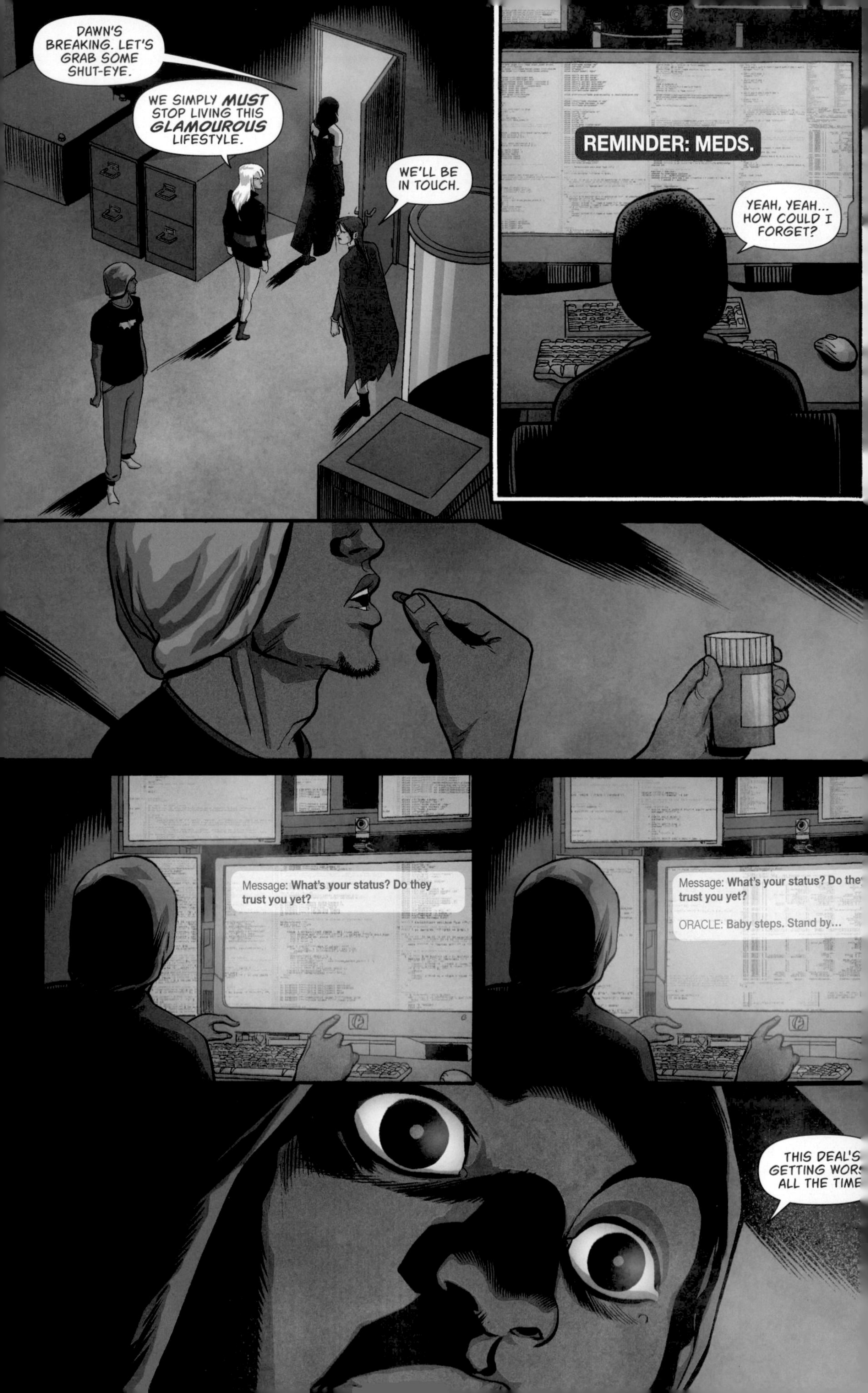
DAWN'S BREAKING. LET'S GRAB SOME SHUT-EYE.
WE SIMPLY MUST STOP LIVING THIS GLAMOUROUS LIFESTYLE.
WE'LL BE IN TOUCH.
REMINDER: MEDS.
YEAH, YEAH... HOW COULD I FORGET?
Message: What's your status? Do they trust you yet?
Message: What's your status? Do the trust you yet?
ORACLE: Baby steps. Stand by...
THIS DEAL'S GETTING WORS ALL THE TIME

BATGIRL AND THE BIRDS OF PREY: REBIRTH #1 variant cover by BEN CALDWELL

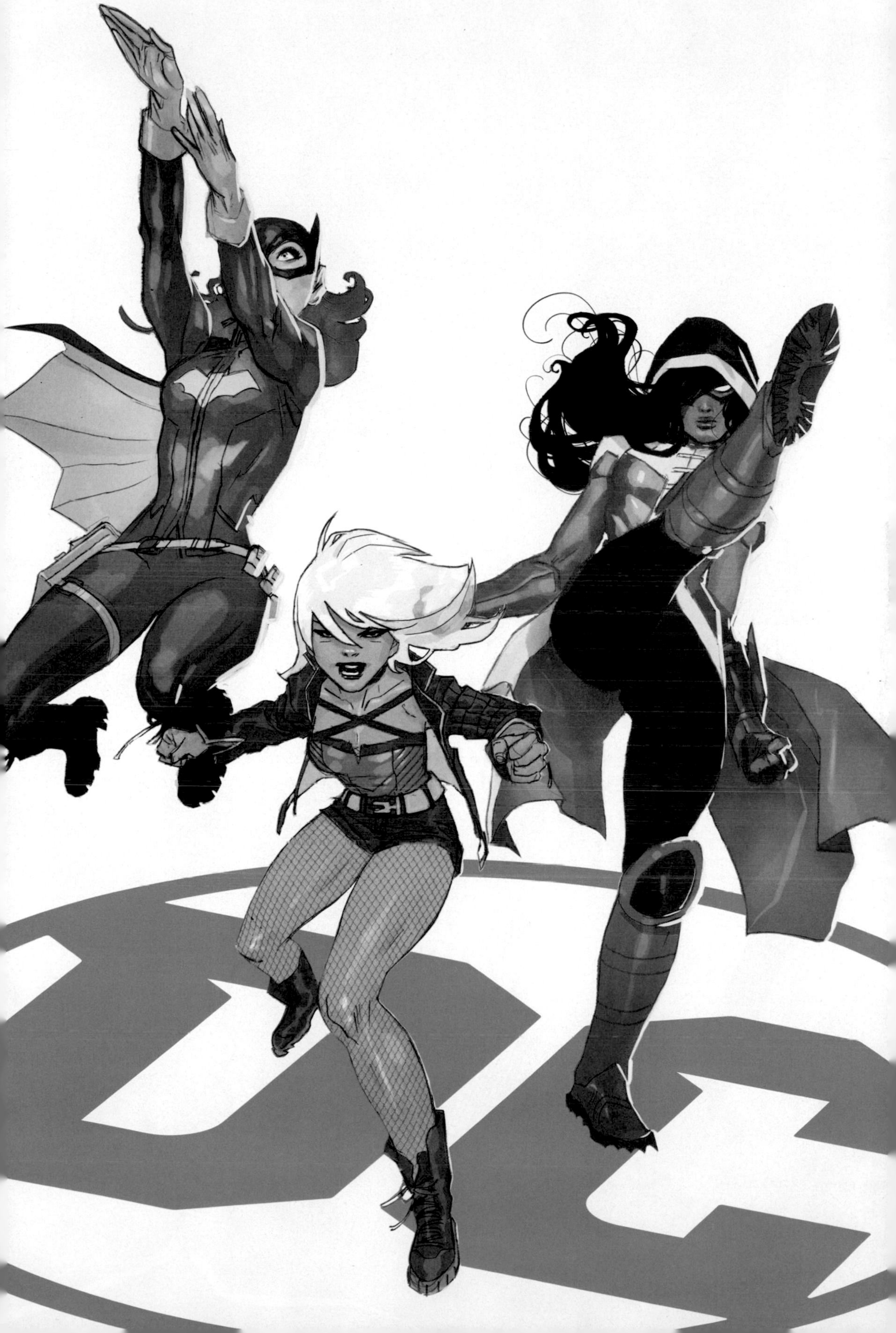

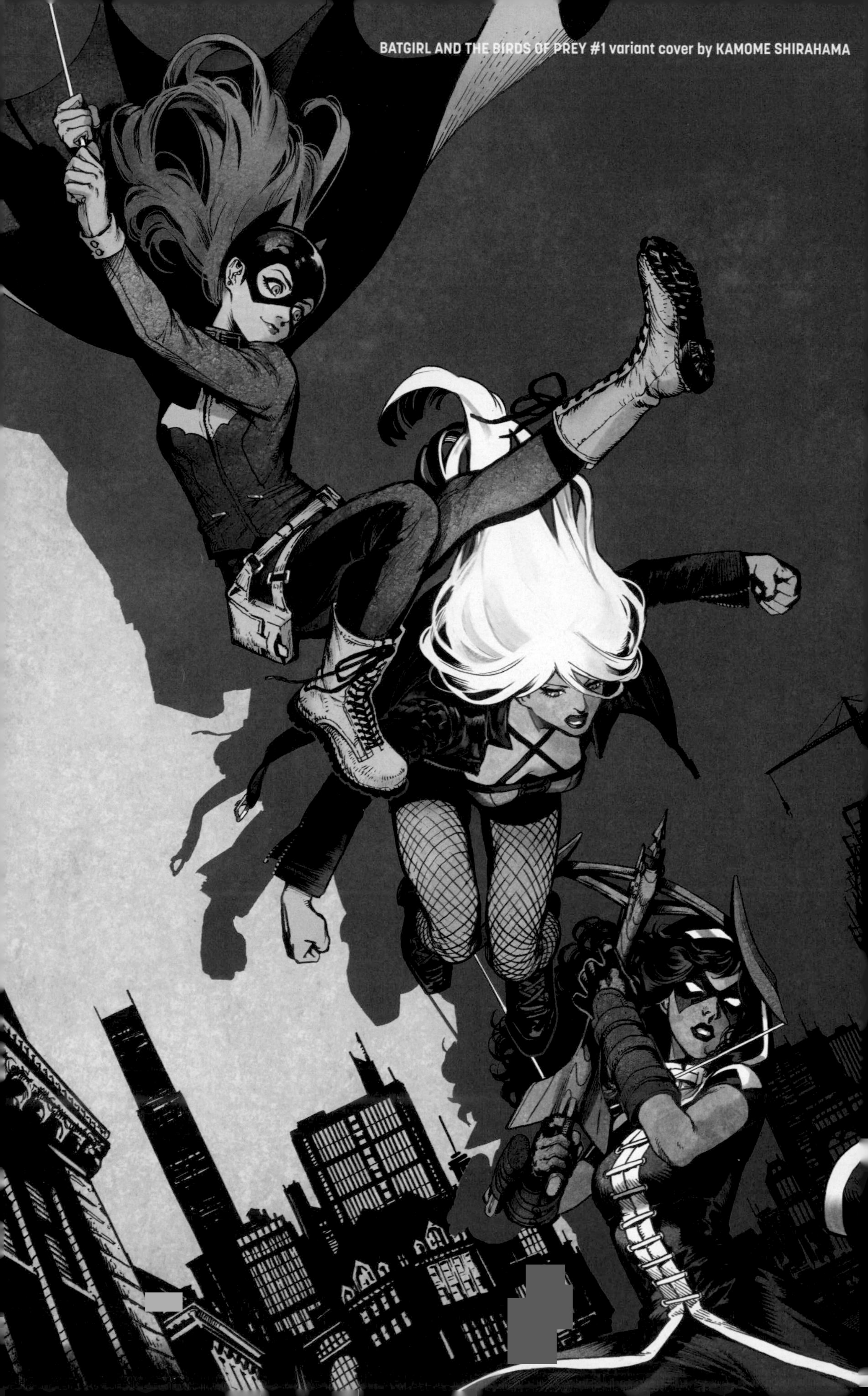

BATGIRL AND THE BIRDS OF PREY #1 variant cover by KAMOME SHIRAHAMA

BATGIRL AND THE BIRDS OF PREY #2 variant cover by KAMOME SHIRAHAMA

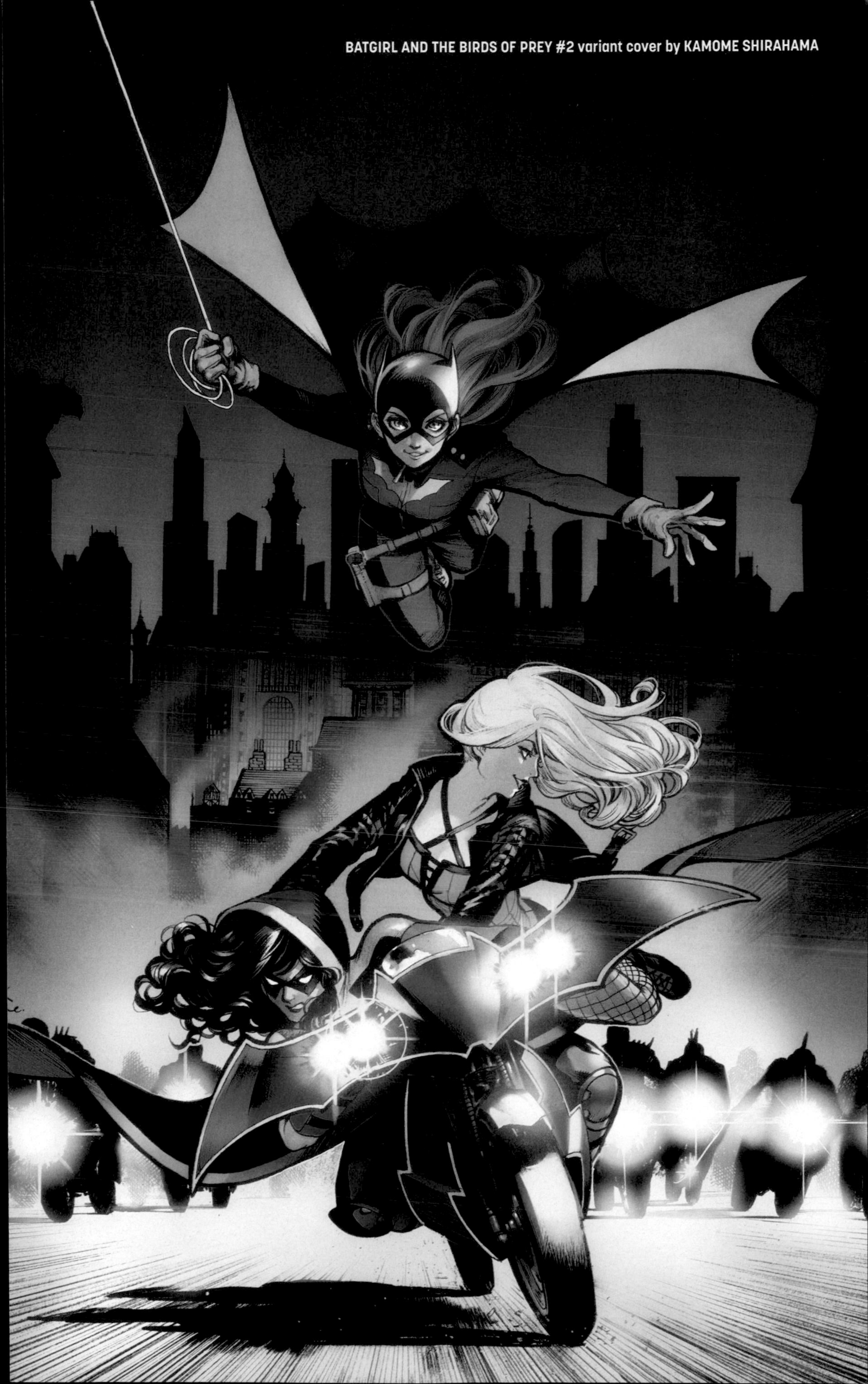

BATGIRL AND THE BIRDS OF PREY #3 variant cover by KAMOME SHIRAHAMA

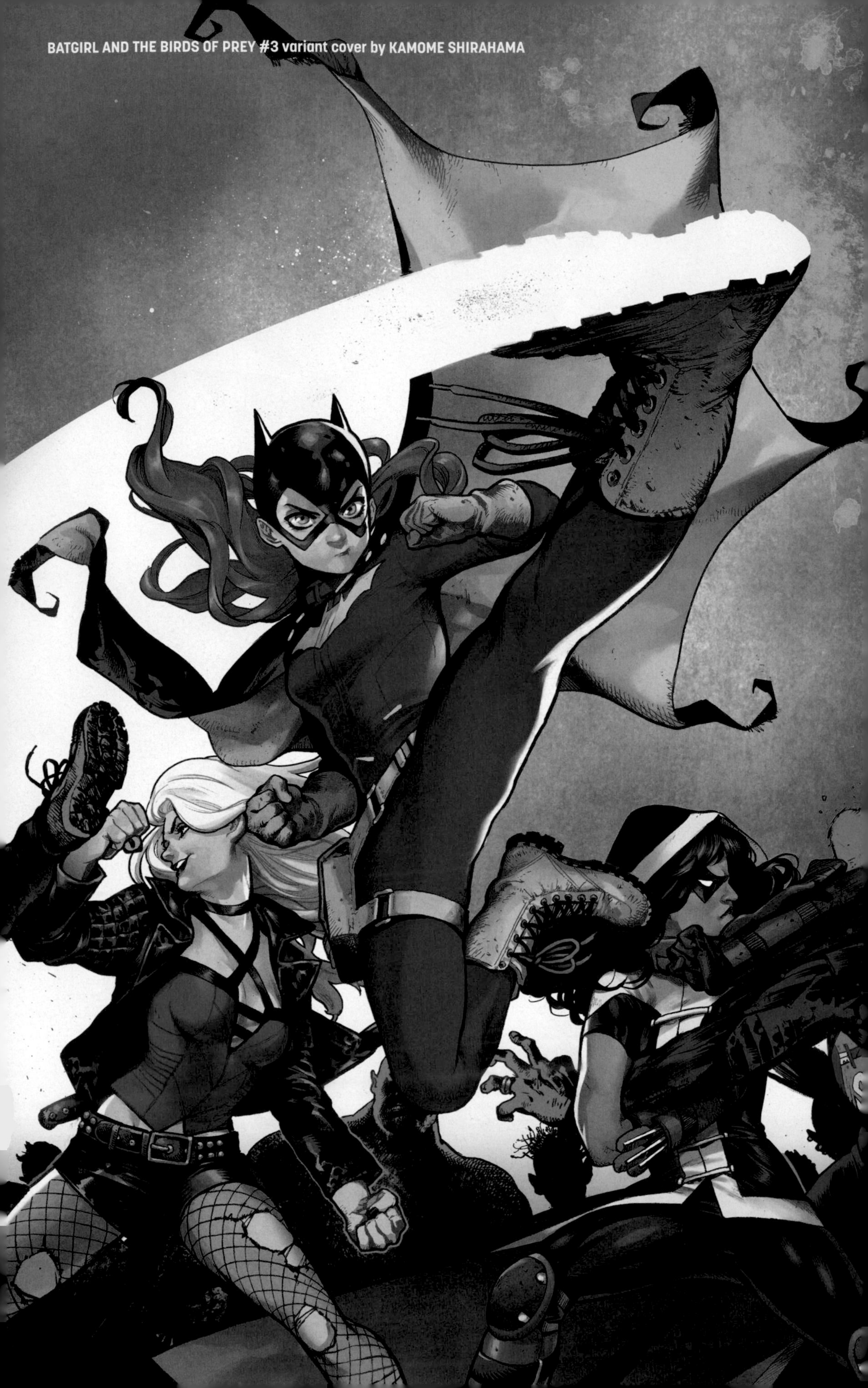

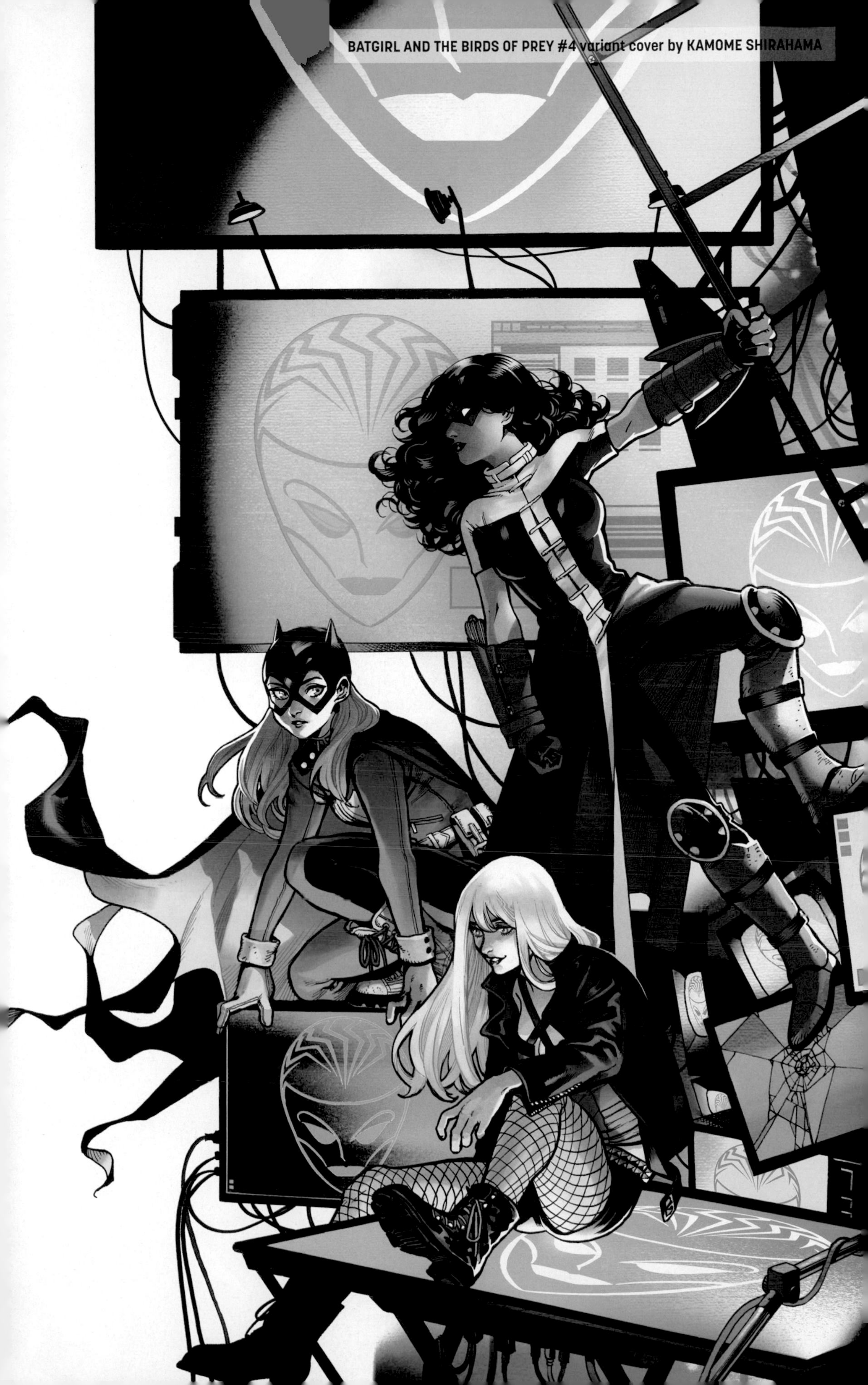

BATGIRL AND THE BIRDS OF PREY #4 variant cover by KAMOME SHIRAHAMA

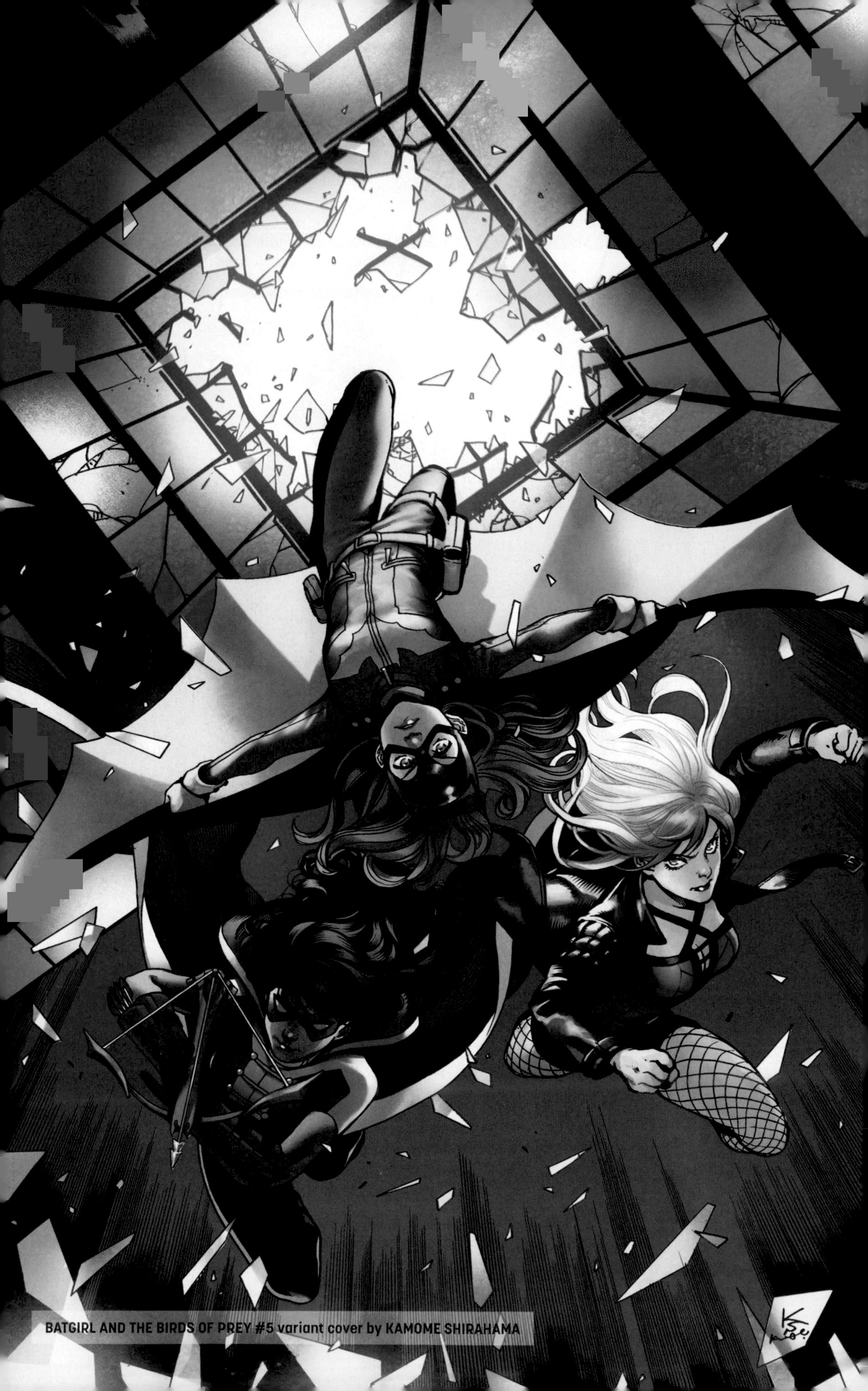

BATGIRL AND THE BIRDS OF PREY #5 variant cover by KAMOME SHIRAHAMA

BATGIRL AND THE BIRDS OF PREY #6 variant cover by KAMOME SHIRAHAMA

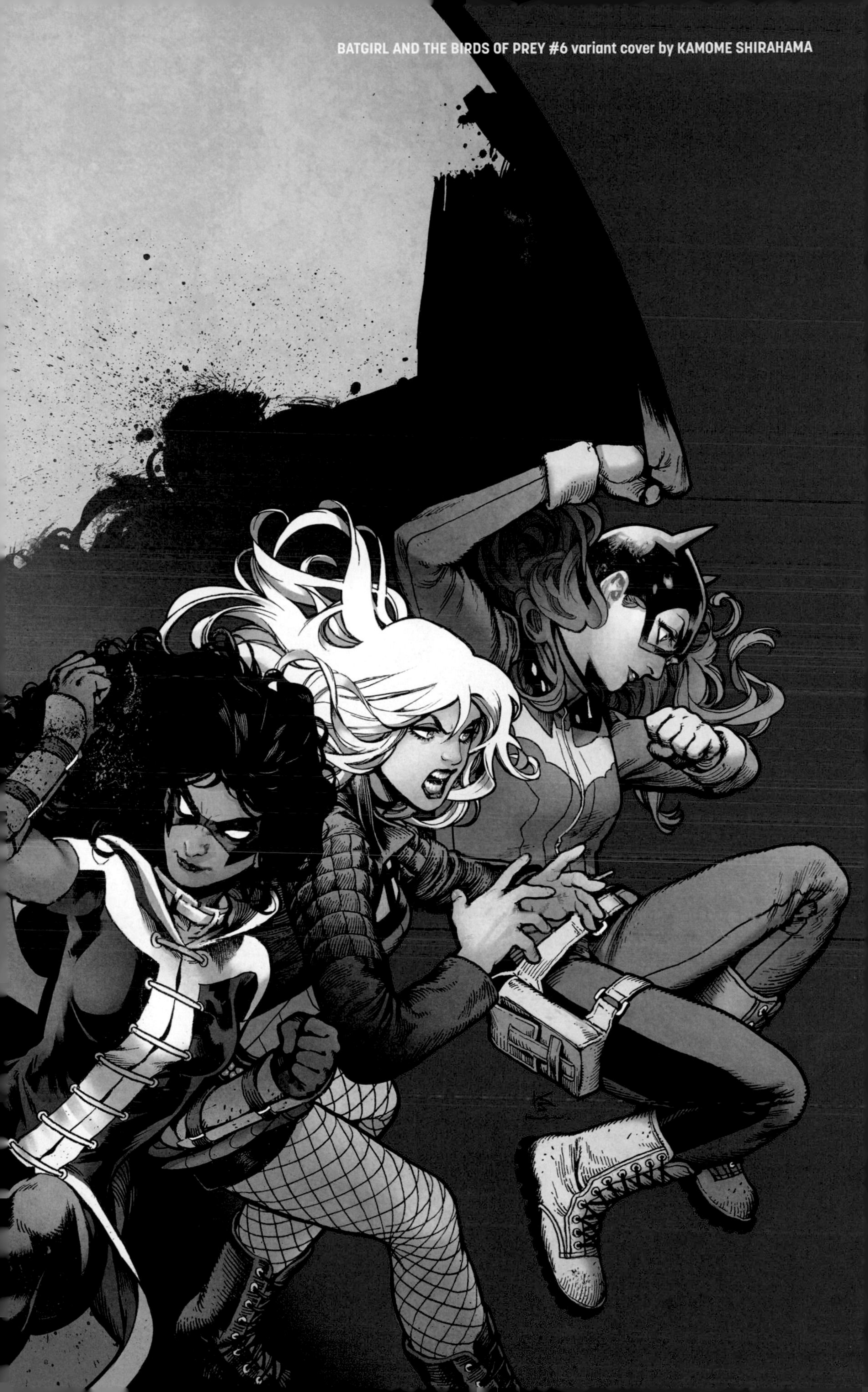

HUNTRESS DESIGNS
by Yanick Paquette

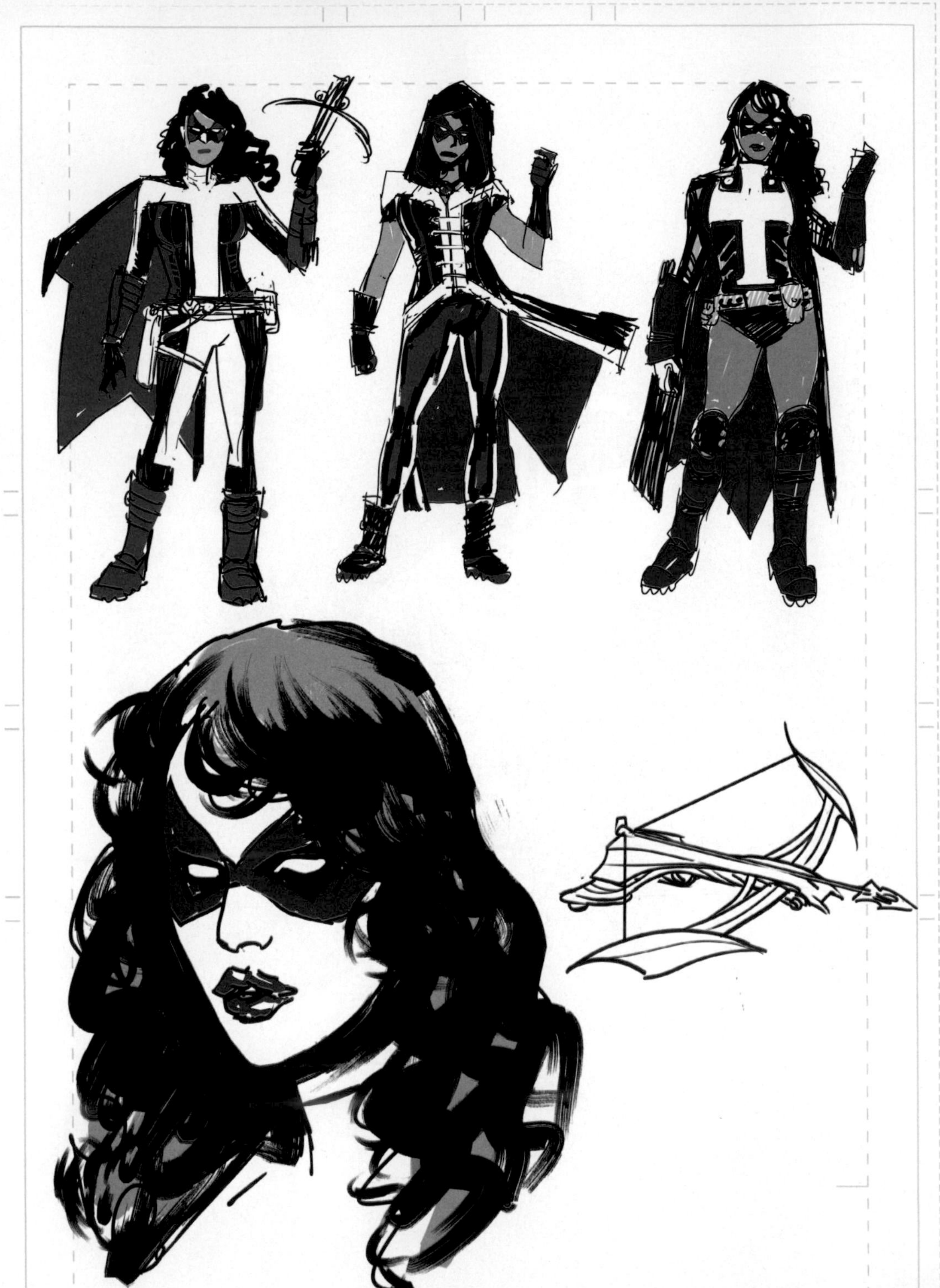
LIVE AREA
CROP
BLEED

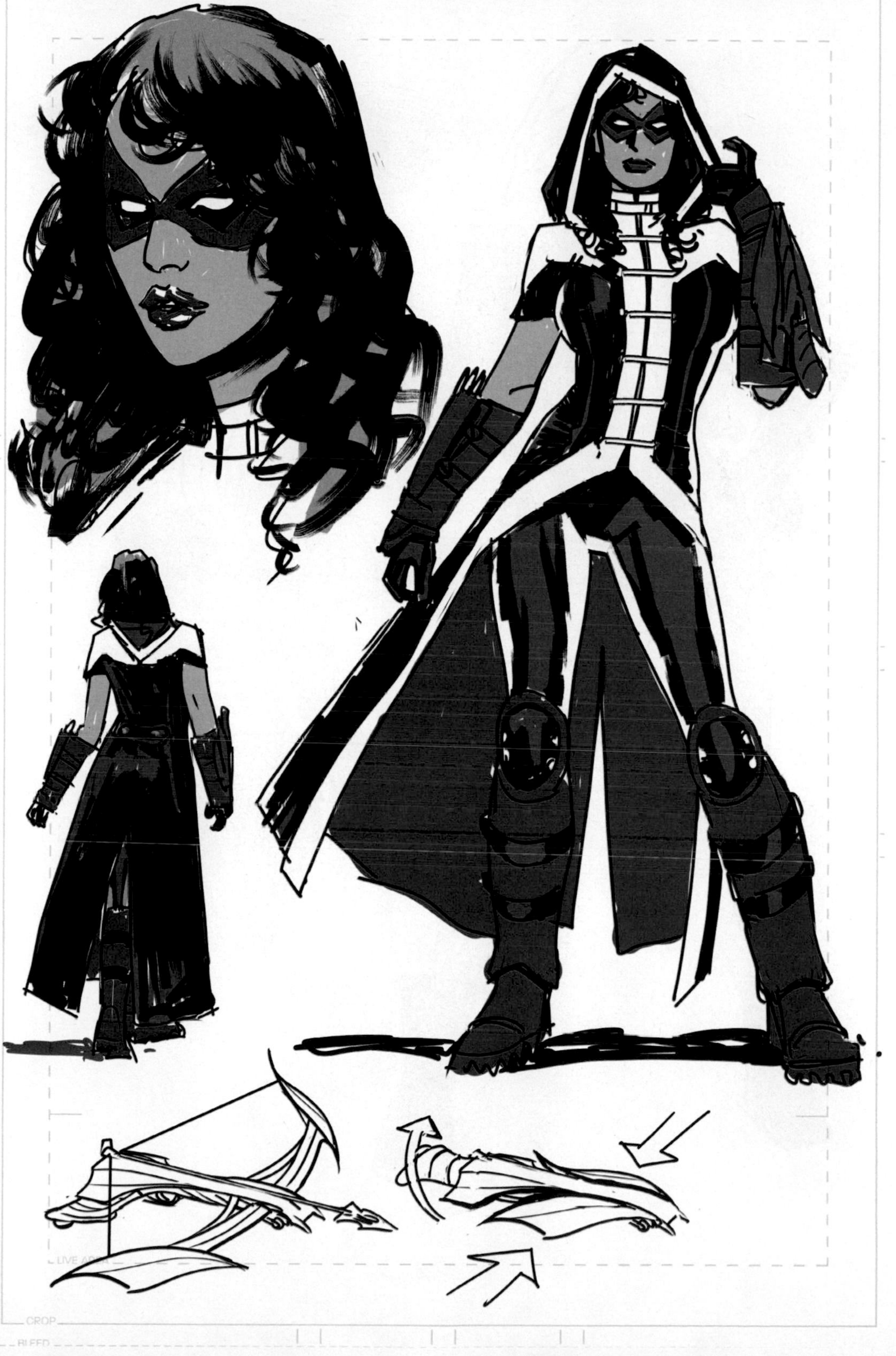

BLACK CANARY DESIGNS
by Yanick Paquette

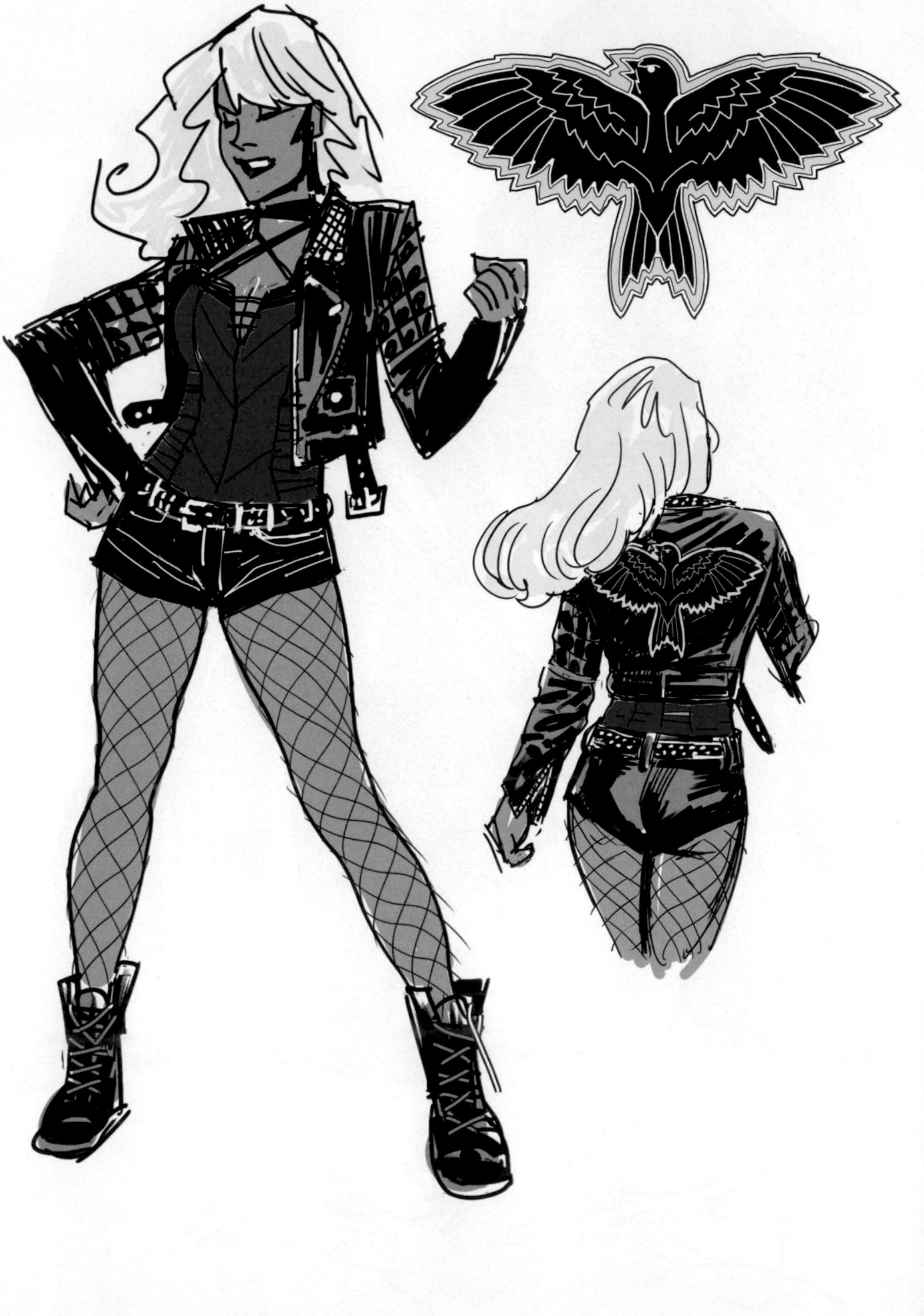

BLACK CANARY SKETCHES
by Claire Roe

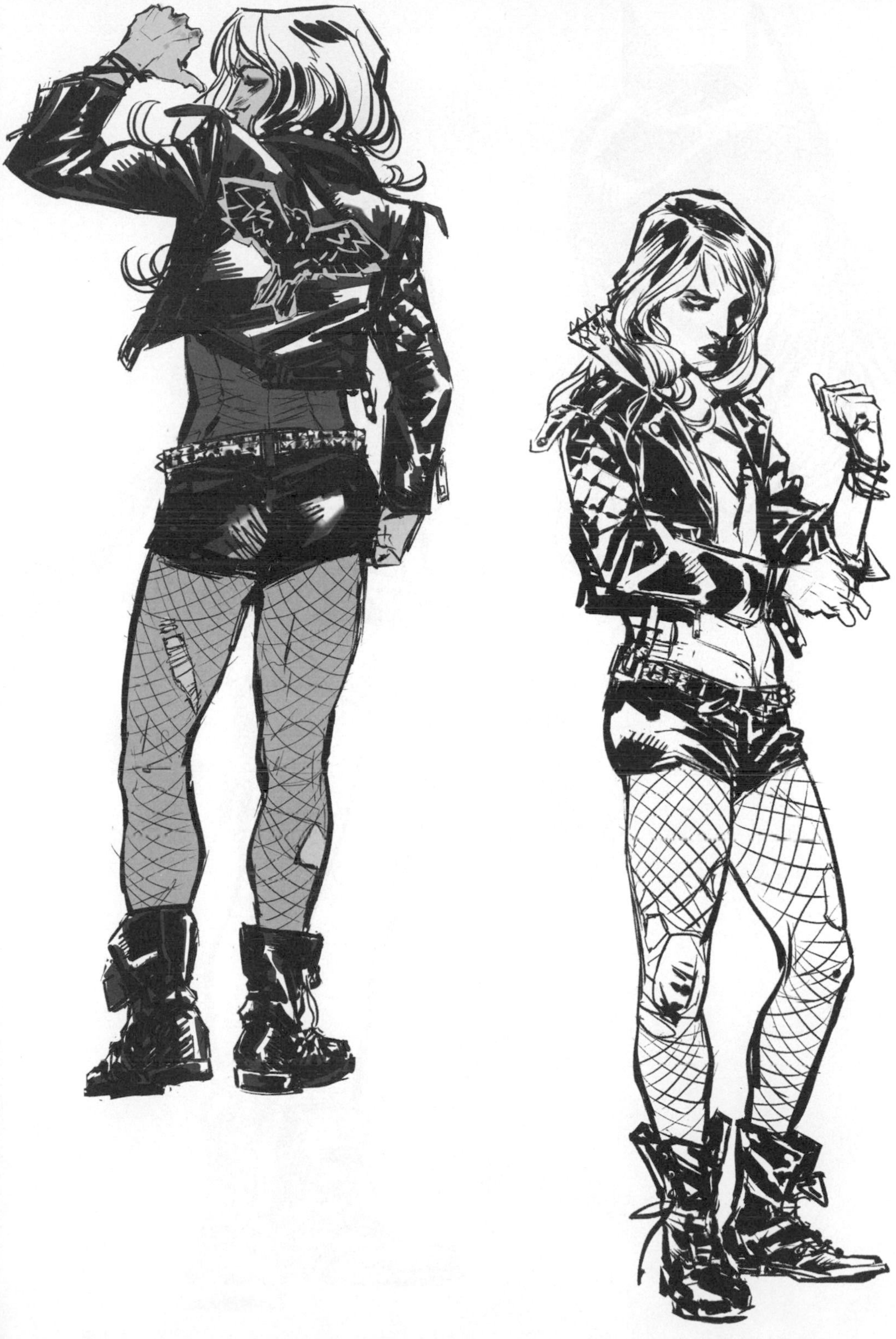

BATGIRL SKETCHES
by Claire Roe

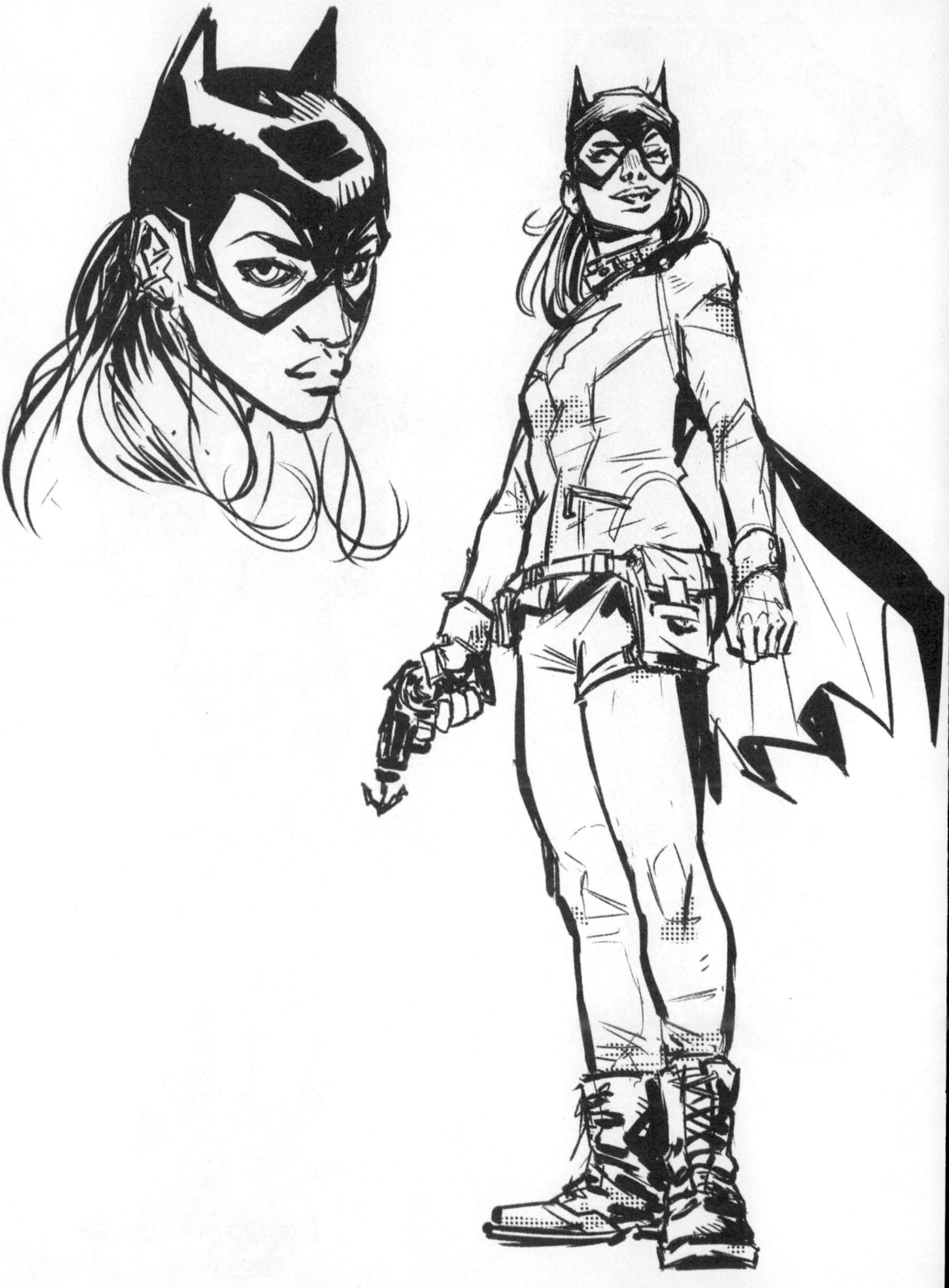

HUNTRESS SKETCH
by Claire Roe

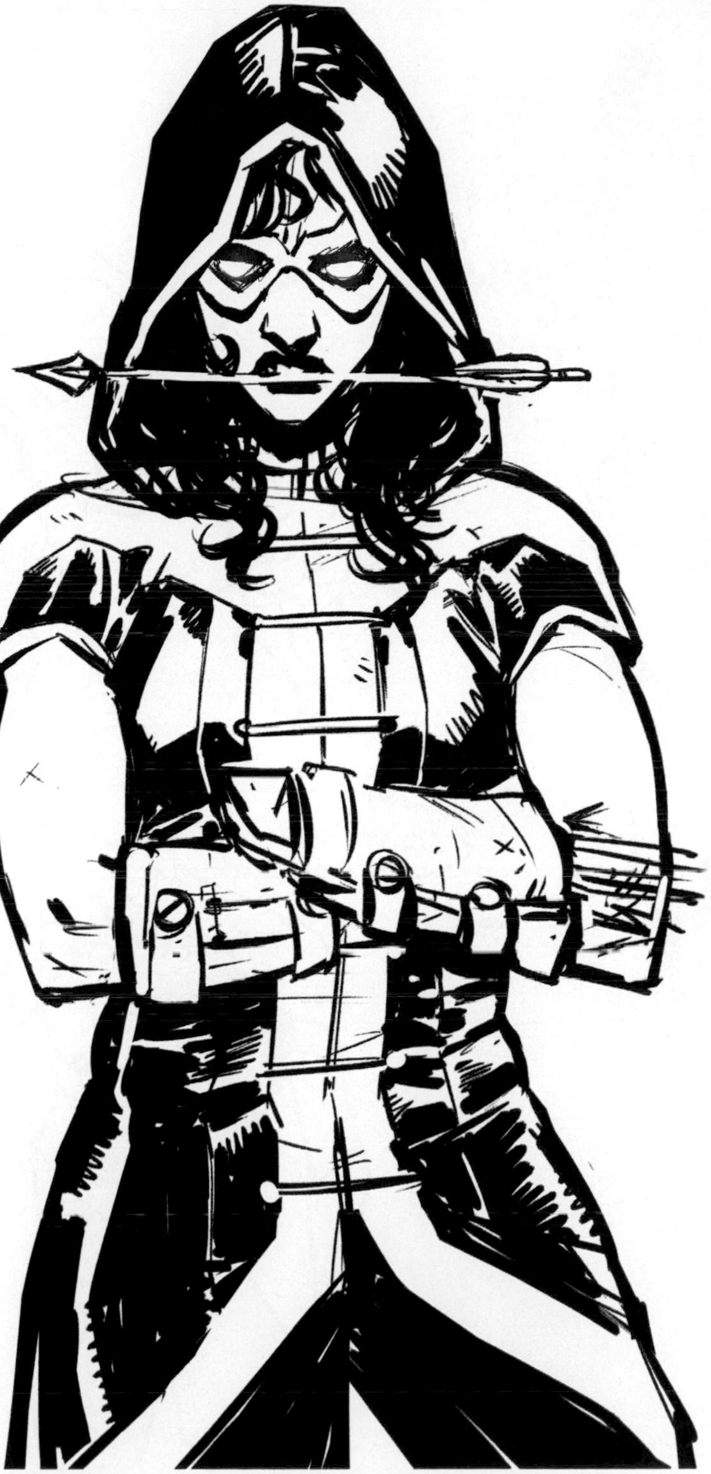

ASP DESIGNS
by Claire Roe

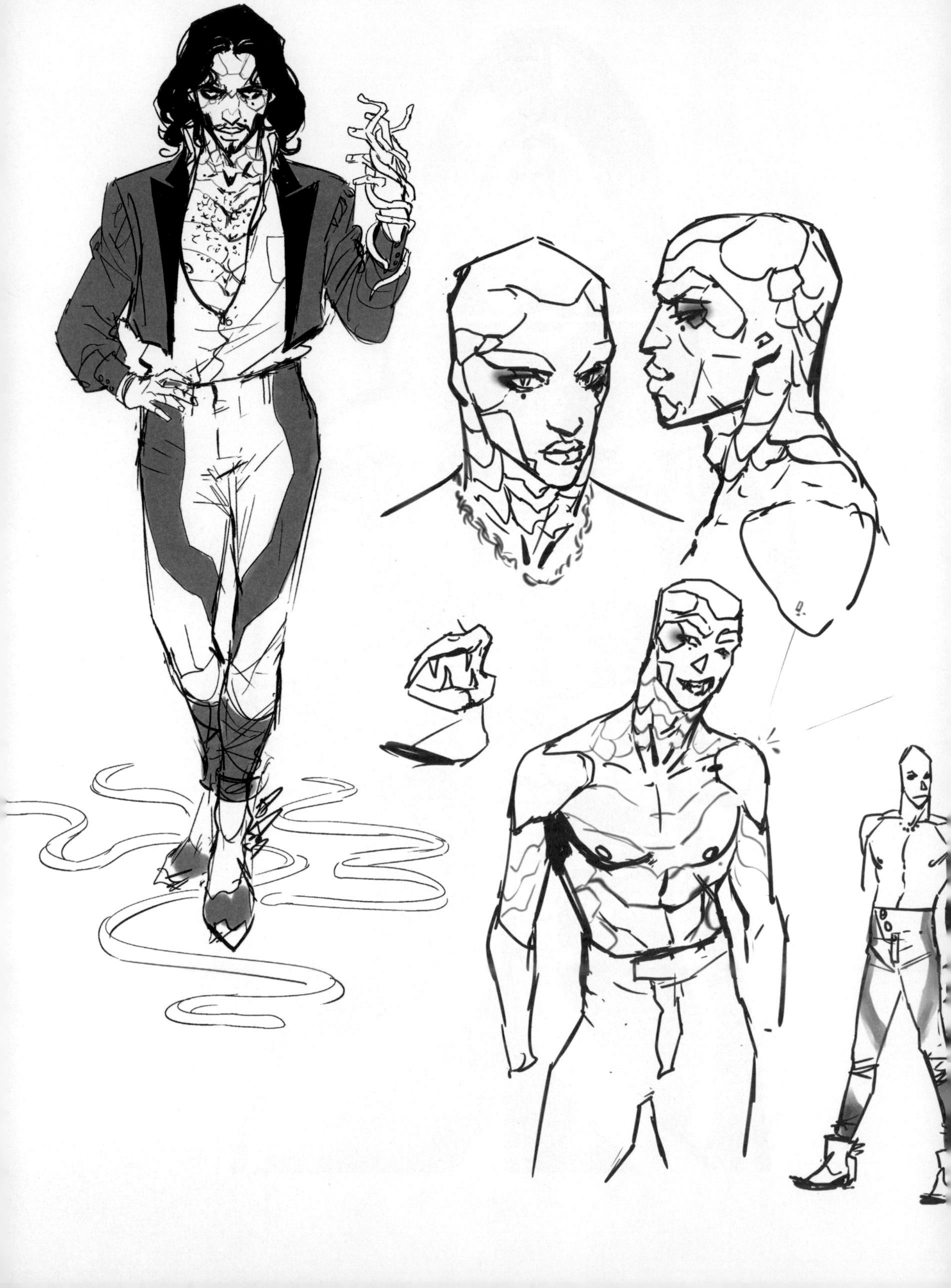

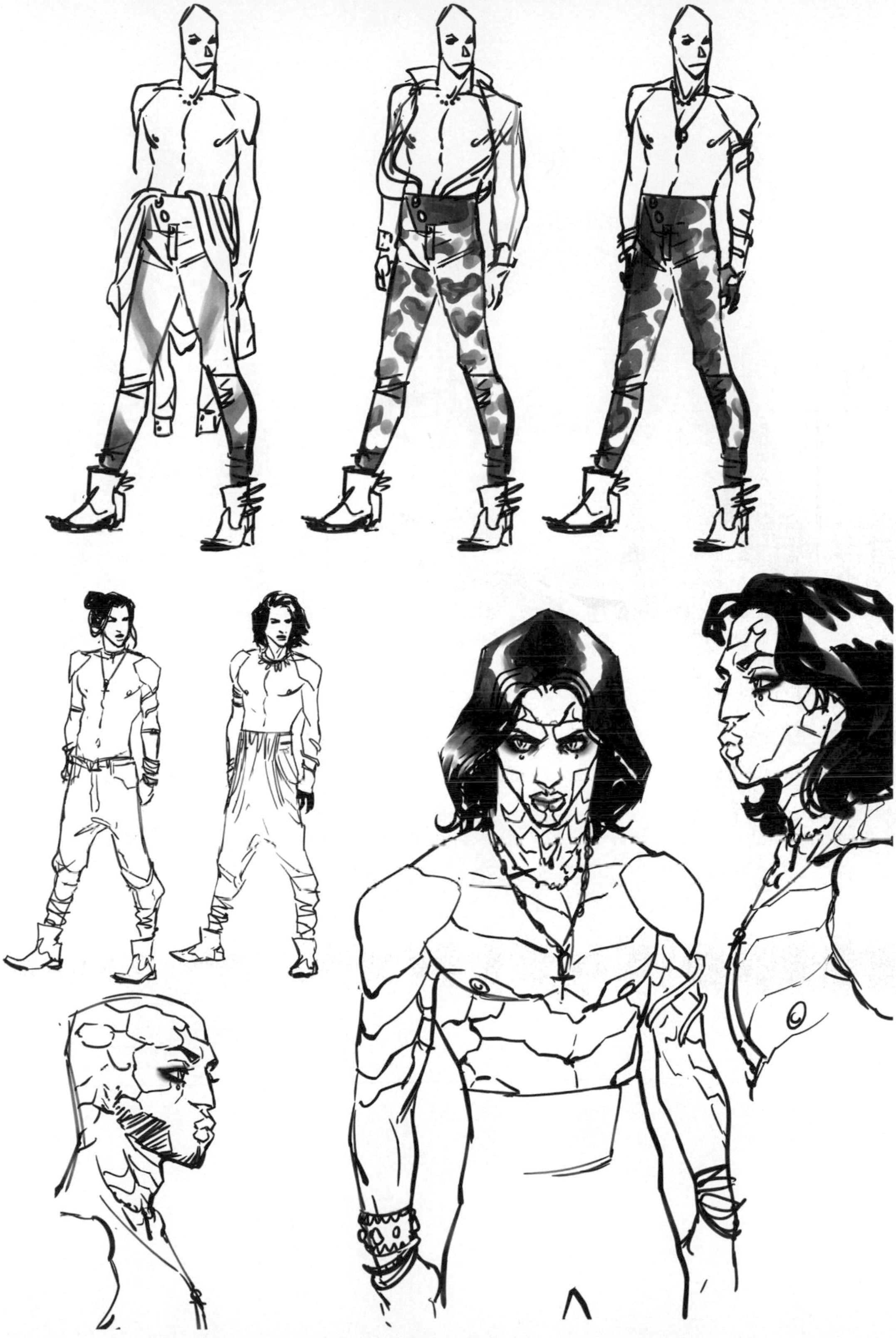

FENICE DESIGNS
by Claire Roe

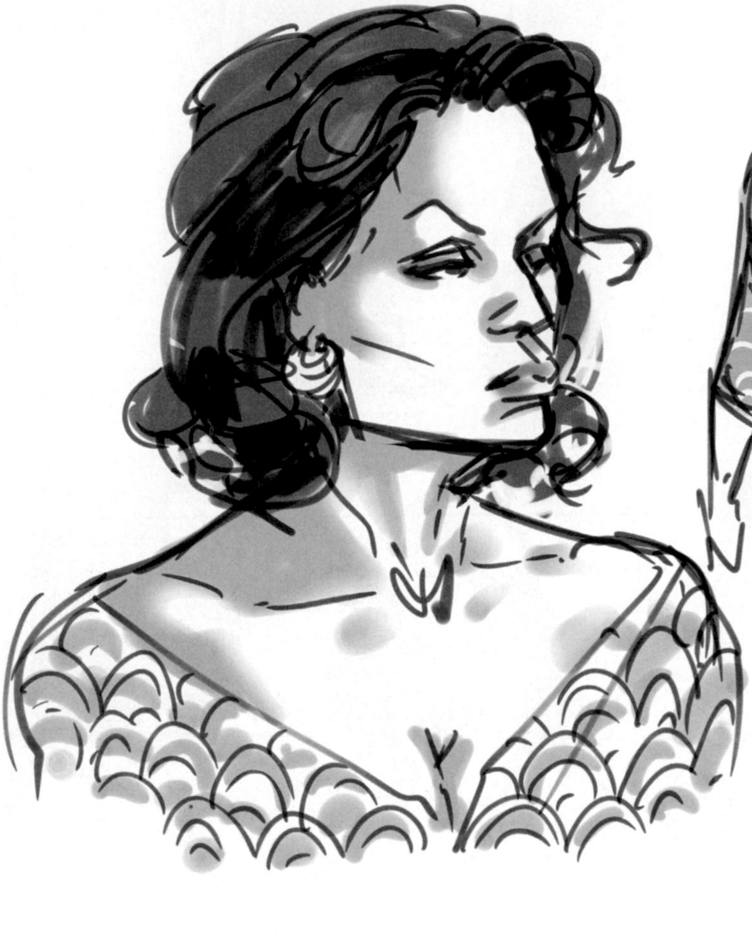

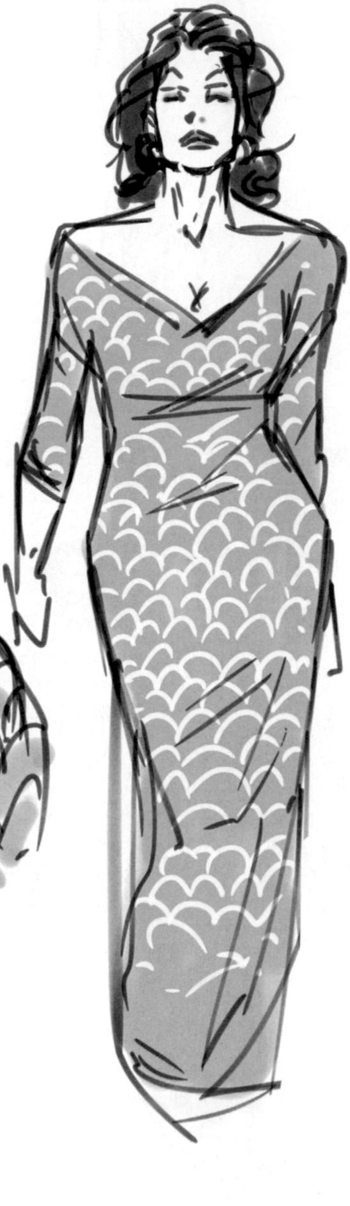

DC UNIVERSE REBIRTH

WONDER WOMAN

VOL. 1: THE LIES

GREG RUCKA
with LIAM SHARP

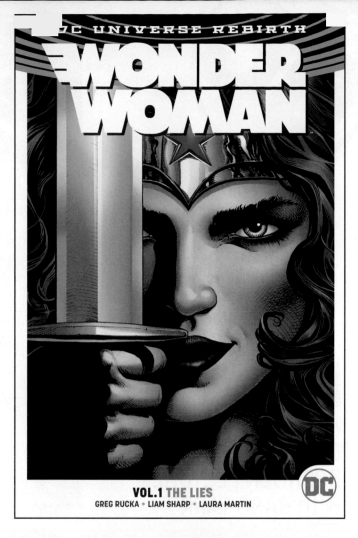

VOL. 1 **THE LIES**
GREG RUCKA ★ LIAM SHARP ★ LAURA MARTIN

JUSTICE LEAGUE VOL. 1: THE EXTINCTION MACHINES

SUPERGIRL VOL. 1: REIGN OF THE SUPERMEN

BATGIRL VOL. 1: BEYOND BURNSIDE

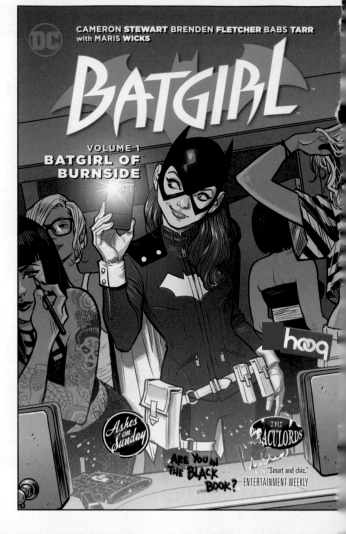